African Pentecostalism and World Christianity

african christian studies series (africs)

This series will make available significant works in the field of African Christian studies, taking into account the many forms of Christianity across the whole continent of Africa. African Christian studies is defined here as any scholarship that relates to themes and issues on the history, nature, identity, character, and place of African Christianity in world Christianity. It also refers to topics that address the continuing search for abundant life for Africans through multiple appeals to African religions and African Christianity in a challenging social context. The books in this series are expected to make significant contributions in historicizing trends in African Christian studies, while shifting the contemporary discourse in these areas from narrow theological concerns to a broader inter-disciplinary engagement with African religio-cultural traditions and Africa's challenging social context.

The series will cater to scholarly and educational texts in the areas of religious studies, theology, mission studies, biblical studies, philosophy, social justice, and other diverse issues current in African Christianity. We define these studies broadly and specifically as primarily focused on new voices, fresh perspectives, new approaches, and historical and cultural analyses that are emerging because of the significant place of African Christianity and African religio-cultural traditions in world Christianity. The series intends to continually fill a gap in African scholarship, especially in the areas of social analysis in African Christian studies, African philosophies, new biblical and narrative hermeneutical approaches to African theologies, and the challenges facing African women in today's Africa and within African Christianity. Other diverse themes in African Traditional Religions; African ecology; African ecclesiology; inter-cultural, inter-ethnic, and inter-religious dialogue; ecumenism; creative inculturation; African theologies of development, reconciliation, globalization, and poverty reduction will also be covered in this series.

SERIES EDITORS

Dr. Stan Chu Ilo (DePaul University, Chicago, USA)
Dr. Esther Acolatse (University of Toronto, Canada)
Dr. Mwenda Ntarangwi (Calvin College, Grand Rapids, MI, USA)

African Pentecostalism and World Christianity

Essays in Honor of
J. Kwabena Asamoah-Gyadu

EDITED BY
NIMI WARIBOKO AND
ADESHINA AFOLAYAN

PICKWICK *Publications* • Eugene, Oregon

AFRICAN PENTECOSTALISM AND WORLD CHRISTIANITY
Essays in Honor of J. Kwabena Asamoah-Gyadu

African Christian Studies Series 18

Copyright © 2020 Nimi Wariboko & Adeshina Afolayan. All rights reserved. Except for brief quotations in critical publications or reviews, no part of this book may be reproduced in any manner without prior written permission from the publisher. Write: Permissions, Wipf and Stock Publishers, 199 W. 8th Ave., Suite 3, Eugene, OR 97401.

Pickwick Publications
An Imprint of Wipf and Stock Publishers
199 W. 8th Ave., Suite 3
Eugene, OR 97401

www.wipfandstock.com

PAPERBACK ISBN: 978-1-7252-6635-3
HARDCOVER ISBN: 978-1-7252-6636-0
EBOOK ISBN: 978-1-7252-6637-7

Cataloguing-in-Publication data:

Names: Wariboko, Nimi, 1962–, editor. | Afolayan, Adeshina, editor.

Title: African Pentecostalism and World Christianity : essays in honor of J. Kwabena Asamoah-Gyadu / edited by Nimi Wariboko and Adeshina Afolayan.

Description: Eugene, OR: Pickwick Publications, 2020 | African Christian Studies Series 18 | Includes bibliographical references and index.

Identifiers: ISBN 978-1-7252-6635-3 (paperback) | ISBN 978-1-7252-6636-0 (hardcover) | ISBN 978-1-7252-6637-7 (ebook)

Subjects: LCSH: Pentecostalism—Africa | Pentecostalism | Pentecostals, Black

Classification: BR1644.5 W37 2020 (print) | BR1644.5 (ebook)

Manufactured in the U.S.A.   09/11/20

For Theodora Asamoah-Gyadu

Contents

Preface and Acknowledgements | xi

Introduction: The Worlding of Christianity in Africa and African Pentecostalism | 1
—*Nimi Wariboko and Adeshina Afolayan*

I: Christianity in History

Chapter 1
Bird's Eye View of Contemporary Christianity in Africa | 15
—*Opoku Onyinah*

Chapter 2
Independent, Enthusiastic, and African: Reframing the Story of Christianity in Africa | 30
—*Harvey C. Kwiyani*

Chapter 3
From/To the Ends of the Earth: Mission in the Spirit | 45
—*Kirsteen Kim*

Chapter 4
The First Non-Jewish Christian Was from Africa | 57
—*Craig S. Keener*

Chapter 5
Religious Reforms and Notions of Gender in Pentecostal Christianity: A Case of the Church of Pentecost | 75
—*Charles Prempeh*

Chapter 6
World Christianity and the Global Leadership Crisis: Forming Servant Leaders in the Age of the Strongman | 88
—*Kenneth R. Ross*

II: Spiritual Reality, Worldviews, and Formations

Chapter 7
Kwabena Asamoah-Gyadu: A Measured Critique of Africa's Use of the Holy Spirit's Healing Gifts | 107
—*Trevor H. G. Smith*

Chapter 8
Sighs and Signs of the Mind? Pentecostalism, Renewal, and a Ghanaian Mind Folk Theory | 123
—*Vivian Dzokoto*

Chapter 9
"One of the Greatest Prayer Weapons . . .": A Religio-Cultural Practice of "Libations" in Cameroon Neo-Pentecostalism | 137
—*Chammah J. Kaunda and Felix Kang Esoh*

Chapter 10
Proclaiming Good News to the Poor (Isa 61:1–2; Luke 4:18–19): Pentecostalism and Social Justice in Ghana | 153
—*Patrick Kofi Amissah*

III: Media, Mediatization, and World Christianity

Chapter 11
Second Generation Africans and the New Media as Agents of Demystification in the African Diaspora Church | 171
—*Caleb Nyanni*

CONTENTS

Chapter 12
Mass Media and the Dynamics between African Pentecostalism and African Neo-Traditionalism | 185
—*Marleen de Witte*

Chapter 13
Hallelujah Testimonies: Miracles, Memory, and Mediatization of Pentecostal Performances | 201
—*Oluwaseun Abimbola*

IV: African Pentecostalism in Context

Chapter 14
"Rise Up and Walk!" The Role of Pentecostals in Economic Development and Poverty Eradication | 221
—*Philomena Njeru Nwaura*

Chapter 15
The Need for Theologizing from the Experience of the "Other" in Contemporary Christianity in Africa | 234
—*Faith Lugazia*

Chapter 16
Religion and Development in European-African Dialogue: Exploring Learning Processes with Independent and Charismatic Churches in Africa on Sustainability and Integral Social Development | 245
—*Dietrich Werner*

Chapter 17
African Pentecostalism and Prosperity: Continuity and Discontinuity | 259
—*Allan H. Anderson*

Bibliography | 275
Name Index | 301
Subject Index | 303

Preface and Acknowledgements

AFRICAN PENTECOSTALISM HAS ALWAYS occupied a prominent place in World Christianity. We might even say that the history (in the last fifty years) of World Christianity has been disproportionally shaped, if not defined, by African Pentecostalism. The objective of this volume is to investigate and interrogate the critical junctures at which World Christianity invigorates and is invigorated by African Pentecostalism. The essays of the thinkers gathered in this book interrogate the general relationships between World Christianity and Africa, and the specific interplays between World Christianity and African Pentecostalism. Scholars from multiple continents and countries examine how the theological scholarship and missional works of eminent African intellectual Johnson Kwabena Asamoah-Gyadu have contributed to the scholarly understanding of how World Christianity has been mediated by its reception in Africa. They also investigate how African Pentecostalism has been shaped by its contact with diverse forms of Christianity in Africa and the rest of the world.

Asamoah-Gyadu is a significant scholar and theologian of African Pentecostalism. His contributions derived not only from scholarly engagements with Pentecostal and Christian practices, but also from a personal involvement through a participant observation as a minister of the Gospel. His entire scholarly outputs have done a lot to redefine the way Pentecostalism in its African incarnation is perceived in the trajectory of World Christianity. And in several other publications on the relationship between African Pentecostalism and the new media technologies, Asamoah-Gyadu has also continued to interpret and reinterpret the multiple ways by which the spread of the Gospel is motivated by the Holy Spirit as well as mass mediation which in turn configures Pentecostal and Christian practices and experience in multiple other ways.

All the contributors to this volume are united not only in their deep and abiding respect for Kwabena Asamoah-Gyadu's influential intellectual impact on the signification of African Pentecostalism. They are also unanimous in their collective enthusiasm in exploring the multidimensional reach of his ideas, arguments and discursive direction, first in the understanding of the extent and limit of African Pentecostalism; and second, in the relationship between African Pentecostalism, global Pentecostalism and world Christianity.

Our gratitude goes first to a friend and colleague, Professor Kwabena Asamoah-Gyadu, who continues to be a source of inspiration to both the old and new generations of theologians and Pentecostal scholars and ministers all across the world. This volume is a proof that Asamoah-Gyadu has not only generated sufficient ideas and theories to transform our reflection on Pentecostal and Christian practices especially in Africa, but that those very ideas and theories have become the instigation for more reflections. We are also very grateful to all the contributors who responded in record time, and with quality and outstanding essays, to the call for contribution to celebrate this great scholar.

Finally, we appreciate Baker Academic for granting permission to Dr. Craig S. Keener to adapt six thousand words from pages 1550–78 of his 2013 book, *Acts: An Exegetical Commentary, Vol. 2*, in chapter 4 of this volume.

Introduction

The Worlding of World Christianity and African Pentecostalism[1]

NIMI WARIBOKO AND ADESHINA AFOLAYAN

Christianity across the World

SINCE THE INAUGURATION OF the concept of World Christianity in the mid-twentieth century, it has gone on to define a multiplicity of the conceptual manifestations of Christianity all across the globe. When it first emerged, its objective was to understand the scope and extent of the Christian community across the globe, and especially to define the understanding of Christian unity and Christian missions. World Christianity, therefore, redefines the need to limit the regulatory boundary between Christians and non-Christians, to understand Christianity outside the

---

1. The concept of "worlding" is one of Martin Heidegger's contributions to philosophy. It involves the transformation of the noun "world" into an active verb, "worlding," which signifies a process of world-becoming and world-making as an ongoing process of meaningful being. Since its emergence in Heidegger's magnus opus, *Being and Time* (1927), the concept of worlding has been applied to several aspect of human endeavors, from international politics to globalization and from secularization to the "enfleshment" of God in the world. We are adopting the term here to reflect the expansion and the deepening of Christianity across the world and in multiple theologies that provide meanings for several people.

West as not just mere manifestations of Western Christianity, and to expand the universal sense of catholicity.

One of the most interesting issues in its conceptual emergence is its insertion into the ideological contexts of globalization, and the critical distinction between the global North and the global South. A growing number of literatures has explored the complex relationship of Christianity with different regions and contexts in ways that led to distinct and dramatic social, religious, political and cultural changes to both the contexts and regions themselves as well as to Christianity.[2] Some other scholars have focused specifically on the historical and theological implications of World Christianity, especially as it manifests in the Global South.[3]

Dana Robert argues for the emergence of World Christianity as a reputable academic discourse from the transformation of historical missionary activities across the world into mission studies as an academic discipline. European imperialism and the globalization motivated by the infrastructural consequences of the Industrial Revolution gave way in the late nineteenth century and the early twentieth century to a huge enthusiasm for missionary journeys and the vision of world evangelization, from the West to Asia, Africa and Latin America. By 1910, according to Roberts, the World Missionary Conference at Edinburgh represented "a convergence of Protestant missionary interests from around the world."[4] The rigorous Protestant missionary movement provided the fuel for the robust discussions and projections that led to the emergence of mission studies as a serious discourse:

> Preliminary reports conducted the first survey of worldwide Christianity by Protestants. Analysis of such issues as missions and governments, the missionary message in relation to non-Christian religions, world evangelization, and missionary preparation relied on information gathered from hundreds of informants around the world. A comprehensive missionary atlas documented the spread of missions worldwide. The Edinburgh Conference provided visible inspiration for a multicultural Christianity.[5]

---

2. Farhadian, *Introducing World Christianity*; Sanneh and McClymond, *Wiley Blackwell Companion to World Christianity*; Pachuau, *World Christianity*.

3. Hassan, *Religion and Development in the Global South*; Kim, *Rise of the Global South*; Daughrity, *Rising*; Sanneh and Carpenter, *Changing Face of Christianity*.

4. Robert, "Naming 'World Christianity.'"

5. Robert, "Naming 'World Christianity,'" 2–3.

This understanding of the multicultural credentials of Christianity was the signal for the blossoming of interest in its relationship with the non-Western world. Yet, by the early 1900s, colonialism still eclipsed the idea of Christian multiculturalism in a way that gave global cooperation for mission and the growing recognition of an enlarged and extended understanding of the "Kingdom of God" a limited global configuration. The idea of Protestant unity still largely possesses a European imprint. Yet, the ardent desire for the unity of the church of God led to the birth of an ecumenical movement in the 1940s, around the worldview of one world under God. Ecumenism was particularly fueled by the horrors of the Second World War and the palpable fear of a spreading Communism. And these led to the growing desire, founded on the mission experiences, for an alternate totalizing worldview that brings God's people worldwide under "one church."[6] John Joseph Considine published *World Christianity* in 1945. And in 1947 Henry P. Van Dusen published a book titled *World Christianity: Yesterday, Today, Tomorrow* that was defined around a new world order founded on a Christian ecumenical base. In other words, for the world to survive as one, there is an urgent need for a world church—"To an age destined to survive, or to expire, as 'one world,' we bring a world Church," says Dusen.[7]

When the World Council of Churches was founded in 1948, Dusen's view about the organic unity of World Christinaity (rather than just a Christian multiculturalism that grounds Europe as Christendom) was vindicated. Robert argues that the emergence of the World Council of Churches was, for Dusen,

> both the culmination and the end of the historic expansion of Europe and the beginning of the new age of World Christianity. The centrifugal movement of missions gave birth to the centripetal movement of church unity, which together characterized the world church of the twentieth century. Van Dusen not only used missions and ecumenism as the two poles of his historical analysis, but he worked to unite them visibly in his role as chairman of the joint commission for the integration of the International Missionary Council and the World Council of Churches in 1961.[8]

Yet, like the idea of multicultural Christianity before it, the optimism heralded by Dusen and other Protestant ecumenists was to fail in the shadow

---

6. Robert, "Naming 'World Christianity,'" 4.
7. Robert, "Naming 'World Christianity,'" 4.
8. Robert, "Naming 'World Christinaity,'" 5.

of the Cold War and the militant rise of anticolonial movements in Africa and Asia. The triumphalism of world ecumenism, according to Robert, was overtaken by a different interpretation of history that was grounded on conflict rather than consensus. In other words, "the ecumenical movement failed to recognize the full-blown implications of the so called fourth self of mission theory—that of self-theologizing."[9] The ecumenical spirit of World Christianity was colored by the tragedy of European imperialism, colonialism and racism.

It was the 1970s that gave birth to a postcolonial model of a renewed World Christianity on the ashes of mainline mission theology and evangelization. The reconfiguration of World Christianity along a postcolonial dynamics was inaugurated around the emergence of multiple and culturally inflected indigenous forms of Christianity in Africa, Asia and Latin America. And there began to grow the institutional recognition of a switch from the "center" of Christianity to its "margins"; or, as Robert puts it, several institutional endeavors began to bring home the realization of "how the 'margins' of Christianity were becoming the 'center.'"[10] By 1989, and with the fall of USSR and international communism, World Christianity was rejuvenated and relaunched as a serious theological and academic discourse. First, Christianity became untethered from Cold War politics to become a significant indigenous form which "stressed multiculturalism, numerical growth, diversity, and multiple nodes of authority."[11] And Robert recognizes the publication of Lamin Sanneh's book, *Translating the Message* (1989), as a game changer that unhinged mission from colonialism, and grounded on a new understanding of mission as the motivation for indigenous Christianity everywhere. Thus, "Asian, African, and Latin American Christians were not clones of northern Europe and North America but had embraced Christianity on their own terms."[12]

Africa represents one of those ideologically volatile contexts within which Christianity has unfolded its theological and ideological underpinnings. This becomes so significant with the complicity of Christianity in the *mission civilatrice* of colonialism. The engagements of Christianity with the divergent cultural and social formations in Africa led to several transformations both in the internal theological mechanism of Christianity

9. Robert, "Naming 'World Christianity,'" 6.
10. Robert, "Naming 'World Christianity,'" 8.
11. Robert, "Naming 'World Christianity,'" 8.
12. Robert, "Naming 'World Christianity,'" 9.

itself and in the religious dynamics on the continent. While Christianity, in its incarnation in the African Initiated Christianity or African Independent Churches (AIC), has remained a solid entry point by which scholars attempt to understand the postcolonial religious trajectory of the continent, Pentecostalism has achieved a tremendous growth and presence that have insinuated it into the important sectors of the African life, from politics to economic development.

Several scholars have focused on the relationship between World Christianity and Africa.[13] Only few, however, have explicitly interrogated the fundamental dynamics involved in the critical engagements between World Christianity and African Pentecostalism. Even fewer still have been interested in the critical influence of the media and digital media technologies on the transformation of African Pentecostalism and World Christianity. One of such scholars is Johnson Kwabena Asamoah-Gyadu. He is one scholar of Pentecostalism who has assiduously dedicated himself to pushing the boundaries of understanding of the relationship of World Christianity to African Pentecostalism. His research interest spans the nature and manifestation of Christianity in Africa to the different dimensions of African Pentecostalism. From the pneumatological movement to the mediatization of religion, and from the deployment of religious symbols in sport to the relationship between witchcraft and Christianity, Asamoah-Gyadu has done a lot to advance knowledge on how African Pentecostalism has evolved in relation to world Christianity.

This volume investigates and interrogates the critical junctures at which World Christianity invigorates and is invigorated by African Pentecostalism. In exploring the dense connections between World Christianity and African Pentecostalism, the volume pays particular attention to how their dynamics are responding to, are reenergized, and are reworked by the media and mediatization. The scholars who have been assembled to flesh out this argument constitute one of the most distinguished groups of experts on Pentecostalism ever assembled to investigate the intersection of World Christianity and African Pentecostalism.

In trying to outline the critical juncture at which World Christianity and African Pentecostalism intersects, this volume becomes a distinct contribution to the discourse about the nature of these two Christian formations,

---

13. Sanneh and Carpenter, *Changing Face of Christianity*; Bediako, *Christianity in Africa*; Bongmba, *Routldge Companion to Christianity in Africa*; Maxwell and Lawrie, *Christianity and the African Imagination*; Barnes, *Global Christianity and the Black Atlantic*.

or rather, one complex formation with multiple sides. The dynamics and practices of this complexity have done a lot to re-inscribe our understanding of the evolution of Christianity especially within the African context. In this particular context, multiplicity of historical circumstances (mediated by coloniality and postcoloniality) and sociocultural disarticulations have not only facilitated the penetration of Christianity as a religious system, but also the transformation of Christian practices into diverse forms and formations. How has World Christianity affected the condition of the African continent? How has African Pentecostalism mediated the theological assumptions of World Christianity? What are the specific African elements of Pentecostalism? The scholarship of Professor Johnson Kwabena Asamoah-Gyadu, the President Trinity Theological Seminary, Legon-Accra, Ghana helps us to tackle these questions, and many more.

Asamoah-Gyadu and African Pentecostalism

We have discerned three basic ways of interpreting African Pentecostalism in the course of our studies. More precisely, we can say that there are three regnant regimes of discourse. There are those (such as theologian Amos Yong and Frank Macchia) who interpret Pentecostalism at its strongest theological perspective. There are others (such as Ruth Marshall and Nimi Wariboko) who read it at its theoretically most accessible point. There is yet another group (including Matthews Ojo and Allan Anderson) which interprets it at its contextually most engaged corner. Professor Johnson Kwabena Asamoah-Gyadu institutes a fourth regime, which we are naming for the first time here as the "Legon" discourse (Legon is the capital city of Ghana, from where Asamoah-Gyadu operates). He does this by making a diagonal cut through the three other forms of discourse. He accomplishes his objective by adopting a wide-angled lens which sees African Pentecostalism more deeply, more perceptively, and more sympathetically at the dense intersection of the "theologically strongest" and the "contextually most keen" than any scholar today. He brings theology and context together in brilliant analyses and discussions that are theoretically inflected. In his works, theology, theory, and context interact dialogically to shed ample light on African Pentecostal situations.

His scholarship is a rich tapestry of sophisticated academic analyses and profound sensitivity to the Africanness of Pentecostalism, the aim of which is to uncover the unique contributions of sub-Saharan Africans to global Pentecostalism and World Christianity. In his work, African Pentecostals are neither the venerable saints that some scholars in the declining centers of Christianity in the northern hemisphere make them out to be, nor the contaminating, transgressive devotees excreted by African traditional religions into the pure body of Christ. African Pentecostalism is instead a bold development whose dynamism and creativity forge new paths and ideas in ways that are supremely relevant to Christianity today. African Pentecostals are relevant not only for Africa, but also for the world. He states that he has found them "very fascinating, serious, religiously innovative and very entrepreneurial in their approach to Christianity. I do not support everything that I have seen them do in the name of Christianity, However, I find their general argument that God has raised them to undertake a fresh assignment in mission very compelling."[14] In this same text, he consistently and insistently argues that African Pentecostals are claiming territories for Christ in tandem with "God's Spirit of renewal that has been at work in them."[15]

In the quotation, above we see his scholarly temperament of "Yes-and-No" to the practices and ideas of African Pentecostals on display. In his writings there are no easy or cheap resolution of the contemporary tension between the distortions and achievements of Pentecostalism in Africa. He both affirms and criticizes, fully living into the tension and in this way, he forges his own stance.

The tension is clearly observable in his analysis of the prosperity gospel as it is instantiated in Sub-Saharan Africa. He writes that contemporary African Pentecostals "have developed a certain penchant and proclivity for things that reflect glory and power, which includes seeing material acquisitions as reflective of God's favor almost to the total exclusion of any discussion of why people suffer."[16] When they do discuss suffering, he maintains, they attribute it to witchcraft.[17] Yet he is also astute and careful enough to understand the contextual dynamics that have made this gospel or, indeed, Pentecostalism so successful in Africa. Pentecostalism, according to him, "affirms traditional worldviews of mystical causality and provides the

---

14. Asamoah-Gyadu, *Taking Territories*, 7.
15. Asamoah-Gyadu, *Taking Territories*, 2–8.
16. Asamoah-Gyadu, *Contemporary Pentecostal Christianity*, 113.
17. Asamoah-Gyadu, "African Pentecostalism," 31.

appropriate Christian ritual contexts within which the fears and insecurities of ordinary people may be dealt with."[18]

All this is not saying that Asamoah-Gyadu is a dialectical theologian or philosopher. He does not proceed by arguing that the affirmative is always fissured by negation, and from which another positive is engendered. Though the "Yes and No" are included in all his analyses and discussions—the sense of the novelty of Pentecostalism conserving and sublating the traditional context contoured by African Traditional Religions—he goes beyond simple dialectical movement. The "Yes" and "No" are two distinct movements, one does not inevitably entail the other. The good accomplishments of African Pentecostalism are not stated to merely balance the negatives. They come from a careful and sympathetic understanding of what God's Spirit is doing in Africa; they come from a sense of mission. In a sense the accomplishments are "subtractive"; they represent irruption of new meanings that names the void that exists in historic mission-church Christianity. Pentecostalism is an affirmative subtraction of Christianity in Africa from the path of irrelevance.

On the whole, Asamoah-Gyadu's work has helped the academy to critically reflect on the role of Pentecostalism in the advancement of Christianity or in mission work. He defines Christian mission as knowing what God is doing and allowing God to engage you in it.[19] In his scholarship, there is an underlying thread that runs through: the tracing, mapping, and analyzing the work of the Holy Spirit in Africa. He considers the purpose of his scholarship as that of recognizing what God's Spirit is doing in the world and allowing God to engage him in the enterprise. Put differently, his scholarship is about recognizing God's work in Africa and being interpellated by such divine work.[20] In this sense, his scholarship is a work of mission and mission is his study.

In his fervent pursuit of recording the work of the Holy Spirit in the world or the body of Christ, Asamoah-Gyadu has developed a theological framework that has five dimensions. It focuses on the "promise, experience, fulfillment, impact and significance" of Africa's encounter with the Spirit.[21] The essays gathered in this volume (in various ways that are not only complementary but also innovative) shed ample light on these five

18. Asamoah-Gyadu, "Spirit and Spirits," 50.
19. Asamoah-Gyadu, *Taking Territories*, 25.
20. Asamoah-Gyadu, *Taking Territories*, 7, 8, 25.
21. Asamoah-Gyadu, *Taking Territories*, 10.

dimensions of Africans' encounter or engagement with the Holy Spirit, Creator-Redeemer.

In this book eighteen scholars delineate the contours of his scholarship, highlighting how it deeply reflects his African context and how it celebrates the universal truths of Christianity as a religion, practice, and a thought system—and they join him to tell beautiful stories of what God is doing in Africa. In the pages ahead we will see how Asamoah-Gyadu's work has become very influential in the global academy, how he has become one of the best interpreters of African Pentecostalism, and, indeed, one of the fiercest critics of its excesses.

Chapter Outline

The volume is divided into three distinct parts that allow the contributors to address different dimensions of Asamoah-Gyadu's work. In the first part—Christianity in History—six essays take a historical critical look at the trajectory of Christianity in Africa. These chapters are significant because they provide the theological and historical understanding of what Christianity has become; essentially, a non-western religion. This is what Opoku Onyinah did in chapter 1. He attempts to tease out Asamoah-Gyadu's definitive role in the Pentecostalization of Christianity in Africa, as different from the American Evangelical Pentecostal Christianity. The new direction charted in Africa seeks "a direct, victorious, supernatural encounter with God, who transforms all aspects of their lives." In chapter 2, Harvey Kwiyani further pursues the theological contours of this "enthusiastic Christianity" in Africa. An enthusiastic Christianity, emerging through what Kwiyani calls the "charismatization of the Christian experience" is fundamentally one that engages "the spirit world just like the old African traditional religions did." And it is in this enthusiastic form that African Christianity makes a unique contribution to the understanding of Christianity in the world. However, he argues, a proper contextualization of the experiences of Christianity in Africa demands that we generate new terms which interrogate what it means to be "pentecostal," "charismatic" or "neo-pentecostal."

Kirsteen Kim's "From/To the End of the World" is a unique reading of the Book of Acts of the Apostle that demonstrates the apostolicity and catholicity of the church. Juxtaposing the central objective of mission (as sending the disciples to the ends of the earth) with the career of Christianity throughout the world (seen as from the ends of the earth), for

Kim, provides a critical move that enables the decentering of Christianity away from Europe. Craig Keener, in chapter 4, declares categorically that "the first non-Jewish Christian was from Africa." And this is with regard to Luke's reference to the Ethiopian official in Acts 8:27. If Luke is taken to be motivated by the task to take the Gospel to the end of the earths, then Kim argues that his interest in the African official cannot be taken to be "exotic," as scholars have argued. And this interest in the official reveals, for Kim, that Africa produced "the first gentile Christian." Both chapters 5 and 6 provide specific critical perspectives that draw on the development in world Christianity and Pentecostalism in Africa. Charles Prempeh interrogates the notion of gender in Ghana's Church of Pentecost (CoP), and how the emergence of a "modernist" orientation, defined around the use of English, seems to undermine the "primitive solidarity" which the CoP shares with global Pentecostalism as a spiritual movement for those on the fringe of society. In chapter 6, Kenneth Ross explores the implications that World Christianity could have in a world that is gradually being taken over by what he calls the "strongman." According to him, "When measured by biblical standards, the shortcomings of today's strongman leaders are clearly exposed."

Part two of this volume—Spiritual Reality, Worldviews, and Formations—contains four essays that fundamentally take their starting point from Asamoah-Gyadu's fundamental third way that balances between what Trevor H. G. Smith, in chapter 7, calls "a hyper-spiritualized (the global South's temptation) and hyper-materialized (the West's temptation) cause and effect understanding of reality." Smith then engages with Asamoah-Gyadu's biblical hermeneutic and ecclesiology "developed out of Africa's single-tiered ontological understanding of reality, an understanding that holds material and spiritual cause and effect as equally important and necessary for understanding this world God has given us." Vivian Dzokoto, in chapter 8, is more concerned with what she calls the "Akan folk theory of mind," and "how these representations of the mind help explain the success of the pneumatic Pentecostal Christian movements that Johnson Kwabena Asamoah-Gyadu focuses on in his prolific program of research on Christianity in Africa today." In chapter 9, Chammah J. Kaunda and Felix Kang Esoh investigate the concept of libation, a key concept in Asamoah-Gyadu's research, as a point of investigating the continuity and discontinuity between African Pentecostalism and African traditional religions. They conclude that the practice of libation amongst the neo-Pentecostals in

Cameroon demonstrates a deep tension between continuity and discontinuity. Lastly in chapter 10, Patrick Kofi Amissah critically interrogates the relationship between Pentecostalism and social justice in Isaiah 61:1–2 and Luke 4:18–19. Specifically, the chapter explores how the issues of poverty and oppression in Ghana can be confronted by Pentecostal and Charismatic Christians from the twin perspectives of spiritual and social justice that these two scriptural texts espouse.

Three critical chapters make up the third part of the volume titled "Media, Mediatization and World Christianity." The idea of the mediation of Pentecostal and Christian practices plays a crucial role in the theological oeuvre of Asamoah-Gyadu. The three essays by Caleb Nyanni, Marleen de Witte and Oluwaseun Abimbola extend Asamoah-Gyadu's interest in the African diaspora, in Ghana and in Nigeria respectively. Chapter 11 critically engages with the role that the new media technologies are playing in refocusing and redefining the religious worldviews of second generation African migrants in the United Kingdom. Chapter 12 is a reflection "on the possibilities and limits of 'African Pentecostalism,'" especially with regard to those who are distinctly not a part of it, like the neo-traditionalists in Ghana. The chapter then interrogates the ways in which mass mediation complicates the relationship between the Pentecostals and the neo-traditionalists in Ghana. In Nigeria, on the other hand, Abimbola's essay is concerned with the enhancement of pentecostal performances, on the one hand; and on the other hand, the "ways in which religious rituals are also shaping an online culture that gives agency to anonymity and performativity."

The last and final part of this volume—African Pentecostalism in Context—with four essays, takes up specific substantive issues relating to African Pentecostalism and the African predicament. Philomena Mwaura's exploration of the role of Pentecostalism in economic development and poverty eradication connects with the issues of poverty and oppression raised by Patrick Amissah in chapter 10. Mwaura argues that the significance of Pentecostalism in economic development is not due to its "consciously defined development activities but rather through the very nature of Pentecostal beliefs and practices"; that is, the nature of its worldview that links the secular to the spiritual under the supervision of God. The issue of development is also the focus of Dietrich Werner in chapter 16. With the call for the recognition of the role that religion, and Faith-Based Organization (FBO) can play in the achievement of sustainable development on the continent. Chapter 15 is also continuous with the gender issue raised by

Prempeh in chapter 5. But here, Faith Lugazia deploys a critical feminist stance and a feminist hermeneutical method to tease out the implications, for Pentecostalism, of theologizing from the experience of the woman as the "other" in religious practices. The last chapter, by Allan H. Anderson, takes up the challenge of new term to characterize religious phenomena in African Pentecostalism and Christianity raised by Kwiyani (chapter 2), by interrogating the issue of "prosperity gospel" crucial to African Pentecostalism. A productive analytic strategy, according to Anderson, demands examining prosperity gospel in African Pentecostalism "from the perspective of ancient African beliefs on prosperity and success, and discuss whether it represents continuity with African religious beliefs or a transformative discontinuity with past beliefs."

In all, these brilliant essays provide a critical tour through the excellent and enlightening oeuvre of Kwabena Asamoah-Gyadu on how African Pentecostalism has extended itself through mass mediation, and has transformed our understanding of World Christianity. The uniqueness of this volume is in its specific focus on the complex relationship between World Christianity and African Pentecostalism, and how all these intersect with media and mediatization. This is one dimension of the historical and theological trajectory of the Christianity discourse that has not received much scholarly attention in the literature on World Christianity. It is our hope that this volume will enable scholars of African studies to critically engage with the trajectory of World Christianity and African Pentecostalism in conceptual, cultural and historical interactions. It will assist theologians and religious studies scholars to understand the transformations and transmutations of Christian doctrines, practices and spiritual forms in different contexts. In the sociology of religion, the volume, we hope, will facilitate a deep assessment of the sociological elements that go into the articulation of Christianity, and specifically Pentecostalism in various contextual forms. Finally, it is our hope this volume will provide valuable resources for students and scholars of religions, and of Christianity, specifically in seeing how the works of Asamoah-Gyadu and the contributors to this volume enable diverse perspectives, paradigms and models that ground the understanding of Christianity itself in its various and variegated multiplicity across space and time.

Section I

Christianity in History

1

Bird's-Eye View of Contemporary Christianity in Africa

Opoku Onyinah

I FIRST MET PROFESSOR J. Kwabena Asamoah-Gyadu when I was studying at the Regent Theological College at Nantwich, in the UK, and our meeting was providential and fortuitous. The Director of Studies at Regent had recommended that I pursue a Doctor of Philosophy degree in theology, but he preferred that my supervisor be a Pentecostal theologian. During this time, our school hosted a Pentecostal conference, and a student from the University of Birmingham attended. This student gave me a greeting and a telephone number from Kwabena Asamoah-Gyadu, who was then a PhD student at Birmingham. I contacted Kwabena, who introduced me to Professor Allan Anderson, one of the premier scholars of Pentecostalism, and he graciously agreed to be my PhD supervisor. This was in perfect accord with what my director of studies had recommended. Soon, my family moved to Birmingham, and we stayed at Griffin Close, next door to Asamoah-Gyadu and his family, and a great friendship developed. We shared things together and often joined in prayer. He told me that when he finished his course, he wanted to return to Ghana and equip people in Christian education.

Like a prophet, Professor Anderson (who was Asamoah-Gyadu's internal examiner) told me that Kwabena had the potential to become a great scholar. Indeed, that is what has happened. Asamoah-Gyadu is a world-renowned African Christian educationist.¹ His writings and teachings have proven to be timely and relevant for African Christians now that the Western missionary enterprise in Africa has significantly declined, and the Christian faith is in African hands. The missionary effort resulted in the spread of Western Christianity across sub-Saharan Africa. Missionaries sought to evangelize the continent and to keep the faith—and its followers—pure, with no syncretism. To achieve this, missionaries often removed believers from their homes and placed them in so-called "*Salem*" environments. But those days of partitioning African Christians from Africa are long gone. In the latter part of the twentieth century, Christian churches in Africa transitioned to be led by African leaders.

This chapter looks at what African Christians consider to be the vital, essential parts of the faith. In short, they seek a direct, victorious, supernatural encounter with God, who transforms all aspects of their lives. Under African leadership, this reformed Christian experience, dubbed as the "Pentecostalization" of Christianity, evolved through African ingenuity in the transformation of Evangelical Pentecostal Christianity, which had been tied to American Pentecostal/Charismatic spirituality. Professor Asamoah-Gyadu has helped guide this shift. His writings and teachings are evidence of what David Barrett predicted in 1970, that "African Christians might well tip the balance and transform Christianity permanently into a non-western religion."[2] This is not just happening on African soil. African Christians who have traveled abroad have transported their Christian experience to the diaspora, where many of them worship the Lord in the same manner in which they worship Him in Africa. In this chapter, I will also take note of that very significant movement.

I shall begin by giving a historical overview of Christianity in Africa. The emergence of the Pentecostal movement and its impact on the mainline churches follows. Then I will end with the contemporary Christianity in Africa and its worldwide influence.

Early Christian Activities and Nineteenth-Century Missionary Activities

Christianity entered Africa as early as the New Testament times as we see Philip ministered to the Ethiopian eunuch in Acts 8:26–40. We assume that

---

1. See Asamoah-Gyadu, "Theological Education."
2. Barrett quoted in Asamoah-Gyadu, "Growth and Trends," 67.

the eunuch carried the Gospel back to Africa. Quite quickly, North Africa became the center of Christian activities and this lasted from the second through the fifth centuries. Africa produced notable Christian leaders such as Tertullian, Clement of Alexandria, Cyprian, Origen of Alexandria, Athanasius, and Augustine of Hippo. The African faith was strong. During times of Imperial Roman persecution, many chose death rather than recant their faith. However, from the sixth century, the faith waned, and the church in North Africa was divided through doctrinal issues and internal struggles. The desire for ecclesiastical and political power replaced the evangelistic zeal. These factors facilitated the spread of the new Islamic religion across North Africa from the seventh century onward.

Though Christianity survived for hundreds of years, ultimately, only the Coptic Church in Egypt was left standing (though we also affirm the tenacity of the Church in Ethiopia). Currently, the Coptic Orthodox Church represents 10 to 15 percent of Egypt's population.[3] This crippling of the Church in North Africa denied Christianity to the rest of Africa until later missionary enterprising activities. Christianity was introduced to sub-Saharan Africa in the fifteenth century. The Portuguese commercial voyages maintained some Roman Catholic priests to minister among their settlements. In Southern Africa, this began in 1458, while in West Africa this began in 1471. During this period, attempts were made to present the Christian faith to the Africans, but not much was accomplished. As of the beginning of the nineteenth century, only a few converts, some ruins of churches, sculptures, crucifixes, and archival records could be identified.[4]

In the eighteenth century the Moravian Church of Denmark or the United Brethren and the Society for the Propagation of the Gospel also made various attempts to plant the Christian faith, but very little success was recorded.[5] Christianity was, however, steadily established in the nineteenth century across Africa through the missionary activities of societies such as the Basel Mission, the Bremen Mission, Church Missionary Society (CMS) of the Anglican Church, the Wesleyan Methodist Society, and the Catholic Mission.[6] In this paper, churches which are associated with these mission societies are referred to as "mainline churches." The missionaries came with

---

3. CIA, "Africa: Egypt." Note that in 1974 *Operation World* placed the number at 8 percent (Johnstone et al., *Operation World*, 233).

4. Denis, "Christianity in Southern Africa"; Agbeti, *West Africa Church History*, 3.

5. Falk, *Growth of the Church in Africa*, 118.

6. Olwa, "Christianity in Eastern Africa"; Hasting, *Church in Africa*.

zeal. However, some of them had been impacted by the Enlightenment and were sympathetic to rationalism, critical biblical interpretation, and liberal theology.[7] One hallmark of liberal theology is that it denies the belief in the supernatural, especially the belief in the devil, witches, and demons.

At the same time, other missionaries influenced by pietism still upheld the traditional "diabology" and the coexistence of God and the devil. Whereas both views—liberalism and pietism—had, until then, peacefully coexisted, from the second decade of the nineteenth century onward, the Protestant (and partly Catholic) Awakening heavily attacked rational and liberal theology in particular and secularization in general. As McLoughlin has shown, the aim of the Protestant Awakening was to restore and maintain the "old-time religion and traditional way of life."[8]

The "old-time religion" was based upon the traditional interpretation of the Scriptures that the church had practiced from its inception through medieval times. This resulted in the denunciation of idol worship, the demonization of the Gentile gods, and the need to exorcize those who worshiped them. "To restore old time religion" inevitably meant that the Protestant Awakening sought to restore belief in the reality of the devil, life after death, the reality of heaven and hell, and the need to evangelize the "heathen."[9] Klaus Fiedler rightly points out that prominent among new initiatives and organizations, which each revival brings, are evangelistic efforts, social activities and foreign missions.[10]

The nineteenth-century missionary awareness, therefore, was the product of the Protestant Awakening. But slumber can still attack those who are wide awake. Harvey Cox brought to light Ralph Waldo Emerson's warning to an audience at Harvard Divinity School in 1838, "The danger of a steady diet of other people's religion is that it can dry up one's own resource."[11] Keith Thomas argues that the "disenchantment of the world" during the Enlightenment[12] did not extinguish traditional Christian belief in the devil and witchcraft; however, it still had a great impact on Protestant

---

7. Gerrish, *Prince of the Church*, 47.

8. McLoughlin, *Revivals, Awakenings, and Reform*, 108.

9. For instance, Orr records that in 1860, in Edinburgh, the Carrubber's Close Mission ejected an Atheist Club from their premises; they described the house of prostitutes as "a fortress of the Devil" (Orr, *Second Great Awakening in Great Britain*, 74).

10. Fiedler, *Story of Faith Mission*, 113.

11. Cox, *Fire from Heaven*, 14.

12. Thomas, *Religion and the Decline of Magic*, 571–85, 640, 655.

thinking. It was with this type of thinking—traditional Christian beliefs in the devil, weakened by the critical scholarship during the Enlightenment—with which missionaries began their ministries in Africa. This is reflected in David Livingstone's oft-cited motivation, "I go back to Africa to make an open path for commerce and Christianity."[13]

To be sure, missionary Christianity contributed immensely to the advancement of African society. The major contributions included the introduction of Western medical systems, the establishment of schools, and the abolition of slavery. Additionally, the missionaries promoted translation, including the development of vernacular alphabets and the production of grammars and dictionaries. However, as an effort to evangelize and civilize the indigenous people, the missionaries taught that the belief in the African spirit-forces—including witches, the deities or gods, and elves or dwarfs—was superstitious. Yet, at the same time, they also promoted the devil and demons as the power behind these spirit-forces. By the introduction of a personalized devil and identifying the gods with demons, the missionaries unwittingly strengthened the belief in them and the fear of them. However, the missionaries did not adequately answer this fear. For the Africans, these forces were real and life-threatening, but the missionary teaching left them stranded. In the light of this inadequate theology, some Africans started their independent churches.

African-Initiated Churches

The first counter-response to missionary Christianity in Africa was that of a black nationalist group, labeled, "Ethiopians," who wove a network of cultural protest against white domination in power and culture over the church.[14] A few of the elite broke off to form African churches that resembled the mission churches. A second group, often called prophets, was poor in resources and in education, but also challenged the authority of the missionaries through the demonstration of healing with a blend of Christianity and African traditional religious practices. These prophets were not commissioned by missionaries, yet their mission activities helped to spread the Christian message in Africa. Prominent among them were William Wade Harris, Joseph Babalola, and Garrick Braide in West Africa; Isaiah Shembe in South Africa; and Simon

---

13. Price, "Missionary Struggle with Complexity," 101
14. Ogbu, "Third Response," 3.

Kimbangu in Zaire.[15] The battle to find a place for such prophets within the mainline churches was a problem until the 1920s and 1930s, when another trend emerged: these prophets broke away from the mainline churches and established their own independent churches. Asamoah-Gyadu's doctoral research, following his professor C. G. Baëta, centers around these churches. He is very sympathetic to them, and, like Allan Anderson, he describes them as "Indigenous Pentecostal-type churches."[16] Accordingly, he points out that "they were the first group of mass Christian religious movement to transform the religious landscape in Africa."[17]

In their churches, worship is a blend of the Bible and all the colors of the African traditional spectrum. Their activities, growth, and creativity have engaged the attention of scholars as they have attempted to identify African contributions to world Christianity.[18] Despite the fact that these African-initiated Churches have attracted many followers, the lack of theological understanding and little pastoral accountability have drawn some into unethical practices, such as exploitation and immorality. This has caused a decline in their patronage and paved the way for the popularity of the classical Pentecostal Churches."[19]

Classical Pentecostal Churches

The origin and growth of Pentecostalism in Africa is a complex story. Asamoah-Gyadu observes that "classical Pentecostal denominations of both Western missionaries and indigenous kinds started in sub-Saharan Africa from the same time."[20] Some of the classical Pentecostal churches were originally initiated and established under the auspices of foreign Pentecostal missions. But in other churches, Africans initiated the process. They had read some gospel tracts that shared the Pentecostal practices, and they had experienced some of the phenomena. In consequence, they invited foreign

---

15. For discussion on the prophetic and how it has been reinvented into the contemporary prophetic practices in Africa, see Asamoah-Gyadu, "From Every Nation Under Heaven," xxx.

16. Anderson, *Bazalwane*, 7; Asamoah-Gyadu, "Renewal within African Christianity," 22.

17. Asamoah-Gyadu, "Introduction into the Typology of African Christianity," 63.

18. Turner, *Church of the Lord*; Parrinder, *Religion in an African City*; Welbourn and Ogot, *Place to Feel at Home*.

19. Asamoah-Gyadu, "Renewal within African Christianity," 133.

20. Asamoah-Gyadu, "Growth and Trends," 70.

Pentecostal missions to come to take control of their groups. Those churches that came to Africa included the Apostolic Faith Mission, the Assemblies of God, the Apostolic Church, and the Foursquare Gospel Church. Soon, especially, in West Africa, churches emerged as independent, indigenous, classical Pentecostal churches. The notable ones include the Christ Apostolic of Nigeria, the Gospel Faith Mission of Nigeria, and the Church of Pentecost of Ghana. Some of these churches not only have branches in neighboring West African countries but across the globe.[21]

South Africa became an important influence in the spread of Pentecostalism in Central Africa, especially with regard to the Anglophone countries such as Zimbabwe, Zambia, and Malawi. Most of the classical Pentecostals who evangelized Central and Eastern Africa were from Pentecostal denominations in North America and Europe. The prominent ones include the Apostolic Faith Mission and Full Gospel Church. Similarly, the independent Pentecostal denominations from Europe and North America also expanded the Pentecostal faith in East Africa. Some well-known ones among them were the Pentecostal Assemblies of Canada, the Elim Pentecostal Church from the UK, the New Testament Church from the US, and the Pentecostal Holiness Church from the US.

Pentecostal Beliefs and Practices

Pentecostal beliefs and practices are very appealing to Africans, and these beliefs and practices resounded across the entire Christian spectrum in Africa. Thus, yes, it is a Pentecostalization of the faith, but it is also an Africanization because it has been shaped by Africans and it reveals what elements of the faith they most clearly embrace: a God who engages and lifts His people supernaturally and victoriously.

Pentecostalism presents the Bible in a way that speaks directly to the African worldview in both confirmation and condemnation. On the one hand, the gods, demons, sorcery, and witchcraft are taught as real and powerful. They can destroy people's lives and destinies. Yet, on the other hand, God is taught as almighty, and His power supersedes those of the devil and the gods. Those who worshipped the gods, practiced traditional religion, got involved in witchcraft and sorcery are invited to denounce them and come to Jesus. The power of God can be given to anybody who believes and accepts His Son Jesus. To receive Him is to be born again. The fullness of

---

21. Onyinah, "African Christianity."

His power is received through the baptism of the Holy Spirit with emphasis on speaking in tongues. This is considered a powerful weapon for evangelism. Healing and exorcism are to accompany those who are baptized in the Spirit in their evangelistic efforts.[22]

With these teachings about the power and presence of God, the early Pentecostals were addressing the basic problems of Africans. These problems had also been presented to the missionaries, but the missionaries had failed to respond adequately. Because it connected with the people, Pentecostalism swept over the continent by winning many converts and drawing members from the mainline churches. Such members from the mainline churches were asked to receive Jesus again and be re-baptized by immersion.[23]

Contribution of Para-Church Organizations to Pentecostalization

In the 1980s, the parade of members from the mainline churches to the Pentecostal churches was boosted by those who had experienced new life in various parachurch organizations in Africa, especially those in tertiary institutions. The Fellowship of Christian Union (FOCUS) in Kenya facilitated the expansion of the Pentecostal renewal in the neighboring countries. In Ghana, the members of the Scripture Union (SU) and University Christian Union who had Pentecostal backgrounds spread the experience among their colleagues. Some Nigerians who did their language study in the francophone countries in West Africa (Togo, Benin, Guinea, and Cote d'Ivoire) also spread the experience.[24]

The Full Gospel Business Men's Fellowship (FGBMF), which was created in the US in 1951, spread throughout the continent in the 1980s. It contributed to the Pentecostal experience immensely through its breakfast meetings. The female counterpart of the FGBMF was the Women's Aglow. These groups invited businessmen and women to their meetings. Through the sharing of testimonies, many people were won to Christ and were encouraged to seek for the baptism of the Holy Spirit with the evidence of speaking in tongues.[25] Many people who joined the student

---

22. Asamoah-Gyadu, "You Shall Receive Power," 45–66.
23. Onyinah, "African Christianity," 305–14.
24. Ojo, "Church in the African State."
25. For reading on the Full Gospel Businessmen Fellowship International, see Asamoah-Gyadu, *Sighs and Signs of the Spirit*.

movements and the business fellowships crossed over from the mainline churches to join the Pentecostal churches.

Response of Mainline Churches

As they lost members to the Pentecostal churches, the mainline churches soon raised an alarm. In Ghana, some of them established committees to investigate and make recommendations as to why people were leaving their fold to join the African-initiated Churches.[26] Eventually, because of the spreading of the Pentecostal faith, and, in a way, as a response to the finding of such committees, renewal groups were organized within the mainline churches. Currently, the prayer meetings of such renewal groups follow the practices of their Pentecostal counterparts. Often it is difficult to notice a difference between a Pentecostal/Charismatic church and a renewal movement in a mainline church. Sometimes, after a mainline church has finished its liturgy, it will shift to the informal Pentecostal way of worship, which includes singing choruses, drumming, clapping hands, dancing, and simultaneous congregational prayer. This is the type of Christianity in Africa now. This is what some pastors and theologians see as the "Pentecostalization" of Christianity in Africa.[27] It has changed the theology and form of Christianity in Africa, and it reveals a supernatural, active, victorious God.

Pentecostal Spirituality and the Resultant Proliferation of Churches

Pentecostalism depends greatly on charisma with no requisite of theological training. Based on 1 Peter 2:9–10, the priesthood of all believers is promoted. A major feature of Pentecostal spirituality is spontaneity, demonstrated in orality. Worship does not depend upon a scripted, written-and-taught liturgy. Therefore, preaching does not demand hermeneutical accuracy. The hermeneutics of Pentecostals is action based, with experience and Scripture handled in partnership. The Holy Spirit is believed to uphold the truth in life experience. Thus, priority is placed on experience, emotions, relations, and the freedom to interpret and appropriate the multiple meanings of biblical texts.

---

26. Asamoah-Gyadu, *African Charismatics*, 63.
27. Anderson, *African Reformation*; Asamoah-Gyadu, "Growth and Trends."

The preference is on narrative—or story—texts. Pastors read them eschatologically as the intrusion of the kingdom of God into the present and as empowerment for living out its promises. The sermon is presented in a transformative way so that the hearers must respond. Pentecostal Christians come to churches with their Bibles, iPads (or notebooks), smartphones, and pens to take notes. Many of the churches record the messages and sell CDs, DVDs, books, and magazines for congregational consumption. In addition to such traditional media, Pentecostals are active with new media (websites, Facebook, Twitter, Instagram) as tools for ministry. Considering how some Pentecostals and Charismatics touch the TV and the radio during preaching and prayer, Asamoah-Gyadu rightly asserts, "For contemporary Pentecostals, mass resources tend to be seen . . . as possessing a certain sacramental value."[28]

One of the main challenges that accompanies Pentecostal spirituality is its liberty. A Nigerian Church historian, Ogbu Kalu, rightly observes, "Leadership thus becomes dependent upon proved worth and charisma and not upon inherent right. As soon as some detect a fault, a weakening of charisma or autocratic exercise of power, a split occurs."[29] With this freedom, new churches spring up daily. Many churches have arisen from renewal groups within the mainline churches and even the classical Pentecostal churches. There are many new Charismatic churches on the continent—and more are added regularly. Six or more churches can worship in one school block, each one in a different classroom. In many African cities, churches are found at every corner and in every vacant space. Their names are all different, and they tell of the excitement inside.

African Initiatives Enriched by Western Pentecostal Preachers

The ministries of some Western Pentecostal preachers fueled the efforts of Africans to change the face of Christianity on the continent. This began in the 1970s when African ministers eagerly read the books and listened to the cassettes of the Western Pentecostal preachers in order to enhance their ministries. In addition, many of them—such as T. L. Osborn, Reinhard Bonnke (Germany), and Morris Cerullo—were invited to hold crusades on the continent.

28. Asamoah-Gyadu, *Sighs and Signs of the Spirit*, 64
29. Kalu, "Third Response," 18.

In Africa, however, was the special role of Archbishop Benson Andrew Idahosa (1938–1998) of Nigeria, who was perhaps the most significant person in the history of Nigerian and Ghanaian Pentecostalism. (He also influenced other African countries.) Idahosa was greatly influenced by many North American Pentecostal preachers. He studied at the Christ for All Nations in the US, which was started by Gordon Lindsay. Afterward, he established the Church of God Mission International and a Bible School in Benin City, Nigeria, where he offered scholarships for people to study. Idahosa received many invitations from Pentecostals and Charismatics across the globe to speak and conduct healing services at their programs. Idahosa's message was centered on faith and healing, and he was not labeled as a "Prosperity Gospel" preacher as such. However, his "flashy" lifestyle challenged ministers of the gospel to shed the poverty mentality and embrace prosperity as integral aspect of Christian living. He can rightly be labeled as a *precursor* to the Prosperity Gospel preaching in Africa.

Spiritual Warfare

Following this, in the early part of the 1980s, was the beginnings of the spiritual warfare movement and the associated books and cassettes (both video and audio) that increased people's awareness of demons and how to exorcize them.[30] In the latter part of the 1980s and early 1990s came an intensification of how to deal with these powers through deliverance, breaking generational curses, and exorcisms. Then, in the latter part of the twentieth century, the movement altered from demon possession to levels of "spiritual warfare." Two levels were explained. Charles Kraft championed the "ground-level," while Peter Wagner was concerned about "cosmic level," which he called "strategic-level warfare." Ground-level warfare is supposed to deal with evil spirits that inhabit people, while strategic-level warfare is supposed to deal with territorial spirits (Dan 10:13, 21), intuitional spirits, spirits assigned to supervise and promote special functions and vices, spirits assigned to spaces, as well as nonmaterial entities and ancestral spirits. Those in this camp tell us that strategic-level spirits

---

30. Irvine, *From Witchcraft to Christ*; Brown, *He Came to Set the Captive Free*; *Prepare for War*; Prince, *Blessings or Cursing*; *From Cursing to Blessing*; *They Shall Expel Demons*; Basham, *Can a Christian Have a Demon?*

are in charge of ground-level spirits and assign and supervise them as they carry out their various assignments.[31]

The spiritual warfare dimension resonated with the African concept of salvation. Salvation is considered transformation and empowerment. This means salvation must produce transformation in the lives of believers, such as the discontinuation of smoking, disco dancing, drinking, and fornication. Salvation must necessarily include prosperity, fruitfulness, healing of sickness, and deliverance from the demonic. Failure to experience these benefits as a Christian is interpreted as the presence of demons or ancestral curses in the person's life and thereby calls for spiritual warfare.

Attempts to Oust All Evils in African Christianity

Spiritual warfare teachings led to a practice in African Christianity which I call "Witchdemonology."[32] Witchdemonology is the synthesis of the practices and beliefs of African witchcraft and Western Christian teachings of demonology and exorcism. These beliefs include the acceptance of the reality of witchcraft, demons and gods; the belief in territorial spirits and mapping them out; the belief in ancestral curses, and the identification of demonic realities and curses in both Christians and non-Christians. In order for people to be set free to prosper in life, special prayer sessions called "deliverance meetings" are held, either in groups or in private sessions.[33]

Witchdemonology opened the door for two types of prophetism. Dr. Emmanuel Anim, a Ghanaian Pentecostal theologian, identifies the first as the "Super-Charismatic Prophetic Movement."[34] These super-charismatic ministers speak to people about their future, reveal the causes of their problems, interpret dreams, reveal ways of dealing with difficult issues, and then pronounce blessings of prosperity and a bright future. Ministers in this category diagnose people's problems through words of knowledge or prophecy. The ministry happens at normal church services, revivals, crusades, "all-night prayer services," and through the media. This is not new; it is similar to divinatory-consultation, which I consider as the live wire of African Traditional Religion. The desires of many people are to prosper, enjoy

---

31. Kraft, *Defeating the Dark Angels*; *Christianity with Power*; Wagner, *Warfare Prayer* [1991]; *Warfare Prayer* [1992]; *Engaging the Enemy*; *Confronting the Powers*.

32. Onyinah, "Contemporary 'Witch-Demonology.'"

33. Onyinah, *Pentecostal Exorcism*.

34. Anim, "Who Wants to Be a Millionaire?," 122.

good health, and be protected from evil forces.³⁵ Ministering to people in this way serves as the charismatic substitute for the old shrine practices in African traditional religions.

The second category is the arena of "quasi-prophets." While the super-charismatic ministers may be genuine Christians who embrace an unbiblical understanding of the spiritual gifts, the quasi-prophets are people whose identification with Christ is questionable. These are "prophets" who promote themselves through any means, including asking people to fake illnesses and claim to be healed after prayer is said for them.³⁶ These so-called prophets are wreaking havoc on the continent.

In other words, what is happening on the continent of Africa is a mixture of Christian and non-Christian activities, all taking place in the name of Christ. Some researchers label everything as the "prosperity gospel," but many of the practices do not fit neatly in that category. Still, Dr. Anim has succinctly argued that prosperity is an important part of the African worldview:

> In African cosmology, the belief in, and pursuit of prosperity is paramount. Africans do not "honor" or accept suffering or poverty. It is a battle they have always sought to fight. The belief in the gods is, primarily, to ensure prosperity and well-being. The influence of the American type of prosperity teaching only served as a catalyst and also reinforced what was already prevailing in the matrix of primal worldview. Thus, local primal considerations offer important perspective in interpreting contemporary African Christianity.³⁷

Against this backdrop, it can rightly be argued that the desire to worship in the biblical pattern, through the lens of primal spirituality, has resulted in the contemporary state of African Christian liturgy and activities, which has a strong emphasis on prosperity. Good health, fullness of life, fertility and prosperity were important aspects of those who were obedient to the Lord in the Old Testament, while wasting disease, premature death

---

35. Quayesi-Amakye, "Prophetism in Ghana's New Prophetic Movement"; Anim, "Prosperity Gospel and the Primal Imagination"; Hackett, "Charismatic/Pentecostal Appropriation."

36. Some claim even frequently to raise the cripple, open the eyes of the blind and open the ears of the deaf, release the mouth of the dumb, and even raise the dead. Some in the attempt have duped the rich and poor, and as a result are placed in prison. Some of these are trending on social media.

37. Anim, "Prosperity Gospel and the Primal Imagination," 30. See also Anim, "Who Wants to Be a Millionaire?"

and dire poverty were the curses for those who disobeyed (e.g., Exod 15:26; 23:24; Deut 11:26–32; 28:15–68). Thus, wellbeing and prosperity have been important parts of both biblical and primal spirituality.

The right application of the prosperity teaching has enabled many churches in Africa to achieve what the early missionaries struggled to achieve: churches that are self-supporting, self-propagating, and self-governing. On the other hand, the abuse that often accompanies the so-called Prosperity Gospel is alarming, and African Christian leaders must address this.

Africa Churches in the Diaspora

The 1980s and 1990s saw a great migration of Africans to the West. Initially, many of them contributed to the growth of Western churches. Yet they could not find their identity and enjoy the services. These types of divisions have a long history. Roswith Gerloff, a German scholar, writing about the African-American slaves rightly said, "The religion of the slaves [Africans] and the religion of the slave master [Whites] were never identical, even when both referred to the same Bible."[38] Contemporary African immigrants faced the same challenge. Thus, in the attempt to find their identity, they began to establish their own churches in the West. By the close of the twentieth century, the African churches had proliferated in the whole of the West, conducting services as they do at home. Currently this has attracted the attention of many scholars. Commenting on the African-initiated churches that he studied, Bengt Sundkler, a Swedish-Tanzanian Church historian and missiologist, said, "In these churches one would be able to see what the African Christian, when left to himself, regarded as important and relevant in Christian faith and Christian church."[39] The issue that remains is whether this form of Pentecostalization of Christianity in Africa will continue to meet the needs of diasporan Africans and how it will relate faithfully to the Christian faith. Time will tell.

Conclusion

The chapter has shown that the Christian missionary enterprise that began in the nineteenth century in Africa, was from one perspective, enormously successful. Christianity flooded sub-Saharan Africa to the extent that it

---

38. Gerloff, "Holy Spirit and the African Diaspora," 91.
39. Sundkler, *Bantu Prophets in South Africa*, 17.

can be assumed that Africa is now Christianized. Nevertheless, the sort of Christianity that the missionary expected to remain in Africa has changed drastically. African Christianity has been Pentecostalized; that is, it is the sort of Christianity that Africans think will benefit them. This new Christian experience in Africa evolved through African ingenuity in the appropriation of the Evangelical Pentecostal Christianity, which was tied to Western, mostly American Pentecostal/Charismatic spirituality. This modern Christianity has replaced the missionary Christianity and that of the early African-initiated churches, yet it is still adorned with the colors of the initial missionary strand. How the Africans can effectively and attractively manage these various colors is the task of African theologians and missiologists.

2

Independent, Enthusiastic, and African

Reframing the Story of Christianity in Africa

Harvey C. Kwiyani

Exploring Africa's Enthusiastic Christianity

My intention in this essay is to discuss the significance of Kwabena Asamoah-Gyadu's expansive work on African Pentecostal and Charismatic Christianity in the context of Africa's widespread enthusiastic Christianity.[1] To do this, I will attempt to situate Asamoah-Gyadu's work in the wider story of the development of African Christianity. I will draw connections between the early African encounters with the missionaries in the nineteenth century and the currently ongoing *charismatization* of African Christianity. I will also attempt to locate it in the wider subject of world Christianity as Africa will shape Christianity in the world for this century. I make use of a historical phenomenology to make sense of the twentieth-century narrative of Africa's spirit-centered Christianity and to make two suggestions. First, a properly contextualized Christianity will be enthusiastic in its outlook. Thus, I argue that only a Christianity that can engage the spirit world just like the old African traditional religions did would be viable both in colonial and post-colonial sub-Saharan Africa. The emergence of African

1. "Africa" in this essay is used to describe what would be rightly called "sub-Saharan Africa."

independent churches suggests that on the one hand, attempts to limit expressions of Christianity in Africa to non-charismatic denominations are often a form of miscontextualization (or undercontextualization, or even non-contextualization) and can only result in a religious and theological identity crisis for Africans.

On the other hand, the labels that we use for African Christianity do not sufficiently describe what is happening on the ground. Many African independent churches precede Pentecostalism and most of them do not subscribe to Pentecostal theology even though they are often lumped together as Pentecostals. Second, I argue that Asamoah-Gyadu's work is of greater and broader significance as it (inadvertently, I believe) announces the full arrival—or the *mainstreaming*—of spirit-centered expressions of Christianity in the form of Pentecostal, Charismatic, and Neo-Pentecostal movements in the continent in Africa. Looking back at the body of his literature, it becomes rather clear that he presents to us African Christianity at a tipping point where it confidently assumes its identity as African Christianity both in the continent and in the diaspora, and in the process, it begins to influence world Christianity. He catches the story at a moment when Africa Christianity is able to actually become African. I attempt to connect this current development to the African independent churches of old. Of course, it is in the past two decades that African Christianity has begun to let go off its western robes, theological and otherwise, and Asamoah-Gyadu has provided a critical commentary to the process. Indeed, he captures for us the story of the *africanization* of Christianity, first in Ghana in his *African Charismatics* but later, in his subsequent works, in the wider African context including that of the African diaspora. I argue that this *africanization* of Christianity reflects the momentum of African independent churches and is shaped largely by the encounter between African culture and Christianity (and not Pentecostalism).

Appropriating Asamoah-Gyadu in African Christianity

Asamoah-Gyadu's work stands tall in a long line of important scholarly writings on African Christianity. Before him are towering figures of such scholars of renown as Andrew Walls, John Mbiti, Lamin Sanneh, Kwame Bediako, Allan Anderson, and many others. He picks up the baton in the late 1990s and emerges to make a critical commentary on subsequent developments in African Christianity in a period when it begins to reshape itself as an African religion. Asamoah-Gyadu has dedicated a great deal of his work for the past two decades to making a very important commentary—a *critical* one for that matter—on the ongoing *africanization* and *charismatization* of Christianity in Africa. This story of African Christianity does not begin in the second half of the twentieth century when Africa emerges to be a significant Christian heartland while Europe's secularization continues at a shockingly rapid pace. Thus, Asamoah-Gyadu's work serves to connect contemporary Christianity in Africa both with its past and its future. The *africanization* that we are seeing is in its very early stages. Africa will shape a great deal of ecclesial history for the next few centuries. This time that we live in, following the great works of Asamoah-Gyadu, will be recognized as the tipping point when African Christianity embraced its enthusiastic nature and rose up to re-energize world Christianity. This story will not be told without the mention of the eloquent words of J. Kwabena Asamoah-Gyadu. But to appreciate his impact, we have to start at the beginning.

Why Did You Hide the Spirit from Us?

The emergence of spirit-oriented forms of Christianity in Africa precedes the birth of the Pentecostal movement by at least two decades. Early African spirit-oriented churches began to appear in West Africa in the 1870s, long before the partitioning of the continent at the Berlin Conference of 1884, the scramble for Africa that followed, and the colonizing of Africa by European powers. Indeed, they appeared long before the rise of the Pentecostal movement in California in 1906. We could actually look to the charismatic tendencies in early Christian communities of North Africa (e.g., the Montanists and Saint Anthony, 100–500 CE) and the Kongo (e.g., Kimpa Vita, 1500–1700 CE) to say that enthusiastic Christianity actually precedes the arrival of the nineteenth-century missionaries in Africa. However, that said, my argument in this essay only focuses only on those enthusiastic expressions of Christianity that emerged after the missionaries arrived in Africa in the 1800s. These spirit-oriented churches were labelled African independent churches right from the moment they emerged—and in the course of the decades that followed, they have been called African *instituted* churches or African *initiated* churches, or in some cases, African *indigenous* churches.

African independent churches first appeared in West Africa where many European missionaries begun to work in the early decades of the nineteenth century. They emerged largely because of two factors; access to education and the presence of African religions. Often, the missionaries started with education partly because they needed their new converts to be able to read the Bible. They established schools for the teaching of the children of their converts and used them to convince and coerce others to conversion. Along with education and evangelism came the need to translate the Bible into African vernaculars. But above all this, education was the only perceivable way to civilize the heathens out there, so they reasoned. It was largely through education that they would civilize and *christianize* the Africans.[2] Thus, education fit well with the missionaries' agenda to bring civilization to Africa. Practically speaking, educated Africans—and by this, in the context of nineteenth-century Africa, I have in mind primary-school-educated Africans—could be more helpful in serving the missionaries both in the church as altar boys or deacons, for instance, and at home as gardeners and cooks. All in all, educated Africans were beneficial to the missionaries. In addition, many African leaders were open to having their subjects go to school under the missionaries as they understood that "you could only defeat the white man if you had the white man's education."[3] Before long, quite a few Africans were able to read the Bible in their own languages. Some Africans actually learned to read and write in European languages and could, therefore, read the Bible in English, French, Dutch, or German. This direct access to the Bible meant they could interpret the Bible for themselves without needing the help of the missionaries. Consequently, Africans could also confidently disagree with the missionaries on how they understood the text of the Bible.

One subject of contention between the Africans and the missionaries was that of the Spirit and the spirit-world. On the one hand, African converts were informed by traditional religion, from which they had converted, and which had a vibrant and dynamic spirit-world that shaped the entirety of their lives, from birth to death. It has been said numerous times by African scholars from John Mbiti[4] to Kwame Bediako[5]

---

2. It is also because of education—the access given to Africans to learn the *white man's book*—that Europe's colonization of Africa only lasted eighty years.

3. Both Chinua Achebe and Ngugi wa Thiong'o are clear about this in their novels *Things Fall Apart* and *The River Between* respectively.

4. Mbiti, *African Religions and Philosophy*.

5. Bediako, *Christianity in Africa*.

and Laurenti Magesa[6] that for Africans, the spirit-world is not a distant reality and that spirits can break into the material world of human beings at any time. This is normal and generally expected and accepted among Africans, especially those outside Christianity and Islam. Indeed, for most cultures in sub-Saharan Africa, the gap between the material and the spiritual worlds is so thin that it is considered non-existent and whatever of it exists, it is thoroughly permeable that humans and spirit interact constantly. Indeed, for precolonial Africans, it was impossible to tell a people's religion apart from their culture as the two are generally inseparable. Precolonial Africans understood religion to be entirely about staying connected with the spirit-world (of ancestors and other spirits, including that of god, whatever that god was called in each of their tribal languages), and they shaped their culture accordingly. Until today, almost two hundred years after the arrival of the missionaries, and even after a majority of sub-Saharan populations are Christian, the belief in a spirit-world among Africans is unaffected. If anything, as Asamoah-Gyadu shows us, this belief in an active spirit-world has made Christianity catch fire in the continent. It is spirit-centered Christianity that has exploded in Africa in the past fifty years. I cannot count how many times I heard as a young African growing up in Malawi that "the spirit-world is more real than the physical world," and that "human beings are essentially spirits that have (and live in) human bodies." This attention to and awareness of the spiritual world shaped—and continues to shape—the ways in which Africans engaged with the missionaries and read the Bible.

The missionaries, on the other hand, were shaped in modernity in Europe and would find it difficult to understand and acknowledge the vibrancy of African religions and their openness to the spirit-world. Of course, by 1800, the Enlightenment had been shaping European culture for almost 200 years. In this time—and this would go on for another 200 years—science and reason were the drivers of European life. Religion slowly gave way to science, losing its place on the public sphere in the process. European Christianity would have to keep adapting itself to a culture that was constantly shifting towards secular humanism. Even its theology would eventually lose its ability to understand and engage the spiritual nature of Christianity as a religion. Bultmann, a German theologian of the twentieth century, would become famous for having demythologized

---

6. Magesa, *What Is Not Sacred?*

the miracles of the New Testament."⁷ Consequently, when the missionaries came to Africa, they arrived equipped with a theology that could not fathom African spirituality, let alone its religion. Many of their converts would find this new religion, the Christianity of the missionaries, devoid of the Spirit. Without an active spirit, the Christianity of the missionaries would leave its converts unprotected from contrary spirits (both of their abandoned deities and ancestors and those sent by their enemies to harm them), and this was a real danger that cost people their lives. Victor Hayward is correct in his diagnosis:

> Christianity was too Western, too rationalistic and otherworldly, to gain the confidence of its adherents at their deepest levels of experience. This showed up most plainly in those times of personal crisis, such as barrenness and sickness, when many baptized believers, thinking that Jesus Christ did not have any interest, or worse, the power to improve their state of affairs, felt they had to visit the traditional healer.⁸

Gottfried Oosterwal would be more direct in 1973:

> For it is precisely the absence or lack of the power of God as a reality people can live by that has been a precipitating factor to these movements. In the African traditional religions, power is as the center of their thinking, life, and experience. And the *spirit*—of God, the gods, or the ancestors—was a tangible reality. How remote, how intellectual, how powerless seems to be the God and the Spirit the missionaries preach about, or the Westerners show in their lives. As one leader once expressed it in a conversation with the missionary, "*You have held back the Spirit!*"⁹

One of my ancestors, a spirit medium and herbalist, refused for a long time to convert to the Christianity of the Western missionaries saying, "Your religion has no sense of mystery and wonder. Its spirit is too passive; one would think it does not exist at all. Therefore, your religion is no religion at all." Towards the end of his life, after he converted, he told me,

---

7. Bultmann, *Jesus Christ and Mythology*. John Mbiti tells a fictitious yet tragic story of a young African PhD graduate majoring in theology who returns home after many years of study abroad and cannot exorcize his sister (as expected by his family and community) because Bultmann had demythologized demon possession. See Mbiti, "Theological Impotence."

8. Hayward, *African Independent Church Movements*, 50.

9. Oosterwal, *Modern Messianic Movements*, 36 (my italics).

"A religion that fails to connect with the spirit is only a moral philosophy whose only good news is either moral legalism or moral liberalism." When I asked him to explain why he converted, he said that when he discovered the Holy Spirit it reflected the spiritual world in its purest form and it was more powerful than anything he had worked with. It is to people like him that African independent churches were attractive. The Africans who initiated independent churches had converted from traditional religion to Christianity only to find that (1) Christianity—as it was presented by the missionaries—did not know how to meet to their spiritual needs and (2) being a Christian meant they had to let go of everything to do with African culture. As a result, it was generally impossible for a person to be a Christian and an African at the same time. Christianity and African culture were mutually exclusive. Naturally, many converts to Christianity sought ways to keep their newly found faith without losing their *Africanness*. To do this, they had to reinterpret the Bible to make space for the active spiritual world they knew from the African religion. It was a great delight when the African converts discovered the Spirit in the Bible.

As Africans came to understand the Bible more, the gap between African independent churches and the missionary-led churches would widen. Often, the missionaries did not appreciate African independent churches and incited the colonial governments to frustrate them. In the Congo, for instance, Baptist missionaries would incite the colonial government to imprison Simeon Kimbangu in 1921 for establishing an independent healing ministry that proved more popular than the mission churches.[10] Even though both William Wade Harris and Garrick Sokari Braide were wildly successful in their evangelism efforts in West Africa, reaching many thousands more than the missionaries could and challenging Africans in ways that actually resonated with their cultural sensibilities (for instance, to burn their fetishes and trust the spiritual powers of Jesus Christ to protect them), they both were maltreated by the colonial government while the missionaries nodded and looked away.[11]

---

10. For the fascinating story of the Prophet Kimbangu, see Mokoko Gampiot and Coquet-Mokoko, *Kimbanguism*.

11. Harris was deported from Ivory Coast for disturbing peace through his evangelism. Braide was jailed because his ministry threatened lowering tax on alcohol as people were convicted to stop drinking beer. See Isichei, "Soul of Fire"; Tasie, *Christian Missionary Enterprise*.

African Independent Churches in the Colonial Era

African independent churches started as a protest form of Christianity, first against the spiritually deficient Christianity of the missionaries and later against colonialism, especially where colonialism worked hand-in-hand with the missionaries (which was almost everywhere). Generally speaking, European colonialism took full advantage of the presence of the missionaries in Africa.[12] To many, it actually appeared like the sending of missionaries to Africa was intended to prepare the way for colonialism, especially as Europeans needed to replace the trade of kidnapping and enslaving Africans to sell them in the Americas which had run for more than four hundred years with a new one. Edward Andrews argues that even though many modern mission historians—Kenneth Latourette and Stephen Neill inclusive—have portrayed missionaries as "visible saints, exemplars of ideal piety in a sea of persistent savagery" wider Western scholarship often labels them as the religious arm of European colonialism.[13] Indeed, some missionaries actually worked for their European governments, pacifying the people before the full wrath of colonialism was unleashed and keeping them subservient to their colonial masters, forcing upon them racist ideologies of white supremacy—that everything African was evil and inferior. David Silverman adds that "by the time the colonial era drew to a close in the last half of the twentieth century, missionaries became viewed as 'ideological shock troops for colonial invasion whose zealotry blinded them,' colonialism's 'agent, scribe and moral alibi.'"[14] While, of course, there existed many missionaries who sought to undermine colonialism, it is unthinkable that the colonial agenda did not aid mission in any way. The mere presence of a European colonial governor with his agents and numerous white traders made the work of the missionary somewhat easier.

Surprisingly though, Christianity began to take root in Africa during the colonial era. Even the missionaries themselves did not expect Christianity to gain traction in Africa. At the World Missionary Conference in Edinburgh in 1910—at the peak of both the colonial scramble in Africa and

---

12. Mongo Beti's classic novel, *The Poor Christ of Bomba*, narrates an excellent story that reflects the complex relationship between mission and colonialism. However, this is a theme that has been explored to a great depth by many scholars in the past century. See Beti, *Poor Christ of Bomba*. I would also refer the reader to Robert, *Converting Colonialism*. Another good resource is Carey, *God's Empire*.

13. Andrews, "Christian Missions and Colonial Empires Reconsidered," 663.

14. Silverman, "Indians, Missionaries, and Religious Translation," 144.

of the Western missionary movement—they believed that Africa appeared to be on the verge of converting to Islam. They were wrong. Christianity continued to grow in Africa. It grew exponentially and unexpectedly in the African independent churches, away from the gaze of the colonial governments and the mission scholars. William Wade Harris's story of travelling to and through Cote d'Ivoire, baptizing an estimated one hundred thousand converts in an eighteen-month period and impacting the lives of an estimated two hundred thousand people over the three years[15] when European missionaries could convert only one thousand people would play itself many times over in other parts of Africa. In addition, mission churches generally thrived where they allowed marginal movements of revival to exist in their midst. The Anglican Church in Kenya, Uganda, and Rwanda would benefit greatly from the East African Revival that operated between the Church and charismatic independent groups in the region. Allan Anderson is right to suggest that the growth of African independent churches is akin to an *African Reformation*—the title of his book that explores their development in the twentieth century.[16] Citing Bengt Sundkler, Anderson says that African independent churches grew from forty-two thousand members in 1900 to fifty-four million in 2000.[17] Gina Zurlo and Todd Johnson project that they will be at one hundred eighty million in 2025.[18] This suggests that almost 25 percent of African Christians are in independent and unaffiliated churches. While this phenomenal growth is to be celebrated, I wish to suggest that their greatest impact is that they prepared the way for the Pentecostal, Charismatic, and Neo-Pentecostal churches that emerged in postcolonial Africa.

During the colonial era, Europeans were essentially in charge of both governance and religion over millions of Africans even though they did not understand the religious sensibilities of Africans. Consequently, they sought to do away with African traditional religion and they frowned upon

---

15. Isichei, "Soul of Fire," 24.

16. Anderson, *African Reformation*.

17. Anderson, *African Reformation*, 7. He adds that the World Christian Encyclopedia put the figure at eighty three million, and this only highlights the problematic nature of these statistics, especially when they have to do with Christianity in Africa.

18. 151 million for Independents plus 29 million for Unaffiliateds. Zurlo and Johnson, "Religious Demographics of Africa," 155. Both Pentecostals and African independent churches are included in this figure, and that makes the figure seem rather conservative. This is part of the challenge of depending on Western categories to explore African Christianity.

African independent churches, often persecuting their members. The existence of such churches allowed Africans some space out of European reach to practice a form of Christianity that the Europeans did not understand. This was a great cause for concern for Europeans as they needed to monitor the Africans at all times for fear of anticolonial uprisings. In Malawi, an insurrection in 1915 led by John Chilembwe, a Malawian evangelist, caused the British colonial government to pass laws that made it impossible for Malawians to register Christian churches unless they were led by white Westerners.[19] Those laws were abolished after Malawi gained her independence from Britain in 1964.[20]

Second, African independent churches differed quite significantly from Europeans both in their theology and their ecclesiology. William Wade Harris's calabash and cross, the *Aladura's* white garments, Isaiah Shembe's music and dancing, Simeon Kimbangu's healing ministry, all these plus the prominent role of the charismatic leader (in the likeness of the oracle or the medium of traditional religion) made it difficult for Europeans to trust members of African independent churches as fellow Christians. Since most of their leaders were not advanced in the Western system of education, and that they were either illiterate or semi-literate in the eyes of the Europeans, there was always concern about syncretism—that Africans were mixing their Christianity with aspects of African religion. Of course, the operational belief was that all Christians would worship and behave just like European Christians. Many missionaries believed that there was only one way to be a Christian—the European way. Every Christian in the world would have to believe and behave like a European. Any deviation was suspect. Consequently, African independent churches were politically suspicious and religiously unwelcome. Therefore, by their very existence, African independent churches critiqued this belief and showed that Christianity without European culture is possible. Whatever the Europeans thought of as syncretism, the Africans believed to be contextualization. Thus, the Africans risked syncretism in order to be—a charge that we still hear today even though it is true that every expression of Christianity has some syncretism in it. Yet, by the time colonialism came to an end, they had grown at a significantly faster rate than missionary-led denominational churches.

---

19. Shepperson and Price, *Independent African*.
20. Strohbehn, *Pentecostalism in Malawi*.

SECTION I: CHRISTIANITY IN HISTORY

Pentecostal, Charismatic, Neo-Charismatic, and Beyond

At the center of the argument of this chapter is the proposition that African independent churches have made African Christianity as we know it today possible. What Harris and Kimbangu did earlier on in the twentieth century, at the height of the colonial era became the template for the multiplication that we see in African Christianity in postcolonial Africa. Their spirit-empowered prophetic and healing ministries that critiqued and protested against the missionaries and the colonists foreshadow the many charismatic ministries that have emerged in Africa since the end of colonialism. They were both extremely successful in their evangelizing efforts. They understood how to engage their audiences from within their own cultures—the missionaries could never do this. They not only spoke local languages, they also understood the spiritual needs of Africans. Through prophetic and healing gifts, they presented to Africans a God who was both touched by their needs and was close enough to help. The Jesus of Harris and Kimbangu was not only concerned with saving souls from hellfire. Yes, people had to be saved, but they also had to trust Jesus' Spirit for protection and healing. They had to burn their fetishes and be healed of their diseases through prayer. It should be no surprise that beginning in the 1960s and 1970s when European colonization of Africa started to unravel, and the colonial representatives and agents returned to Europe, it is the Harris or Kimbangu type of Christianity that emerged across sub-Saharan Africa. The process of decolonizing Christianity took much longer (and is said to have been a lot harder) than that of the political states but when it happened, a spirit-oriented Christianity emerged. Many Western missionaries tried to stay on, arguing that the "younger churches" of Africa were not mature enough yet to stand on their own. A majority of them had to be pushed to move on.[21] But once the leadership of African churches was handed over to Africans, many churches began to allow some aspects of African culture shape their theology and ecclesiology and just like in the African independent churches of old, the Spirit came rushing in. Overall, it became clear that a decolonized African Christianity had to liberate itself from European thought systems.

Since the 1970s, the Christianity of African independent churches has come to shape a great deal of African Christianity. Without the widespread

21. John Gatu's request for a moratorium on Western missionaries in Africa in 1971 was inspired by the process of political decolonization that swept through sub-Saharan Africa in the 1960s. See Reese, "John Gatu and the Moratorium on Missionaries."

misunderstandings and persecutions from the missionaries and colonial governments, African independent churches have themselves thrived and multiplied. They are home to millions upon millions of Christians in sub-Saharan Africa. For instance, both the Harrist and Kimbanguist churches have continued to grow. In southern Africa, Apostolic and Zionist churches have also continued to spread across many countries. Altogether, these classical African independent churches have millions of members both in Africa and in the African diaspora.[22] Many other African independent churches have modernized and rebranded as Pentecostal denominations. Several large West African Pentecostal denominations started out as *Aladura* groups of praying people. Both the Redeemed Christian Church of God and the Apostolic Church of Nigeria—with more than ten million members between them—have their roots in the *Aladura* movements of the 1920s. In addition, of course, the Pentecostal movement made it possible for many who wanted a spirit-oriented Christianity to find a home outside the mission-established and -controlled churches. Classical Pentecostal denominations like the Assemblies of God and Foursquare have also benefitted, but in the context of Africa, they are far outnumbered by other enthusiastic expressions of Christianity. Neo-Pentecostal churches are generally modernized African independent churches. They have emerged in Africa after colonialism.

Consequently, they have a different set of concerns from those of the early AICs. In addition, most of them have Western connections and are largely informed by American popular Christianity. In addition, data coming out of America research organization puts African Pentecostal, Charismatic and Neo-Pentecostal Christians at 25 percent of the entire African Christian population. However, anecdotal reports coming from the continent are saying otherwise. Spirit-oriented Christianity influences almost all of African Christianity. Even those denominations that have come out of strict Reformed and cessationist movements have had to *pentecostalize*. Anglicans, Baptists, Catholics, Presbyterians, and all other mission-established churches have gone through a process of *pentecostalizing*. They have had no choice but to follow the crowd and transform themselves to allow African culture and worldview influence their theology and ecclesiology. We joke of Bapticostals and Prescostals as a way of I have heard from many friends, Lutherans from Nigeria, Anglicans from

---

22. For example, the Kimbanguist Church has a significant presence in Belgium. The Apostolic Church of Zimbabwe has several congregations in England.

Kenya, and Presbyterians from Malawi saying, "If we cannot beat the Pentecostals, we better join them, otherwise we will lose all our members." One would be hard pressed to find a denomination that has not been affected, some kicking and screaming. Back in the 1980s and 1990s, it was common for mission-founded churches to demand that their members should not fellowship with the tongue-speaking Charismatics. Some denominations excommunicated their members for behaving like Pentecostals. Today, we have generations of African Christians who have never belonged in a non-charismatic church, many who cannot imagine being church without the charismatic gifts of the Spirit being manifest.

We Need New Terms

In African Christianity, the lines between the Pentecostals, Charismatics, and Neo-Pentecostals are blurred and very permeable. Most people are not even clear whether they are Pentecostal or Charismatic and why they belong to those camps. Many do not even know what differentiates them from other traditions. A typical "Pentecostal" pastor in rural Africa has never heard of Azusa Street, Amos Yong, or Wayne Grudem. More important though, Pentecostals, Charismatics, and Neo-Pentecostals form only a small section of the many spirit-oriented Christians in the continent. Just like those Christians who formed AICs before the birth of Pentecostalism, African Christians do not need to be Pentecostals, Charismatics, or Neo-Pentecostals to believe in the active power of the Spirit. In addition, the lines between these spiritist denominations and mission-founded churches have also become thinner in Africa by the year. African Christians can be in a Catholic or a Presbyterian church and yet be filled with the Holy Spirit with the evidence of speaking in tongues and find it normal. Generally speaking, Africans do not even need to be Christians to believe in the power of the spiritual world. The power of the spirits is part of their worldview. Such Africans find a Christianity without an active spirit-world impotent and strange. A religion whose spirit cannot perform miracles does not make sense to most Africans. A god that cannot help its people in times of need is not a god at all.

For this reason, when we use these generalized labels to describe African Christianity, we risk being vague and out-of-context. Of course, labels are important; they help us categorize whatever it is that we are working with, based on similarities, differences or any other criteria. Labels help us box similar things together and, at the same time, keep those things that are dissimilar, and do not belong, out of the box. However, labels always make sense in the perspective of the people doing the labelling. They hardly reflect the self-understanding of those being labelled. This explains why people reject labels given to them by others. In this conversation, all the labels that we use—Pentecostal, Charismatic, Neo-Pentecostal and/or Neo-Charismatic—are imported from the West. They work well when used to describe some sects of Western (and usually American) Christianity. However, it appears to me that, more often than not, when we import them to Africa, we often fail to recognize that what we identify as African Pentecostalism is in many ways different from American Pentecostalism. Even when we are talking about one and the same Pentecostal denomination operating in the United States and in Africa at the same time, (for instance, the Assemblies of God—a classical Pentecostal denomination in the United States that has found its way to many African countries), its American and African members do not always believe the same things. Their theologies are not congruent on all issues pertaining the Spirit. Even their belief in the gifts of the Spirit does not lead to the same behaviours and manifestations. Here in Britain where this writer resides, the Ghanaian-originated Pentecostal denomination, the Church of Pentecost, looks and behaves nothing like its British sister-denomination, the ELIM Pentecostal Church. I am even more intrigued when I see that the Ghanaian members of the Church of Pentecost in Britain are happier to belong to their Ghanaian denomination and not the British ELIM even when it takes more effort to do so.

In Europe, where there exists today a significant presence of African Christians, it is well-accepted that the type of Christianity that has come from Africa is Pentecostal in nature.[23] The term "African Pentecostalism" has almost become synonymous to African Christianity. The largest African denominations in the diaspora are Pentecostal, and they have become representative of African Christianity outside Africa. Be it the Redeemed Christian Church of God with their one thousand congregations in the UK alone, or the Church of Pentecost that has almost two hundred assemblies in the UK, or even Sunday Adelaja's Blessed Embassy of the Kingdom of God in Kiev, Ukraine, when researchers write about African Christianity in Europe, it is usually these Pentecostal churches that are in focus. However, both the ethnocentric label, "African," and the theological one, "Pentecostal," are problematic, especially in the diaspora.

23. Kwiyani, *Sent Forth*, 110.

"African Pentecostals" forms a double fronted missional barrier to Westerners who, while finding "African" exotic and interesting, are suspicious of Pentecostalism—it is foreign to the Western Enlightenment-shaped worldview. I believe that if African Christianity is taken for what it is, and understood to be necessarily enthusiastic because of the culture that shapes it, it has a great deal to offer to the world.

Conclusion

Africa's enthusiastic Christianity makes a unique contribution to the world. The circumstances around its emergence are unique. The historical realities of Africa's encounter with Europe—the four hundred years of the Trans-Atlantic slave trade and the ensuing attempts to evangelize and colonize Africa—plus the spiritual realities of African cultures make a distinct flavour of Christianity inevitable. Several decades after the Scramble for Africa, we see Christianity gain traction in the continent, even when the Africans were beginning to agitate for independence. Most of those Africans who found Christianity attractive needed a type of Christianity that was strong enough to meet all their spiritual needs. An enthusiastic Christianity emerged that continues until today. It is this Christianity that has reshaped the religious landscape of Africa. It is larger than any of our current labels can contain. It arises out of Africa with the potential to reach the world in the power of the Spirit. One of its major scribes is Asamoah-Gyadu. As the next generation will write about it, they will owe a great deal of that history to him.

3

From/To the Ends of the Earth
Mission in the Spirit

Kirsteen Kim

Dr. Kwabena Asamoah-Gyadu is known in World Christianity especially for his sympathetic studies of African Pentecostalism. Many studies of Pentecostalism have explained it in purely sociological terms, or criticized it using Western theological categories. However, Asamoah-Gyadu offers cultural and theological explanations drawn from his expertise in African Traditional Religion and African spiritualities. His thick description helps to set issues of power encounter, prosperity, and other criticisms of African Christianity within a broader context of the reinvention of the church in Africa by Africans which takes as its paradigm the experience of the church at Pentecost. As such, Asamoah-Gyadu is able to present new theological insights from a vigorous part of world Christianity to the other parts.

In honor of Dr. Asamoah-Gyadu's work and following its spirit, I will re-read the Pentecost narrative and the Book of Acts in a way which is informed by the study of mission and world Christianity. First, reflecting on Pentecost and its aftermath in Acts, I will offer a new model of the apostolicity of the church. Second, I will suggest that the interface of mission—sending to the ends of the earth—and world Christianity—described as from the ends of the earth—offers a new way of understanding the church's catholicity. Both these moves contribute to a de-centering of Europe in world Christianity.

Mission in the Spirit: A New Approach to Apostolicity

Pentecost: From/to the Ends of the Earth

The annual report for 2013–2014 of the Evangelische Missionswerk in Deutschland (EMW), which brings together the Protestant churches and missions in Germany, took as its title for a study of world mission "*From* the Ends of the Earth."[1] It derived this title from the record of the diaspora Jews gathered in Jerusalem at Pentecost (Acts 2:5). But as we know, the Pentecost event is more readily seen as the fulfillment of Jesus' promise to his disciples: "you will receive power when the Holy Spirit has come upon you; and you will be my witnesses in Jerusalem, in all Judea and Samaria, and *to* the ends of the earth" (Acts 1:8). The problem with that verse today, after more than five hundred years of Christendom, is that "To the ends of the earth" sounds suspiciously like the colonial paradigm of mission in which missionaries, along with adventurers and colonizers, went out from Europe as far as they could go. In a post-colonial world, some of the problems of this model have necessitated re-thinking it, together with its theological foundations. Much attention has already been given by David Bosch and others to the re-interpreting the "Great Commission" of Matthew 28:18–20, but the same treatment needs to be given to the rest of the New Testament.[2]

The book of Acts is foundational for understanding the mission of the early church. Does "*to* the ends of the earth" imply that Luke shared the expansionist vision of the contemporary Roman emperors or the colonial vision of the modern West?[3] I think not, for several reasons.[4] First, we cannot accuse Luke of imperial attitudes. The mission of the apostles is described as "witnessing to Christ" (Acts 1:8). That is, it has the same self-sacrificing character as Jesus' mission. The apostles are vulnerable—even Paul, the

---

1. EMW, *Von allen Enden der Erde*. This chapter originates in the guest lecture which I gave at the invitation of the Evangelisches Missionswerk (EMW) to their General Assembly, in Breklum, Germany, October 8–10, 2014. I thank Dr. Michael Biehl and the EMW for their kind hospitality and also their framing of the topic which stimulated my thinking.
2. See Bosch, "Structure of Mission."
3. See Burrus, "Gospel of Luke and the Acts of the Apostles."
4. Shillington, *Study of Luke-Acts*.

Roman citizen, gets imprisoned for the faith. The early Christians were Jews, an oppressed group within the empire, and not agents of any political power. Like Jesus, the apostles rejected the adulation of the people (Paul and Barnabas, Acts 14:8–17) and did not gain materially from their missions. The apostles condemned demons but not people (with the possible exception of Elymas, Acts 13:6–11). And, most strikingly of all, the apostles did not impose their Jewish culture on Gentile converts.

Second, although the spread of the gospel according to Luke is often thought of in terms of expanding concentric circles—*from* Jerusalem, to Judaea, Samaria, and the ends of the earth—and was used in colonial mission histories as a prototype of expansionist history,[5] this image of expansion is a misperception. There are several reasons why; first, because the call to witness is *in* each of those locations; second, because they do not form concentric circles. Jerusalem may be central to Judaea but not to Samaria. These first three places represent the ministry of Jesus himself, and the progress of the gospel in Acts 2:1–8:25. "The ends of the earth" is clearly the new departure, the mission to the gentiles, which we read about from Acts 8:26 onwards, mostly in connection with Paul. However, it is clear that Paul is not the only missionary to the Gentiles—there were other missions like those of Philip (Acts 8:4–40; 21:8), Barnabas (Acts 15:36–40), and Apollos (Acts 18:24–28; 1 Cor 1:12; 3:4–6, 22). But even though they went to the Gentiles, there is no record in Acts of Paul or any other apostle reaching the end of the earth.

What we hear about in Acts is mostly about a spreading of the good news within the Roman Empire. Like most empires, it dispossessed and displaced individuals and whole communities. Persecutions—like those recorded in Acts 8; 11; and 18—caused Christian communities to break up, scatter or re-locate in a random fashion. As well as such involuntary movement, the empire also facilitated mobility for some, like Paul himself, his fellow tent-makers Priscilla and Aquila, and Lydia, the business woman (Acts 16).[6] But in this period, Christianity was not the imperial power; it was subject to imperial whims. The spread of the early church was not one of relentless expansion and its limited growth was not by conquering territory. Third, expansion is a misnomer because it misses half of

---

5. E.g., Latourette, *History of the Expansion of Christianity*.

6. For insight into the colonial and diaspora context of early Christian mission, see, inter alia, Wright, *New Testament and the People of God*; Schnelle, *Apostle Paul*; Wedderburn, *History of the First Christians*; Irvin and Sunquist, *History of the World Christian Movement*; Harris, *Mission in the Gospels*.

the story. As the EMW report points out, the direction of spread was not only outwards from Jerusalem; at Pentecost there is also a movement in the opposite direction.[7] Moreover, later in Acts we read that Paul himself frequently returns to Jerusalem, sometimes bringing Gentiles with him (Acts 12:25; 15:4; 18:22; 21:17).

Luke may have an agenda to lay the ground for peace between Christianity and Rome, but—and this is the third reason why he cannot be charged with imperialism—Luke is at the same time subversive of Roman power. Luke's narrative, with its message of "good news to the poor" (Luke 4:18), has equally provided a key foundation for liberation theology. Luke may admire elements of the Roman Empire; for example, as in the Christian community, within the empire Jew-Gentile distinctions are transcended; and in Acts, Paul calls on Roman justice and experiences Roman protection. But Luke is all the while claiming supremacy for the kingdom of God, which transcends and sometimes counters Rome because Jesus is revealed as "Lord" (e.g., Acts 9:1–28).

Finally, Luke's narrative, which follows Paul around Asia Minor, into Greece, and on to Rome, does not imply a special place for the West in Christian history. It is true that Luke does not refer to Paul's years in Arabia (Gal 1:17; 2 Cor 11:32–33) but he does mention the spread of the gospel to Africa—Ethiopia—by a native of that place (Acts 8:27–39), and this is the implication also of the reference to diaspora representatives in Acts 2. We are meant to assume that they took they gospel back with them and that this is therefore not only the best record of the Jewish diaspora in that period but also, plausibly, a record of the location of the first churches. They extended from Pontus in the north of Asia Minor south to Egypt, from Rome in the west to Elam, which is east of Arabia.

In this connection, it is important to note that the "Macedonian call" (Acts 16:9–10) is not described by Luke as a call into Europe—that is a later European interpolation. It is true that, after his circular journeys, Paul travels from Jerusalem to Rome. However, this is not primarily because it is west but because it is the heart of empire. There is no indication in Acts that Jerusalem, or Antioch, or any of the other centers mentioned are superseded by Rome as a Christian center. The witness in the other places continues. Arguably neither Jerusalem nor Rome nor anywhere else is the center for Luke, but only heaven, where Jesus is. The book begins with Jesus' ascension to there (Acts

---

7. EMW, *Von allen Enden der Erde*, 3.

1:1–11) and the most exemplary witnesses in Acts—Stephen and Paul—both have visions of heaven (Acts 7:55; 9:3; 10:11, 16).[8]

It is often said that Luke's second volume, the Acts of the Apostles would be better named "the Acts of the Holy Spirit." It is true that the Holy Spirit initiates, guides and empowers the church's mission in Acts.[9] We could also say that the filling of the Holy Spirit is a prerequisite for all Christian witness—not only in the iconic case of the disciples at Pentecost but in every case. Following the first Pentecost there are repeated pentecosts in Acts. The believers in Jerusalem received the Holy Spirit a second time (4:31) but in most cases the reference is to the Spirit coming on different communities. After their baptism, the Samaritans received the Holy Spirit through the ministry of Peter and John (8:14–17). The Gentiles associated with the Roman centurion Cornelius received the Holy Spirit in the same way as the Jews had, which convinced Peter and the church in Jerusalem that the Gentiles had also gained the new life of salvation (10:44–48; 11:17–18) and contributed to their being counted as Christians on equal terms as Jews by the Jerusalem Council (15:8–9).[10] The Holy Spirit came upon the Ephesians through Paul's ministry with the same manifestations of power (19:1–7). The ending of Acts leaves open the possibility of continued manifestations of the Spirit's power. Pentecostals—as their name implies—but also Pietist, Holiness, charismatic and other movements before them—expect such continued blessing and look for the signs of the Spirit described by Luke.[11] They see themselves as undergoing the same experience as that of the early church. Luke's somewhat idealized picture of the early church is directly informing the identity and practice of many newer churches today

We could take one example of a contemporary Pentecostal-charismatic movement to illustrate this. Protestant Christianity in Korea experienced a revival movement in 1903–1907, the period in which Pentecostalism emerged in the USA, and which has much in common with it and other similar movements in Wales, India, and other parts of the world around

---

8. E.g., Gooder, "Gospel of Luke."

9. Bosch, *Transforming Mission*, 114.

10. The Jerusalem Council might be seen as drawing back from Peter's conclusion and qualifying the status of Gentiles, but Gonzales points out that in Acts 15:9–11 Peter goes beyond what he claimed in chapter 10 and Gaventa argues that Acts 10:34–38 forms the climax of the first part of Acts and the Council's intention is rather to protect the Gentiles from idolatry and polytheism. See Gonzales, *Acts*, 173; Gaventa, *Acts*, 163–82, 210–27.

11. See Yong, *Spirit Poured Out on All Flesh*, 83.

that time.[12] Its effect in Korea was not to create separate Pentecostal churches but to strengthen and indigenize the existing Presbyterian and Methodist churches which were inclined to accommodate it. Because of its parallels with Acts, the revival was described as "the Korean Pentecost" and descriptions of the event are heavily influenced by the account in Acts, chapter 2. For the Koreans and the foreign missionaries who experienced it, this was a watershed moment in which the Koreans understood that they, having the Holy Spirit, were now an autonomous Korean church, and the missionaries came to believe that the Koreans believers really were Christians as much as they were because they manifested the Spirit in the same way.[13]

A New Approach to Apostolicity

All the autonomous churches in existence to this day, including European ones, have at some point been through such a moment, whether they express it in Pentecostal terms or not. At some point they were recognized as churches in their own right, endowed with the Spirit of God, and therefore able to determine their own futures. We read about such a moment in Acts in the history of the church of Antioch when the mixed community of Jews and Gentiles became a distinct community known as "Christians" (11:26). From this point on in the narrative, Antioch stands in mutual relationship with the Jerusalem church and it becomes an independent center of mission activity.[14]

It is difficult to determine historically if the original Jerusalem community descended directly from that first Pentecost is extant today. The different churches that exist all over the world, and which we encounter in our ecumenical and mission relations, each have a distinct origin that was after the first Pentecost. The logic of the Pentecostal narrative of the book of Acts is that all "there is no distinction" (Acts 15:9). If other churches also manifest the same signs of the Spirit, then they are Christian every bit as much as those who brought the message to them. They are "filled with the Spirit" and there are no half measures. So, whether it was two thousand years ago, two hundred years ago, twenty years ago, or two years ago makes no essential difference. Their apostolicity is confirmed by the evidence of their baptism in the Spirit. Pentecostals, like other free or

---

12. See Anderson, *Introduction to Pentecostalism*.
13. Kim and Kim, *History of Korean Christianity*, 93–106.
14. Gonzales, *Acts*, 142–43.

independent churches claim apostolicity on the grounds of faithfulness to the apostles rather than the apostolic succession in the sense of a continuous historical line back to the apostles through a series of bishops. If they claim to be filled with the Spirit as we do, then, as Peter asked, what is to prevent us recognizing them as partners in the same mission, brothers and sisters in Christ? (Acts 10:44–48)

Luke's application of the word "apostle" to individuals is notoriously slippery. At first, he seems to apply it only to the Twelve, who are eyewitnesses of Jesus' ministry (1:21–22). But later, both Paul and Barnabas are (14:4, 14) are referred to as apostles. Furthermore, although Stephen and his fellows are appointed deacons in a way that seems to give them an inferior place to the original apostles, Luke gives two of these "Seven"—Stephen and Philip—great prominence in his narrative and it is clear that they combined the waiting on tables with the prayer and preaching that the Twelve apparently considered more important. Noting the prominence and unqualified praise of Stephen particularly, and considering the fact that the Lord Jesus gave considerable importance to waiting on tables, David Pao wonders if Luke is actually criticizing the Twelve here?[15] At any rate, it is clear from the narrative that the apostolic function is carried out most fully like people like Stephen, Philip, Barnabas, and later Paul, who were filled with the Spirit of God, regardless of the credentials possessed by the Twelve. Apostolicity is Acts is defined by the evidence of the Spirit at work. Furthermore, the apostles were missionaries, those commissioned with a particular task, sent ones, and missionaries were apostles. Apostolicity then comes down to the question of who has the Spirit that was in Jesus Christ? Who truly manifests the "power from on high" that Jesus promised? (Luke 24:48)

The Indian liberation theologian Samuel Rayan SJ wrote about "mission in the Spirit."[16] Mission is not primarily about the task to be accomplished, the goals and the strategy to get there, it is about the call to be filled with the Spirit. "The Spirit of the Lord is upon me," said Jesus as he announced his mission (Luke 4:18). Mission is not primarily an action but a spirituality, a way of being in Christ. Furthermore, the Spirit in whose power we do mission, and in which Jesus carried out his mission, is sent from the Father and at work in the whole creation. The Spirit in which Jesus was conceived, grew up, was baptized and performed wondrous deeds was already known to the people as the Spirit of God manifest in the prophets,

---

15. Pao, "Waiters or Preachers."
16. Rayan, *Holy Spirit*. See also Kim, *Mission in the Spirit*.

even the Spirit of life itself (Nicene Creed). Since the work of the Spirit is much wider than our particular community, mission can be thought of as "finding out where the Holy Spirit is at work and joining in."[17] This is the gist of the current statement of the World Council of Churches on mission and evangelism, *Together towards Life: Mission and Evangelism in Changing Landscapes*. It concludes: "We understand that our task is not to bring God along but to witness to the God who is already there (Acts 17:23–28). Joining in with the Spirit, we are enabled to cross cultural and religious barriers to work together towards life."[18]

World Christianity: A New Approach to Catholicity

World Christianity

The concept "world Christianity" owes its origins largely to the work of Andrew Walls, whose long career has taken him to Aberdeen, Edinburgh, Princeton and Liverpool Hope universities, and to his disciples and colleagues, most notably the late Lamin Sanneh. However, it has been appropriated by others as well and serves several purposes. It is debated whether it is purely descriptive or somehow normative; whether it is an observation or a new paradigm.[19]

From Walls's work, world Christianity is partly a neat way of explaining the statistical fact that, somewhere around the year 1970, the number of Christians in the global South began to exceed that in the global North. With this statistic in mind, many have treated world Christianity as a product of European colonialism as if Christianity was a European religion that went global only in the last few centuries. The study of world Christianity tends to be dominated by a historical approach that locates it in the postcolonial and globalization eras. However, Walls, together with Todd Johnson, points out that Christianity is Asian in origin, that its early spread was in multiple directions and that up until the year 923 AD, there were more Christians living south of the latitude of Jerusalem than above it.[20]

Statistics should not be allowed to determine understanding of Christian faith—there is much more to it than that. Moreover, the sources

---

17. Kim, *Joining in with the Spirit*; cf. Bevans, "Plenary Address."
18. CWME, "Together Towards Life."
19. For recent debate, see Cabrita et al., *Relocating World Christianity*.
20. Johnson and Ross, *Atlas of Global Christianity*, 48–51.

of such statistics could be questioned as well as the underlying assumptions about what defines a Christian. But the use of numbers is not forbidden in theology—Luke himself concludes the Pentecost story with a head-count (Acts 2:41, 47). They are certainly significant, among other measures of Christian-ness—such as social impact and cultural change—in the study of Christianity.[21]

Sometimes it is assumed that "world Christianity" represents a sociological alternative to ecumenical *theology* or church *history*, and for some theologians this is a reason for dismissing it. It is true that "world Christianity" is a sociological term and that the subject provides a way in which sociologists have been drawn into the study the church or churches. It is also true that the study of world Christianity involves treating Christianity as a social movement and that critical tools from social studies are applied. However, world Christianity is best thought of as a multi-disciplinary topic. Most of the leading figures—such as Walls, Sanneh, Dana L. Robert, Brian Stanley, or Klaus Koschorke—are historians who also take theology very seriously. So seriously in fact that a historian or sociologist might sometimes worry that theology is driving their historical interpretations. World Christianity is, and should be, primarily an empirical study. But empirical findings can and should challenge theological claims—explicit or implicit—that do not reflect ground realities; for example, any claim that a certain theology developed in in a particular time and place (Aquinas, Luther, Barth, etc.) is somehow normative for all Christians everywhere.

"World Christianity" is sometimes used to imply an approach to Christianity that focuses on developments outside the West, like the terms "world music," "world film," or "world religions." Much of the study of world Christianity does indeed do this in that it redresses a balance and moves beyond colonial approaches. However, as a movement that continues to have significant centers of power in the West, world Christianity must also attend to these—especially Christianity in Europe and the USA—if it is do justice to the whole.

In many respects, world Christianity studies what is so often treated as a European religion in the same way as the other religions which are often referred to under the broad heading "world religion," such as Islam, Buddhism, and so on. They are studied both in their countries of origin and also in their global spread and manifestations in different continents. Although, the term "world religion" is a contested and ideologically loaded

---

21. Kim and Kim, *Christianity as a World Religion*, 4–8.

one, it is not necessary to assert the parity of certain religions in order to apply religious studies methods. In any case, Christianity has a strong claim to be a truly world religion on empirical grounds because it is "locally rooted," "globally widespread" and "interconnected."[22] The contemporary discipline of religious studies treats religions as the lived practices of people rather than as systems to live by. World Christianity tends to study Christianity this way as well, although theology is more recognized than in the discipline in general.

In the UK and North America, professorial chairs in "world Christianity" have rapidly replaced chairs in mission studies and ecumenics. In the case of mission studies or missiology, this is primarily because the colonial associations of mission have been difficult to overcome; second, because the paradigm shift to God's mission (*missio Dei*) suggested to many that mission from one community to another should cease; and third, because in secular university settings mission appears as a narrowly church pursuit. Personally, I think this is short-sighted; first, because churches and their mission agendas are far from marginal to society, even in places of high secularization; and second, because now that most churches think of themselves as missional and globally missionary movements are on the increase, especially in and from the global South, it is all the more important to be doing mission studies. Similarly, with ecumenics, the growth in Christian diversity makes issues of unity all the more urgent and greatly increases the dialogue to include churches beyond Protestant, Catholic and Orthodox. World Christianity challenges a view of church history that assumes that in the beginning there was one united church which was subsequently rent asunder by schisms. This view of the origins of Christian diversity, which has dominated the ecumenical movement, sees diversity negatively and suggests that a unity that heals these divisions should be the main priority in inter-church relations. Although it was considered necessary at various times and places to unify, regularize or codify Christian belief and practice in one place, region or within one jurisdiction, such uniformity was secondary and diversity was more normal.[23] Moreover, there always existed churches beyond these jurisdictions. Through the ecumenical councils, limits to diversity were set but these still allowed for regional variations. Such variations have come down to the present day in the Orthodox and Catholic

---

22. Kim and Kim, *Christianity as a World Religion*.
23. For the case of liturgy, see Bradshaw, *Origins of Christian Worship*.

churches; many have probably been lost. Furthermore, the churches have continued to be founded in different regions and cultures.

A New Approach to Catholicity

All the above definitions of world Christianity are true to an extent but at the heart of the shift to world Christianity in mission theology lies a rediscovery of the nature of the church's catholicity. World Christianity shifts interest away from understanding Christian diversity primarily in terms of doctrine and polity and toward spatial or geographical diversity, which was the primary sense in which the first councils of the church understood catholicity. No longer is the unity envisaged mainly a denominational one; it is also a cultural and regional one. The ecumenism of the colonial period which gave birth to the World Council of Churches tended to assume that overcoming the doctrinal and liturgical differences between the churches of Europe would unite Christians globally. Today, this is no longer the case and new expressions of catholicity are being sought, for example through the Global Christian Forum.

However it is treated, the study of world Christianity tends to de-center Europe. World Christianity approaches to history reinforce the fact that Europe rose to dominance late in Christian history and that the early spread of the faith was in all directions. Early Christianity was polycentric and the faith has always been expressed in diverse ways. Christianity has multiple histories and a number of orthodoxies.[24] In the light of two thousand years of Christian history and with the rise of Christianity in Asia, Africa, the Americas, and other regions, the dominance of Europe begins to look like a one-thousand-year aberration, an accident of history, soon to be superseded. Not only does it critique Euro-centrism, the world Christianity approach relativizes *all* regions and theologies. It is not only the study of non-Western Christianity but should include the critical study of Christianity in the West as well.

One of the strands of Walls's theory is that Christianity undergoes "serial expansion." Use of this term is often misleading and misguided,[25] but it does make the valid point that Christianity both waxes and wanes in different parts of the world at different times. There is no guarantee that Christian

---

24. Perhaps the best example of a world Christianity approach to Christian history is Irvin and Sunquist, *History of the World Christian Movement*.

25. See Kim, *Joining in with the Spirit*, 14–16.

growth is inexorable. From a historical point of view, the prime example is the Middle East and North Africa, in which there were once strong Christian centers. Another is the suppression of Christianity under Communism and its subsequent revival in many areas. From a theological point of view, we have the New Testament warnings to churches by Paul and the writer of Revelation, and the metaphor of pruning being necessary for growth. So one reason for de-centering Europe is that its numerical decline suggests—although it does not necessarily imply—that European Christianity will become a less significant player in world Christianity in future.

The new catholicity must recognize that many of the newer churches are organized differently from the traditional churches of Europe, which are national churches with parish systems. They may be megachurches, or new denominations, which describe themselves as "international." Or they may be "migrant churches"; that is, they are not yet settled or integrated into the local religious landscape.[26] These are "Christians without borders" and "churches on the move"—arguably much like the churches of the book of Acts.[27] In view of the historical diversity of world Christianity and the different contexts in which faith is practiced, the new catholicity will keep an open mind about models of church polity and the limits to Christian diversity, while encouraging a truly "global conversation" to discern the Holy Spirit.[28]

The study of world Christianity not only poses conceptual challenges for understanding the context of mission, but it also suggests a re-reading of the biblical narrative and a new appreciation of mission as "in the Spirit," which contribute to new approaches to the church's apostolicity and catholicity. Theology is always done in context; mission theology especially must respond to the changing landscape of mission and take into account the vision of partners whose theology and view of the world may be different from our own.

---

26. See Kim and Kim, *History of Korean Christianity*, 280–82, 299–315. For an in-depth study of an African megachurch, see Gitau, *Megachurch Christianity Reconsidered*. For a study of African migrant churches, see Hanciles, *Beyond Christendom*.

27. Kim, "Christians without Borders."

28. See Kim, *Holy Spirit in the World*. For theology of conversation, see Haers and Mey, *Theology and Conversation*.

4

The First Non-Jewish Christian Was from Africa[1]

CRAIG S. KEENER

Introduction

How historical is Luke's narrative concerning the African official? Some scholars suggest that it reflects the style of legend,[2] but this judgment is fairly subjective, since ancient historians used many of the same narrative techniques employed by storytellers and novelists.[3] C. K. Barrett wryly warns, "There is no means of checking the historicity of the narrative unless it can be assumed that angels do not exist."[4] Whether or not it pleases modern readers, most of Luke's contemporaries assumed such events not only in novels but in their own real world. Others have suggested that the story is "completely

---

1. This article adapts Keener, "Novels' 'Exotic' Places and Luke's African Official (Acts 8:27)," with permission from *AUSS*; and material from Keener, *Acts: An Exegetical Commentary*, 4 vols., with permission from Baker Academic. See also Keener, *Acts*; "Aftermath of the Ethiopian Eunuch."

2. Dibelius, *Studies in the Acts of the Apostles*, 5; Conzelmann, *Commentary on the Acts of the Apostles*, 67–68.

3. For shared techniques, see, e.g., Burridge, *What Are the Gospels?*, 245; Aune, *Westminster Dictionary of New Testament*, 285; Marguerat, *First Christian Historian*, 29; Rothschild, *Luke-Acts and the Rhetoric of History*, 175; Soards, "Review of *Profit with Delight*," 309.

4. Barrett, *Critical and Exegetical Commentary on the Acts*, 1:422.

mythical" because so many details have symbolic value;[5] but parallels between different accounts in Plutarch show that stories laden with narrative connections and allusions could have historical bases.[6]

Other scholars counter with various arguments favoring the narrative's historical accuracy (not least of which is the overall historical genre of Acts).[7] If Philip did meet a pilgrim from Nubia, such a pilgrim might well have been a person of means to make such a journey.[8] If Philip was Luke's oral source, as 21:8–10 might well suggest,[9] Luke may have known and wished to reveal to his audience an event that prefigured the church's official story in Acts 10. Other scholars argue forcefully from the apparent narrative tension with Luke's account of Cornelius works that Luke would not likely have invented this account, though he certainly enlists it to good effect once he has it.[10]

Here I focus on a particular literary question. Richard Pervo argued that Luke includes the story of the African official because the latter was "exotic," being from a distant and fabled land.[11] By contrast to this approach, Luke's narrative lacks the fictitious elaborations about a distant land characteristic of reports in novels and novelistic sources. Luke's details, sparse as they are, display a higher proportion of accuracy than in many historians' speculations; they certainly lack the colorful but inaccurate depictions common in fiction.

---

5. Goulder, *Type and History in Acts*, 195.

6. See, e.g., Plutarch, *Sert.* 1.1; *Demosth.* 3.2; cf. *Cimon* 3.1–3.

7. For Acts as ancient historiography, see, e.g., Plümacher, *Geschichte und Geschichten*; Johnson, *Acts of the Apostles*; Eckey, *Die Apostelgeschichte*; Flichy, *L'oeuvre de Luc*. For implications of this genre for the degree of factual content, see, e.g., Hemer, *Book of Acts*; Byrskog, *Story as History*; Keener, *Acts* [2012]; Keener, *Acts* [2020].

8. Whether he was really a eunuch is harder to test historically, but if the person was of such means as to be an official of the Kandake, the eunuch claim makes sense. Further, it would explain why the traveler would make such a long journey to Jerusalem yet not be a proselyte (his Gentile character being a component Luke would not invent, given the Cornelius story). While the eunuch claim implicitly fits Isa 56:3–6, it remains plausible historically as well.

9. Cf. Ramsay, *Pictures of the Apostolic Church*, 66; Barrett, *Acts*, 51; Witherington III, *Acts of the Apostles*, 169, 280.

10. See Lüdemann, *Early Christianity*, 105, for a historical nucleus here; cf. Spencer, "Waiter, a Magician, a Fisherman, and a Eunuch"; Kollmann, "Philippus der Evangelist."

11. Pervo, *Dating Acts*, 32 (among other arguments against the narrative's historical nucleus). I am not addressing here some of Pervo's other, more accurate literary observations. Ancient audiences did appreciate novelties. Seneca, *Controv.* 4. pref. 1.

The Official's Nation (8:27)

Although writers often engaged in fanciful tales about distant lands beyond the realm of corroboration (e.g., the later "Wonders beyond Thule"), Luke's account takes place in the Roman province of Syria, not a distant land impossible to verify. Often people confused material about distant lands (e.g., the "Ethiopian" Trogodytae with northern Troglodytae, or cave-dwellers),[12] but others reported data accurately, and Luke's report tends to match these more accurate reports.

For example, the Kandake (Acts 8:27) is clearly a historical personage (or series of persons), in contrast to mythical Memnons or exotic novelistic details such as appear in Heliodorus's *Ethiopica*. My focus here will be to compare the treatment of "Ethiopia" in myth and in history and to show that Luke's brief data about "Ethiopia" fit history rather than myth. While myth and fiction could draw on valid historical information, they usually included historically impossible material as well. Were Luke composing novelistically (in contrast to the historical genre in which he writes), we should not expect him to know, any better than other fictitious storytellers did, which kind of source was which.

At a minimum, Luke's sparse portrayal of the official's nation fits historical fact at most of the few points it offers. The Greek title "Ethiopia" technically included all of Africa south of Egypt,[13] but the Candace's title has convinced nearly all scholars that the Nubian kingdom of Meroë is specifically in view here.[14] James Bruce discovered Meroë in 1722, and John Garstang's work (1909–1914) identified the site archaeologically.[15]

That the treasurer is journeying southward toward Gaza would surprise no one and probably cannot be counted either for or against historical authenticity. Meroë's Nubia was what was then a centuries-old black African kingdom between Aswan and Khartoum, the two leading

---

12. Morkot, "Trogodytae," *OCD* 1555. Quintus Curtius Rufus 4.7.18 has the Trogodytes as Arabians south of the Ammon oracle, with Ethiopians to its east; in 4.7.19, the Ethiopians to the west are called "snub-nosed."

13. It included other Ethiopians besides Meroë. See Diodorus Siculus 3.8.1; Herodotus 3.17–24; 4.183, in Snowden Jr., *Blacks in Antiquity*, 105.

14. E.g., Lake and Cadbury, *English Translation and Commentary*, 4:95; Haenchen, *Acts of the Apostles*, 310; Bruce, *Acts of the Apostles*, 190–91; Munck, *Acts of the Apostles*, 78; Eckey, *Apostelgeschichte*, 202–3. For Meroë as Ethiopia in early imperial sources, see, e.g., Losch, "Der Kämmerer der Königen Kandake," 499; cf. Roeder, "Die Geschichte Nubiens und des Sudans," 72–76.

15. O'Connor, "Meroë," 472.

cities of which were Meroë and Napata.¹⁶ People in the Mediterranean world depicted "Ethiopia" as near¹⁷ or directly south¹⁸ of Egypt, likewise describing Meroë as south of Egypt.¹⁹ Such basic information was widely available; even a later novelist who fictionalized freely about Ethiopia recognized its capital as Meroë.²⁰

Information and Myths

As noted, Richard Pervo argued that Luke includes the story of the African official because the latter was "exotic," being from a distant land;²¹ but whatever appeal a remote land might have for the story, Meroë was a real place, and Luke does not elaborate at any length on the location. Whereas many indulged in wild speculations about exotic distant lands, both fictitious and real, Luke avoids adding speculations; while he is interested in the symbolic spread of the gospel to the ends of the earth, his interest is not in fact "exotic."

Unlike Luke, even some nonfiction writers speculated, in some cases more plausibly than others. Based on their knowledge of the Sahara, some Romans thought that "Ethiopia" and the interior of Africa were mainly desert,²² just as much sand lay between Ethiopia and Egypt;²³ all knew

---

16. It had endured since about 760 BCE, since at least the early third century BCE from its capital in Meroë. See especially Leclant, "Empire of Kush," 278–95; Hakem et al., "Civilization of Napata and Meroe." For the transfer of sovereignty from Napata to Meroë as late as 270 BCE, see O'Connor, "Meroë," 472.

17. Plutarch, *Exile* 7; *Mor.* 601DE.

18. Josephus, *Ant.* 2.239; *War* 4.608; Appian, *Hist. rom.* pref. 9; Juvenal, *Sat.* 10.150. Thus a plague beginning there spread to Egypt and thence to Greece (Thucydides 2.48.1). They were thought the people to the furthest south (Pausanias 1.33.3–6).

19. Arrian, *Ind.* 25.7. The boundary came up to the Nile's first cataract in Augustus's day. Losch, "Kämmerer der Königen," 479.

20. Heliodorus, *Eth.* 9.16, 20, 24; 10.3, 5. He depicted it as a triangular island surrounded by three navigable rivers, including the Nile (10.5), but claimed that it was so big it looked like a mainland (10.5); others claimed that a river surrounded Meroë (Vitruvius, *Arch.* 8.2.6). The island did in fact lay "between the White Nile, the Blue Nile, and the Atbara River" (Yamauchi, *Africa and the Bible*, 165). Nero's expedition claimed that the town Meroë lay a full seventy miles from the entrance to the island (Pliny, *Nat.* 6.35.185).

21. Pervo, *Dating Acts*, 32.

22. Seneca, *Nat. Q.* 3.6.2; *Dial.* 5.20.2.

23. Seneca, *Nat. Q.* 1.pref.9.

that it was hot.[24] Some thought that Ethiopia north of Meroë lacked trees, except for those yielding cotton.[25] For lack of more accurate data, many writers simply compared Ethiopia with India, comparing their rains and crocodiles.[26] But an expedition sent in the time of Nero confirmed that desert began giving way to foliage around Meroë, with more forest and even elephant and rhinoceros tracks.[27]

In contrast to information and at least plausible surmises, some exotic "knowledge" was pure invention designed to "sell" on a popular market.[28] Polybius complained about the fables invented by various writers about Ethiopia—and other distant locations—in his day.[29] Thus the Ethiopians were said to mine metal by pulling it up only by magnets.[30] One swift monster considered native to Ethiopia supposedly had a lion's body with a human face, and three rows of teeth useful for eating humans.[31] Ultimately writers often mixed genuine and fictitious information, lacking resources to distinguish them: thus Ethiopia produced not only hyenas and monkeys, but also "winged horses armed with horns."[32]

Pliny the Elder offers some of the most thorough information about what the Roman world thought of Meroë in Luke's era. In *Nat.* 6.35.178–80, he lists towns and peoples reported south along Nile to Meroë, but notes (6.35.181) that most no longer exist, as attested by Nero's scouts who found there only desert. While researching his work on Ethiopia, one Greek writer allegedly lived in Meroë for five years (6.35.183). Nero's scouts found few

---

24. Arrian, *Ind.* 6.7. Vitruvius, *Arch.* 8.2.7, opined that Africa had few rivers, because it was hot and moisture comes from the north.

25. Pliny, *Nat.* 12.8.19; 13.28.90. Pliny, *Nat.* 12.8.17, notes that Herodotus 3.97 attributes ebony to Ethiopia, but with Virgil, *Georg.* 2.116–17, he attributes it to India.

26. Arrian, *Ind.* 6.8.

27. Pliny, *Nat.* 6.35.185.

28. Some stories told to Herodotus fit this description (see Herodotus, 3.17–24; 4.183, in Snowden, *Blacks in Antiquity*, 105), as in novelistic works (e.g., Ps.-Callisthenes, *Alex.* 3.21; Heliodorus, *Eth.* 10.4–5) and rabbinic speculations (e.g., *b. Pes.* 94a; *Taan.* 10a; *y. Ber.* 1:1, §12; *Song Rab.* 6:9, §3; cf. similarly fanciful dimensions in Heliodorus, *Eth.* 10.5).

29. Polybius 3.38.1, 3; 3.57.1–59.9, esp. 3.57.1–9; 3.58.2.

30. Sil. It. 3.266–67. Somewhat more plausibly, their companion Nubians wore no armor, but linen, including on the head, and they tipped their javelins with poison (Sil. It. 3.269–73).

31. Pliny, *Nat.* 8.30.75 (attributing this "information" to Ctesias).

32. Pliny, *Nat.* 8.30.72 (LCL 2:53).

buildings in Meroë (6.35.185); while it apparently had a sizeable population, it was apparently spread out.

The Roman world claimed knowledge of some other African, "Ethiopian" regions in addition to Meroë, sometimes with the same sort of admixture of fact and fiction. Besides north African regions and Axum, these included explorations in west Africa in the second century BCE, likewise preserved for us in Pliny the Elder (5.1.9–10). Discoveries included forests (5.1.9) and rivers with crocodiles (5.1.9–10). Elsewhere in Africa, after a desert and the Egyptian Libyans, came the "white Ethiopians"; and after them, "the Ethiopian clans of the Nigritae, named after the river."[33] But the further Pliny moves from his known world, the less certain (and often more skeptical) we can be of his information. He speaks of mute, snake-eating cave-dwellers (5.8.45);[34] the naked Gamphasantes (5.8.45); the Blemmyae, whose mouth and eyes are on their chests (an unfortunate necessity because they lack heads; 5.8.46); leather-footed people who crawl rather than walk, along with Satyrs and other creatures (5.8.46).

Even around Meroë, he assures us, strange peoples lived: on the east some flat-faced peoples lack noses; some had neither mouth nor nostrils, but one opening both for breathing and for sucking in fluids through "oat straws," using gestures instead of speech (6.35.187–88). Likewise (but now again more reliably), some also report a race of Pygmies closer to where the Nile originates (*Pygmaeorum*; 6.35.188).[35] All quadrupeds around "Nubian Ethiopia" (*Nubaei Aethiopes*), including elephants, lacked ears; a still more distant people "have a dog for a king and divine his commands from his movements" (6.35.192).[36] Some plants around Meroë were useful

---

33. Pliny, *Nat.* 5.8.43 (LCL 2:249, 251); the river is the Niger (among African tribes called Tarraelii and Oechalicae, 5.8.44), though not necessarily the modern river by this name. "Niger" was a common river name, perhaps partly because in the Libyan language *gher* (or *ghir*) applied to "any flowing waters" (Werner Huß, "Niger," BNP 9:749).

34. Unfortunately following Herodotus 4.183. Pliny deals further with the Trogodytice, the cave-dwellers, at 6.34.169; beyond Meroë, all were cave-dwellers (6.35.189). In Pliny, *Nat.* 5.5.34, cave-dwellers lived seven days to the southwest of Libyan desert-dwellers who built houses of salt; Rome's only contact with the cave-dwellers was carbuncle imported through Ethiopia. Reports of "cave-dwellers" might confuse the "Ethiopian" Trogodytae with northern Troglodytae, or cave-dwellers (Morkot, "Trogodytae").

35. Beyond Meroë, Philostratus, *Vit. Apoll.* 6.25, lists nomadic Ethiopians (living in wagons), elephant-hunters, cannibals, and pygmies; plus people who were "shadow-footed"; nevertheless, the travelers found hospitality in a village there (6.27).

36. Some ideas, like a ruling dog, may have grown from outsiders' views of sacred totems, but plainly Pliny's sources are not accurate at these points.

medicinally, whereas others caused suicidal madness.³⁷ A mineral category including diamonds was found in mines near Meroë (37.15.55), though also in India and Arabia (37.15.56).

Although all educated people knew of Africa south of Egypt, some of the most widely circulated stories about particular Africans south of Egypt belonged to myth and legend. One of the most popular characters was Memnon, though his Ethiopia was placed in the "east," the land of the dawn.³⁸ (Some later writers, however, also associate him with Egypt.³⁹) Dawn, a goddess who lived in the east, consorted with the mortal Tithonus and bore him two sons, including Memnon, in Ethiopia.⁴⁰ Memnon was black (*nigri*),⁴¹ and Odysseus claimed that Memnon was the handsomest man he had ever seen.⁴² By all accounts, he was a mighty warrior, yet he finally was killed by Achilles.⁴³ In some versions, after Achilles slew Memnon, Zeus made the latter immortal.⁴⁴ Pliny reports the view of some that birds fly annually from Ethiopia to fight over Memnon's grave at Troy, and that another source claims that the birds do the same around his

---

37. Pliny, *Nat.* 24.102.163; cf. 27.1.2; detailed in 27.3.11–12.

38. E.g., Silius Italicus 3.332–34; Seneca, *Troj.* 10. For fragments of the *Aethiopis*, including dealing with Memnon, see West, *Greek Epic Fragments*, 108–17. On Memnon, see also Scherf, "Memnon."

39. See Rose and March, "Memnon (1)," 955 (citing Pausanias 1.42.3).

40. Hesiod, *Theog.* 984–85; Apollodorus, *Bib.* 3.12.4. In less detail, also Ovid, *Ex Ponto* 1.4.57; *Am.* 1.8.3–4; Philostratus the Elder, *Imag.* 1.7.

41. Virgil, *Aen.* 1.489. Further, Ovid, *Am.* 1.8; *Ex Ponto* 3.3.96–97. But his mother Aurora (Latin for Eos, Dawn), as a goddess, had golden hair (Ovid, *Am.* 1.13.2)! In Philostratus the Elder, *Imag.* 1.7, his skin has a trace of ruddiness mitigating the black. Greek vase-paintings portray him according to Greek heroic conventions, but often his attendants as black Africans (Rose and March, "Memnon").

42. Homer, *Od.* 11.522.

43. Apollodorus, *Epit.* 5.3. Also Pindar, *Nem.* 3.62–63; 6.49–53; *Isthm.* 8.55; Pliny, *Nat.* 6.35.182; Dio Chrysostom, *Or.* 11.114, 117; for his war exploits, e.g., Philostratus the Elder, *Imag.* 2.7.

44. *Aethiopis* 1–2, excerpted, hence preserved, in Proclus, *Chrestomathia* 2 (in Hesiod [LCL 506–7]; also West, *Greek Epic Fragments* [LCL 113]). A revisionist version claims that the Memnon slain at Troy was a Trojan (Philostratus, *Hrk.* 26.16–17), though Memnon of Ethiopia ruled during the Trojan War, and is worshiped in Ethiopia and Egypt (*Hrk.* 26.16; cf. similarly *Vit. Apoll.* 6.4).

palace in Ethiopia.[45] For centuries, his death remained a subject for Greek art and of rhetorical descriptions thereof.[46]

Some suggested that the Ethiopians originated astrology.[47] Others claimed that they stole their wisdom from India (Philostratus, *Vit. Apoll.* 6.11), from which they were expelled for murdering many Indians, including King Ganges, the river's son (3.20). Ethiopian sages could make the trees salute Apollonius (6.10); after Apollonius argues that the Indian sages are superior to them (6.5–11), the youngest of the Ethiopian sages follows him as a disciple (6.16). Ethiopians were as wise due to their warm climate as Scythians were fierce due to their harsh climate.[48]

The Roman public proved infatuated with any stories about Ethiopia after the return of Nero's expedition (61–62 CE).[49] By contrast, Luke (versus, say, the later novelist Heliodorus) does not even describe Ethiopia; moreover, we know that Nubians were a *real* people (unlike Amazons), and that Kandake was a *real* queen. Comparison with ancient fictions show us that Nubia would be of interest to Luke's audience; but unlike some other locations fictitious reports claim, Nubia was not fictitious. Far from indulging speculations about distant lands, Luke stays close to the most sober model of historiography. Though he could not have known which reports of his contemporaries were reliable and which were not, what he reports (in contrast to what many others report) does not contradict what we know.

"Exotic" Analogies

Against the claim that Luke would invent the African official because he hails from an unverifiable, "exotic" land, Luke's brief report is barely comparable to sources genuinely interested in exotic matters. Many Greeks had long enjoyed speculating about distant, exotic lands, where life differed from what was known as far as imagination could allow. Comparison with

---

45. Pliny, *Nat.* 10.37.74. On this myth, see further Scherf, "Memnonides," 8:652–53. Memnon's statue in Ethiopia could speak, and was so realistic it helped Eos to stop mourning her son (Callistratus, *Descr.* 9).

46. Philostratus the Elder, *Imagines* 1.7.

47. Lucian, *Astr.* 3, suggesting also (5) that they passed it to Egyptians; but Lucian is being satirical in this essay.

48. Pliny, *Nat.* 2.80.189. For climate theories of race in antiquity, see McCoskey, *Race*, 46–48.

49. Klauck, *Magic and Paganism in Early Christianity*, 25–26, following Plümacher, *Lukas als hellenisticher Schriftsteller*, 12–13.

some other peoples helps set their speculations about Ethiopia in context. In the far north lived the Hyperboreans,[50] who enjoyed such longevity that finally, when they tired of living, they would banquet and then hurl themselves into the sea.[51]

Likewise, some claimed that India had rivers of milk, honey, wine and olive oil,[52] and people ate the lotus that grew without need for cultivation;[53] their Brahmin sages drank from the "fountain of truth," making them incapable of lying.[54] Ants larger than foxes dig gold, and at midday, when the ants retreat underground due to the heat, Indians steal their gold, often leading to ensuing battles with the ants.[55] Arrian had such fantasies in mind when he complained about unverified tales of water monsters, griffins, and gold-mining ants in India.[56]

Speculation (mixed with more accurate knowledge)[57] had also been rife about the Scythians, with whom Ethiopians were sometimes linked,[58] because they were remote enough[59] that knowledge about them was limited. Thus some felt that Scythia was too cold for thunderbolts, just as Egypt was too hot for them.[60] One plant there reportedly preserved one from hunger and thirst, so long as one kept it in one's mouth.[61] In their

---

50. See, e.g., *Epigoni* frg. 5 (so Herodotus 4.32); Hesiod frg. 150.21 M.-W. (West, *Greek Epic Fragments* [LCL 59]).

51. Pliny, *Nat.* 4.12.89, though himself unsure if the reports were correct.

52. Dio Chrysostom, *Or.* 35.18 (noting that all flow one month of the year only for the king, as his tribute).

53. Dio Chrysostom, *Or.* 35.19. The trees brought their fruit down to whomever wished to eat (35.21).

54. Dio Chrysostom, *Or.* 35.22.

55. Herodotus 3.102–5 (claiming that he learned this from the Persians); Dio Chrysostom, *Or.* 35.23–24.

56. Arrian, *Alex.* 5.4.3.

57. For some research, see, e.g., Minns, *Scythians and Greeks*.

58. McCoskey, *Race*, 143.

59. On their remoteness, see, e.g., Aeschylus, *Seven* 728, 817; Cicero, *Nat. d.* 2.34.88 (mentioned alongside Britain). In Josephus, *Ant.* 1.123, they are Magog.

60. Pliny, *Nat.* 2.51.135. They are contrasted with Egyptians also in Philo, *Mos.* 2.19; Maximus of Tyre, *Or.* 23.4.

61. Pliny, *Nat.* 25.43.82.

land, a wild country,[62] one hairy animal changed its color to blend in with its surroundings.[63]

Another major area of exotic geographic speculation involved the renowned Amazons, though by this period they are more often mentioned with regard to the past. Amazons were essentially the opposite of how Greek men conceived of Greek women, hence a fertile ground for imagination. It was thought that Amazons had once subdued much of Asia and Europe;[64] it was more difficult for more recent people to believe such reports, one historian opined, because their strength had died out.[65]

Most ancient historians and other writers took for granted the historical authenticity of the Amazons.[66] Herodotus assumes the existence of Amazons.[67] Xenophon did not see any Amazons in the east, but notes that his colleagues captured a man with weapons like those attributed to the Amazons.[68] Pompey's Asian captives included women thought to be Amazons; but it was uncertain whether they belonged to a separate kingdom or these "barbarians" simply called any warrior women "Amazons."[69] Later, Strabo still apparently believes in Amazons, but thinks that, despite various claims, no historian in his day really knows their location.[70] Arrian reports that some in Alexander's day claimed the existence of Amazons,[71] but suspects that they must have died out by Alexander's day, since he did not run into them.[72] In the second century CE Pausanias still treats them as real

---

62. Aristophanes, *Birds* 941.

63. Philo, *Drunkenness* 174.

64. Diodorus Siculus 2.44.2–3. More fully, see Diodorus Siculus 2.44.2–46.6.

65. Diodorus Siculus 2.46.6.

66. E.g., Lefkowitz, *Women in Greek Myth*, 22–23; in Greek historians, see Sobol, *Amazons of Greek Mythology*; in literature and art, 91–112. For the question of their actual existence, see Sobol, *Amazons*, 113–47, doubting that historicity can be proved either way.

67. E.g., Herodotus 4.111–17.

68. Xenophon, *Anab.* 4.4.16 (the weapons are not all that distinctive).

69. Appian, *Hist. rom.* 12.15.103. Since local language was presumably translated into Greek and Latin, the "Amazons" may be the translators' doing.

70. Strabo 11.5.1, 4.

71. Arrian, *Alex.* 4.15.4. Some claim that the Amazon queen came to meet Alexander (Diodorus Siculus 17.77.1; uncertainly, Plutarch, *Alex.* 46.1–2), or sent tribute (Ps.-Callisthenes, *Alex.* 3.26, an unreliable source). In *Pesiq. Rab Kah.* 9:1, a place inhabited only by women, possibly in Africa, dissuades Alexander from warring with them.

72. Arrian, *Alex.* 7.13.4–6.

figures, citing earlier historians.⁷³ Some philosophers offered arguments that depended on their authentic existence.⁷⁴ Others proved more skeptical about their existence, though sometimes simply because such warlike women seemed to them unthinkable.⁷⁵ Although Greek art contains many Amazons, they do not appear in the art of other peoples, for whom Amazons would also have been a matter of interest.⁷⁶

Luke's Plausible Details

The few features Luke reports about the official relevant to his culture appear both in historical and novelistic works, but what is significant is that, in contrast to novelistic works, none of Luke's essential claims is improbable.

A Meroitic Treasurer

Luke's claim that the African was an official is not implausible. The journey was a significant one; any of Luke's contemporaries who derived information from sources like Herodotus might expect Meroë to be nearly a two months' journey south of Elephantine, and more fabled expanses yet two months further south.⁷⁷ As noted above, if Philip did meet a pilgrim from Nubia, such a pilgrim might well have been a person of means to make such a journey.

To supervise the queen's wealth was no small matter, given the famous wealth of Meroë.⁷⁸ Meroë was known for its wealth,⁷⁹ hence a novelist could

---

73. Pausanias 1.2.1.

74. E.g., Crates, *Ep.* 28. The artistic portrayal of Pericles fighting Amazons in the historical period (Plutarch, *Per.* 31.4) is an artistic recollection of Theseus's and the Athenians' battle with them.

75. Tatian 32.

76. Lefkowitz, *Women in Myth*, 22.

77. Herodotus 2.29–32. See also Snowden, *Blacks in Antiquity*, 105. Pliny, *Nat.* 2.112.245, estimates 705 miles from the Ethiopian coast to Meroë, and 1250 from Meroë to Alexandria; in 6.35.184, he notes that Nero's scouting expedition reported 945 miles from Syene to Meroë. Note the fanciful proportions of Ethiopia in *b. Pes.* 94a; *Taan.* 10a; *y. Ber.* 1:1, §12; *Song Rab.* 6:9, §3.

78. Smith, "'Do You Understand What You are Reading?,'" 64. On Kush's economy (including in the Meroitic period), see especially Welsby, *Kingdom of Kush*. Among legendary portraits, Ethiopians valued gold less than Mediterranean peoples valued lead (Herodotus 3.23; Dio Chrysostom, *Or.* 79.3).

79. Diodorus Siculus 1.33.1–4. See also Taylor, *Egypt and Nubia*, 46–47; Crocker,

claim that Ethiopians cared little for gold or jewels, heaps of which the royal palace had in storage.[80] Its wealth was not, however, purely novelistic. At about one square mile, Meroë is, apart from Egyptian cities, "the earliest large-scale city" we know of in Africa.[81] Although plunderers ravaged much of Meroë's wealth over the centuries, excavators found many expensive imports, as well as hoards of gold jewelry.[82]

Even those writing fictitious geography recognized the strategic location for trade, but again, this connection was not itself fictitious.[83] As the link between the Mediterranean world and Egypt on the one hand and the wealth of Africa's interior on the other, Meroë was strategically positioned for trade.[84] Not far from Meroë was the strategic horn of East Africa, from which the Axumite empire would eventually rise to challenge Meroë's dominance.

Greeks apparently had widespread contacts with Africa south of Egypt as far back as the Minoan period;[85] Nubia's contacts with the northern Mediterranean world were even more prominent in the Roman imperial period.[86] "Ethiopia" was considered a source for ebony and ivory,[87] though at this time some elephants also existed in North Africa.[88] Ships trading in Roman Egypt would make "a two year round trip" along the

---

"City of Meroe."

80. Heliodorus, *Eth.* 9.24; cf. 10.5, for its marvelous fertility, including three-hundred-fold harvests.

81. O'Connor, "Meroë," 472. This archaeological evidence may conflict with and should then be preferred to Pliny, *Nat.* 6.35.185.

82. O'Connor, "Meroë," 473.

83. See Xenophon, *Eph.* 4.1.

84. See Adam and Vercoutter, "Importance of Nubia." Pliny, *Nat.* 6.35.18, claims that another island joined with its own to form a harbor; Philostratus, *Vit. Apoll.* 6.2, claims that Ethiopia-Egypt trade was more equitable than Greek trade.

85. See Hansberry, *Africa and Africans*, 37–39. For the history of Greek contact with Africa, see the survey in Huß, "Africa." For Greek sources in translation, see Burstein, *Ancient African Civilizations*.

86. See Taylor, *Egypt and Nubia*, 48; Burstein, *African Civilizations*, 53–75; cf. Yamauchi, *Africa*, 165–66; Seidlmayer, "Nubia," BNP 9:867–70.

87. Pausanias 1.42.5. It had access to elephants (Seneca, *Ep. Lucil.* 85.41; Pliny, *Nat.* 8.13.35; Juvenal, *Sat.* 10.150; Heliodorus, *Eth.* 10.5) and ivory (Polybius 34.16.1; Pliny, *Nat.* 8.47). One could also secure these from India (e.g., Catullus 64.48; Pliny, *Nat.* 8.11.32; Dio Chrysostom, *Or.* 79.4), and ivory was more available to the Roman world in Egypt (at least by the period of Philostratus, *Vit. soph.* 2.21.603).

88. Cf. Weeber, "Environment, Environmental Behavior," 1007; Simpson, "Bone, Ivory, and Shell," 346; Schneider, "Ivory."

east African coast "as far south as Zanzibar," purchasing "ivory, tortoise shell, myrrh and incense" en route.[89]

Naturally the nation's prosperity also affected that of the queen, whose treasurer this official is. Meroë's art typically depicts their queens as laden with jewels and many-fringed robes, and notably corpulent; their wide girth, probably intended as a display of prosperity, persisted in representations from the third century BCE to the fourth century CE.[90]

Queen Candace

Presumably the queen the official served worshiped traditional deities of Meroë; nevertheless, she (and perhaps her society) must have known and tolerated Jewish faith. The treasurer could hardly have taken an excursion for months, along with his presumed entourage, without the queen's approval (cf. Neh 2:5–8).

Most scholars, including nearly all commentators on Acts,[91] hold that "Candace" (pronounced *kan-dak'e*) was not the queen's name but her dynastic title, presumably comparable to Pharaoh or Ptolemy;[92] Pliny claims that this name was passed on to each queen ("through a succession of queens for many years").[93] Although Greek and Roman authors thought it a proper name, it is a Meroitic construction, *kdke* or *ktke*, from "woman" (*kd*) and the titular suffix *-ke*.[94] Historically, we know of several Candaces from the late first century BCE to the mid-first century CE; the title seems to stop in the mid-first century CE.[95] This observation could suggest that Luke's source predates that time and the time of Luke's own writing, though

---

89. Kraybill, *Imperial Cult and Commerce*, 4; cf. Reynolds, "Africa (Libya)," 33; for details on the first-century mariners' guidebook for this voyage, including the merchandise acquired there (such as spices, ivory, and tortoise shell), see Casson, *Ancient Mariners*, 203–4.

90. Yamauchi, *Africa*, 172.

91. E.g., Lake and Cadbury, *Commentary*, 96; Haenchen, *Acts*, 310; Bruce, *Commentary*, 186; Munck, *Acts*, 78; Conzelmann, *Acts*, 68. Much earlier, see also Bede, *Comm. Acts* 8.27b (Martin 82).

92. See, e.g., Pausanias 1.8.6, commenting on the line of Ptolemies (with distinct individual surnames).

93. Pliny, *Nat.* 6.186. LCL 2:477. Often noted, e.g., Abbott, *Acts of the Apostles*, 102; Bruce, *Commentary*, 186n43 (citing also Strabo 17.1.54; Dio Cassius 54.5.4).

94. Lohwasser, "Kandake."

95. Yamauchi, *Africa*, 171.

we dare not infer too much from it (since Greco-Roman writers later than he continue the tradition of employing the title).

Because the kings were considered sons of the sun god (similar to ancient Egypt's pharaohs), Bion of Soli claims that they did not specify their fathers, but only their mothers, the mother of each king being called the Candace.[96] Because of the king's holiness, it was thought, the queen was then left with tasks of secular administration.[97] Nero's scouting expedition claimed that a queen ruled Meroë.[98] As late as Eusebius, the Roman Empire believed that queens ruled in Meroë.[99]

Though not entirely accurate, Greco-Roman conceptions of this queen were close enough for ordinary purposes.[100] Nubian society was not matriarchal, but its queens were wealthy and did exercise significant power, sometimes as regents for sons.[101] One scholar argues that "Candace" appears to have been "a corruption of a Meroitic title (*kdke*) which was borne by all the royal consorts or queen-mothers of Kush; it does not specify a queen regnant."[102] From a minimalist perspective (that is, based on only the extant evidence and not inferences from it), though "at least five queens" reigned directly "during the latter centuries of the Kushite dynasty," no two of these known queens are known to have "reigned in succession, and it is not certain that they bore the title *kdke*."[103]

Did Luke's informant (again, possibly Philip) know the details of the Candace, or did he fill in this information relevant to the official's position based on the popular Greco-Roman view of his era? "Candace" was the

---

96. Bion, *Aethiopica* 1; Lake and Cadbury, *Commentary*, 96; Bruce, *Commentary*, 186n43.

97. Bruce, *Acts*, 191. Examining also novels, Weever, "Candace in the Alexander Romances," 530, notes that in Ps.-Callisthenes, *Alex.*, "Candace, rather than her adult son, rules the country."

98. Pliny, *Nat.* 6.35.186, *regnare feminam Candacen*; undoubtedly true in the generation of their visit.

99. Eusebius, *Hist. eccl.* 2.1.13; Johnson, *Acts*, 155.

100. Cf. the Nubian inscription noting the reigning queen in 13 BCE. Deissmann, *Light from the Ancient East*, 352; Bruce, *Acts*, 191.

101. Adams, *Nubia*, 260. He notes cases of patrilineal and possibly some matrilineal succession but points out that brother-sister marriages may have been common (Adams, *Nubia*, 260). These were also common in Egypt, see, e.g., Diodorus Siculus 1.27.1; Sextus Empiricus, *Pyr.* 1.152; Ptolemy, *Tetrab.* 4.10.203; and in the Ptolemaic royal house, e.g., Pausanias 1.7.1; Lucian, *Icar.* 15.

102. Adams, *Nubia*, 260.

103. Adams, *Nubia*, 260.

title by which she was known to the Greco-Roman world, and Adams concurs that this designation is apparently connected to the indigenous Nubian title for all queens. Further, this eunuch could work for her without implying that no king held power at the same time.[104] Whether the queen would have her own wealth and her own treasurer is a subject meriting further exploration, but we need not rule it out a priori; there can be no question that the queen mothers in this period held significant political power.[105] Even at this point, where we could most readily forgive Luke if he (like some other historians) were slightly confused, his sparse report does not clearly conflict with certainly known facts.

Still, it is not impossible that this Candace was also a queen regnant. Although some have suggested that a Candace named Amanitare (25–41 CE) ruled in this period, the newer chronology identifies a different queen for this period, for whom the particular title Candace is not yet attested. She may well have borne this title (alongside a name, like other Candaces), or Luke may simply employ the title familiar to a Greco-Roman audience (or to his source); as noted above, the wife or mother of any king could bear the title. We know of four queen mothers who actually ruled (holding the title *qore*, "ruler") in this period, the last being Queen Nawidemak, ruling in the first half of the first century CE. The Candace here could thus possibly be Queen Nawidemak, who is attested as *qore*, hence ruled Nubia.[106]

Mediterranean Perspectives on Candace

For Luke's audience, this queen unquestionably held high status. Although Roman sources claimed that Augustus defeated the Candace's troops, the concessions he granted her suggest that this is one of the empty claims to victory so common among losers' boasts in antiquity. Likewise, as Snowden observes, Meroë's own reliefs and other evidence could suggest a Meroitic victory.[107] Rome continued diplomatic relations with Meroë, working to-

---

104. E.g., even a general could have his own treasurer (Aeschines, *Tim.* 56).

105. See Hakem, "Napata and Meroë," 302–4; Oliver and Fage, *Short History of Africa*, 32. Cf. the high status of queens in some traditional African societies, including the Amhara in East Africa. Mbiti, *African Religions and Philosophies*, 234, 243.

106. Yamauchi, *Africa*, 172.

107. Snowden, *Blacks in Antiquity*, 133.

gether in the time of Nero[108] and even in later times after the kingdom's strength vis-à-vis Axum was waning.[109]

Even novelists knew of the Candace, and seem to have preferred alliances with Ethiopian queens to battling them.[110] In a work praising Alexander, a novelist portrays the Candace as extremely tall, looking like "a demigod"; she proves smarter than Alexander and freely tells him so.[111] Greek and Latin sources tend not to describe the Candace's color, since it may be assumed from her being Ethiopian;[112] but it is certainly only some of the later European romances that portray her as European.[113] Another Greek novel, set in the Persian period, makes Ethiopia's queen, Persinna, the priestess of the Moon (Heliodorus, *Eth.* 10.4) and attributes to her a revelatory dream (10.3); like all women, she was barred from attending special sacrifices lest she accidentally defile them (10.4). The story's heroine, her daughter, is nearest to the throne for succession (10.12, 15). Luke shows little interest in such novelistic expansions, but his more modest assumption of a wealthy and powerful queen is accurate.

The Official's Communication with Philip

That the official is reading (or perhaps has another reading to him, especially given likely bumps in the road) an Isaiah scroll, or can converse with Philip, is not implausible. Meroë had its own language, with (by this period) an alphabetic script,[114] but we cannot expect Philip to have acquaintance with that language. If Philip was primarily Greek-speaking (cf. Acts 6:1–5), how could he talk with the Ethiopian or understand that

---

108. See Seneca, *Nat. Q.* 6.8.3; Losch, "Kämmerer der Königen," 495. On Nero's expedition, see, e.g., Pliny, *Nat.* 6.35.178–85.

109. See Snowden, *Blacks in Antiquity*, 133–36.

110. Ps.-Callisthenes, *Alex.* 3.19–21; cf. Josephus, *Ant.* 2.252–53 (less helpfully to the other Ethiopians). This approach does not stem from favor toward women in general; both Achilles and Theseus supposedly slaughtered Amazons freely (e.g., Plutarch, *Thes.* 26–28).

111. Ps.-Callisthenes, *Alex.* 3.22. Also emphasized in Du Bois, *World and Africa*, 140.

112. See Weever, "Candace," 533.

113. See Weever, "Candace," 537, 540–44.

114. Hawass, "Nubia," in *OEANE*, 4:170–71; cf. the use of Egyptian hieroglyphs and its own alphabet in Seidlmayer, "Nubia," 869. From no later than the mid-second millennium BCE, Meroitic, apparently a north-Sudanese language like Nubian, used "eighteen single-sound characters (fifteen consonants and three vowel signs) and four syllabic signs in a hieroglyphic form and the usually employed cursive form" (Lohwasser, "Meroitic").

he was reading from Isaiah? It is possible that Philip could have known enough Hebrew to recognize a Scripture text, but we need not suppose that this Nubian God-fearer reads Hebrew poetry as well as converses with Philip in (presumably) Greek.[115] There is no question that the Septuagint was widely available in Alexandria and probably in Jerusalem as well, and that is the version Luke quotes (though the version we might expect Luke to quote from would be a Greek version in any case).

Luke's Greek audience would know that Ethiopians were not normally among Greek-speaking peoples (cf. Acts 2:10; *Sib. Or.* 3.516). No person of means would come from Ethiopia to Jerusalem without either a translator or some knowledge of the language; in this case, the latter situation is far more probable. As a presumably educated member of the Nubian elite and one perhaps involved in discussing trade, this treasurer would likely speak several languages, including those relevant for trade ties with places like Greek-speaking Alexandria in Egypt to Meroë's north. Greek appears in Nubian inscriptions, including one mentioning the queen in 13 BCE.[116] Coins from nearby Axum, dated before Ezana's conversion (in the early fourth century), use Greek inscriptions as well as a Roman design and gold standard.[117] An earlier king of Meroë appearing in Greek sources is said to have had a Greek education, which suggests one or more teachers of Greek there.[118] Certainly knowledge of Greek would have been essential in relations with Ptolemaic Egypt;[119] likewise in this period, the ruling elite in Egypt, as in much of the eastern empire, continued to speak Greek.

Conclusion

Various factors support Luke's dependence on genuinely prior tradition. One is that whereas Luke's brief information about Nubia comports with known historical data, he lacks the fictitious elaboration characteristic of most fictitious and speculative sources. This difference also suggests that

---

115. Fitzmyer, *Acts of the Apostles*, thinks the scroll "in Hebrew, or less likely Greek." But while Hebrew Torah scrolls may have been preferred, MSS of the LXX show that Greek versions also existed, and if anyone needed a Greek scroll this official may have been among them.

116. Deissmann, *Light*, 352.

117. Heldman, "Axum," in *OEANE*, 1:239–41.

118. Welsby, *Kingdom of Kush*, 194–95, noting Diodorus Siculus 3.6.3 and an alphabet inscribed perhaps for educational purposes.

119. Welsby, *Kingdom of Kush*, 67.

Luke's source, however limited, may reflect a genuine historical encounter between Jewish and Nubian culture. Correspondences with genuine information also appear in novels, but they (and sometimes historical works citing misinformation) also include fictitious elements (usually abundantly). While the present state of research does not prove that some of Luke's details (such as a current "Candake" having her own treasurer) will never be open to question, even those details do not differ substantially from what we find in basically accurate portrayals in contemporary historical works. Luke lacks interest in fictitious elaboration about the official's homeland (on account of which he lacks even the inadvertent fictitious elements often found in histories).

While such correspondences and lack of elaboration do not prove that Luke has a source, they do show that his interest is more in recounting his historical source than in adding the "exotic" developments characteristic of novels. That is to say, at the least, that Pervo's suggestion of Luke's novelistic interest in the account is at this point misplaced. On the whole, then, it seems likely that Luke's account reflects genuine information about an actual encounter with a real historical figure. We thus have good reason to believe that the first gentile Christian was from Africa.[120]

---

120. Some debate persists as to whether he was actually gentile, but the fivefold mention of his eunuch status, appropriate for a queen's attendants, would preclude full conversion to Judaism. See Keener, *Acts* (2013), 2:1544–45, 1565–71.

5

Religious Reforms and Notions of Gender in Pentecostal Christianity
A Case of the Church of Pentecost

Charles Prempeh

English Assemblies, PIWC, and Class and Social Conflict in the CoP

IN THE 1980S, THE Church of Pentecost (CoP) led by Apostles Albert Amoah, A. T. Nartey, Gyasi Addo, Pastors Stephen Nyarkotey Kwao, and Joshua Adjabeng introduced the English Assembly concept in the church. The pro-English policy was as a result of pressure from the youthful constituency of the CoP who had formed the Pentecost Students and Associate (PENSA) on tertiary campuses and local churches in the late 1980s. Because language is the vehicle for the storage and transmission of cultures,[1] the introduction of English in the CoP meant that new cultural practices had to be endorsed (however grudgingly it was). The strict rules about dress code, sitting arrangement, youthful leadership position, and courtship were relaxed in the English Assemblies and Pentecost International Worship Centers (PIWCs). Consequently, while the local churches retained strict rules on the above practices, the English

---

1. Sapir, *Culture, Language, and Personality*, 18.

Assemblies and PIWCs relaxed them and, in the process, are said by church leadership to have grown in population.[2]

The introduction of the English language at some assemblies of the Church of Pentecost has been criticized by some members of the church. In an informal conversation with one of the members at the Maamobi English Assembly, she intimated that the singing of English songs during worship has destroyed the spiritual fervor of the church. In her opinion, singing in the local languages connects one spiritually with God than singing in the English language that one may not fully understand.[3] These concerns should be located within the broader framework of local cultures and languages in Ghana. Following the function of language as a storehouse and vehicle for the storage and transmission of culture, many church members have expressed concerns about the future of Ghanaian cultures, as more of the youth prefer to worship with an English assembly or PIWC over the local assemblies. The challenge is broadened to see how it challenges the quest for multilingualism in Ghana. More recently, some scholars, including Dr. Gladys Ansah, a senior lecturer at the Department of English, University of Ghana, have been pushing for linguistic pluralism, where English will coexist with other Ghanaian languages equally.[4]

The state has intensified its efforts to promote the use of Ghanaian languages as the medium of instruction at the lower primary schools. But this project of linguistic pluralism is obstructed by two main sources: the English assemblies of the Church of Pentecost and the ubiquity of social media. The introduction of English assemblies and PIWCs in the CoP is gradually overshadowing the use of local languages in service. The proliferation of the internet in Ghana since the late 1990s has also sustained the construction of many Ghanaian youth as cyber beings. Gradually, many Ghanaians are opting for online friends (in the cyber world) as opposed to offline friends (social world). The overwhelming use of social media is undermining linguistic plurality. This is because on social media in Ghana the youth mostly use the English language that is readily accessible and mutually intelligible to their peers. Hardly do most Ghanaian youth use the local language on social media. And even when they do, they code-mix

---

2. Four years after the 2010 reforms, the youthful population of the Church of Pentecost was 624,647 while the general church population was 2,407,545. But by 2018, the youthful population had increased to 1,046,114, while the general population of the church stood at 3,147,939 (Church of Pentecost, "Annual Statistics Report").

3. Personal conversation with Deaconess Elizabeth Dzakpasu, March 2019.

4. Ansah, "Harnessing our Multilingual Heritage."

English and the local languages, which only succeeds in corrupting the right use of the languages (possibly because most of them do not have the script for the local languages or simply do not care about the accurate use of the language). For example, the expression, "I am tired *koraa*" (to wit I am very tired) is written, "I am tired *kraa*." This development adds to the assertion that some local Ghanaian languages are on the tipping point of extinction, as many speakers of local languages do not speak the language or pass it on to the succeeding generation. The idea of language shift, which denotes the replacement of one language by another as the primary means of communication and socialization within a community,[5] is already having a telling effect on some language communities in Ghana.

There is also another challenge associated with the increasing promotion of the English language in the CoP. While language is generally used to convey ideas, beliefs, and inform action, it also signals one's social class, status, region or origin, gender, age group and so on.[6] In Ghana, the English language is an index of social class. The prestige attached to the use of the English language is such that the language is used as a coterminous to social class and elitism. People who speak English fluently are considered to have access to the lifestyles that are associated with the affluent in society. Consequently, there is some form of social stratification creeping into the CoP, following the introduction of English Assemblies and PIWCs. Some members of English Assemblies and PIWCs tend to have an elitist posture. In a sermon delivered at one of the assemblies of the CoP, Apostle Alexander Nana Yaw Kumi-Larbi, the General Secretary of the CoP, bemoaned the near demise of the "primitive solidarity" that shaped the collective conscience of the church. This concern reflects global concerns in Pentecostalism. Globally, Pentecostalism popularly emerged among those on the margins of society.[7] The CoP similarly emerged among those who were on the fringes of society in the Akan areas and endorsed communal living with members supporting one another, and participating in communal work.[8]

Because the CoP began as a grassroot movement, the elite derided the CoP as "the clapping church" (*abo nsem asore*) because the church hardly had money to buy "modern" instruments for service. Any elite who joined the church was jeered for having retrogressed in terms of the

---

5. Mesthrie et al., *Introducing Sociolinguistics*, 245.
6. Mesthrie et al., *Introducing Sociolinguistics*, 6.
7. Cox, *Fire from Heaven*, 24.
8. Church of Pentecost, *Ministerial Handbook*, 18.

social ladder. Since the church began as a grassroots movement in society, the collective sense of deprivation ensured "primitive solidarity" among members. This "primitive solidarity" shaped the capacity of the CoP to survive its challenges at the nascent stage. Apostle Alexander Kumi Larbi narrated in his "Apostolization"[9] sermon at the Downtown Ofakor Officers Retreat on March 22, 2019, that in the 1970s, members of the CoP were so kind to one another, who shared their material blessings and also shared information about job opportunities. He said that in the 1970s, members of the church who drove commercial vehicles (what was popularly called Bedford or "Bone Shaker") will freely give a lift to church members. For example, Mrs. Christina Obo-Mends gave all her ornaments—which wealthy women wore—to James McKeown to be sold to finance the penniless church.[10] But this sense of care and we-feeling has collapsed in the church, under the heavyweight of social classism. In a conversation with a septuagenarian member of the CoP in a village in the Central Region of Ghana, he intimated that *nnoboa* was a common practice among the early members of the CoP.[11] Given that the church began in a rural area at a time when farming was largely subsistence among peasants, organic solidarity was strong among them.[12] The sociological essence of the *nnoboa* system was that it helped church members to share each other's burden in a country where technology in farming was still rudimentary in the 1950s. The shared challenge on the farm helped them to bond around the communion that they took at church.

The establishment of English Assemblies and PIWCs has also contributed to social segregation between the rich (elite) and the poor in the church. It has undermined the sense of egalitarianism that the shared

---

9. "Apostolisation" is a term that was coined in 2004 by Apostle Prof. Opoku Onyinah to describe a retreat he used to organize for ministerial students at the Pentecost University College, the CoP's tertiary institution. It was called "Apostolisation" because he normally invited apostles, both active and retired, to teach the pastor students, share their practical experiences with them, and lead them in prayer. Since Opoku Onyinah became the chairman of CoP in 2010, the term became associated with the annual officers' retreat organized for all CoP leaders.

10. Leonard, *Giant in Ghana*, 43.

11. Informal conversation with Samuel Okwam, a septuagenarian and one of the early converts of the Pentecostal movement, March 31, 2019, Budu Atta, Ghana.

12. *Nnoboa* was a practice "involving rotating self-help system of cooperative labor involving two or ten young male friends in their late teens and early twenties. When the group works together, one gets the benefit from the toil of all; next time around, another member directs the benefits" (Boni, *Clearing the Ghanaian Forest*, 203).

common deprivation enforced. The poor in the church are attracted to the local churches, where group solidarity is strong, while the elites are attracted to the English Assemblies where class consciousness and sense of privilege is high. This is also affecting persons who are called into ministry. Until the 1990s, the CoP nominated persons for ministry based on the person's demonstrable spiritual gifts like healing, prophecy, and evangelism. Persons were also called into ministry based on a recommendation by a serving pastor or an apostle of the church. But since the introduction of English assemblies, reflecting on the force of modernity, nomination into pastoral ministry is, in addition to one's spiritual gifts, based largely on whether or not one has had sufficient western education (usually undergraduate degree). Some of the elders I had informal conversations with expressed worries about the current criteria used in nominating potential pastors. An elder at one of the local assemblies told me, "You, the educated ones, with your western education, are quenching the spirit of the church."[13]

The concerns and trepidation of some church leaders is that western education tends to diminish Ghanaians' pride in their culture and spirituality. Some also think that the rationalistic proclivity of western education tends to affect the spirituality of the CoP. For example, while speaking tongues features prominently in the CoP, an elder told me, "Nowadays, the educated ones in the English assemblies hardly give concern to speaking the heaven language (speaking in tongues)."[14] The consolidation of the gains of the church since its beginning in the 1930s requires shared norms, values, beliefs, and practices. While the differences in lifestyle in the English Assemblies/PIWCs and the local churches have not led to any conflict, there is some sense of implicit tension. The point at which the pro-English policy led to a schism in the CoP was when the language policy resulted in the liberalization of some church policies about head covering for women, women wearing trousers, and men with dreadlocks being allowed. In the next section of this chapter, I do show that the tensions that characterized the reforms brought to the fore the notions some members of the church had about women. Consequently, while many church members envisioned the reforms to constitute the tipping point of the destruction of Pentecostal ethics, it was the "liberation" women in the church felt that was the implicit source of tension.

13. Informal conversation with Elder Moses Oklu, February 5, 2007.
14. Elder Sampson Yeboah, an Elder of the Maamobi English Assembly, November 2019.

SECTION I: CHRISTIANITY IN HISTORY

Religious Reforms and Notions of Gender

Since the inception of the CoP in the 1930s, head covering had become deeply entrenched in the church. Over the years, a nebulous text in the book of Corinthians 11:2–16 was adduced to enforce and legitimize the practice. While the exact interpretation of Paul's admonition for women to veil is not universally shared among Christian theologians, the text became the basis for some of the leadership of the CoP to consciously or unconsciously enforce head covering among female members of the church. It is said that Sophia McKeown, the wife of James McKeown, decided to cover her hair as part of identifying with the cultural normative practice of the Akan women she encountered on the mission field. It is, however, said that while McKeown himself did not make a fuss about head covering, he freely allowed it to obtain in the church since it did not affect one's salvation. Accordingly, allowing head covering in the CoP was part of McKeown's supposed accommodation of Akan culture.[15]

But given that culture is dynamic, after years of head covering in the CoP, the practice became a major hindrance to church mission and growth. This was because some female members of the church who had tasted the vibrancy of charismatic service on tertiary campus became disenchanted with the practice. For these female charismatic Christians, head covering was antiquated and emblematic of a "primitive" past. Some of the youth of the CoP felt the same way and decided to sever alliance with the church to join the thriving charismatic movement, which emerged in the 1970s. The issue of head covering also discouraged other female non-members from joining the CoP. In one of my informal conversations, a female non-member of the CoP told me she refused to marry a man from CoP because she did not want to be subjected to wearing a headscarf. Her response follows the practice in most churches (including the CoP) in Ghana, where a female who married a man from a different Christian denomination had to join the church of her husband. The lady was emphatic in saying that she found head covering in the CoP as archaic and an infringement on her rights as a female to worship freely. While head covering still holds sway in most of the local assemblies I visited across the country during my fieldwork, the practice is less enforced in the English Assemblies, PENSA, and the PIWCs. At the PIWCs, most deaconesses do not use the headscarf.

---

15. Personal communication with Aps. (Retired General Secretary of the Church of Pentecost) Rigwell Ato Addison, March 15, 2019.

At instances where females in English Assemblies and PIWCs use the headscarf, it is more of part of fashion (adornment) rather than a religious practice. Some of the older members in the local churches of the CoP feel that the relaxation on the headscarf is part of the attempt by the elites in the church to enforce their elitism on all. It is also seen as a deviation and watering down of the "Pentecostal holiness," which is believed to be enshrined in the covenant the church has with God.

In 2010, after years of contemplation, the CoP, led by its immediate past chairman, Aps. Prof. Opoku Onyinah, decided to relax the rigidity that had built around headscarf and the use of trousers by females in the church. Just when the CoP had rolled out its reforms that relaxed dress code, and while I was pursuing my postgraduate studies at the Institute of African Studies, University Ghana, on my way to campus, I met a female member of the CoP at the 37 (Accra) and, knowing she was clad in the uniformed cloth of the Women's Movement of the CoP, I greeted her with the usual greetings of the Movement, "Holiness," she replied, "unto God," and followed up with a question, "Gentleman, are you with the church?" When I responded in the affirmative, she said, "You, the young educated ones, are those destroying the church. What we inherited from the founders, the covenant (*apam*) you with your education are messing the legacies of our founders." She added with an imprecation, "God will punish anyone who seeks to destroy the covenant the Lord has with the church." After she said that, I was speechless and only managed to assure her that "God is in control of His church" and left.[16] The response of the woman was shared by many church members. The leadership of the Executive Council and General Council were cursed, insulted, and prayed against. The year 2010 was a major challenge to the leadership of the CoP.

The controversies that met the reforms point to two main things: the politics of cloth and the notion about the female's body. A dress does not merely cover the body, it is part of the social construction of gender, character, wealth, and status, and it determines negotiated social relationships.[17] A dress is also imbued with a political language capable of unifying, differentiating, challenging, contesting, and dominating.[18] In many religions, a dress is an important index that is used to gauge the commitment and conformity

---

16. Informal conversation with a female member of the Church of Pentecost, July 2010.

17. Byfield, "Dress and Politics in Post-World War II Abeokuta," 32.

18. Allman, "Fashioning Africa," 1.

of a member to the norms of behavior that is understood to be a significant part of a group membership.[19] In the case of the CoP, it is the headcover that gives a visible and non-verbal identity to a female member and also set her apart from societal mainstream. A female member who fails to cover the hair during worship service is considered deviant from the established norm of the church. As one member of the CoP, Auntie Bettie, recounted, "Most women in the church still prefer to cover their hair to church. That is what differentiates us from others."[20] This was reiterated by Georgina Nkrumah, also a member of the church, "We should maintain what we wear to church. That is the surest way to identify a member of the Church of Pentecost."[21] In the same way, the headscarf had also become a standard used to determine female church members who cross the religious and social norms and as a result, expose themselves to church discipline. Much as the head covering had crept into the church to become a visible symbol of identity in the CoP, it had simultaneously become a hindrance to non-conformists who want to feel "liberated" in the church. It had also become a major stumbling block to some of the female youth to join the church.[22]

The church's policy was to incorporate "modernists" into the church. This was articulated by Mr. Ofinam-Antwi, the-then Public Relations Officer of the CoP:

> The motive behind the measure was to offer the opportunity to all persons to get the chance to know Christ, saying that members of the church are still under obligation to adhere strictly to the church's way of doing things. . . . The dynamics of the world we are creating a divergent cultural society, it had become necessary to create an open-door policy to enable as many people as possible to be accommodated in the church so that they could also to be reached with the gospel. In the past, Ghanaian ladies, generally, were not accustomed to wearing trousers. But times have changed and many young ladies wear trousers more than the cloth now. The church must acknowledge such social changes. The idea behind the changes was to create the opportunity for people to feel

---

19. Dutton, "Fashion," 247.
20. Cobba-Biney, "Do Our Churches Need Dress Codes?," 23.
21. Cobba-Biney, "Do Our Churches Need Dress Codes?," 23.
22. Personal communication with Aps. (Retired General Secretary of the Church of Pentecost) Rigwell Ato Addison, March 15, 2019.

welcome once people come to the church, the message of the gospel will do its work of causing changes in their hearts.[23]

While the leadership of the CoP saw the reforms as recasting the image of the church to invest in modernity, the main discussion over women's dress code centered around the question of the body of a woman and whether women have agency in the church. Many of the male and female discussants of the CoP and other Pentecostal churches whose views were sampled by the newspapers sexualized the body of females. It was widely believed that the body of a woman could seduce a man and lead him into amorous living. Hence, women must cover their hair and their entire body to avert the challenge of causing men to lose concentration in the church. A woman wearing a pair of trousers is misconstrued as showing the contours of her feminine body that could lure a man into lustful thinking. This was the position of Georgina when she said, "And that would force some of the men to look at the women without paying attention to the teachings of the church."[24] For many of the discussants, a female in a pair of trousers is the next step to endorsing nudity in the church. Nudity is a politically charged and socially constructed notion. Historically, the idea of covering the African, particularly females, was part of the "civilizing mission" of the European colonizers. Nudity was considered barbaric, primitive, and antithesis to "modernity."[25] Colonial mentality feeds into the minds of many members of the CoP. For many such members, any hint of "nudity" is considered a relapse to a pre-Christian "pagan" past. The idea of the nudity of the woman is part of the structures of a patriarchal society. The body of the woman must, therefore, be controlled because it is dangerous and tempting. The female body is sexualized much more than that of the male, and throughout history, the female body has been an object of attention, desire, and lust.[26]

Thus, not only is the woman's blood considered dangerous during menstruation,[27] her body is also considered to be seductive. This was clearly articulated in the communique, that "the wearing of seductive or sexually-provocative dress should be discouraged in the church; that women must avoid the practice of cleavage (the partial exposure of the breasts) as that

23. Markwei, "Church of Pentecost Relaxes 'Morality' Rules," 1.
24. Cobba-Biney, "Do Our Churches Need Dress Codes?," 23.
25. Allman, "Let Your Fashion Be in Line with Our Ghanaian Costume," 146–47.
26. Tamale, "Nudity, Protest, and the Law in Uganda," 12.
27. Douglas, *Purity and Danger*, 150.

does not glorify the Lord."[28] The same idea was articulated by Apostle Alfred Koduah, the past General Secretary of the CoP, when he prescribed the clothes a Christian woman must avoid:

> Christian women should be educated to avoid the use of indecent sexually-provocative and seductive dresses such as the infamous skin-tight ladies trousers, usually without any waits band, popularly called "I am aware" that exposes their lower back. Other types of such dresses include the skin-tight short skirts called *Apuskeleke*, the short blouse known as "show your belly" and the bare, popularly referred to as, Ma trick Jesus (I have tricked Jesus). There is even the single sleeve woman's top dress popularly called Accident, which exposes parts of the chest and breast to the public. All this cleavage must be avoided by Christian women as they do not glorify the Lord.[29]

The sexualizing of the breast of the female is at odds with the indigenous Akan notion of the female's breast. The breast of the female in the Akan conceptual framework is not a sexual object for voyeurism; it is rather a symbol of life since every human being feeds on the breast to survive.[30] The relationship people drew between a pair of trousers and nudity is interpreted as stifling the agency of females in the church. Their subjectivity as females is constructed by males, and sometimes less of the Bible. Thus, to challenge the discourse about females in the church, Vicky Wireko, a columnist for *Daily Graphic*, asserted:

> The key changes as announced no doubt have generated some debate. The question of discrimination even in the house of God has also been raised. So why was the mode of dressing directed only at women in a world where men are wearing earrings and neck chains? Where the plaiting of the hair and wearing of sleeveless shirts have become fashionable and some of the youth will wear same for church. Questions have been asked. So, what is wrong with a woman wearing trousers for church or not covering her hair at a time when Jesus Christ asked His followers not to retreat from association with the "world." Definitely, dressing appropriately for the house of God is the moral duty of every Christian man and

---

28. Annor-Antwi, *Myth or Mystery*, 574.
29. Koduah, *Woman's Head-Covering in Church*, 180–81.
30. Personal communication with Prof. Kofi Asare Opoku, February 1, 2019.

woman, boys and girls. The decision as to what is decent and appropriate should be left to the conscience of the individual.[31]

The idea of a sexualized body of the female also fed into seating and dancing arrangements in the church. In the communique, the church indicated that "couples or families desiring to sit together at church be allowed to sit under the feet of Jesus to learn."[32] The need for this directive was because in the local church men and women were segregated. Men and women could neither sit nor dance together during church services. This practice was believed to have been inherited from the Apostolic Church, UK, which practiced the segregation of the sexes during church services.[33] In the case of Ghana, the practice emerged from the Akan concept of sexual purity and ethics, where a married woman is not to mingle freely with a non-relative male. For example, Apostle Alfred Koduah, recounted as follows:

> When Pentecostalism started in Ghana, it introduced the singing of simple choruses with clapping and dancing as part of its worship. As more women were converting into the Pentecostal churches, there was suspicion with some communities that the men could misbehave with the women in the church. Some jealous husbands even sent out people to spy on their wives who had gone to church. If these spies saw a man seated on the same bench with someone's wife, that could confirm the suspicion. The leaders of the Pentecostal churches, therefore, thought it wise to segregate the men from the women to avoid any suspicion.[34]

It follows from the above that the female's body is not just a biological material, but needs to be understood both as a material and a political entity.[35] The way the body is viewed is based on a narrative that has been historically, socially, and culturally constructed,[36] particularly by the European missionaries. The Pentecostal ethics for women is framed in the Women's Movement slogan, "Holiness unto the Lord." The slogan imposes moral inscriptions on the female's body. It spells out the normative lifestyle expected of a female member of the church. And this finds expression in what they

---

31. Wireko, "Invitation to Worship," 7.
32. Annor-Antwi, *Myth or Mystery*, 575.
33. Koduah, *Woman's Head-Covering in the Church*, 176–77.
34. Koduah, *Woman's Head-Covering in the Church*, 177.
35. Tamale, "Nudity, Protest, and the Law in Uganda," 14.
36. See Foucault, *History of Sexuality*.

wear, their hairdo, whom they marry, and how they relate with the opposite sex. Just like the colonial era, the idea of cloth, particularly concerning the covering of the body has often been associated with females.[37] In the CoP, the issue of cloth has always revolved around the body of the female members. Females in the church must not be seen in certain clothes; they must conform to certain social and church norms. This was articulated in the reform that was meant to allow women to freely worship. For example, part of the communique stated that "women should fashion their hairstyle in a decent, modest, and appropriate manner to the glory of God." But to show that the church was not making ruptures with its conservative history, the former PRO of the church at the time of the communique said that the measures should not be misconstrued as bending the traditions of the Church of Pentecost in the sense of membership drive.[38]

While head covering became a major issue for discussion in the CoP, head covering or headgear has been part of the adornment of many African cultures since pre-colonial times. Although it varies in forms and, at times, materials may vary, headdresses, hats, caps, coiffures, veils, and headscarves serve similar functions of practicality, propriety, status, fashion, and identity for women and men.[39] The headcover had had different symbolic expressions in different cultures. As a marker of status, the Himba girl's wig called *ehando* serves to announce the unmarried status of a young girl.[40] Also, Yoruba girls, generally, wore two wrappers, the *irobinrin*, and a small headscarf the *idiku*, to signal their unmarried status whenever they went out.[41] Married women also used a third cloth, the *iborun*, as a shawl or as a covering for the head and back. The headdress, or *gele*, finished a woman's outfit. Elderly women and the exclusive right to another headscarf, known as *ikaleri*, which they sometimes used to carry gifts presented to them.[42] The CoP started among the Akan. Consequently, Akan cultural practices made headways into the church and were canonized as biblical sanctioned practice. This was acknowledged in the communique when it stated that that "the practice of head covering might have crept into the Church's practices from the fact that it was traditionally required of women in Ghana

---

37. Foucault, *History of Sexuality*, 149.
38. Markwei, "Church of Pentecost Relaxes 'Morality' Rules," 1.
39. Kreamer, "Practical Beauty," 91.
40. Kreamer, "Practical Beauty," 91.
41. Byfield, "Dress and Politics in Post-World War II Abeokuta," 32.
42. Akinwumi, "Commemorative Phenomenon of Textile Use," 32.

to cover their head before speaking to their kings and this might have led foundational women of the Church to insist on appearing before the Lord, the King of kings, with their head covered."[43]

In the past and even now, the most common practice among some Akan women was/is to wear a scarf as a mark of seniority. There is no extensive explanation for this practice, beyond the fact that it marked the age of an Akan woman. Another Ghanaian ethnic group that claims to have practiced head covering since the pre-colonial times is the Ewe people of the Volta Region. From the perspective of the communique, the practice of head covering entered the CoP because of the Akan cultural context of the church.

Conclusion

While the reforms in the CoP created a new form of cultures that were considered at variance with Pentecostal ethics, it did not engender gender parity in the CoP. As I have indicated, the contention that marked the relaxation in dress code had an androcentric stint that undermined women agency in the church. Women's lack of agency in the CoP resonates with their exclusion from the offices of pastors, apostles, evangelist, and prophets. While some of the church leaders I interviewed had an interest in females in the church taking up leadership positions, they were reluctant to discuss the subject, even when I probed for detailed conversation. The lead reformer of the CoP, Opoku Onyinah, concerning female ordination, said that he considered the issue based on what the Holy Spirit says to the church at a particular time, but he has not personally received any guidance from the Holy Spirit that would allow him to advocate for women in full-time ministry.[44] Since male-only policy remains a major challenge to the CoP in the "modern" world, it is important to discuss the specific and general role women play in the CoP and the factors that have militated against their rise through the ranks to be ordained into the pastoral ministry.

43. Annor-Antwi, *Myth or Mystery*, 573.
44. Ofoe, *"Newness" Theology of Opoku Onyinah*, 143.

6

World Christianity and the Global Leadership Crisis
Forming Servant Leaders in the Age of the Strongman

KENNETH R. ROSS

Global Leadership Crisis

WORLDWIDE A NEW FORM of political leadership has come into place during the early part of the twenty-first century. While political systems vary from country to country, there are significant points in common when we consider the leadership being offered by, e.g., Donald Trump in the USA, Jair Bolsonaro in Brazil, Boris Johnson in the UK, Matteo Salvini in Italy, Viktor Orban in Hungary, Recip Erdogan in Turkey, Vladimir Putin in Russia, Narendra Modi in India, Xi Jinping in China and Rodrigo Duterte in the Philippines. All are "strongman" leaders, authoritarian and mercurial in style, strongly nationalist, hostile to the rules-based international order, socially conservative, allied to vested interests, and anti-immigration. In terms of character and track record, all are open to question as regards their suitability for national leadership. When Boris Johnson was running to become Tory Party Leader and Prime Minister in 2019, his former boss at the *Daily Telegraph* Max Hastings, denounced "his moral bankruptcy, rooted in a contempt for truth," and stated that "he cares for no interest save his own fame and gratification."¹ This appraisal was amply vindicated when Johnson took office in July 2019.² Similar withering assessments have been offered of other strongman leaders yet without impeding their advance. Indeed, they are buoyed by confidence that the tide of affairs is flowing their way. On the eve of the G20 summit in Osaka, Japan, in mid-2019, Vladimir Putin hailed the growth of national populist movements in Europe and America, claiming that liberalism is spent as an ideological force.³

Few would disagree with Putin's assessment that a wave of populism is shaping the contemporary global political environment. As Jan-Werner Müller explains, "Populists always claim that they—and they alone—properly represent the people. This perhaps initially innocuous-sounding rhetoric has two pernicious consequences. First, all other political contenders are condemned by populists as being part of a self-serving, corrupt elite. Second, citizens who do not support the populists will have their status as proper members of the people put into doubt."⁴ Populism thus entails a dismissive and condemnatory attitude towards other political parties or movements and a tendency to close down the space available to citizens who wish to advocate alternative views. Complex issues are reduced to a binary choice between good and evil and anything less than unquestioning support for the populist leaders is portrayed as morally degenerate. This is well illustrated by the political environment in the UK following the vote to leave the European Union ("Brexit"). Riding a wave of populist fervor, the right-wing Tory Government immediately questioned the integrity of anyone who challenged its determination to drive through a "hard" Brexit.

Populist movements also nurse grievances and promote exclusionary nationalist politics. The movement propelling Donald Trump to the American Presidency provides a good example. In his inauguration speech, he declared: "From this day forward, it's going to be only America first, America first. Every decision on trade, on taxes, on immigration, on foreign affairs, will be made to benefit American workers and American families. We must protect our borders from the ravages of other countries making our products, stealing our companies, and destroying our jobs. Protection will lead

---

1. Hastings, "I Was Boris Johnson's Boss."

2. Within weeks, he had suspended Parliament, which could only resume sitting when the Supreme Court unanimously found Johnson's action unlawful. See Bowcott et al., "Johnson's Suspension of Parliament Unlawful."

3. Barber et al., "Vladimir Putin."

4. Müller, "In the Name of the People," 14. See further Müller, *What Is Populism?*

to great prosperity and strength. . . . We will follow two simple rules: buy American and hire American."[5] An *Observer* editorial commented on the speech, noting that its crass nationalism

> appeals to the darker side of human nature, bolstering the insidious claims of jealousy, envy, greed, and hubris. It thrives on fear, chauvinism, discrimination, and not always subliminal notions of ethnic, racial, and moral superiority. It is a product of our times. But it is not too much to say Trump's ranting scream of "America first, America first!" carries an echo of the "Sieg Heil" (hail victory) of another, not-forgotten era of brutish nationalist triumphalism.[6]

The International Fellowship of Mission as Transformation has expressed similar concern from an explicitly Christian viewpoint:

> A new form of dangerous political leadership is emerging in different parts of the world. Although this is not the first, and likely not the last time, the threat today of what can be called the new fascism is real. As an ideology characterized by fundamentalist, militant, nationalistic, and racist policies, fascism threatens especially the "other," be it the poor, the oppressed, or the disenfranchised—people for whom God has a special concern.[7]

Here is a litmus test when it comes to leadership and the shortcomings of the strongman are soon exposed.

Metropolitan Mor Geevarghese Coorilos, the Indian Syrian Orthodox bishop, has suggested:

> There are "new King Herods," a new imperial age and numerous "little empires" being formed in the orbit of the "mega-empire" and working in hegemonic ways. In India, for example, an unholy alliance of religious fundamentalism, caste mentality and the ideology of neo-liberalism is creating a fascist empire. Division, fundamentalism, violence, and discrimination are all on the increase.[8]

Among many points of concern, two that stand out are the attitudes of the strongman leaders to the question of truth and the question of the "other."

---

5. Trump, "Inauguration Speech."
6. "Editorial," *Observer*, January 22, 2017.
7. Adeleye et al., "Call for Biblical Faithfulness amid the New Fascism."
8. Keum, "Transforming Discipleship."

There can be little doubt that the reason "post-truth" became the word of the year for the Oxford Dictionaries in 2016 is because of the nature of the campaign in the UK's referendum on membership of the European Union.[9] In earlier times, if a politician were found to have stated something that was demonstrably false, their credibility would collapse and their cause would be lost. In a post-truth situation, a politician can carry on repeating a claim, even when it has been shown to be untrue by convincing independent analysis. Perhaps the most notorious illustration of this was the claim by the Vote Leave campaign that EU membership cost the UK £350 million each week. Despite convincing analysis from a whole range of authorities showing that this was an inaccurate and misleading figure, the Vote Leave campaign continued to use it as a centerpiece of their campaign until the very day of the referendum, after which everyone agreed that it had not been an accurate or realistic figure.

As the journalist John Lanchester observed: "I don't think there has ever been a time in British politics when so many people in public life spent so much time loudly declaring things they knew not to be true."[10] The point, however, is that whereas once it would have been fatal to one's political prospects to be found to be deliberately lying, in a post-truth era it is possible for politicians who have achieved their ends through being untruthful to be rewarded and to flourish. The referendum on EU membership demonstrated that the prevailing political culture has changed. Much less importance is attached to the issue of whether or not a claim is factually true.

As the commentator Andrew Sullivan has observed about demonstrably false statements issued by the Trump administration: "They are direct refutations of reality and their propagation and repetition is about enforcing his power rather than wriggling out of a political conundrum. They are attacks on the very possibility of a reasoned discourse, the kind of bald-faced lies that authoritarians issue as a way to test loyalty and force their subjects into submission."[11] Likewise, Michael Gerson has observed, "Trump is not only speaking a series of lies. He is inviting millions of loyalists to live in a political reality conjured by his deceptions. . . . How is any political conversation or policy discussion possible when citizens inhabit

---

9. English Oxford Living Dictionaries, https://en.oxforddictionaries.com/word-of-the-year/word-of-the-year-2016 accessed 8 March 2017.

10. Lanchester, "Brexit Blues," 6.

11. Sullivan, "Madness of King Donald."

separate universes of truth and meaning? This is Trump's most dangerous innovation: epistemology as cult of personality."[12]

The loss of high standards of truthfulness in political life thus becomes a tool in the hands of authoritarian, populist leaders. Truth and power, however, are not only political issues but also religious. As regards truth, the Christian vision offers a perception of reality that arises from obedience to Christ. In the post-Enlightenment Western world, the challenge to Christian discipleship has been how to express that vision of faith in a context where great authority was accorded to human reason. That authority is now being diminished as we enter a post-truth era. The Christian vision now has to be advanced in a context where the raw assertion of power by authoritarian regimes creates a climate that is in many ways antithetical to biblical faith. Power as domination and control stands in sharp contrast to power as love and service. As the Common Call of Edinburgh 2010 stated: "Disturbed by asymmetries and imbalances of power that divide and trouble us in church and world, we are called to repentance, to critical reflection on systems of power, and accountable use of power structures."[13] The hermeneutic of suspicion in regard to the exercise of power that is built into the Christian tradition may be crucial to faithful witness in our time.

Another distinguishing feature of today's strongman leaders is xenophobia, particularly hostility towards immigrants. A key plank in Donald Trump's Presidential campaign was his pledge to build a "great, great wall" on the Mexican-American border. He justified his plan by alleging that, "[Mexico] are sending people that have lots of problems, and they are bringing those problems to us. They are bringing drugs, and bringing crime, and their rapists."[14] It is clear that a nation largely composed of immigrants will now take a hostile attitude toward future aspiring immigrants, even those seeking asylum from violence and insecurity in their countries of origin. Trump also called for all Muslims to be banned from entering the USA, seeking a "total and complete shut-down" of the country's borders to Muslims.[15]

Meanwhile in the UK in July 2016, the month after the vote for Brexit, there were 5,468 "hate crimes," an increase of 41 percent from the

---

12. Gerson, "Trump Isn't Just Speaking Lies."
13. Edinburgh 2010 Common Call §4, in Kim and Anderson, *Edinburgh 2010*, 1.
14. Gabbatt, "Donald Trump's Tirade."
15. Pilkington, "Donald Trump."

previous year.[16] As John Lanchester observed: "There is a real darkness in this country, a xenophobic, racist sickness of heart that is closer to the surface today than it has been for decades. That is a direct result of the referendum campaign. The campaign's dual legacy is the end of the idea that politics is based on rational argument, and *a new permission to hate immigrants*."[17] Achille Mbembe for his part suggests that, "With the triumph of this neo-Darwinian approach to history-making, apartheid under various guises will be restored as the new old norm. Its restoration will pave the way to new separatist impulses, the erection of more walls, the militarization of more borders, deadly forms of policing, more asymmetrical wars, splitting alliances and countless internal divisions including in established democracies."[18] Strongman leaders around the world are actively pursuing exactly such policies.

This direction of travel stands clearly in contrast to the view of others, strangers and immigrants that meets us in the Bible. Thirty-six times in the Old Testament alone, God's people are commanded to care for the foreigner and the stranger in their land. Jesus commanded his disciples: "Love your enemies and pray for those who persecute you" (Matt 5:44). At a time when prejudice, hatred, racism, misogyny and xenophobia are returning the mainstream and being validated by those in power, the onus is on disciples of Christ to show that they offer a very different kind of leadership. The way of Christ, writes Alan Lewis, tells us that "trust, defencelessness, and vulnerability are in themselves, despite all appearances, finally more productive and protective than all stratagems for aggression or defence, attack or retaliation, self-assertion or self-protection." Following Christ means being willing "to lead risky, unprotected, costly lives, open to others and committed to self-expenditure on their behalf."[19] When measured by biblical standards, the shortcomings of today's strongman leaders are clearly exposed.

A Failure of Leadership

To some extent the strongman leaders of our time have become figures of fun. Their foibles and pronouncements are often so ridiculous as to

16. Weaver, "Hate Crimes Soared After EU Referendum."
17. Lanchester, "Brexit Blues" (my italics).
18. Mbembe, "Age of Humanism Is Ending."
19. Lewis, *Between Cross and Resurrection*, 321, 454.

provoke mirth and their many critics on social media can have a field day. Yet it is not long before the sobering awareness dawns that the issues at stake are no laughing matter. While political culture is being degraded and human society being polarized, there are imminent threats to the earth and its peoples that remain unaddressed. Worse still, two of the gravest threats to our common future are being exacerbated by the kind of leadership that prevails today. Consider the effect of the strongman leader when it comes to the issues of inequality and climate change.

In a report issued on the occasion of the World Economic Forum at Davos, Switzerland, in January 2017, Oxfam pointed out that the world's eight richest individuals have as much wealth as the 3.6 billion people who make up the poorest half of the world, that since 2015, the richest 1 percent has owned more wealth than the rest of the planet, and that over the last thirty years the growth in the incomes of the bottom 50 percent has been zero, whereas incomes of the top 1 percent have grown 300 percent.[20] The report concluded that: "As growth benefits the richest, the rest of society—especially the poorest—suffers. The very design of our economies and the principles of our economics have taken us to this extreme, unsustainable and unjust point. Our economy must stop excessively rewarding those at the top and start working for all people."[21] Under strongman leadership the direction has been exactly the opposite, e.g., with Donald Trump's administration in the USA prioritizing tax breaks for the wealthy.

We cannot underestimate the extent to which deeply entrenched economic inequalities drive the destructive social and political trends identified above. As Pankaj Mishra has argued: "An existential resentment of other people's being, caused by an intense mix of envy and sense of humiliation and powerlessness, *ressentiment*, as it lingers and deepens, poisons civil society and undermines political liberty, and is presently making for a global turn to authoritarianism and toxic forms of chauvinism."[22] These in turn find their counterpoint in militancy and terrorism with a vicious circle developing as the two monsters feed one another.

In the crisis of our time it is not only the future of humanity that is at stake but the future of the earth itself. The international agreement on action to tackle climate change, achieved at the UN summit in Paris in December 2015, signalled a moment of hope, albeit fragile, in regard to the gravest

20. See "Economy for the 99 Percent."
21. "Economy for the 99 Percent," 1.
22. Mishra, *Age of Anger*, 14.

threat facing the human community and the earth itself in our time. However, on the campaign trail Donald Trump was openly sceptical about the scientific consensus on the causes of climate change and eager to promote businesses that depend on the exploitation of fossil fuels. On his first day in office, the White House website's expansive section on climate change was deleted and replaced by an "American energy first plan" in which Trump promised to scrap the "harmful and unnecessary" climate action plan.[23] His appointment of Scott Pruitt, a raucous supporter of fossil fuel companies, as head of the Environmental Protection Agency, indicated the direction of travel. It was no surprise, though still a source of profound dismay, when the USA withdrew from the Paris Accord.

These moves by the Trump administration are part of a global trend. Why is such apparently self-destructive action taking place? Naomi Klein suggests that: "This is happening because the wealthiest countries in the world think they are going to be OK, that someone else is going to eat the biggest risks, that even when climate change turns up on their doorstep, they will be taken care of."[24] There is need to reckon with the hard reality that "climate change isn't just about things getting hotter and wetter: under our current economic and political model, it's about things getting meaner and uglier."[25]

As Philip Alston, United Nations Special Rapporteur on extreme poverty and human rights, reported in June 2019: "Climate change will have devastating consequences for people in poverty. Even under the best-case scenario, hundreds of millions will face food insecurity, forced migration, disease, and death. Climate change threatens the future of human rights and risks undoing the last fifty years of progress in development, global health, and poverty reduction."[26] In this context he highlights a failure of leadership: "Governments, and too many in the human rights community, have failed to seriously address climate change for decades. Somber speeches by government officials have not led to meaningful action and too many countries continue taking short-sighted steps in the wrong direction."[27] Pope Francis has declared a global "climate emergency," and warned that failure to take urgent action would be "a brutal act of injustice toward the

---

23. Rushe et al., "What You Need to Know."
24. Klein, "Let Them Drown," 14.
25. Klein, "Let Them Drown," 14.
26. UNHRC, "Climate Change and Poverty," 1.
27. UNHRC, "Climate Change and Poverty," 1.

poor and future generations."[28] Yet the strongman leadership prevailing in today's world is making things worse rather than better.

To consider no more than these two vast and urgent issues of inequality and climate change, it is abundantly clear that the strongman leaders of our time are failing to provide the leadership that is required. The scale of the challenges facing the human community today would test the greatest of leaders. Instead of making any serious effort to engage with pressing issues, today's strongman leaders compound the problem. At the heart of our crisis lies a failure of leadership.

Leadership: A Question for World Christianity

Given that the political direction worldwide seems to be fostering a form of leadership that is ill-equipped to meet the challenges of our time, from where can a renewal of leadership come? This is a question that World Christianity cannot evade. Surveying the global context in the early twenty-first century, Doug Birdsall, former Executive Chair of the Lausanne Movement, arrived at this conclusion: "As I have travelled the world the last several years on behalf of the Lausanne Movement, I am increasingly convinced that the greatest needs are not about new strategies and programs, nor are they about better buildings, more personnel, additional financial resources, and innovative use of technology, as important as these issues are. No, the greatest need is for leaders, men and women with Christ-like character, faith, and vision."[29] The need of the day is for leaders with personal integrity, sound values and far-seeing vision.

It might be hoped that World Christianity would be in the business of producing such people. At its best it has done so. Sadly, however, it has not been immune to abuse of power and self-serving forms of leadership. The Lausanne Movement's *Cape Town Commitment* observes that: "The rapid growth of the Church in so many places remains shallow and vulnerable, partly because of the lack of discipled leaders, and partly because *so many use their positions for worldly power, arrogant status or personal enrichment.* As a result, God's people suffer, Christ is dishonored, and gospel mission is undermined."[30] Any consideration of the role of World Christianity in rela-

---

28. Harvey and Ambrose, "Pope Francis Declares 'Climate Emergency.'"
29. Birdsall, "Foreword," in Jørgensen, *Equipping for Service*, x.
30. *Cape Town Commitment* §3 (my italics).

tion to leadership must begin with self-criticism. Yet this only underlines the importance of the question.

When the World Council of Churches convened its World Mission Conference in Arusha, Tanzania, in 2018, it recognized that leadership is a key question in today's world. What is leadership? What kind of leadership does our world need? What kind of leadership are the churches called to offer? The Arusha Call to Discipleship included the affirmation that, "We are called to be formed as servant leaders who demonstrate the way of Christ in a world that privileges power, wealth, and the culture of money."[31] In line with its central theme, the Arusha Call set the question of leadership in the context of discipleship. It recognized that a call to *servant* leadership very much goes against the grain so far as today's prevailing culture is concerned: "The human soul and human community are stunted by the institutionalization and amplification of greed in an unrestrained market society. The integrity and well-being of creation is directly and dangerously threatened. We must engage in a determined attempt to present, for this generation, a faithful alternative to the spiritual formation offered by the culture of money."[32]

In this context, the Arusha Conference was very clear about the required direction: "Alongside the need to denounce the greed for power, wealth and privilege in the life of our churches, the Conference also pointed out the ways in which leadership is understood and exercised in our communities, churches, and Christian organizations. Unfortunately, some in our leadership structures today seem more preoccupied with privilege and power that come with their positions rather than with their calling to responsible stewardship."[33] They have succumbed to the wrong kind of formation.

Besides exposing destructive patterns of leadership in the world at large, there is a prophetic critique to be brought to bear on the church itself: "Too often the church has been moulded by prevailing patterns of the surrounding world, its leaders seeking power and wealth for themselves rather than modelling the sacrificial service seen in Christ. Today we urgently need church leaders who are, first and foremost, disciples, walking in the Spirit, forming and guiding communities that take the way of Jesus."[34]

31. Jukko and Keum, *Moving in the Spirit*, 46.
32. Jukko and Keum, *Moving in the Spirit*, 16.
33. Jukko and Keum, *Moving in the Spirit*, 15.
34. Jukko and Keum, *Moving in the Spirit*, 15.

SECTION I: CHRISTIANITY IN HISTORY

Jesus as Prototype

In the perspective of Christian faith, leadership is not something that we seek to invent by ourselves. Rather it is a matter of discipleship—of learning from a master, of following Jesus.

When we take this as our cue, we find that it points us in the direction of servant leadership. This is a major theme of the Gospel, powerfully expressed, for example, in Luke:

> And Jesus said to them, "The kings of the Gentiles exercise lordship over them, and those in authority over them are called benefactors. But not so with you. Rather let the greatest among you become as the youngest, and the leader as one who serves. For who is the greater, one who reclines at table or one who serves? Is it not the one who reclines at table? But I am among you as the one who serves." (Luke 22:25–27)

So far as disciples are concerned, Jesus' life of service sets the pattern when it comes to leadership. Their destiny and calling is, in the words of the apostle Paul, to be "conformed to the image of [God's] Son, that he might be the firstborn among many brethren" (Romans 8:29). The way that Jesus led his life sets the tone. The leadership that he offered provides the prototype for his disciples.

As the question of leadership becomes a crucial one today there is need to revisit the way that Jesus lived his life, the choices he made, the people with whom he associated, the words he spoke, the actions he took and the kind of leadership that he offered. The distinctive quality offered by World Christianity is the call to follow Jesus that rings out in every Christian tradition as a gospel imperative. The leadership that is needed today depends on faithfulness in discipleship, on a close and committed following of Jesus Christ. Wesley Granberg-Michaelson recalls the ministry of Dietrich Bonhoeffer, comparing today's challenges with those that arose when the darkness of Nazism and the Second World War descended on Europe:

> The public witness of so many who follow Christ lacks the spiritual depth and clarity to proclaim the true meaning of Christian faith for the life of society in this time. Discipleship falters without the strength to follow Jesus into the world. Courage is dissipated, bereft of spiritual power and biblical discernment.... Once again we are in grave need of basic, enduring spiritual formation to acquire both the clarity and strength that equips us to follow Jesus and

answer the question posed by Bonhoeffer: "Who is Jesus Christ for us today?"[35]

Servant Leaders

The "who" question is also one that we are prompted to ask of ourselves. Who are we? Leadership springs first from who we are. Before the doing comes the being. Rowan Williams begins his recent study of the Christian life by observing: "Discipleship . . . is a state of being. Discipleship is about how we live; not just the decisions we make, not just the things we believe, but a state of being."[36] The World Council of Churches mission affirmation *Together Towards Life* states the matter in spiritual terms: "Life in the Holy Spirit is the essence of mission, the core of why we do what we do and how we live our lives."[37] The Lausanne Movement's *Cape Town Commitment* concludes with the affirmation that: "Biblical mission demands that those who claim Christ's name should be like him, by taking up their cross, denying themselves, and following him in the paths of humility, love, integrity, generosity, and servanthood. To fail in discipleship and disciple-making, is to fail at the most basic level of our mission."[38] To be a disciple is, first and foremost, a personal matter. It is about an inward encounter with Christ, the formation of Christ-like character and the embarking on a way of life that corresponds with the path that Jesus followed. As Knud Jørgensen observed: "The person, who has not learned to be a disciple, cannot be a leader."[39]

Or, to state the matter in positive terms, it is through growing as disciples that we become servant leaders. Christian discipleship is not primarily about adopting a political position, protesting against injustice or advocating certain ethical standpoints—even if it may in due course lead to such commitments. Nor is discipleship primarily a matter of adopting a belief structure or becoming a member of an institution—even if such developments may in due course be entailed. Christian discipleship is first of all personal—a matter of a transforming encounter with Jesus Christ, the risen Lord, in the power of the Spirit. It is from this encounter that a distinctive kind of leadership grows.

35. Granberg-Michaelson, *Future Faith*, 157.
36. Williams, *Being Disciples*, 1.
37. Keum, *Together Towards Life* §3.
38. *Cape Town Commitment*, s.v. "Conclusion."
39. Jørgensen, *Equipping for Service*, 35.

The Arusha Conference offered a clear idea of the qualities required of leaders: "This vision of discipleship is geared to the formation of leaders who are equipped not only intellectually, but particularly at the level of spiritual discernment and personal transformation. It fosters a radical openness to the Spirit of God that finds expression in leadership marked by mutuality, reciprocity, humility and interdependence. It provokes a radical openness to others that is life-affirming and profound in its integrity."[40] Likewise, the *Cape Town Commitment* observes that: "some leadership training programmes focus on packaged knowledge, techniques and skills to the neglect of godly character. By contrast, authentic Christian leaders must be like Christ in having a servant heart, humility, integrity, purity, lack of greed, prayerfulness, dependence on God's Spirit, and a deep love for people."[41] When Jesus sent out the first disciples he required them to go without money or material protection, vulnerable and dependent on the hospitality of those to whom they went (Matthew 10:9–10; Luke 10:1–9). Leaders whose project is to acquire power and wealth for themselves have taken a very different direction. The Arusha Conference found that, "Humility and sacrifice are urgently needed to liberate the gospel from captivity to projects of self-aggrandizement."[42]

Knud Jørgensen reminds us, "The overriding biblical perspective on leadership is service."[43] To become a servant leader one must be ready to swim against the tide, one must be intentional in opting for a way of life different from the prevailing norm. As noted in the Arusha Conference Report: "A spirituality of resilience is at the center of the theological and missional formation for discipleship."[44] Such resilience holds the key to servant leadership. It involves a radical identification with all who are vulnerable, excluded or afflicted. As the *Cape Town Commitment* reminds us: "The Bible tells us that the Lord is loving toward all he has made, upholds the cause of the oppressed, loves the foreigner, feeds the hungry, sustains the fatherless and widow. The Bible also shows that God wills to do these things through human beings committed to such action. God holds responsible especially those who are appointed to political or judicial leadership in society, but all God's people are commanded—by the law and prophets, Psalms and

---

40. Jukko and Keum, *Moving in the Spirit*, 16.
41. *Cape Town Commitment* §3.
42. Jukko and Keum, *Moving in the Spirit*, 13.
43. Jørgensen, *Equipping for Service*, 23.
44. Jukko and Keum, *Moving in the Spirit*, 16.

Wisdom, Jesus and Paul, James and John—to reflect the love and justice of God in practical love and justice for the needy."[45]

True leadership today involves a prophetic stance in relation to prevailing trends. On the occasion of Donald Trump's inauguration as US President in 2017, the International Fellowship of Mission as Transformation led by example:

> As a challenge to the new fascism, we call the whole church to biblical faithfulness in:
> - the merciful and just treatment of immigrants, refugees, strangers, and racial and religious minorities;
> - the rejection of all sorts of objectification of women and commercialization of sex;
> - the responsible and just regard for the care of God's creation, including taking seriously the reality and dangers of climate change;
> - the commitment to world peace in the face of the war industry, military rhetoric and action; and
> - the courageous and self-sacrificing pursuit of the welfare of the poor, marginalized, people with disabilities, and other vulnerable groups, including children and youth.[46]

Of course, even if the whole church does offer such a challenge there is no guarantee that it will have any effect at the level of political leadership. However, the Christian movement has a record of working from unexpected angles to reshape the way people think and act. Modelling servant leadership in situations of adversity might introduce the leaven that has transformative effect. Consider a picture that is sketched by Ivan Satyavrata:

> The following scene is from the largest red-light district in South Asia, an evil hellhole of brutal sexual exploitation in a thriving commercial metropolis. The corpse of a young woman, covered with a white sheet, was being carried through the streets. She had been ill for a while with a terrible disease. The last few days of her life were agonizingly painful, lonely and terrifying. The madam who ran the brothel had forced four of her terrified girls to hold the corners of the bedsheet as they dragged her body out and tossed it into the street near a garbage dump. It lay there all day while neighbors yelled out their complaints and passers-by covered their faces in disgust. Then a group of strangers came with

---

45. *Cape Town Commitment* §7c.
46. Adeleye et al. "Call for Biblical Faithfulness."

a stretcher, some sheets and flowers. These were not paramedics, family members or friends. People wondered who they were as they watched them sing and pray softly as they wrapped the sheets around the body gently and lovingly.

The efforts of this Teen Challenge-Project Rescue team to begin work in the district had been frustrated and stonewalled at every corner, until the leader saw a window of opportunity when he heard that the girls who died of AIDS were being dumped into the streets. He and his workers began to pick up these corpses and give them in death something that they never had all through their lives—dignity. That's when the wall in the red-light district began to crack open to Christian influence. Today there is a church of more than four hundred people at the edge of the red-light district, while a fifty-acre community called Village of Hope on the outskirts of the city houses a rehab center and a rescue home for the children of scores of women from the district.[47]

Such scenes might be far removed from the presidential palace. Yet it is from such marginal contexts that we can see the emergence of a form of leadership that is diametrically opposed to that which prevails in the corridors of power. It is in its outreach, in its missionary dimension, that World Christianity discovers the servant leadership that is among its outstanding characteristics.

> Mission . . . is much more than the work we do; in itself it becomes a means of ongoing transformation of our own lives," writes theological educator Madge Karecki. She suggests that: "Mission leads us into a more profound sharing in the paschal mystery of Christ. It makes possible a kenotic participation in this mystery of the humility of God made visible in Jesus the Christ as we allow ourselves to be broken and poured out for others in the service of mission. This kind of spirituality, which is not for the faint-hearted, can be embraced only through the work of the Holy Spirit.[48]

Commenting on the biblical text "He that findeth his life shall lose it; and he that loseth his life for my sake shall find it," J. H. Oldham unfolded a paradox: "The human heart is so constituted that its fullness comes of spending. When we serve we rule. When we give we have. When we surrender ourselves we are victors. We are most ourselves when we lose sight

---

47. Satyavrata, "Pentecostals and Charismatics," 299.
48. Karecki, "Missiological Reflection," 192.

of ourselves."[49] Our calling, as Bishop Festo Kivingere often said to younger leaders within the East African Revival, is to be "broken bread and poured out wine."[50] A lifetime in the missionary movement allowed John Taylor to conclude, "Every opening of one's whole self towards another, every taking upon oneself the burden and the gift of another, contributes a little to that quiet tide which is flowing back and forth, carrying us with it into the very being of God, sweeping us back with God into the life of the world."[51] Such are the dynamics that create servant leaders. It is as these take effect that World Christianity will bring its distinctive contribution to the challenge of meeting the global leadership crisis.

---

49. Oldham, *Devotional Diary*, s.v. "Second Month, Day 19."
50. Festo Kivingere quoted in Jørgensen, *Equipping for Service*, 40.
51. John Taylor quoted in Wood, *Poet, Priest, and Prophet*, 210.

Section II

Spiritual Reality, Worldviews, and Formations

7

Kwabena Asamoah-Gyadu
A Measured Critique of Africa's Use of the Holy Spirit's Healing Gifts

Trevor H. G. Smith

Introduction

I do not come to this essay on the contributions of the Rev. Dr. J. Kwabena Asamoah-Gyadu as an impartial scholar—as though such a thing is either possible or desirable. His help and influence in my own doctoral studies preclude the possibility of impartiality. Instead, I come as a western scholar who believes that the time is right for a robust, global conversation on what it means to be a follower of Jesus, a conversation whose agenda needs to be strongly influenced by Africa's fully Trinitarian understanding of the god *Yahweh*. He is the god who has revealed himself to this world in Scripture and in the person of his Son, Jesus and now empowers his people by the presence of his Holy Spirit in us.

In this essay I will demonstrate how Kwabena Asamoah-Gyadu's ability to sort through the various theological and practical issues involved in a fully Trinitarian understanding and practice of the Christian life, achieves a necessary balance between a hyper-spiritualized (the global South's temptation) and hyper-materialized (the West's temptation) cause and effect understanding of reality. In other words, his work has the potential to offer a third way that balances the strengths of both the global West and South to take seriously both spiritual and material cause and effect to understand this God-created world in which we live and move and have our being. In particular I will show how he has developed a biblical hermeneutic and ecclesiology out of Africa's single-tiered ontological understanding of reality, an understanding that holds material and spiritual cause and effect as equally important and necessary for understanding this world God has given us.

As a scholar of African Christian theology, which necessarily makes him a scholar of what he himself calls "pneumatic" Christianity, Asamoah-Gyadu distinguishes what is happening in theology in Africa from where it has ended up in the West. Because the African church's experience of God is rooted in the transforming power of the Holy Spirit, belief and practice now form the boundaries of her life. Both are essential for understanding what is happening in the church of Africa. This, Asamoah-Gyadu notes, differs from the West where, he observes:

> Theologizing invariably involves rational systematic analyses of the "content of faith," that is, the nature, purposes, and activity of God in relation to the world. Pentecostals theologize too. But . . . they center their Christianity on the experience of God the Holy Spirit, seeing this experience as the heartbeat of their faith. It is more appropriate, therefore, especially within oral cultures like that of Ghana, to speak of "Pentecostal beliefs and practices" rather than of "Pentecostal theology."[1]

Single-Tiered Ontological Structure of Reality

I made reference above to Africa's *single-tiered ontological understanding of reality*. This is a term that requires further explication. When I began to read texts in African Christian theology, I noticed almost immediately that virtually every African author, whether a professional theologian, historian, philosopher, or social scientist, made note of one particular phenomenon: a "unitive perspective" towards the world that did not separate the visible from the invisible or the spiritual from the material, but held them together

---

1. Asamoah-Gyadu, *African Charismatics*, 7.

such that any explanation of life in this world required both spiritual and material cause and effect.²

Eventually I concluded that behind this unitive perspective was an understanding of reality rooted in what I call Africa's *single-tiered ontology*. The genesis of this term began when I read how Kwame Bediako referred to the West's division of the world into two tiers,³ the secular and the sacred. At that point the term *single-tiered* suggested itself as a way of differentiating this African approach to reality from the approach common in the West. A single-tiered perspective rejects the privileging of the secular (that is, the material and natural part of reality that can be studied using the scientific method) over the sacred (or the unseen and spiritual world that cannot be studied using mere natural cause and effect), treating them as equals while recognizing that they are not the same. Africans perceive the world as a single-tiered reality where both the spiritual and material are necessary to understand the world we live in. I do not suggest that Africans collapse the material and spiritual into one another, but instead, that they perceive them as at once distinguishable but inseparable. Africans, as Bediako notes, experience life and reality as a single, unitive whole—this is what is normal in the African context.

The second element in the phrase, *ontology*, draws our attention to an understanding of what is real where the interpretive landscape is bounded on every side by horizons which include both the natural and supernatural in a unitive whole. I use this word, ontology, as defined by the Kenyan scholar, John Mbiti. Readers familiar with this word in its western context will need to understand that Mbiti felt under no obligation to use it in its western sense and has, in fact, defined it from his own African perspective. Mbiti uses the term "African ontology" to describe an understanding of the world constructed out of five delicately balanced

---

2. We see this starting as far back as Carl Christian Reindorf, a native Ghanaian whose historical study of the Gold Coast was translated and published in English in 1895 (see Reindorf, *History of the Gold Coast and Asante*). Kwame Bediako put Reindorf's work "in the same category as Bede's and Gregory's histories—essentially national histories with, and arising from, Christian interest" (Bediako, *Christianity in Africa*, 4). In a very helpful introduction to Reindorf's life and work, Heinz Hauser-Renner notes that Reindorf's *History* embraces "the idea of society comprising ancestors, living beings, and the yet unborn; a strong reverence for the past; and the hand of the ancestors at work in both the present and the future" (Hauser-Renner, "'Obstinate' Pastor and Pioneer Historian," 68–69). No western theologian I am aware of would, or possibly could, write of society existing in this way.

3. Bediako, *Christianity in Africa*, 176.

features—(1) God, (2) Spirits, (3) humans (born and unborn), (4) animals and plants, and (5) phenomena and objects without biological life—such that none can be removed without destroying the whole.[4] Consequently, this phrase, "single-tiered ontological structure of reality," combines two essentially African terms—in the sense that neither has any prior reliance on western thought—into a single phrase. And I use this term, *single-tiered ontology*, to describe what is normal to Asamoah-Gyadu and the other scholars discussed in this essay, an approach to understanding the world that sees spiritual and material cause and effect as equally necessary to an understanding of the world God created.

This phrase *single-tiered ontology*, or more fully, *single-tiered ontological structure of reality*, provides a hermeneutical tool that is essential for properly understanding and appreciating the contribution of a scholar like Kwabena Asamoah-Gyadu. He perceives this world as a robust, permeable material/spiritual reality. Benezet Bujo captures something of the essence of this single-tiered unitive perspective when he writes,

> In African religion and ethics, everything in the world is intimately connected. All the elements in the universe are related to each other in an interlocking way. One cannot touch one of them without causing the whole to vibrate. Humans are not the only part of the cosmos; they are also a microcosm within the macrocosm, or a miniature version of the universe. Black Africans belong at the same time to the world of the living, the dead, and the yet-to-be-born, and they can identify with spirits, animals, plants and minerals. They know that they exist within the vital flux of all creation, which ultimately connects them to the Supreme Being, God, the source of all life.[5]

Throughout this essay, I will use the term, single-tiered ontology, or its longer form, single-tiered ontological structure of reality, to point to this understanding of reality which holds together the seen and unseen, the material and spiritual, the natural and the supernatural. At times, I will use more simply, Africa's *unitive perspective* where *unitive* connotes the idea of a coherent whole while *perspective* points to Africa's interpretive landscape bounded on every side by both the natural and supernatural. In each instance, however, the basic idea is the single-tiered ontology. That it is a nuanced feature

---

4. Mbiti, *African Religions and Philosophy*, 15–16.
5. Bujo, "Distinctives of African Ethics," 81.

requires my using these several different phrases in order to capture its several different facets along with what I consider its intellectual beauty.

The Single-Tiered Ontological Structure in the Work of Asamoah-Gyadu

There is no doubt that Asamoah-Gyadu operates fully out of Africa's single-tiered ontology. We see this fact evidenced in his both/and approach to spiritual and material cause and effect. We then see his application of this approach in his use of Scripture, and in his understanding of the church, particularly in his description of the democratization of the *charisms* in the African church. We note, for example, his use of the term *religio-culture* to describe the African context. Asamoah-Gyadu has borrowed this term from Kwesi Dickson who developed it to make clear that religion in its African context is not a sub-set of culture. Asamoah-Gyadu argues that Christianity's phenomenal growth in Africa took place because it paid attention to Africa's religious consciousness—this both/and understanding of reality which requires taking into account both the material and the spiritual. African Christianity grew from ten to five hundred million adherents during the twentieth century because the gospel found a ready landing place within the African single-tiered ontology. Consequently, Asamoah-Gyadu notes that the church grew because of the sensitivity it showed "towards African religio-cultural ideas and realities in the mediation of the gospel. The African religio-cultural reality has maintained its dynamism and vitality in the African religious consciousness in the face of Christianity's phenomenal growth and impact."[6]

By way of contrast with the mission founded churches, many of which in the nineteenth and twentieth centuries came out of the Evangelical movements in Europe and North America and would be expected to take seriously the supernatural, it was the Sunsum Sorè, and early African leaders like William Wade Harris, who acted on the reality of the spiritual, supernatural forces at work in Africa and thus met the very real needs of the people—needs left unmet by the mission founded churches. Consequently, "rather than deny the reality of the African supernatural world, the Sunsum Sorè virtually institutionalized what they considered to be more effective ways of dealing with that world."[7] This demonstrated "an acceptance of the

---

6. Asamoah-Gyadu, *African Charismatics*, 39.
7. Asamoah-Gyadu, *African Charismatics*, 41. People reported that Prophet Harris

supernatural, and the provision of ritual contexts within which to engage it" which Asamoah-Gyadu argues gave them both a "pastoral and theological edge over Western missionary Christianity."[8]

In summarizing his own work and research on African charismatics, Asamoah-Gyadu again draws attention to the unseen, spiritual, transcendent reality apart from which it simply is not possible to understand African, and more specifically, Ghanaian religious practice. No one can understand Africa's religiosity, he writes, apart from

> the recognition that there is a transcendent dimension to life. There is very little in Ghanaian traditional life that lies outside the jurisdiction of Onyame, God, and spirit powers such as the ancestors.... Pentecostal spirituality thus speaks to the African experience in a very relevant manner because it affirms the immediacy of God's presence.[9]

Along with other African scholars, most notably Kwame Bediako, but also western scholars like John V. Taylor,[10] Asamoah-Gyadu sees both Africa's traditional religions and Christianity as a response to the underlying African primal imagination. And because the pneumatic or Pentecostal churches in Africa are themselves a response to this primal imagination, characterized as I have said by the single-tiered ontology, Christianity, once freed from the two-tiered approach of western missionaries,[11] flourished. Asamoah-Gyadu's thesis is that the response he has analyzed fits African religio-culture on the one hand while reflecting the biblical understanding of reality on the other.

---

would engage ATR priests in Elijah type spiritual battle and win. In this way he demonstrated the superior power of the Christian God.

8. Asamoah-Gyadu, *African Charismatics*, 41.

9. Asamoah-Gyadu, *African Charismatics*, 236.

10. Taylor discusses the phrase, "traditions of response," in chapter 9 of Taylor, *Go-Between God*. In chapter 4 of *Jesus in Africa*, Bediako discusses "world-view" in the context of Taylor's understanding of religion as "traditions of response." Bediako understands world-views as a people's response to God's revelation of himself to them prior to the coming of Scripture that, in a sense, completes the story begun in their primal traditions.

11. Opoku Onyinah has demonstrated that the first missionaries to arrive in Ghana were German pietists whose belief in the supernatural, while still present, was weakened by the tacit assumptions of the Enlightenment that had swept across Europe. See Onyinah, "Akan Witchcraft," 133.

The Significance of the Single-Tiered Ontology in Asamoah-Gyadu's Methodology

Asamoah-Gyadu's description of African Pentecostal spirituality, with its focus on an immediate experience of the power of God in their lives through the Holy Spirit, emerges from his observation that for any religious tradition to succeed in Africa it must meet the needs of the whole person. Consequently, his research methodology, following in the tradition of C. G. Baeta, whose seminal work on the Spiritual Churches of Ghana[12] is the precursor to Asamoah-Gyadu's own research, required that he focus on both experience and belief in his work. He writes, "the method adopted for this study, has been arrived at by participating, observing, listening and asking for the meanings of what Ghanaian Pentecostals preach, sing, say, do and sometimes write about."[13]

In participating, observing, and listening, however, Asamoah-Gyadu cannot avoid the unitive perspective of the single-tiered ontology. It simply is not possible to isolate Pentecostal belief from Pentecostal practice because of the holistic nature of the African understanding of reality. And this, as he points out, sets his work apart from that of Western thought.

> In Pentecostal spirituality generally, there is a strong link between the physical, emotional, psychological and spiritual dimensions of life. Mind, body, and spirit "trichotomy" associated with Western thought is not present. This makes possible the employment and normalization of healing, prophecies, dreams, and visions in Christian worship. There is much in the Pentecostal attempt to end the fragmentation of body, mind, and spirit that coheres with African ideas of human holism. The important point for our purposes is that these components are inter-related and the condition of each affects the others. By extension, Africans view life in holistic terms with "body and spirit," the "sacred and secular," and the "psychological and theological" being held together as one whole. The result is that health in traditional terms is symptomatic of a balanced relationship with one's self and with the cosmos.[14]

What we see here is, of course, as assertion of both independence from western scholarly norms on the one hand with an assertion of African scholarship's right to work according to its own set of scholarly norms on the other.

12. Baeta, *Prophetism in Ghana*.
13. Asamoah-Gyadu, *African Charismatics*, 8.
14. Asamoah-Gyadu, *African Charismatics*, 47.

Such norms necessarily take into account the both/and of material and spiritual causality. The West barely retains spiritual categories of the sort still operative in Africa and so, in many instances, has neither the eyes or ears to see and hear what is happening in Africa.[15]

I now move on to discuss how Asamoah-Gyadu's understanding and use of Scripture, and his understanding and analysis of the church, emerge from Africa's single-tiered ontology.

Asamoah-Gyadu's Use of Scripture as It Emerges from the STO

To begin, Asamoah-Gyadu contrasts Africa's approach to Scripture to the liberal demythologizing perspective of some western Christians. In his essay honoring Kwame Bediako's Christological work, Asamoah-Gyadu compares his friend and mentor's understanding of Scripture to that of Rudolph Bultmann: "We know that stalwarts of Western theological scholarship, such as Rudolf Bultmann, refused to accept the reality of the historical Jesus and treated the things of the Spirit as biblical myths. Not so with Kwame Bediako."[16] Later, in *Contemporary Pentecostal Christianity*, Asamoah-Gyadu contrasts the contemporary Pentecostal approach to Scripture to that of the "Western academy." For Pentecostals, the Bible is imbued with the holiness of God who, by their account, is its author. This does not allow for the relativizing that Africans observe in the West.

> In contradistinction to this Western liberal position, African Christians, particularly those who belong to the independent indigenous charismatic streams, celebrate the divinity and supernatural status of the Bible. . . . If the contents of the Bible are to be taken seriously as God's inspired word, the status of the Bible as a sacred book must first be recognized. The word of God in textual form is essentially material to be read and meditated upon, material that provides guidance through life and in relationships with God (Deut 6:3).[17]

---

15. See, for example, the work of Ellis and ter Haar, "Religion and Politics in Sub-Saharan Africa"; Hackett, "Revitalization in African Tradition Religion," 135; Meyer, "Christianity in Africa." Each questions the ability of the West to understand what they are no longer able to "see."

16. Asamoah-Gyadu, "Kwame Bediako," 51.

17. Asamoah-Gyadu, *Contemporary Pentecostal Christianity*, 167.

We see Asamoah-Gyadu's full recognition of the supernatural realities that Scripture describes, and its coherence with Africa's religio-culture, in those places where he examines the African church's practice of healing and deliverance. As in Scripture, the Ghanaian church believes that the Holy Spirit is able "to provide release for demon-possessed, demon-oppressed, broken, disturbed and troubled persons, in order that victims may be restored to 'health and wholeness.'" People are freed from demonic influence and curses to enjoy God's fullness of life available in Christ.[18] As he notes, fighting off evil spirits has always been a high priority in Ghanaian religion and a high priority for pastoral care today. Christians there take great solace from passages like Acts 8:1, 4–8, where demonic exorcism and physical healing are part of the church's ministry. These fit well in the religio-culture of Ghana. It hardly needs stating that such practices are at best a fringe practice within churches in the West. And the reason, I am suggesting, is that the West is virtually devoid of the categories for demonic possession, spells cast by sorcerers, or for understanding physical healing outside of purely material or psychological causes.

Asamoah-Gyadu shows his critical skills, however, when he points out that neo-Pentecostal deliverance ministries have not worked out an entirely coherent understanding of sin, suffering, and demonic influences, and are sometimes guilty of giving Satan too much credit. He notes that while Paul and Jesus both saw demonic power at work in some instances of suffering and illness, they didn't always. Sometimes suffering was to educate, as Paul's thorn in the flesh, or to show God's power, as with the man born blind. He notes that in traditional Ghanaian thought, emerging itself from the single-tiered unitive perspective, there was a differentiating between natural and supernatural causation.

> The biblical thought that suffering and misfortune may not always be explained in terms of mystical causation is not alien to African traditional thought either. Most Ghanaian traditions distinguish between what the Akan call *sunsum mu yarba* (spiritual sickness) and *honam muyarba* (literally sickness of the flesh, that is natural ailments). . . . There is room for the belief that a person's own untoward behavior—laziness, careless living, stupidity, lack of industry, etc.—may suffice as explanations for his or her misfortunes. The "uncompromising link" made between misfortune and

---

18. Asamoah-Gyadu, *African Charismatics*, 165.

mystical agents create the danger of diminished individual and corporate responsibility that the Bible also upholds.[19]

He concludes, however, by emphasizing that neo-Pentecostals are getting something right that the West no longer has the capacity to understand. He references John Mbiti's famous parable of the young African Bible scholar who returns to his African village with a PhD in New Testament, yet when his own sister falls ill, all his learning is useless to help her because he now sees only the West's remedies for healing to be real. Asamoah-Gyadu follows this parable with the story of a Presbyterian pastor he knew who was confronted by a priestess who wanted to be delivered from a water spirit. Not knowing what to do, he called on some of his members who were part of the charismatic Bible Study and Prayer Group in his church who did, with the result that this pastor became a believer in their work and in the reality of the foes they were fighting. Asamoah-Gyadu suggests that these stories provide "further evidence of the practical difference between Ghanaian indigenous Pentecostal thought and the inability of traditional Western mission Christianity to respond to the theological questions raised by African Christians."[20]

Asamoah-Gyadu's understanding of God as Scripture's author, reflecting God's being, means that both the supernatural and natural are expressions of God's power and truth. Asamoah-Gyadu's contribution, however, is his critical, rational analysis of both material and spiritual cause and effect. He maintains a healthy critical perspective of both approaches without dismissing either because both are represented in Scripture. He avoids the either/or temptation and adopts instead a critical both/and. God uses natural and supernatural means and has given us human reason to help us discern when a particular practice or interpretation has gone off the rails, that is, when it no longer has biblical support.

Asamoah-Gyadu can appreciate the African church's healing practices while at the same time retaining a critical eye towards those practices because he himself is grounded in the African single-tiered ontology. He implicitly invited the western church to recognize and begin again to use all Scripture's categories, including the supernatural, which might then lead to a rediscovery of the power of God absent from the demythologized world of Rudolph Bultmann.

19. Asamoah-Gyadu, *African Charismatics*, 196–97.
20. Asamoah-Gyadu, *African Charismatics*, 198.

Asamoah-Gyadu's Use of the Single-Tiered Ontology for Understanding the Church

We see Asamoah-Gyadu's understanding of the church emerging from the single-tiered ontology when he notes that first, in the Sunsum Sorè, or Spiritual Churches, then in Africa's later charismatic movements, and finally in his examination of contemporary African Pentecostalism, spiritual gifts are of first importance in the life of the church. Writing specifically of the charismatic movements, from which many of the contemporary Pentecostals then developed, he writes:

> Within the ecclesiology of the CMs, the basis of ministry becomes a person's encounter with the Spirit and not theological competence or dynastic succession. The emphasis on experiencing the Spirit and making use of one's gifts in ministry stands as one of the key factors accounting for the growth of the CMs, which would also ensure their survival for generations.[21]

In his judgment, one of the most important contributions of the charismatic movement in Ghana was "the space created for young people to exercise their spiritual gifts within an ecclesiastical environment."[22]

Asamoah-Gyadu notes in particular two main themes among those involved in the charismatic movements. First, they saw themselves as God's end time militia raised up for this time to fight Satan and the powers of darkness. Second, they use people based on their experience of the Holy Spirit, transforming them and empowering them, and the gifts God has given them, both natural and supernatural, to do ministry. The New Testament scholar, James D. G. Dunn, applauds this as closer to the New Testament model than one which uses seminary training alone. Asamoah-Gyadu refers to this as the "democratization of charisma" with the result that, "the laity have been mobilized on the basis of their spiritual gifts and talents to minister in the power of the Spirit in leading worship, personal evangelism, healing, deliverance and others."[23] Asamoah-Gyadu contrasts

---

21. Asamoah-Gyadu, *African Charismatics*, 130–31. The Sunsum Sorè churches largely confined the exercise of the spiritual gifts to individual leaders which led, in part, to their decline. Attendees became "clients" rather than "members" and those wanting to exercise their own gifts had to go elsewhere.

22. Asamoah-Gyadu, *African Charismatics*, 120.

23. Asamoah-Gyadu, *African Charismatics*, 131.

this practical manifestation of the "priesthood of all believers" with the practice of churches in the West. He writes:

> There is much reference in traditional Western denominations to the priesthood of all believers and to the ministry as belonging to the "whole people of God." In spite of this the ordained clergy in these churches hold a virtual monopoly over things pertaining to ministry just as the prophets of the Sunsum Sorè tend to monopolize access to spiritual gifts.[24]

What we see then is an ecclesiology which in both its theology and its practice emerges out of the working of the Holy Spirit to affect transformation and empowerment for ministry in the lives of all people. This makes sense in a context where the natural and supernatural, the seen and the unseen are equally real, and why, in the West where the unseen and spiritual are more or less optional, we see relatively little emphasis on the reality and power of the Holy Spirit in the life of the church. The world described by the single-tiered ontology requires the church to respond to the peoples' need for protection from evil spirits, for exorcism, for protection against spells, and for healing—physical, emotional, and spiritual. Not so in the two-tiered West where such phenomena tend to be seen as the fruit of superstition or psychological delusion—categories natural in a two-tiered context.

One of the great doctrines in trinitarian theology is an understanding of the perichoretic relationship of the three persons of the Godhead to one another. If one understanding of what it means to be a Christian is to be a person who has entered into that "divine dance," then the church Asamoah-Gyadu describes is a church already participating with joy and purpose in that great dance.

A Case Study: A Ghana Airways Prayer Vigil and Its Implications for Religion, Evil, and Public Space[25]

In his article, "'Christ is the Answer: What is the Question?': A Ghana Airways Prayer Vigil and its Implications for Religion, Evil, and Public Space,"

---

24. Asamoah-Gyadu, *African Charismatics*, 130. He adds: "Within the ecclesiology of the CMs, the basis of ministry becomes a person's encounter with the Spirit and not theological competence or dynastic succession. The emphasis on experiencing the Spirit and making use of one's gifts in ministry stands as one of the key factors accounting for the growth of the CMs, which would also ensure their survival for generations" (131).

25. Asamoah-Gyadu, "Christ Is the Answer."

Asamoah-Gyadu considers the case of Ghana's national airline which, after a series of mechanical problems, called in an evangelist, Dr. Lawrence Tetteh, to conduct a service of healing prayer for the airline. Needless to say this is not something that would ever happen in the West. So why might it make sense in the African context? Asamoah-Gyadu's answer is that such a practice "takes African worldviews of mystical causality seriously."[26] Asamoah-Gyadu notes that this understanding of mystical causality, which understands that material cause and effect alone is not capable of explaining all of life's events, has not gone away with the introduction of modernity. Even as the missionaries, who counted things like witches and demons as mere superstition,[27] established churches, schools, and hospitals, and as the impact of modernity was felt in business, and technology, the both/and explanatory power of the single-tiered ontology remained. He writes:

> In the face of modernization, development and globalization, the African universe still remains a sacramental one that does not sharply dichotomize between the physical and the spiritual realms of existence. The physical thus acts as a vehicle for developments in the supernatural realm, a worldview that we constantly see being played out in African public space.[28]

In this world, prophets are proved by their success because such prophetic and healing practices are "underpinned by the African belief in mystical causality."[29] The result is that the healing and deliverance beliefs and practices of the Pentecostal/Charismatic churches are being used to intervene in all facets of African life, not only to heal, but to ensure prosperity. This is what Asamoah-Gyadu means by the *encroachment* of religion on *public space* that appears in the title of this article.[30]

In the specific case of Ghana Airlines, it was when a "pattern of failure" showed up that people began to suspect that "malevolent powers" were at work to "hijack the situation and worsen the plights of victims."[31] They were not, of course, oblivious to the fact that human mistakes were also being made; but that alone could not explain the "pattern of failure."

---

26. Asamoah-Gyadu, "Christ is the Answer," 93.

27. See again Onyinah, "Akan Witchcraft," 133, where he discusses the influence the Enlightenment had on the early missionaries to Africa.

28. Asamoah-Gyadu, "Christ is the Answer," 95.

29. Asamoah-Gyadu, "Christ is the Answer," 96.

30. Asamoah-Gyadu, "Christ is the Answer," 98.

31. Asamoah-Gyadu, "Christ is the Answer," 102.

Consequently, the airline called in the help of someone they believed had the "anointing" to offer healing prayer for the airline. They chose the evangelist, Dr. Lawrence Tetteh. While such an approach would be scoffed at in the West, the operative worldview here made this a reasonable, rational next step to take. Asamoah-Gyadu writes, "in African contexts like that of Ghana, health and wellbeing are both personal and communal. Anybody who does not work towards the total wellbeing of the community could therefore be what the Akan of Ghana describe as *abonsam*, devil."[32] Thus, by the "prophetic prayer" of Dr. Tetteh, the anointed leader, such evil could be exorcized, and people could be freed from the power of the demonic and the airline healed.

Asamoah-Gyadu places this particular episode within the context of the role religion plays in African public life. Religion serves as a survival strategy in Africa—and always has. While modernity has nudged God out of the picture in the West it has done nothing similar in Africa. Africans understand the distinction between natural and supernatural causality, but because they live in a both/and world, solutions to whatever problems they face must account for what is happening in both the seen and unseen spheres of this present world. He writes:

> The belief in a sacramental universe means that in dealing with personal or public decisions on life, economics, health or politics, religion may be employed in Africa for purposes expressed by Robin Horton as "explanation, prediction, and control." In traditional Africa, as we have noted, prayer, sacrifice and offerings, in fact religious ritual in general, often aims to achieve the practical ends of success, prosperity and general wellbeing.[33]

Asamoah-Gyadu argues then that it is proper to take the supernatural into account but to be very careful not to give Satan credit for the incompetence of mechanics or shoddy supervision of airline managers. So, pray but also be sure that proper maintenance records are kept, mechanics are well trained, and people at every level are held accountable for their decisions. He writes:

> The problems of Africa are real, and life remains incomplete and meaningless without the complement of the transcendent. Always to cast human problems in super-naturalistic terms, however, also runs the risk of blinding people to their responsibility

32. Asamoah-Gyadu, "Christ is the Answer," 103.
33. Asamoah-Gyadu, "Christ is the Answer," 114.

to remove the causes of disease, and allowing those in power to avoid accountability for decisions made or how public resources are handled.[34]

Of importance for us in this essay is that Asamoah-Gyadu takes seriously both the spiritual and material, the seen and the unseen. In this he is faithful to his own single-tiered sacramental universe. At the same time he does not privilege either the spiritual or material; instead he uses reason as a tool to discern what weight to give to one or the other.

This, I am suggesting, is the methodology that African theology brings to the global theological conversation which needs to take place, especially in the West. In so doing he avoids the temptations of both the global West (an over-reliance on exclusively material explanations), and the global South (ascribing demonic causality for every human failure).

Conclusion

With the passing of such scholars as Ogbu Kalu and Kwame Bediako, both mentors of Asamoah-Gyadu, he has risen to the top rank of scholars in Africa. His two works, *African Charismatics* and *Contemporary Pentecostal Christianity*, form both an introduction and update to the state of the church, and it beliefs and practices, in Africa. Asamoah-Gyadu is himself aware of the contribution Africa has to make to the worldwide church and the reticence of many in the West to listen. Part of his argument is that the West mistakes Africa's single-tiered ontology for mere superstition instead of a rational approach rooted in Scripture itself. In addition, as the immigrant church grows in Europe and North America, the opportunity now exists for the West to benefit from the vitality and contributions of these churches.

> Africa has learnt much from European theology, but Europe in turn may need to learn a few things from the types of immigrant charismatic communions working in their midst. In the words of Wahrisch-Oblau, "instead of feeling threatened by the New Mission Churches and rejecting their criticism of 'mainline' Protestantism as fundamentalist and culturally irrelevant, the Protestant churches . . . could in grateful joy, perceive the work of the Holy Spirit outside the confines of their own organized pastoral

---

34. Asamoah-Gyadu, "Christ is the Answer," 115.

activities, and recognize the genesis of new churches and congregations on European soil as 'the grace of God.'"[35]

In the work of J. Kwabena Asamoah-Gyadu, the West has ready at hand a scholar of the first rank to help shape a global Christian theological conversation that, like iron sharpening iron, cannot help but result in a more thoughtful and more effective Church.

---

35. Wahrisch-Oblau, "We Shall be Fruitful in the Land," 46, quoted in Asamoah-Gyadu, *Contemporary Pentecostal Christianity*, 15.

8

Sighs and Signs of the Mind?
Pentecostalism, Renewal, and a Ghanaian Mind Folk Theory

VIVIAN DZOKOTO

Introduction

> Jesus replied: "Love the Lord your God with all your heart and with all your soul and with all your mind." (Matt 22:37 NIV)

WHAT IS THE MIND and what does it do? The answer to this question is partly contingent upon culture.[1] In a recent paper,[2] I explored the folk theory of mind in Ghana's Akan ethnolinguistic group. Delineation of what the Akan of Ghana consider to be the role of the human mind contributes to understandings of how the Akan make sense of and map out the non-biological boundaries between the human interior and the surrounding physical, spiritual, and interpersonal worlds. It supplements extant philosophical writings[3] on the interplay between personhood, the *sunsum*, and the *okra*.[4] Given the conceptual overlap between Akan and other Ghanaian

1. Luhrmann, "Thinking about Thinking."
2. Dzokoto, "Adwenhoasem."
3. Wiredu, "Concept of Mind," 153–79.
4. Gyekye, *African Philosophical Thought*.

and African worldviews, it contributes to understandings of African epistemology. These in turn, impact how Christianity is internalized and represented in African settings. In particular, as I demonstrate in this chapter, these representations of the mind help explain the success of the pneumatic Pentecostal Christian movements that Johnson Kwabena Asamoah-Gyadu focuses on in his prolific program of research on Christianity in Africa today. To make this case, I first provide a summary of the Akan folk theory of mind. Next, I review some of the foci of Asamoah-Gyadu's work. Third, I draw parallels between the two.

The Akan Mind: Summary of a Folk Narrative

My work on the Akan mind formed part of a large, multi-country research project about spiritual experiences and the mind: The Mind and Spirit project.[5] We worked in five different countries: China, Ghana, Thailand, Vanuatu, and the US, with some work in the Ecuadorian Amazon. In each country, we included a focus on an urban charismatic evangelical church, with additional work in a rural charismatic evangelical church, and in another urban and rural religious setting of local importance.

To glean the Akan folk theory of mind, I used multiple sources of data (interviews, proverb analysis, and lexical analysis), and found that each of these sources of information about Akan culture consistently reflected particular attributes of the mind. I found four dimensions of mind that transversed local, linguistic, and proverbial representations of what constitutes the mind and its qualities. First, for my Akan interviewees (all adults), using the mind to set up and execute a plan for the future (e.g., setting up a profitable business, purchasing land, generating income to build a house) was a crucial means to creating an optimal future for the self. Thus, facilitating self-advancement is considered the primary function of the mind. Everyone needed a plan, and the mind was responsible

---

5. The Mind and Spirit project is a Templeton-funded, Stanford-based comparative and interdisciplinary project under the direction of anthropologist TM Luhrmann (PI), drawing on the expertise of anthropologists, psychologists, historians, and philosophers. The project asks whether different understandings of "mind," broadly construed, might shape or be related to the ways that people attend to and interpret experiences they deem spiritual or supernatural. We took a mixed-method, multiphase approach, combining participant observation, long form semi-structured interviews, quantitative surveys among the general population and local undergraduates, and psychological experiments with children and adults. (This paragraph is based on a description drafted collectively by the Mind and Spirit team and used to illustrate the joint nature of the research).

for coming up with the plan. Unfortunately, all plans are not created equal: there are good plans and bad plans. Similar to the characteristic of the plans which the mind is responsible for generating, minds are considered to be either good or bad. In other words, Akans consider the mind to be valenced, and this valence shapes behavior. Good minds motivate people to do good things, and bad minds ensure that the bodies associated with them engage in behavior that disrupts social harmony and the wellbeing of others. Similar references to the valenced mind have been documented in East Africa,[6] Trinidad,[7] Jamaica,[8] Barbados,[9] Antigua,[10] and Guyana[11] suggesting that iterations of this model of the mind may be shared in other parts of Africa and its diaspora. Another noticeable dimension about what Akans considered the mind concerns embodiment. Many aspects of mental activities—which western representations would typically locate in the mind (such as feeling)—were for the Akan situated in the body. The body was also central to notions of wellbeing.

Finally, the Akan mind folk representation included a narrative of porosity; a belief in the ability of the mind to directly influence and be influenced by external forces (many of them spiritual). This belief would be perceived as unusual in a western context where the mind is perceived as having a much less permeable boundary with the world.[12] To illustrate, Pentecostal Christians I interviewed believe that the Holy Spirit can insert a specific thought, Bible verse, or message into a person's mind. Such thoughts tend to be distinguishable in experience from self-generated thought. In more dramatic cases of porosity, Pentecostal Christians I interviewed believe that the Holy Spirit can take control over a person's body such that person falls down when slain in the Spirit. This is a common experience in Pentecostal praise and worship services. Similarly, traditional healers that I interviewed as part of the study reported that their gods could insert thoughts (such as specific herbal remedies for clients seeking

---

6. Taylor, *African Aphorisms*.

7. Levisen and Jogie, "Trinidadian 'Theory of Mind,'" 169–93.

8. Hickling and James, "Traditional Mental Health Practices," 465–86; Lewis, "So Black People Stay," 327–42; Sutherland, "African-Centered Jamaican Psychology," 330–32; Wardle, "Concept of Mind," 153–79.

9. Barrow and Aggleton, "Good Face, Bad Mind," 29–52.

10. Kincaid, *Small Place*; Medica, "Influence of Anxiety."

11. Hodari et al., *Lifelines*.

12. Taylor, *Secular Age*.

treatment) into their minds. Their gods also possessed them—as in routinely took complete motor control of the traditional healers' bodies—for short amounts of time (generally from a few minutes to a few hours) during festivals and other religious gatherings to dance, and to demonstrate distinguishing characteristics. Thus, Christians and non-Christians alike considered the mind to be porous: external forces could have a range of influences on the human mind, from individual thought insertion to complete control of motor functions, which is a function of the mind.

To be clear, Christians from other countries in our sample also considered it possible for God to communicate with Christians by placing thoughts in their minds or talking to them. However, the belief was normative in Ghana for Christians and non-Christians alike. Viewing the mind as a porous entity has double-edged implications. On the one hand, this belief system sets the stage for an epistemological orientation in which positive external influences can impact the mind, and a support of engaging in religious practices (such as prayer and meditation) that can make it more likely for such porous events to occur.[13] On the other hand, the belief that individuals are vulnerable to unwelcome negative influences—particularly those from bad minds—served as an existential threat that was a source of great concern. Religion was a default avenue through which people sought to deal with this concern, not as a one-time effort, but in their daily practice.

Asamoah-Gyadu on Pentecostal Christianity in Africa

In *Sighs and Signs of the Spirit: Ghanaian Perspectives on Pentecostalism and Renewal in Africa*, Asamoah-Gyadu makes the case that prayer, prophecy, and healing—which he dubs a charismatic triad—are central to the four revitalization movements of Christianity that Ghana has experienced.[14] In this book and elsewhere[15, 16] he argues that the "gospel of contemporary Pentecostalism is very much a message of upward mobility and redemptive uplift."[17] In other words, successful Pentecostal movements demonstrate a concerted shift towards addressing the tangible, problems, concerns,

---

13. Luhrmann, *When God Talks Back*.
14. Asamoah-Gyadu, *Sighs and Signs*, 5.
15. Asamoah-Gyadu, "Of Faith and Visual Alertness," 336–56.
16. Asamoah-Gyadu, "Learning to Prosper," 64–86.
17. Asamoah-Gyadu, *Sighs and Signs*, 15.

and needs of everyday life—a message of practical salvation.[18] They have achieved this new representation of Christianity and inherent theological change by: emphasizing the power of the Holy Spirit at the level of the individual; promoting a message of dominion (upward mobility) and prosperity as central to the will of God for his people; incorporating the use of technology in spreading their message; and democratizing ministry rather than leaving evangelism to professional clergy. Pentecostals/Charismatics, Asamoah-Gyadu asserts, "have pushed for a practical pneumatology, in keeping with the focus on power, transformation, and expansion "to the ends of the earth."[19] This is because "in Africa, generally, religion is a survival strategy, and people use its resources in ways that allow them to deal with the crises of life."[20] The African pneumatic Pentecostal movement has created spaces—literally and figuratively—where "the troubled could repair in times of distress for aggressive and intense prayer through which they knocked on heaven's door for solutions."[21]

The solution of health problems is an important focus of Ghana's successful Pentecostal movement. Asamoah-Gyadu has written extensively about this, positing that seeking divine healing for ailments is *central* to the practice of Pentecostal/Charismatic Christianity in Ghana. He argues that African Independent Churches operated on the premise that things that happened in biblical times—including divine healing, visions, revelations, and prophecy—also occur in the present.[22] In other words, expectations of healing are supported by a theological emphasis on the power of the Holy Spirit in contemporary life. He writes:

> Under the force of Pentecostalism, the ministry of healing has grown in Ghana, and now straddles all sectors of indigenous Christianity including the historic mission churches. This centrality of healing in Ghanaian Christianity is what has generated innumerable healing practitioners, prayer centers or sacred places generically referred to in this paper as prayer "mountains"—grottoes, residential healing camps, on actual hills and mountains where people spend time seeking God's intervention in the problems that beset them as human beings.[23]

18. Asamoah-Gyadu, "Christianity and Sports," 239–59
19. Asamoah-Gyadu, *Sighs and Signs*, 31.
20. Asamoah-Gyadu, "Christ Is the Answer," 353.
21. Asamoah-Gyadu, "Go Near and Join," 351.
22. Asamoah-Gyadu, "Therapeutic Strategies."
23. Asamoah-Gyadu, "On the Mountain," 85.

SECTION II: SPIRITUAL REALITY, WORLDVIEWS, AND FORMATIONS

Contemporary Pentecostal/Charismatic theology specifically emphasizes personal experience of the power of the Holy Spirit, through which healing and the casting out of evil spirits occurs.[24] It operationalizes salvation as inclusive of general and physical wellbeing, and protection and deliverance from evil.[25] Asamoah-Gyadu observes that African pneumatic churches commonly feature "charismatically anointed leaders"[26] who provide both diagnostic and interventionist healing consultation services. Mystical causal attributions feature prominently in the Pentecostal healing and deliverance ministry, and are taken into serious consideration by the movement. This, Asamoah-Gyadu[27] argues, accounts for the ministry's and movement's mass appeal. Healing and exorcism in the Pentecostal/Charismatic movement, he argues is "an innovative Christianity that has much to teach us about what it means to be both African and Christian without undermining either of these twin identities."[28]

Prayer is not exclusively used in the search for healing. It constitutes a part of the charismatic triad and is an important generalized participatory practice in Ghana's successful Pentecostal movements. In a nutshell, Pentecostal/Charismatic prayer is a participatory, experiential, and pragmatic spiritual practice used to harness the power of the Holy Spirit to effect progress, success, mobility, and healing; thus, opening heavenly doors to provide solutions to earthly problems. Modern Pentecostal/Charismatic theology focuses primarily on existential issues and pays scant attention to eschatological judgment, the Parousia, and heaven and hell—messages that mission churches and classical pietistic Pentecostalism focused on.[29] Pentecostal/Charismatic prayer includes making requests for a variety of concerns considered existential and fundamental to success and wellbeing in Ghana's economy and Ghanaian society. These include employment, securing of visas, access to international travel, general well-being, marriage, children,[30] finances,[31] success in business, academic excellence,

---

24. Asamoah-Gyadu, "Pulling Down Strongholds," 306–17.
25. Asamoah-Gyadu, "On the Mountain," 65–86.
26. Asamoah-Gyadu, "Therapeutic Strategies," 76.
27. Asamoah-Gyadu, "Faith and Visual Alertness."
28. Asamoah-Gyadu, "Pulling Down Strongholds," 317.
29. Asamoah-Gyadu, "Learning to Prosper," 64–86.
30. Asamoah-Gyadu, "Broken Calabashes and Covenants," 437–60.
31. Asamoah-Gyadu, "Learning to Prosper," 64–86.

and victory in sports.³² Thus, prayer in Ghanaian Pentecostal/Charismatic theology is quintessentially pragmatic. Getting these needs met (deemed breakthroughs due to the perspective that misfortunes are supernatural in origin) are viewed as indicative of "good Christianity."³³

In his work, Asamoah-Gyadu has addressed not only the practice of Pentecostal/Charismatic prayer at the individual and congregational level, but also at corporate and national levels. For instance, he deconstructed a prayer vigil organized by a public corporation (Ghana's now defunct national airline) aimed at "exorcizing evil spirits from the affairs of the airline and releasing it from its predicaments."³⁴ He explored church-led prayer meetings scheduled for during "critical moments in Ghana's political history,"³⁵ usually right before elections. In 2015, he noted that due to the widespread belief that success in all life domains including sports could benefit from spiritual influences, "it was actually a regular practice for the national teams of Ghana in all the sporting disciplines to worship with the church at the end of training camp sessions and prior to any competition."³⁶ In other work he has explored specialized prayer and worship services tailored to meet specific goals such as combating childlessness,³⁷ bringing in the new year, and "wrestling with God" over specific concerns.³⁸ He argues that breakthroughs, typically shared in church and social circles through testimonies, boost the image of pastors as possessing the anointing of the Holy Spirit to achieve particular purposes.³⁹ He has also commented on the specialized democratization of charisma, which in the domain of prayer includes the formation of prayer teams (known as "prayer warriors") that make prayer the focus of their involvement with the church.⁴⁰ Typical representations of charismatic prayer practices include: spiritual warfare, travailing prayer, fasting, speaking in tongues, participation in prayer meetings, prayer in conjunction with sowing financial seeds in faith (giving offerings specifically mentally allocated to facilitate breakthroughs in a specific domain),

---

32. Asamoah-Gyadu, "Christianity and Sports," 239–59.
33. Asamoah-Gyadu, "Learning to Prosper," 66.
34. Asamoah-Gyadu, "Christ Is the Answer," 93.
35. Asamoah-Gyadu, "God Bless our Homeland," 177.
36. Asamoah-Gyadu, "Christianity and Sports," 248.
37. Asamoah-Gyadu, "Broken Calabashes and Covenants," 437–60.
38. Asamoah-Gyadu, *Sighs and Signs*, 89.
39. Asamoah-Gyadu, "Christianity and Sports," 239–59.
40. Asamoah-Gyadu, *Contemporary Pentecostal Christianity*.

and the use of blessed objects such as oil and water. Asamoah-Gyadu traces the evolution of such practices in his work. For instance, he argues that seed faith was influenced by the ministry of Oral Roberts[41] and that the use of blessed objects has its roots in both African traditional religion and the Catholic church. He also acknowledges that there is a degree of innovation in the Charismatic Christian movement in terms of practices used to seek spiritual breakthroughs. He observes thus:

> In one new Pentecostal church in Ghana, the King Jesus Evangelistic Ministry, members occasionally carry cane whips to church to symbolically whip Satan into submission. In other places the demons may be hooted at, stamped upon, cursed or even boxed, in the belief that those to whom they are directed in the spirit would feel these physical acts of "holy" violence against them, and loosen their hold on victims.[42]

Finally, Asamoah-Gyadu has argued in much of his work that prophecy and the power of the spoken word—channeled through charismatic mediators with the power to perceive the supernatural realm—are central to the practice of Pentecostal/Charismatic Christianity in Ghana and elsewhere in Africa.[43] He explains that in traditional shrine culture, two common services sought are seeking explanations about destiny (*ebisa* in Akan), and direction in domestic, political, family, occupational, economic, or health domains of life (*akwankyere* in Akan). In Pentecostal/Charismatic Christian circles, prophecy serves this role. Prophetic gifts and words of knowledge are considered oral gifts of the Holy Spirit that may or may not occur in tandem with visions and dreams, which are considered to be gifts of revelation. Providing direction is also informed by the gift of discernment, which in Pentecostal/Charismatic Christian circles is considered to be a Holy Spirit-inspired ability to "determine the extraordinary source of an issue and offer appropriate guidance on how to deal with it."[44]

The Parallels

This chapter only provides a glimpse into the scope of work covered by the Mind and Spirit project, and similarly, only a fraction of Asamoah-Gyadu's

---

41. Asamoah-Gyadu, "Oral Roberts and Mediated Pentecostalism," 230–32
42. Asamoah-Gyadu, "Faith and Visual Alertness," 104.
43. Asamoah-Gyadu, "Therapeutic Strategies," 70–90.
44. Asamoah-Gyadu, *Sighs and Signs*, 103.

impressive body of work. A full treatment of all the overlaps between the Akan mind model generated by the Mind and Spirit Project and Asamoah-Gyadu's work is unfortunately beyond the scope of this chapter. I thus aim to make two major points in this section. First, I observe that both the Akan mind model and Pentecostal/Charismatic Christianity consider self-advancement as crucial to wellbeing. Second, I submit that Christian pneumatic movements in Ghana have thrived because they are consistent with the notion of the mind and self as porous. I discuss each of these below.

The Struggle for Need-Provision and Self-Advancement

My interviewees were asked many questions about their spiritual lives, practices, and experiences. Early in the interview, each person was asked why they pray. Most people gave responses similar to Kweku, a thirty-four-year-old, married father of two, identifying as Christian and resident in a rural area in southern Ghana:

1. I pray so that I would not fall into temptation
2. I pray to put my needs before God
3. I pray to ask for guidelines from God
4. I pray to ask for protection, that God will protect me
5. I pray so that God will give me clear eyes to see (discern) some things

Later in the interview, Kweku elaborates:

> [Praying to God] is better than going to a human being. Matthew says if we ask, he will give it to us, if we knock, it shall be open to us. So, if there is anything, we have to ask God first before we go to human beings. So, before you go the person, God has already prepared the person, then you will receive it.

Collectively, the goal of prayer was getting one's needs met and fostering self-advancement, a theme that is central to the Pentecostal/Charismatic movement in Ghana and elsewhere. Asamoah-Gyadu explains that the new Pentecostal/Charismatic movement is a hub for the production of "alternative Christian rituals that enable people to achieve the desired 'supernatural acceleration' in life."[45] The movement's materialistic focus, which includes

---

45. Asamoah-Gyadu, "Christianity and Sports," 243.

ostentation on the part of some of its leaders, certainly has its critics. But Asamoah-Gyadu presents another important perspective about the impact of the movement: it is a source of empowerment and motivation for self-improvement for young Africans despite a backdrop of challenging socio-economic conditions.[46] The movement motivates people to take charge of their destinies. In particular, he observes that Reverend Mensa Otabil of Ghana's International Central Gospel Church is a persistent champion of self-advancement via advocating "popular liberation theology hermeneutics and black empowerment discourse."[47] Otabil preaches messages about the "positives and possibilities in this life"[48] that offer "practical information for personal development and self-improvement"[49] in order to "inspire Africans to exploit their potentialities and abilities to the full."[50] He notes that Otabil challenges both the internalized perception of the Black race as inferior and simplistic versions of the prosperity gospel; promoting instead a message about wealth-generation through the application of God-given wisdom. It is clear that Asamoah-Gyadu concurs with this position. He notes that "the 'powers of heaven' will continue to be called upon in all situations to help deal with problems that often appear to be beyond human wisdom and ability."[51] But also, he cautions:

> The seemingly problematic destiny of the country should not always be explained in terms of the activities of evil powers when there are very practical things to do to move our democracies and development forward as a people. . . . Always to cast human problems in super-naturalistic terms . . . runs the risk of blinding people to their responsibility to remove the causes of disease, and allowing those in power to avoid accountability for decisions made or how public resources are handled.[52]

Clearly inherent in both the Akan model of the mind and the practices and beliefs of the Pentecostal/Charismatic movement is an understanding of the reality of the hardships of life in a third world country—one in which basic needs are often not met for many, and one in which the state cannot

46. Asamoah-Gyadu, "Transforming Christianity," 337–54.
47. Asamoah-Gyadu, *Sighs and Signs*, 16.
48. Asamoah-Gyadu, *Sighs and Signs*, 17.
49. Asamoah-Gyadu, *Sighs and Signs*, 17.
50. Asamoah-Gyadu, *Sighs and Signs*, 18.
51. Asamoah-Gyadu, "Faith and Visual Alertness," 115.
52. Asamoah-Gyadu, "Faith and Visual Alertness," 115.

provide adequate supplemental support. Thus, the onus for survival lies on the self and associated kinship and communal networks. The mind is seen as a generator of personal advancement strategies. Pentecostal/Charismatic Christianity is seen as a divine avenue to the same goal. I submit that the popularity of Otabil's message is due to its consistency with the Akan model of the mind. Incorporating God-given wisdom into strategic-planning for self-advancement makes sense since divine guidance (*akwankyere*) is likely to result in success, divine guidance helps the mind produce an ideal plan for the individual. In addition, challenging colonial perspectives of an "African mind" (if there is such a thing) that is deficient in function has positive implications for assumptions of self-efficacy, which can positively promote agency. However, just as planning is not considered the only attribute of the mind, self-advancement through applying the self is not the only important attribute of Pentecostal/Charismatic Christianity.

Porous Selves and Objects: Protection, Deliverance, and Anointing

Unlike the accounts by American participants who formed part of the larger Mind and Spirit study, praying for protection was an important motivator of personal prayer practices for my Ghanaian interviewees. When asked to elaborate on why praying for protection as part of regular, personal spiritual practice was important, Kweku (quoted above) had this to say:

> With the protection . . . as we are going and coming we have some people who are watching you—spiritually wicked people like the agents of Satan. So, if you don't pray and ask for such protection then Satan [can harm you]. God has used something to protect us like a fence and he is guiding and protecting us . . . but if you are a Christian and you commit a sin or you disobey God, that means that protection that he has given you, you have created a hole inside it so Satan can come with something like sickness or can let your business collapse or can let a child of yours fall sick or he can even let you die.

Kweku's unprompted use of a fence metaphor involves the imagery of a boundary between the self and the world. He presents a self-world boundary that is permeable and extremely vulnerable to external forces. This is what Charles Taylor means when he talks about the porous self.[53]

53. Taylor, *Secular Age*.

SECTION II: SPIRITUAL REALITY, WORLDVIEWS, AND FORMATIONS

For Christians, according to Kweku's analogy, God fortifies the vulnerable self with a fence-like protective system. However, the efficacy of the protective system is contingent upon proper conduct of the self. Asamoah-Gyadu similarly discusses vulnerabilities thus:

> In both the African traditional and Pentecostal worldviews of mystical causality, the physical serves as a vehicle for the spiritual. So acts of commission and omission or even utterances that serve as "points of contact" with evil powers and give them access into one's life and endeavors are referred to as "demonic doorways."[54]

Collectively, my interviewees portrayed living in a world that was extremely dangerous, both socially and physically. They were acutely aware of ever-present potential threats to the body via illness and vehicular accidents. They all positively endorsed having had experiences in which someone had been deliberately making things hard for them, purposely causing them trouble, trying to hurt them or plotting against them, and they were certain of their belief regardless of what others in their lives thought. In other cultural contexts, such endorsements would suggest paranoia. In my interviewees' world, however, it reflects a quintessential traditional African worldview—a world rife with threats, which pose potential dangers to the self. Asamoah-Gyadu argues that the felt need for protection is neither new to the African condition, nor has it waned in modern times. He notes that historic mission churches are generally viewed as inert against potential threats to wellbeing,[55] and states:

> The sense of the supernatural and the need to anchor one's destiny in it has not declined for Africans; rather the need for powers of protection and salvation has increased.... Globalization, modernity, emigration to western countries, and economic development have created new fears, anxieties, and challenges. This has made resorting to supernatural solutions to problems even more important for many Africans.[56]

Both my interviewees' positions on the need for protection and Asamoah-Gyadu's analysis on the same are reflective of the notion of porosity: that selves are permeable to external influences. Porosity also helps to explain the importance of deliverance as a Pentecostal/Charismatic Christian

---

54. Asamoah-Gyadu, "Faith and Visual Alertness," 100.
55. Asamoah-Gyadu, "Christianity and Sports," 239–59.
56. Asamoah-Gyadu, *Sighs and Signs*, 102.

practice. Asamoah-Gyadu considers spiritual causality a perpetual African ethos.[57] This is particularly salient when tackling misfortunes and obstacles to self-advancement. In his work on healing, for instance, Asamoah-Gyadu discusses a diagnostic strategy used in some healing camps.[58] Healing-seekers fill out questionnaires designed to identify obstacles and patterns of difficulty in their lives and those of their families. This is because individual and familial patterns such as child deaths, specific diseases, mental health and substance abuse concerns, high rates of divorce, and having too many unmarried women are often attributed to demonic origins, demonic oppression, demonic possession, or the demonic exacerbation of naturally-caused problems. Fortunately, deliverance theology provides a way out. God is seen as an all-powerful deliverer.[59] Through the power of the Holy Spirit, curses can be broken and people liberated from their afflictions.[60] Many of my Christian interviewees had participated in deliverance services and reported either having been delivered from various situations in their life themselves or knowing someone who had. Asamoah-Gyadu elaborates on deliverance theology thus:

> Pentecostals thus speak of a different kind of apostolic succession that puts the emphasis not only on ecclesiastical authority and inheritance but also on the power of God that was evident then and now. . . . If he took the Israelites through the Red Sea and brought down the walls of Jericho, then it makes sense to establish a Jericho Hour so that the walls of hostility and the strongholds in the lives of his people can be pulled down even today. Similarly, if those who believe in Jesus Christ must do "greater works" then it stands to reason that those who are possessed by the spirits of the traditional world—ancestors, deities, demons and other malevolent forces—must be cast out in order that "the captives" can be set free.[61]

Again, the belief in porosity makes the idea of deliverance possible. If the self were considered completely bounded and non-permeable, then things could not be cast out of the self. Relating this to the idea of spiritual causality, since illness, poverty, or other misfortune is understood as being caused by evil crossing over the self-world boundary to harm a vulnerable individual,

57. Asamoah-Gyadu, "Christianity and Sports," 239–59.
58. Asamoah-Gyadu, "Faith and Visual Alertness," 336–56.
59. Asamoah-Gyadu, "On the 'Mountain.'"
60. Asamoah-Gyadu, "African Pneumatic Movements," 336–55.
61. Asamoah-Gyadu, "Pulling Down Strongholds," 316.

then using the right spiritual tools (aka deliverance and in some cases exorcism) these harm-causing forces can be made to cross the self-world boundary in the opposite direction, relieving the individual of its impact.

In addition to the notion of porous selves, Akan cosmology sets the stage for a belief in porous objects. Objects can be conduits of spiritual forces, both good and evil. In Pentecostal/Charismatic Christianity, objects can be blessed and used as conduits of God's power. In other words, divine power is symbolically mediated by an object for future transfer to the (porous) self. The most popular of these objects is anointing oil, which is activated by ingestion or topical application to parts of the body. The application of anointing oil is a Pentecostal/Charismatic Christian practice employed (both in church settings and in everyday life) in the search for breakthroughs in the areas of health, wellbeing, businesses, and the like. Asamoah-Gyadu observes that on Ghanaian television, olive oil is represented as a spiritual tool more often than as a culinary ingredient.[62] Also, he notes that anointing services feature prominently in advertised religious programming on television. Pentecostal/Charismatic theology relates anointing—the power and influence of the Holy Spirit—with charismata (gifts of grace). The concept of anointing of objects and persons, its fit with the indigenous worldview, and its centrality in the performance of Pentecostal/Charismatic Christianity, Asamoah-Gyadu argues, accounts for the religious movement's mass appeal.[63]

The success of Ghana's Charismatic/Pentecostal movement is generally pitted against the decline of traditional mission churches. Asamoah-Gyadu argues that for long periods, mission church theology de-emphasized divine intervention in everyday concerns, witchcraft, and an ever-lurking evil.[64] Such theological perspectives are consistent with a non-porous (bounded) view of the self and the world. In contrast, each wave of Pentecostal renewal acknowledged the African traditional view of the self as porous and in need of resources, and consequently developed Christian parallels to traditional rituals of protection and self-advancement. Thus, while both groups subscribed to biblical messages such as "Love the Lord your God with all your heart and with all your soul and with all your mind," it appears that they had different operationalizations of what the mind and the self meant.

62. Asamoah-Gyadu, "Christ Is the Answer," 93–117.
63. Asamoah-Gyadu, *Sighs and Signs*.
64. Asamoah-Gyadu, "Christianity and Sports," 239–59.

9

"One of the Greatest Prayer Weapons..."
A Religio-Cultural Practice of "Libation" in Cameroon Neo-Pentecostalism

CHAMMAH J. KAUNDA AND FELIX KANG ESOH

Introduction

REVEREND PROFESSOR JOHNSON KWABENA Asamoah-Gyadu is one of the pioneers in the field of African Pentecostal Studies. Over the years, Asamoah-Gyadu has made a sustained contribution, devoting much of his attention wrestling with developing more African metholdogies in the study of African Pentecostalism. Chammah J. Kaunda continues to have fruitful encounters with Asamoah-Gyadu both in person through various conferences/workshops and through his publications. In fact, this chapter takes as point of departure from Asamoah-Gyadu's lucid observation that "in modern times [libation] has been sustained in the relationship between African Pentecostal/charismatic leaders and their followers."[1] Ogbu Kalu had earlier observed that "Pentecostalism has produced a culture of continuity by mining primal worldview, reproducing an identifiable character, and regaining a pneumatic and charismatic religiosity that existed in traditional

---

1. Asamoah-Gyadu, "Mediating Spiritual Power," 92–93.

society."² This idea of spiritual and cultural continuity between the practice of libation in African traditional religions and Christianity remain foundational in the studies of African Pentecostalism and Christianity in general.³ Both Africanists and African scholars studying African Pentecostalism and Christianity in general have underlined various degrees of continuities and discontinuities of libation between Africa's cultural past and African Christianity.⁴ Contrary to the initial argument that African Pentecostalism claim "cultural discontinuity,"⁵ empirical evidence demonstrates a creation of a culture of both continuity and discontinuity.⁶ African Pentecostalism functions between continuity and discontinuity with African religio-cultural heritage in varying degrees. This means that while many Africans have converted to Pentecostalism, there are indications that their idea of religion and spirituality remain African in both outlook and practice. Silas Ncozana stresses that for most African Christians, wherever the gospel is in its essence and whatever it has achieved, is made through African religio-cultural heritage.⁷ In his work on "Christian Chiefs," Jonas Dah demonstrates that there is a cultural continuity and discontinuity between the practice of libation and Christianity.⁸ Dah found a methodological and contextual connectedness in the functions of Christians, clergy and laity, who took upon themselves traditional titles that mandated them to pour libations.

This chapter explores the spiritual significance of pouring water and oil within Cameroon neo-Pentecostalism which remain predominantly arenas of healing, deliverance and miracles. We utilized African cultural history to address the nature of continuity and discontinuity in the practice

---

2. Ogbu, *African Pentecostalism*, 186.

3. Idowu, *Olodumare*; Awolalu, *Yoruba Beliefs and Sacrificial Rites*; Mbiti, *African Religions and Philosophy*.

4. Ray, *African Religions*; Dickson, *Theology in Africa*; Essel, "Libation Art in Art of Ghana"; Agyarko, "Libation in African Christian Theology"; Asamoah-Gyadu, *African Charismatics*; "Pentecostalism and the Influence of Primal Realities in Africa"; "Mediating Spiritual Power"; Anderson, *Introduction to Pentecostalism*; Larbi, "Nature of Continuity and Discontinuity."

5. Kato, *Theological Pitfalls in Africa*; *African Cultural Revolution*; *Biblical Christianity in Arica*; Anti, "Libation in the Old Testament"; Maxwell, "Delivered from the Spirit of Poverty?"; Meyer, "Make a Complete Break with the Past"; Dijk, "Pentecostalism, Cultural Memory, and the State"; Engelke, "Discontinuity and the Discourse of Conversion."

6. Kaunda, *Nation That Fears God Prospers*.

7. Ncozana, *Spirit Dimension in African Christianity*.

8. Dah, *Christian Chiefs*.

of libation among neo-Pentecostals.⁹ In view of this, a picture of the history and present context of libation in our research context, neo-Pentecostalism in Cameroon, and the phenomenological method which we used, our findings demonstrate that neo-Pentecostal practices of liberation are characterized by a tension between continuity and discontinuity.

African Cultural History of Libation

Though its practices and functions may differ from one community to another, libation which mostly involves the use of water and other liquid substances contains a mellange of cultural, social and religious elements. Culturally, it is performed in reminiscence of historical and cultural knowledge. It is equally a social ritual which evokes community awareness, ensures stability, gives the individual a sense of identity and self-worth, and the expression of communal vision. Religiously, it is the ritual pouring or sprinkling of water to the ground, on objects, and/or on individuals as a sign of cleansing, blessing, healing and protection from evil powers. Dah mentions that among some tribes in Cameroon, libation is poured for various reasons, including: preparation for battle; to avert a calamity; after a calamity or to solicit blessing and protection on individuals or on the clan.[10] Most often the liquid is not completely poured to the ground or on individuals. Some of it is poured into a "communal drinking pot"[11] for all to drink from during the fellowship meal that usually concluded the ritual. After the ritual process and the incantations, the water is considered blessed, and so, it is believed to have the powers to effect healing on the individuals and the community. This practice has been among the people as long as human beings have existed.

The African cultural historical arena in general and of Cameroon in particular demonstrates that, despite the eruptive presence of the missionaries and other cultural infiltrations, libation continues to pervade human life even in this era of globalization and Christianity. Libation has been part of African history from inception. Although Kimani S. K. Nehusi begins his study on libation from Kemet,[12] the practice of libation can be

---

9. Ayandele, *African Historical Studies*; Kalu, *African Christianity*; Sundkler and Steed, *History of the Church in Africa*.
10. Dah, *Christian Chiefs*.
11. Dah, *Christian Chiefs*, 46.
12. Nehusi, *Libation*.

traced much earlier among most primal communities all of the world. Throughout the ancient world, libation played an important role in a wide range of religious, political, and social practices.[13] It remains an essential ritual in most indigenous oriented societies, permeating their social, religious, political, economic, and spiritual universe. The practice of libation has been understood differently by different people throughout history. Among others, it contains an amalgam of social, cultural, and religious elements. It is the simultaneous pouring of water and making incantations to God or gods, spirits, and divinities for goodwill, protection, and blessings.[14] It is also a communal ritual which bind the people together to their social roots;[15] an activity that unites the living and the dead; and a cultural and religious statement capable of providing social, psychological, and political transformation.[16]

Despite the significant place libation occupies in traditional African societies, it is however regrettable that, like most rituals related to the cult of the ancestors, there has not been an up-to-date treatment and consideration of the subject of libation.[17] The long and weird history of libation on the African continent have followed the bizarre treatment which Africa, its cultures and identity have received from most Eurocentric writers.[18] Like Hegel's categorization of African religiosity as *sorcery* and *fetish*, it was Spencer who bundled libation as worship of the dead (ancestor worship).[19] Although often isolated in the arena of creative writings, the works of Chinua Achebe,[20] Ayi Kwei Amah,[21] Kenjo Jumbam,[22] among others, became the pioneers of

13. Cook, *Zeus*.
14. Sarpong, *Libation*.
15. Mbiti, *African Religions and Philosophy*, 9.
16. Sarpong, *Libation*.
17. Most writers on Christianity and African cultures have pointed out this limitation. Among them is Ayandele, *African Historical Studies*, 230 (as cited above); however, he is not the only one who shares this view. Others include, Ade Ajayi, *Christian Missions in Nigeria*; Ayandele, *Missionary Impact on Modern Nigeria*; *Holy Johnson*; Babalola, *Christianity in West Africa*; Baeta, *Christianity in Tropical Africa*; Baur, *Two Thousand Years of Christianity in Africa*.
18. Hegel, *Philosophy of History*; Spencer, *Principles of Sociology*; Kalu, "Shape and Flow of African Historiography"; Adeoti, "African History"; Ayandele, *Missionary Impact on Modern Nigeria*; Baur, *Two Thousand Years of Christianity in Africa*.
19. Hegel, *Philosophy of History*; Spencer, *Principles of Sociology*.
20. Achebe, *Things Fall Apart*.
21. Amah, *Fragments*.
22. Jumbam, *White Man of God*.

African nationalism, exposing the destructive presence of Christianity and European culture on the African continent. For instance, Jumbam demonstrated how the practice of libation was "demonized" and rejected among the people of Bui in Cameroon. It is this picture that has characterized the long history of libation, especially during the missionary and colonial periods and has continued to contemporary times.

By the 1950s and 1960s, as Kwesi Dickson remarks, a new kind of understanding of culture was emerging, which ushered in a rigorous reconstructive framework, coinciding with the decline of the sources that told the early Eurocentric stories.[23] The enculturation framework came to fill the yawning vacuum created by the inability of the early European missionaries to root the gospel in the African worldview. There was a renewed understanding of libation, not limited to "worship," but, as John Mbiti would refer to it, a symbol of "fellowship, hospitality, and respect."[24] Within the context of cultural revolution with the evolution of ideas, including those in connection with ritual practices, libation has remained resilient and camouflage itself as new religious idea within African Christianity. In his study on the cultural history of libation, Felix Kang Esoh highlights the following as tenets of libation that have continued to permeate contemporary Cameroon: first, it is a distinct ritual for anointing, healing, blessing or a curse; second, it is both an individual and a communal act; third, it is no longer restricted to shrines, but is performed wherever and whenever the need arises; fourth, it involves a strong feeling of religious awe as a way of eschewing falsehood and misrepresentations; fifth, in addition to other elements, like palm wine, water is the most preferred element.[25] In short, libation is dynamic and has involved: the pouring of water on individuals; gatherings of members of the community; objects; private and public properties including houses; during private and public meals and equally used for ritual bath; etc.

A major development in the history of libation is the turn toward its consideration in the practice of contemporary Christianity. Mbiti does represent a major inspiration towards such a consideration, in ways similar to

---

23. Dickson, *Theology in Africa*, 49.
24. Mbiti, *African Religions and Philosophy*, 9; *Introduction to African Religion*, 109.
25. Esoh, "Christianity and Sar'h/Ezul (Libation)," 282–86.

how Benjamin Ray,[26] Kwesi Dickson,[27] Osuanyi Quaicoo Essel,[28] Peter Kwasi Sarpong,[29] Jean Marc Ela,[30] K. K. Amos Anti,[31] Robert Owusu Agyarko,[32] approach their studies of libation from the generality of African Christian theology.[33] Borrowing from this scholarship, Robert Owusu Agyarko concludes that apart from the incantations/prayers offered and its recipient, there is continuity in the practice of libation in traditional religions and Christianity.[34] These writings resonate with Ela's argument that such similarities between Christian and ancestral rituals in Cameroon result from the hesitation by Africans to part with their cultural identity.[35] He blames the elements of discontinuity on the disruptive presence of missionary Christianity in the relationship between the Christian faith and Africa's past. Most of the early missionary bodies who came to Cameroon completely rejected any cultural orientation of the gospel, and in most cases, suggested a total rupture from the African religio-cultural world.[36]

Before the arrival of the Pentecostals, it was the London Baptist, The Basel and the Roman Catholic Missions and their methods of inculturating the gospel that won the allegiance of most Cameroonians.[37] Apart from the indigenous Native Baptists in Cameroon, early Christianity in Cameroon was dominated by a European worldview which emphasized a total rupture with traditional practices. As a result, all those who exhibited such old links in the church were banned. For instance, in 1961, a group of persons within the Presbyterian Church in Cameroon (PCC) continued the traditional wearing of Bangles (*mondo*), which they claimed was a means of healing. Following the condemnation by the church, this group finally

26. Ray, *African Religions*.
27. Dickson, *Theology in Africa*.
28. Essel, *Libation Art in Art of Ghana*.
29. Sarpong, *Libation*.
30. Ela, *My Faith as an African*.
31. Anti, "Libation in the Old Testament."
32. Agyarko, "Libation in African Christian Theology."
33. Esoh, "Christianity and Sar'h/Ezul (Libation)," 34–35.
34. Agyarko, "Libation in African Christian Theology." Also see the works of Dickson and Ellingworth, *Biblical Revelation and African Beliefs*; Dickson, *Theology in Africa*; Bediako, *Theology and Identity*; *Christianity in Africa*; Sarpong, *Libation*.
35. Ela, *My Faith as an African*, 13–14.
36. Ela, *My Faith as an African*; Neba, *Healing Services and Anointing*.
37. Dah, *Missionary Motivations and Methods*; Vries, *Catholic Mission, Colonial Government, and Indigenous Response*.

separated from the PCC and formed "The Native Presbyterians" and later changed their name to their present appellation: "Cameroon Church of Christ (CCC)."[38] Similar waves of revivalist drives had continued within the PCC between the 1970s and 1980s. This nativist prophetic wave which spread through the areas of Moghamo and Ngie in North Western Cameroon was championed by one Sister Sophie Njie and Deborah respectively.[39] Their activities were considered incompatible with Christian teachings, but they attracted many followers, including some Christians who attended their healing and deliverance. Dah has observed that the activities of these groups had great similarities with traditional cultural practices. Possible reason why they were popular among the indigenes.

The entrance of Nigerian—derived Pentecostalism only came to continue the elements already present in the Catholic and Presbyterian Churches that had inaugurated the beginning of a radical shift of cultural allegiance from Europe to Cameroon. Certainly, the revival movements of the 1970s and 1980s in the PCC laid the religio-cultural foundations for the later entrance of Pentecostalism in Cameroon. The Pentecostal movement constitutes the contemporary church tradition that, it could be said, has been most successful in meeting the challenges of inculturation within the Cameroonian setting. Their emphasis on the spiritual awareness found, in Cameroon, an accommodating environment. These churches use anointed water and oil during blessing, healing and deliverance services in ways that are similar with the libation ritual.[40] Clearly, even when they claim discontinuity, these churches still make reference to the past. Most prayers for deliverance are usually about a break from ancestral connections. This could be classified as spiritual paradox. Paradoxically, emphasis on discontinuity with ancestral belief systems, that enshrine the pouring of libation, simultaneously, albeit, subliminally, contentious libation system.[41] By doing so, they are bridging the chasm created by missionary Christianity, knowingly or unknowingly. When water is poured in church, converts see the incorporation of their primal belief systems, and for some, it is a way of identification with their roots within the African cultural heritage.

38. Dah, "Vision and Challenges of an Autonomous Church," 66.

39. Dah, "Vision and Challenges of an Autonomous Church," 70.

40. See the likes of Fomum, *Way of Spiritual Warfare*; Bame, *Supernatural Powers of Evil*; Ndip, *Prayer Blast*; Wara, *Student Prayer Passport*; Dah, *Challenges of Spiritual Healing*.

41. Ecke, "Continuity and Discontinuity," 46.

SECTION II: SPIRITUAL REALITY, WORLDVIEWS, AND FORMATIONS

Research Method and Methodology

The religio-cultural, economic and political context of Cameroon has greatly contributed in determining the missio-cultural trajectory of the country. The move towards democratization with its freedom of association and worship which swept across a number of countries in Africa equally prepared the grounds for the flourishing of Pentecostalism in Cameroon. Robert Mbe Akoko has suggested that, the reintroduction of the liberalization laws in Cameroon in 1990 after the ban on the "born-again" movements in the later part of the 1970s, is among the many reasons for the flourishing of Pentecostalism in Cameroon.[42] At this time, the government needed to respond to the wave of democratization that was sweeping through the African continent. Among other reasons, including the new employment alternatives they offered, Pentecostals professed to offer holistic life to their followers, including, healing through spiritual means, power over satanic influences, and above all, their emphasis on the disconnect with "traditional" beliefs and rituals.[43] Observably, it is estimated that between 1990 and 2018, there have been a monumental growth in other Christian groupings than the denominations established by the Western missionaries.

Among other reasons, this research on Cameroon neo-Pentecostalism/Charismatics is ignited by the introduction of/and the extensive use of "Holy Water,"[44] "anointed water,"[45] or "Morning Water" which according to the Nigerian-born Prophet T. B. Joshua, is anointed by Christ to heal, bless and save.[46] The research thematically focused on the interplay of Christianity and culture in Cameroon. The qualitative research technique employed was setting-based and interpretive approach to social reality and lived religious experience of Cameroonian neo-Pentecostal believers.[47] Data were collected between 2015 and 2019 through participant observation as well as unstructured interview techniques were utilized to find out what attracts most Christians to services of deliverance and healing where water is blessed and used. The study utilized opportunist and purposeful sampling techniques and

42. Akoko, *Ask and You Shall Be Given*.
43. Masok, "How Should the Presbyterian Church," 15.
44. Solomon, *Seven Great Prayer Weapons*.
45. Neba, *Healing Services and Anointing*.
46. Emmanuel Television, *Morning Water Renews You*, is the brand name of water which is bottled and sold to Christians. It is a production of Prophet T. B. Joshua's Synagogue Church of All Nations (SCOAN).
47. Creswell, *Research Design*; Denzin and Lincoln, *Handbook of Qualitative Research*.

targeted mostly neo-Pentecostals with focus on the use of water, and small number of some members of the Roman Catholic Church and Presbyterian Church. The views of respondents expressed were collected through notes and phone recordings during some special services, and equally through WhatsApp chats and voice clips. Such interviews are well suited to the ideologies of neo-Pentecostalism, since they have spatial dimensions with regard to dichotomies between Christianity and the African cultural worldview. In what follows, we present and analyze the findings.

"A Counter Force": Data Presentation and Analysis

In his reinterpretation and understanding of the power of "Anointed Water" or "Holy Water," Che Wara Solomon, a former Presbyterian pastor and neo-Pentecostal pastor, argues: "One of the greatest prayer weapons not yet unveiled fully to humanity is the gift of water."[48] He notes that the introduction of "Holy Water" is to satisfy the aspirations of thirsty Christians who have for a long time gone without this important biblical element that provided for the wellbeing of the people. His analysis is based on his interpretation of the complaint made to Moses by the Israelites who had become thirsty and asked him for water to drink. In a similar way, Solomon narrates a scene which according to him, inspired his theology of "Holy Water":

> A Christian came to my congregation and after attending the service and witnessed how we blessed our water she was so worried. When I enquired from her she said . . . she took some anointed water from her neighbor who attended our prayers, and she drank and sprinkled some in her room. That night she neither had a night husband nor ate in her dream again. But her problem was their pastor did not believe in holy water and this kept other Christians so worried. They are really thirsty and need water to drink. For how long will they spend huge amounts of money for transport just to get water? They are threatening their pastor like Moses: "Give us water to drink, we are spiritually thirsty."[49]

The idea of continuity and discontinuity address the question of the Christian faith and primal cultural dichotomy. While, on the one hand, many of the belief systems which Pentecostals refuse to identify with have primal roots, on the other hand, the solutions to such problems which

---

48. Solomon, *Seven Great Prayer Weapons*, 17.
49. Solomon, *Seven Great Prayer Weapons*, 18.

Pentecostals provide, is informed by primal interpretation of the Bible. Most Cameroonian Christians (rural or urban) continue to maintain an unbroken link with their cultural communities and family heritage. Group affinity based on ethnic and lineage leanings remain very strong, in and out of the church. Such a setting provides an opportunity for them to live lives that are neither urban nor rural, neither Christian nor traditional.

Masok rightly argues that, most neo-Pentecostal churches in Cameroon like their counterparts elsewhere, make good use of the Bible, borrow from the African liturgy and incorporate various facets of primal religion and culture into their worship.[50] As a result, even with the offensive on traditional religious practices by Pentecostals, traditional ontology has continued to pervade existing realities, what John Taylor refers to as "the unbroken circle."[51] Since traditional societies associated misfortunes with spirit attacks, the reality of the primal spirit world is testified by the importance attached to rites, rituals and sacred ordinances. Thus, libation which remain one of the main methods of propitiation in traditional societies, has become a means of liberation from curses and demonic spirits in neo-Pentecostal settings.

This religiosity in the new practices of water seem to have been partly motivated by a need to interpret and find explanations for the past. While some of our informants agree that the traditional practice of libation, in which water is poured to spirits of the death invoke ancestral curses, responsible for the misfortune of members, others hold that libation is equally poured as a means of blessing and the assurance of security. Also, protection and deliverance from evil powers are among the reasons for the use of water in combating the evil originating from traditional past. It is believed that libation was performed for good purposes, as well as others used it for evil purposes. As an informant explained, "A lot of people are being cleansed from ancestral stains and generational curses. Sometimes people are using the 'Holy Water' as a counter force."[52]

These interpretations are more comprehendible when one considers the function of libation in the Cameroonian religio-cultural universe. For much of the Cameroonian religio-cultural history, libation ritual pervades the traditional societies, and are an essential activity to their spiritual, social, economic and political coping in communal life, such as life

---

50. Masok, "How Should Presbyterian Church," 16.
51. Taylor, *Primal Vision*, 59.
52. Solomon, *Seven Great Prayer Weapons*, 18.

circle transitions, economic guarantee, crisis mitigation and blessings for progenies.[53] Although some practices associated with libation may connote worship of other gods and spirits of the dead, the very fact that those who died in suspicious circumstances or committed suicide were excluded from ancestral genealogies of most communities, it is not possible to generalize every practice associated with libation as evil. In addition to its functions as a ritual of identity and to maintain a culture of truthfulness, it equally ensures that the community's socio-economic and spiritual stability is guaranteed.[54] As Esoh has illustrated, libation played a vital role in the religio-psychological and the socio-political liberation of the people from physical and spiritual powers, as well as maintained their community stability.[55] Thus, this could be one of the reasons why the neo-Pentecostals and some other churches are incorporating libation in their effort in blending traditional and ecclesiastical leadership.[56] In the PCC for instance, before now, the use of water as an element for blessing was not common. Today, the pouring of water during blessing ceremonies in church and elsewhere have become regular practices even when it has not been given a full liturgical recognition. On the look of things, it is difficult to differentiate the spiritual pouring of water in different churches today, including neo-Pentecostal churches from the traditional libation rituals.[57]

Most of the neo-Pentecostal churches we visited and the members we discussed with including their pastors, acknowledged the cultural and spiritual similarities and significance of the use of water in their churches and

53. Ela, *My Faith as an African*; Che, "Origin and Evolution of Obang Village"; Jumbam, *White Man of God*; Balz, *Where the Faith Has to Live*; Ardener, *Kingdom of Mount Fako*; DeLancey et al., *Historical Dictionary of the Republic of Cameroon*, 1; Littlewood, "Bamum and Bamileke"; Akoko, *Ngwo Blue Print*; McCulloch, "Tikar," 47; Fossouo, *Croyance Africaine*; Dah, *Angry Gods*, 9; Chief Emmanuel Mbela Lifafa Endeley, interview with the author, Buea, Cameroon, 2005.

54. Mbiti, *African Religions and Philosophy*, 26; Setiloane, *African Theology*, 18; Shabangu, "Gospel Embodied in African Traditional Religion," 159; Bediako, *Christianity in Africa*, 220.

55. Esoh, "Christianity and Sar'h/Ezul (Libation)," 336. See also Sarpong, *Libation*; Nehusi, *Libation*; Porterfield, *Power of Religion*, 20.

56. Dah, *Christian Chiefs*, mentions the Very Rev. Jeremiah Chi Kangson who upon ascending his native throne as Fon, reconceptualized libation by pouring it in the name of the Triune God.

57. A number of Christians with whom we had discussions in relation to the subject actually confessed that there is no difference but for the fact that the prayers offered during libation were offered to "idols," while those offered in church are to God. Both Protestants and Pentecostals share this view.

the local cultures.⁵⁸ While a majority of our informants recognized these similarities, especially in function and performativity,⁵⁹ others consider the appellation "libation" as connoting evil in itself. From every indication, the problems have been with the appellation "libation," the person performing the ritual and the one to whom it is directed. Even those who agreed that there is actually no difference in the performance of water libation in church like in traditional ceremonies, they refused to associate the two due to their parallel connotations. Some simply say libation is practiced by non-Christians and directed to the dead, while anointed water is accompanied by prayers offered to God. While most pastors claim that it must be performed by an ordained person,⁶⁰ others say it can be done by any Christian.

The two other groups involved in the use of water are the Catholics and Presbyterians. Their experience in the use of water predates those of the neo-Pentecostals. While the Roman Catholics retain the oldest tradition of the use of Holy Water, the practice has not been very common among Protestant churches. The use of water among Presbyterians is not a liturgical provision, but a spontaneous act among pastors. Most Presbyterians do this during services for the blessing of church houses, private houses and properties including, cars, and other belongings. Both the Roman Catholic Church and the Presbyterian have established liturgies that include the pouring and/or sprinkling of water during Baptism. However, in the Roman Catholic Church, Holy Water is used for other purposes, including pouring or sprinkling on congregants as a means of purification and blessing, and in some cases, the members are expected to take some to sprinkle around their homes. While the pouring or sprinkling of water is an established liturgical act among Roman Catholics, it remains an act of spontaneity among Pastors of the Presbyterian Church in Cameroon.⁶¹ Although the act of pouring or sprinkling water on individuals or objects and properties is not sanctioned by the liturgy of the Presbyterian Church in Cameroon, pastors have done so without any objection from church authorities:

---

58. There is an agreement among them on the significance of water for Christian spirituality, healing, blessing, and deliverance.

59. The pouring on individuals and objects and sprinkling around the house is usually accompanied by prayers just as it is the case in traditional settings.

60. See Solomon, *Seven Prayer Weapons*.

61. This act is largely discretional among pastors of the Presbyterian Church in Cameroon.

Let us consider the recent ceremony for the dedication of a service car of Kumba Presbytery of the Presbyterian Church in Cameroon. A retired Moderator of the Church . . . who performed the rite took water and after haven recounted the long history of the tradition of and how it became necessary for church leaders to have official administrative cars, offered prayers, poured the water on all the main parts of the car.[62] Later, during the feasting, a pastor asked: "can what the very reverend moderator just perform not be called libation?" The debate that ensued was characteristic of the diverse positions held by pastors of the Presbyterian church in Cameroon on the practice of libation.[63]

Like the blessing of a private or church house, this particular act of dedicating a car is an example of contemporary Christian rites that are visibly similar with traditional libation rituals. We would argue that these and many other practices, which were not officially Christian practices, are of a traditional nature and origin. In some mainline churches, like in Pentecostal churches, practices such as the pouring or sprinkling of Holy Water have become regular than they were when Christianity was introduced in the country. In our observations, these practices which were purely traditional, through which adherents received spiritual and physical blessing and healing,[64] are now being performed by Christian churches with almost the same results. Through our observation and the responses, we received, the practices are similar and a kind of bridges the gap created by early missionary Christianity. This view is held by Roman Catholics, mainline Protestants and some Pentecostals who confessed that their use of water shares many characteristics with libation.

Most of our informants who refused associating libation with the Christian practice of water, base their argument on the fact that it is mostly practiced on graves and sacred sites without a single mention of the name of God but those of ancestors. In contemporary libation, as Esoh argues, there is no particular place for the offering of libation nor is there a confusion as to the recipient of libation. In libation:

---

62. The Very Rev. Dr. Nyansako Ni-Nku is a pastor and retired Moderator of the Presbyterian Church in Cameroon (PCC) and former president of the All Africa Conference of Churches (AACC). He performed this ceremony on January 2, 2019, during the public presentation and dedication of a new car for the Presbytery.

63. Esoh, "Christianity and Sar'h/Ezul (Libation)," 324.

64. Sarpong, *Libation*, 330.

> the service rendered to one's ancestors cannot be equated to worship, because the service is simply the same as to one's living parents . . . for that reason, they try to understand the limitations of their human ancestors without forgetting their legacies, while rendering their worship exclusively to the Supreme Being.[65]

According to Andries Shabangu, "the traditional culture of Africa never allowed the worship of ancestors and thus, never in conflict with the gospel message."[66] Even in areas or settings where the traditional reverence around graves and other sacred sites seemingly connoted worship, those emotional and physical expressions are fast changing, giving preference to divine sovereignty while acknowledging the social roles of ancestors. Unless otherwise, and in cases where the practice may seem contradictory with Christian teachings, Agyarko things only then can it be deemed incompatible with Christianity. In such cases as Allan Anderson points out, Pentecostals contrast the "evil" past with a future that is Christian, modern, and transformational.[67] Unfortunately, most of those converted even to Pentecostalism have rarely completely departed from their primal to Christian worldviews. Some of our informants were Christians of some mainline denominations before converting to Pentecostalism, but it seems they had not been very committed Christians. In their new found religion therefore, some of them have simply tolerated religious concubinage between Christian and non-Christian rituals. Others however feel that they need to intensify their religiosity in order to avoid the traps of syncretic Christianity.

In his reconceptualization, Solomon holds that the similarity of libation and the use of Holy Water in church today simply explains the fact that previous practices are completely turned over to God, to serve His very purpose at creation. He notes:

> When you offer your life to Christ and yet discover that you have bags of charms, bottles, feathers, pots of medicine, shrines etc. If you are willing to do away with them, then the first weapon you need is "clean (Holy) water." . . . That is why Elijah first poured water on the offering at Mount Carmel when the prophets of Baal desecrated the place (1 Kgs 18:33).[68]

65. Esoh, "Christianity and Sar'h/Ezul (Libation)," 234.
66. Shabangu, "Gospel Embodied in African Traditional Religion," 159.
67. Anderson, *Spirit-Filled World*.
68. Solomon, *Seven Great Prayer Weapons*, 22.

Like the Israelites, Solomon mentions how Presbyterian Christians "testified that, secretly they have borrowed holy water from Roman Catholic Christians for private use but still kept it a secret. For how long will this hunger and thirst last?"[69] The tolerance of syncretism between primal beliefs and Christianity is considered one of the dilemmas of enculturation. According to many of our informants, a number of Christians continue to live under the bondage of ancestral spirits in which, for a key informant, "the bible provides an alternative through the use of Holy Water."[70] As some of these informants explained to us, most Christians have cultural attachments to water libation, whose quests can only be satisfied by the Christian practice of "anointing water" or "Holy Water." For instance, many have cited some of the following biblical examples as mandate for the use of water in healing and deliverance: Elisha and the purification of the water of Jericho (2 Kgs 2:19–22); Eliezar and the purification of the spoils of war (Num 31:21–23); Ezekiel and the sprinkling of clean water (Ezek 36:25) etc.

It is within this frame that this study identifies a number of practices within neo-Pentecostal churches in Cameroon, as finding resonances in the though, uncompromising discussions between libation and the practice of pouring water and other liquid substances in church and elsewhere. From the findings above, a number of such practices, which employ the pouring of liquid, have been noted as displaying significant continuities between the traditional practices of libation and Christian rites of blessing and exorcism with water. Neo-Pentecostals use water as elements during special blessings (of cars, houses, land and other personal belongings), for the sick and as a symbol for purification, in ways not different from the traditional Cameroonian practice of water libation.[71]

Conclusion

The rejection of cultural continuities, libation practices, and culture-specific customs may be considered a "break with the past," however, as we have noted above, this break is never complete. On the one hand, while neo-Pentecostals claim to be representing a break from the past in their battle against traditions, it is their desire to fight ancestral spirits that

---

69. Solomon, *Seven Great Prayer Weapons*, 18.

70. This view is shared in Solomon, *Seven Great Prayer Weapons*; Neba, *Healing Services and Anointing*.

71. See PCC, "Administration of the Sacrament"; "Blessing."

inadvertently make them borrow from primal religious practices. As has hopefully been shown, the inability to completely divorce from the past justifies the incorporation of traditional practices. For instance, as Meyer notes, some of those things that neo-Pentecostals have called evil still has some control on them, even if it is just something from which they try to distance themselves as much as possible.[72] These point to the diverse usage and interpretations of what actually constitutes the pouring, meaning and function of water libation, whether among traditional communities or among Christian denominations. These differences highlight the continuities and discontinuities, compatibilities and incompatibilities that have continued to characterize the Christian/Primal religious dilemma. While some Christians try to differentiate libation from Holy Water, others say the use of water revives in them a sense of their cultural identity, evokes their commonality and inspires hope within their new community (the church). In short, the new community (the church) has simply redefined their ancient practices, and that even so, they do not feel a complete disappearance of their sense of cultural continuity.[73] There is still a need for further research on neo-Pentecostal theology of libation.

---

72. Meyer, "Make a Complete Break with the Past."
73. Dah, *Christian Chiefs*.

10

Proclaiming Good News to the Poor (Isa 61:1–2; Luke 4:18–19)

Pentecostalism and Social Justice in Ghana

PATRICK KOFI AMISSAH

Introduction

JESUS CHRIST QUOTED PART of Isaiah 61:1–2, which is a Messianic prophecy in the Old Testament, in the "manifesto" of his ministry (Luke 4:18–19). Both the corpuses demonstrate that the text has both spiritual and social justice implications. However, the tendency has been to stress only one to the neglect of the other. In Pentecostal and Charismatic Christianity, for instance, "proclaiming good news to the poor" could be domesticated in the spiritual, to the neglect of social justice. This is so because Pentecostal and Charismatic Christians place strong emphasis on the works of the Holy Spirit in the life of their members and the ministry of their churches. This pneumatological prominence raises the question of how to address, in a balance, the social and spiritual wellbeing of the human person. It is thus important to focus on a balanced approach to the interpretation of the text. This chapter examines Isaiah 61:1–2 and Luke 4:18–19, delineating the social justice and spiritual dimensions in them. Applying the text to contemporary Pentecostal and Charismatic Christianity in Ghana, the chapter touches on poverty and oppression as two social justice issues in Ghana relevant to the text, exploring how the ministry of Pentecostal and Charismatic Christians in Ghana has dealt with these issues.

Context and Meaning of Isaiah 61:1–2

Isaiah 61 is part of the so called third Isaiah which is believed to be a post exilic application of first and second Isaiah. While scholars agree that almost all of first Isaiah (1–39) is original to Isaiah of Jerusalem and is mostly pre-exilic,[1] second and third Isaiah are attributed to other writers or schools who during and after the exile, tried to make meaning of first Isaiah to bring hope and comfort to the exiles and the returnees.[2] The message of third Isaiah, to which chapter 61 belongs is therefore comfort to a grieving community and hope of restoration of their fortunes. This message has both spiritual and social justice implications and given the overall dominance of social justice themes throughout the three parts of Isaiah, it is detrimental to neglect it in any form of interpretation. The table below presents the Masoretic (MS) text of Isaiah 61:1–2, transliteration and the NRSV translation.

MS	Transliteration	English Translation (NRSV)
1 רוּחַ אֲדֹנָי יְהוִה עָלָי	ruach adonai YHWH alai	The spirit of the Lord God is upon me,
יַעַן מָשַׁח יְהוָה אֹתִי לְבַשֵּׂר עֲנָוִים	ya'an mashach YHWH oti levasser anawim	because the Lord has anointed me; . . . to bring good news to the oppressed,
לַחֲבֹשׁ לְנִשְׁבְּרֵי-לֵב שְׁלָחַנִי	shelachaniy lachavosh lenishberei-lev	to bind up the broken hearted,
לִקְרֹא לִשְׁבוּיִם דְּרוֹר	liqro lishvuyim deror	to proclaim liberty to the captives,
וְלַאֲסוּרִים פְּקַח-קוֹחַ	wela'asurim peqach-qoach	and release to the prisoners;
2 לִקְרֹא שְׁנַת-רָצוֹן לַיהוָה	liqro shenath-ratson Lyhwh	to proclaim the year of the Lord's favor,
וְיוֹם נָקָם לֵאלֹהֵינוּ	weyom naqam leloheinu	and the day of vengeance of our God;
לְנַחֵם, כָּל-אֲבֵלִים	lenachem kol-avelim.	to comfort all who mourn;

1. Collins, *Introduction to the Hebrew Bible*.

2. See Redditt, *Introduction to the Prophets*; Leclerc, *Introduction to the Prophets*, 162; Stulman and Kim, *You Are My People*.

Spiritual Emphasis

The prophecy of Isaiah spans the pre-exilic, exilic and post-exilic history of Israel. In first Isaiah (1–39), the prophet warns of the spiritual degeneration of the people of Israel and the consequent punishment that is eminent. If the people heeded his warning and turned to God, a spiritual awakening would have led to transformation and God would have spared them the punishment of exile. While in exile, second Isaiah (40–54) came as encouragement and hope for a return and restoration if the people spiritually transformed and returned to God. To the returnee exiles who were in despair because the prophecy of restoration in second Isaiah had not been fulfilled as dramatic as they expected, came third Isaiah (55–66) to comfort and give hope. There is no doubt that throughout Isaiah and especially here in Isaiah 61, the prophet looked forward to a spiritual awakening of repentance, renewal and return to God in all aspects of the life of the community. So, it is the sins of the people which led to the Babylonian invasion, that resulted in the exile, which came as God's judgement to a wayward people. While in exile, there was repentance that led to God's intervention and the return to the Promised Land. Back in the land, the same unrighteousness that led to the exile, seem to be rife. The prophet thus called for spiritual liberation that must begin with repentance. According to the *Cambridge Bible for Schools and Colleges*: "The terms 'meek' and 'broken-hearted" [as עֲנָוִים (*anawim*) is sometime translated] denote the religious qualities which characterize the recipients of the prophet's Evangel."[3] In this sense, the Anointed One comes with the power of the Holy Spirit to proclaim good news that will liberate the people from any spiritual perversion and bondage to release them to be right with God.

Social Justice Emphasis

Leclerc's claim that the prophet's description of his call as "anointed" is unusual, is questionable. He is right that only king's and priests were described as anointed.[4] However, since the leadership was singled out for particular attention because it bore a particular responsibility for justice,[5] the prophet describing his call using terminology of kingship and priesthood is to

---

3. "Isaiah 61."
4. Leclerc, *Introduction to the Prophets*, 361.
5. Leclerc, *Introduction to the Prophets*, 181.

legitimize his ministry of social justice. Again, in accepting that some terminologies in the text bothers on spiritual issues, the *Cambridge Bible for Schools and Colleges* affirms that designations such as, "captives," "bound," and "mourners," should not only be understood in the spiritual sense because it is "not unlikely that the immediate reference is to the social evils whose redress is already demanded" (see Isa 58:6, 9).[6] Thus, the good news that is preached cannot be limited to the spiritual domain but properly located in the social justice domain too. It is thus not surprising that the prophecy of Isaiah, tagged the spiritual renewal of the people of Israel, to their day to day behavior. They had to do what was just and righteous, physically showing kindness to and being on the side of the vulnerable in order to be accepted by God.

To strengthen the above claim calls for the acknowledgement that social justice is not alien to Isaiah. Right from the onset, there is a strong emphasis on seeking justice and Zion being redeemed by justice (Isa 1:17, 27). Isaiah calls YHWH the God of justice (30:18), emphasizing the theme of the ideal king who executes justice (9; 11) and Zion being founded on and filled with justice (28:17; 33:5). Again, Isaiah exhibits a "passionate commitment to justice" when he energetically denounces acts of social injustice such as: neglecting and exploiting widows, orphans and the poor (1:17, 23; 10:2; 11:4), corrupt legal practices that legitimizes injustice (1:22; 3:14; 5:23; 10:1), excessive and greedy accumulation of wealth (2:7; 3:16–23; 5:8–9; 10:2–3), violence and bloodshed (1:17, 21; 5:7) and opulence (5:11, 12, 22; 28:1, 7–8; 32:9).[7] To W. A. VanGemeren, "The good news of God is always good news to those who have not found deliverance and meaning in the structure of human society. They are the mourners, the poor, the oppressed in spirit who hunger and thirst for divine deliverance."[8] Thus in Isaiah 61, it is the practical acts of justice and righteousness, creating a level playing field for all and restoring community relationships that was going to lead to the needed revival and restoration of Israel to it pre-exilic glory.

One of the features of Isaiah 61:1–2 with focus on social justice is the language used by the prophet to describe the subject of the ministry of the Anointed One. The first is עֲנָוִים (*anawim*, poor), which raises the social justice issues of poverty and its amelioration. It is the plural of the root עָנָו (*anaw*), which occurs four times in Isaiah (Isa 11:4; 29:19; 32:7; 61:1) and

6. "Isaiah 61."

7. Leclerc, *Introduction to the Prophets*, 180.

8. VanGemeren, *Interpreting the Prophetic Word*, 284.

twenty other times in the Hebrew Bible. *Anaw* is generally translated as "poor," "humble," "afflicted," "meek," or "needy." It normally occurs in parallel with אביון (*ebiyon*, needy) and in the context of other terminology that describe vulnerability due to economic or social depravation (see Isa 11:4; 29:19; 32:7; Job 24:4; Ps 9:18; Amos 2:7; 4:8.).[9] J. A Motyer describes *anawim* as those who are the downtrodden, the disadvantaged, or those held back from progress and amelioration by people or circumstances,[10] which could include economic and political systems that inhibit the ability of the poor and needy to better themselves. Furthermore, *Anaw* and its derivative עני (*ani*) come from common roots and are identical in meaning. In the Hebrew Bible, *ani* refers to the oppressed poor, while *anaw* refers to the poor as an identifiable group. In the Prophets and Wisdom, the *anawim* are found in the context of injustice and oppression. In all the seven appearances of *anawim* in the Prophets (except Zeph 2:3), it is in the context of oppression and injustice (Amos 2:7; 8:4; Isa 6:1; 29:19). Pleins details three contexts in which *anawim* are found in the prophetic texts. These are: economic oppression (Isa 3:15; Ezek 18:12), unjust treatment in legal decisions (Isa 10:2) and victimization through deception (Isa 32:7).[11] The approach of the prophets to the issues of the poor, especially locating them in contexts of oppression, abuse and injustice of various forms indicate their understanding that poverty is the result of injustice and that the poor person is further made vulnerable to oppression, abuse and injustice. It is the appalling situation of the poor that the Anointed One has been endue with the spirit of God to address and bring hope, restoration and prosperity to.

The second term is נִשְׁבְּרֵי-לֵב (*nishberei-lev*), a niphal plural construct of שבר (*shabar*, to break), which is usually translated as "broken hearted." With the niphal of *shabar* also meaning "to be maimed," "to be crippled," "to be wrecked," "to be broken," or "to be crushed," the intensity of the vulnerability and the suffering of the "broken hearted" increases. This broken heartedness might have resulted from disappointment in not realizing fully the promised restoration after the exile. However, it could also emanate from the struggles of the oppressed who are unable to reap and enjoy the fruit of their own labor due to exploitation and extortion.

The third terminology is שְׁבוּיִם (*shevuyim*), a qal plural of שבה (*shavah*), which means "to be taken captive." Only two out of the forty-two uses of the

---

9. See Domeris, "אביון"; *Touching the Heart of God*, 14–26.
10. Motyer, *Prophecy of Isaiah*, 500.
11. Pleins, Poor, Poverty.

verb in the Hebrew Bible occurs in Isaiah. In Isaiah 14:2, the prophet brings hope to Israel that they will take captive their captors and rule over their oppressors. Here in 61:1, the one anointed with God's Spirit comes to proclaim liberty to a people who feel they are still in captivity. The prophet's word for liberating these captives is דְּרוֹר (*deror*). Both in Hebrew and in Ancient Near Eastern contexts, *deror* means "manumission," a period when slaves are set free, debts are forgiven and families are allowed to return to their properties. *Deror* occurs seven times in the Hebrew Bible (Exod 30:23; Lev 25:10; Isa 61:1; Jer 34:8, 15, 17; Ezek 46:17). With exception of Exodus, where *deror* is used to describe the free flowing of *myrr*, all the other uses refer to liberty or freedom. In Leviticus, it is used in the context of the year of Jubilee. In Jeremiah, *deror* is used in the context of the only time in the Hebrew Bible when the Jubilee law was actually carried out. In Ezekiel, *deror* is used in the context of the year of Jubilee, where possessions return to the original owners. Thus, the use of *deror* in Isaiah 61:1 directly links it to the great manumission of the Jubilee Year and the proclamation of the year of the Lord's favor. Motyer argues that it "furthers this thought that the Anointed one comes in an appointed time to resettle all things and to release debtors and slaves."[12] This implies that the text cannot be domesticated in the spiritual but must be seen also from the social justice point of view.

The fourth terminology of interest as far as social justice in Isaiah 61:1–2 is concerned, is פְּקַח־קוֹחַ (*peqach-qoach*). This construct is a hapax legomenon and therefore difficult to translate. On its own, פקח (*peqach*) in the qal means "to open."[13] With exception of Isaiah 42:20, where the object is ears, throughout the Hebrew Bible, the object of *peqach* is eyes.[14] This has led some to translate the construct as "opening of eyes" (see NHEB, JPS). However, it connotes liberation and release. The translation "release from darkness for the prisoners" (NIV) considers the object of *peqach* as eyes. When the prisoner is released, she/he comes out from the darkness of the dungeon and their eyes are opened to light. The translation "release to the prisoners" (NRSV) and "opening of the prison to them that are bound" (KJV) do more justice to this context where there is the binding of the broken hearted and the liberation of the captive. In the context of foreign domination, conquest and exile, most prisoners would have been unjustly

---

12. Motyer, *Prophecy of Isaiah*, 500.

13. Clines, *Dictionary of Classical Hebrew*; Koehler and Baumgartner, *Hebrew and Aramaic Lexicon of the Bible*, 959.

14. Hamilton, "פקח," 666.

imprisoned. Also, in a society where small debts could land one in prison until the full amount is paid, liberation from prison would be seen as serving justice and facing up to the oppressor.

The above terminologies used to describe the objects of the ministry of the Anointed One indicate that the good news that he proclaims and the year of the Lord's favor that he announces comes as hope of liberation from oppression, exploitation, poverty and incapacitation, as a result of social injustice. Motyer concludes, "The *good news* embraces personal renewal and restoration, release from restrictions imposed by people and the rectification of circumstances."[15] Thus when Luke records Jesus' quotation from Isaiah 61:1–2, we cannot lose site of the overwhelming social justice implications discussed above.

The Ministry of Jesus and Social Justice (Luke 4:18–19)

The discussion above on Isaiah 61:1–2 has established that the prophet had to contend with both spiritual and social justice issues of his time and that the text has to be interpreted in both ways. Like most prophets, Isaiah sought to transmit the message that spirituality or a good relationship with God must translate into good neighborliness and ensure social justice by righting the wrongs of oppression, extortion, poverty and exploitation. So, when Jesus read this text in the Synagogue at the beginning of his ministry, they had both spiritual and social justice emphasis. The rest of this section explores that possibility.

---

15. Motyer, *Prophecy of Isaiah*, 500.

SECTION II: SPIRITUAL REALITY, WORLDVIEWS, AND FORMATIONS

Greek	Transliteration	English Translation (NRSV)
18 Πνεῦμα κυρίου ἐπ᾽ ἐμέ,	pneuma kyriou ep' eme	The Spirit of the Lord is upon me,
οὗ εἵνεκεν ἔχρισέν με εὐαγγελίσασθαι πτωχοῖς, ἀπέσταλκέν με κηρύξαι αἰχμαλώτοις ἄφεσιν καὶ τυφλοῖς ἀνάβλεψιν,	hou heineken echrisen me euangelisasthai pt‾ochois apestalken me keryxai aichmalotois aphesin kai typhlois anablepsin,	because he has anointed me to bring good news to the poor. He has sent me to proclaim release to the captives and recovery of sight to the blind,
ἀποστεῖλαι τεθραυσμένους ἐν ἀφέσει,	aposteilai tethrausmenous en aphesei,	to let the oppressed, go free,
19 κηρύξαι ἐνιαυτὸν κυρίου δεκτόν.	keryxai eniauton kyriou dekton	to proclaim the year of the Lord's favor.

Just as Isaiah ministered to a nation that was struggling with oppressive foreign domination and yet broken human relations with religious insincerity, so was it in Jesus' time. While the Jews were struggling with Roman domination, looking forward to a Messiah to deliver them, sin and injustice had driven a wedge between them and God. There was the need for repentance and regeneration to make way for the Messiah. Even though Luke does not present Jesus' ministry beginning with the message of repentance as Matthew and Mark do, the ministry of John the Baptist that preceded Jesus' was a ministry that called for repentance, indicating the need for a spiritual renewal (Luke 3:1–19). So, when Jesus read from Isaiah and announced its fulfilment in him, he was announcing an era of spiritual renewal, revival and a release from every spiritual poverty, oppression, bondage and imprisonment. Yet this spiritual dimension of the text is anchored firmly on human behavior which bothers on social justice.

First, there is a sense in which Luke's gospel projects the issues of social justice of Jesus' day and ministry. Almost 40 percent of the material in Luke's gospel that is not included in the other gospels, teaches about poverty in relations to riches. This demonstrates Luke's advocacy for social justice. It has been asserted that Luke relies on social justice themes from Isaiah and other prophets to portray the social justice focus of Jesus' ministry and that of his disciples.[16] He copiously quotes from Isaiah 40 to 66, which deal with the promised salvation of Israel in the area of social justice. In Isaiah 58, for instance, "the coming of salvation is contingent on the people's change of attitude from supporting injustice to doing justice and righteousness." Thus when Luke reports Jesus' reading and exposition on Isaiah 61, he presents Jesus as God's anointed servant.[17] As justice and righteousness are the core elements of the good news of God's Kingdom, so are practical acts of social justice as exemplified by Jesus and the apostles, connected to the proclamation of the good news.[18] Dyer thus confidently conclude that the material in the Gospel of Luke demonstrably portrays Luke's "intentional emphasis on justice and caring for the poor and oppressed."[19]

Further, J. M Godwin agrees with R. B. Hays that when Jesus made the declaration that Isaiah 61:1–2 has been fulfilled within the hearing of his listeners at Nazareth,[20] he pointed not only to a "spiritual reality" but also to "a social event." It was a "visible socio-political, economic restructuring of relations among the people of God, achieved by his intervention in the person of Jesus as the one Anointed and endued with the Spirit."[21] All these put the emphasis on social justice.

Again, that both Isaiah and Luke place the poor in the context of people of low class and status is evident in the semantic domain they use. Despite the desperate attempt to spiritualize the "poor" in the Gospel, it is clear that in Luke the poor are not only those who acknowledge their need of divine help and who are disposed to waiting on God and to hearing his word,[22] nor are they only those who "most often respond to Jesus [and who are] open to God."[23] Instead, the "poor" are those who lack physical ability to sustain themselves economically and who are either neglected or have become victims of oppression and other forms of social injustice, as demonstrated in the table below:

16. Dyer, "Good News to the Poor," 106.
17. Afulike, "Luke's Portrayal," 44.
18. Afulike, "Luke's Portrayal," 53.
19. Dyer, "Good News to the Poor," 102.
20. Goodwin, "Social Justice," 4.
21. Hays, *Moral Vision of the New Testament*, 241.
22. Marshall, *Gospel of Luke*, 183.
23. Bock, *Luke*, 1:407.

Luke 4:18	Luke 6:20	Luke 7:22	Luke 14:13	Luke 14:21	Luke 16:20, 22
Poor	Poor	Blind	Poor	Poor	Poor
Captive	Hungry	Lame	Maimed	Maimed	Ulcerated
Blind	Mournful	Leper	Lame	Blind	Hungry[24]
Oppressed	Persecuted	Deaf	Blind	Lame	
		Dead			
		Poor			

When Luke places the poor on top of the list in all but one case, he sets the condition of the poor to be interpreted and amplified by the others.[25] Coupled with their reference to people typically of low status and who lacks honor, the poor in Luke are among the marginalized and defined by lack of social status.[26] J. A. Fitzmyer is thus right to conclude that the poor in Luke's context "represent generically the neglected mass of humanity."[27] Thus Jesus' reference to them was to draw attention to their underprivileged condition rather than their spiritual superiority.

More so, in Luke's writings, references to "the poor" signify persons with economic and/or physical need. Further, the common association of "the poor" with other terms of low status and marginalization significantly connects them as a group to those on the outside of the social order. Joel Green argues that "the poor" should be understood as an inclusive term that comprises any person of low status and on the fringe of society.[28] At the very least, "the poor" are closely tied to such persons and themselves represent those overlooked and often excluded from community. We can then understand Jesus' proclamation of "good news to the poor" in Luke 4:18–19 as a dedication of ministry—at least to some degree—to those on the outskirts of society.[29] In developing Jesus' agenda of realizing the kingdom of God, Luke shows that "practical acts of social justice are

---

24. Dyer, "Good News to the Poor," 109.
25. Green, "Good News to Whom?," 68.
26. Malina, "Wealth and Poverty in the New Testament," 357.
27. Fitzmyer, *Gospel According to Luke*, 250.
28. Green, "Good News to Whom?," 74.
29. Dyer, "Good News to the Poor," 110.

inseparable from the preaching of the kingdom of God and also constitute proper evidence of repentance and piety."[30]

Social Justice in Ghanaian Pentecostal and Charismatic Christianity

E. D. Rios is apt that because of the tendency to "choose between evangelism, personal salvation, and political engagement,"[31] the Pentecostal and Charismatic traditions have been accused of often withdrawing from issues of social and political nature. However, there is a drift towards balancing the equation of emphasizing both socio-political issues and spiritual matters both in the past and contemporary times. Robert C. Crosby writes:

> There is a new Pentecostalism emerging, a more meditative movement, a more social justice movement, more concerned about the outside of the church rather than [what goes on] inside. . . . Pentecostalism is on the verge of becoming something radically new. God is calling His Church to move toward maturity, to demonstrate institutional flexibility, to reveal the power of divine love to mankind.[32]

Rios, interestingly, acknowledges that the "Pentecostal movement has always thrived among the underprivileged."[33] It is often emphasized that "Pentecostal churches turned the janitor into the Pastor and the housekeeper into the Deacon."[34] Thus, prophetically, Pentecostals and Charismatics "challenged power structures and hierarchies, as they elevated the lowly and raised up the oppressed."[35] This approach shows that Pentecostal and charismatic churches have the ability and willingness to stand as beacons of hope and to declare "to surrounding culture that through the power of the Holy Spirit, they made treasure out of what society deemed as trash."[36] In Ghana, Pentecostal and Charismatic leaders such as Opoku Onyinah, Mensah Otabil, Eastwood Anaba, Dag Heward Mills and Sam Korankye Ankrah have all focused on raising leaders to influence churches

---

30. Afulike, "Luke's Portrayal," 41.
31. Rios, "Pentecostals, the Church, and Justice."
32. Crosby, *New Kind of Pentecostal*.
33. Rios, "Pentecostals, the Church, and Justice."
34. Rios, "Pentecostals, the Church, and Justice."
35. Rios, "Pentecostals, the Church, and Justice."
36. Rios, "Pentecostals, the Church, and Justice."

and communities. This feat of the Pentecostal and Charismatic movement is in line with the social justice focus of the ministry of our Lord Jesus Christ, which Luke roots deep in the social justice message of Isaiah. The Anointed One of God in Isaiah whose mandate finds fulfilment in Jesus Christ, was to proclaim good news to the poor/oppressed and to bring freedom/release to those under captivity and imprisonment. Two of the main social justice issues relevant for Ghana that come up in the text of Isaiah 61:1–2/Luke 4:18–19 are: poverty and oppression. The rest of the section touches on the role of Pentecostal and Charismatic churches in Ghana in resolving these social justice concerns.

To begin with, poverty is an endemic and perennial social justice issue in Ghana. Though there are official statistics claiming the steady reduction of poverty and rapid alleviation of it, the reality on the ground show that many Ghanaian communities and individuals still live below the acceptable level of financial and material means.[37] Poverty does not solely reflect a lack of resources. It also reflects the inability to make choices with one's life and for one's family. Again, poverty also reflects the power and domination systems that people have upon other individuals, a kind of power and domination that removes life choices. People need the hope for choice that Jesus brings with his message of the kingdom of God. This requires intentionally embracing the needs of the poor and looking for every means possible to engage them at the source of their poverty and to be a part of a solution to offer them choices in their lives. Most churches, including Pentecostals and Charismatics are aware that some of the struggling poor are attracted to church by the hope of both spiritual and physical transformation that the messages of Charismatic and Pentecostal preachers present. Out of their meagre means they support the ministry of the church trusting that the blessings of prosperity will be theirs so that they can escape poverty. The message of good news proclaimed to the poor and oppressed in these churches must therefore go beyond the spiritual and the motivational to practical acts of lifting them out of poverty.

Irrespective of the bad name it has acquired, the preaching of the "Prosperity Gospel" among Pentecostal and Charismatic churches, challenged the traditional African and Christian assumption that poverty was a spiritual virtue.[38] The Prosperity Gospel, which teaches that "believers have a right to the blessings of health and wealth and that they can obtain these

---

37. Amissah, "Reflection on the Prophetic Voice of Amos," 38–41.
38. Schliesser, "On a Long Neglected Player."

blessings through positive confessions of faith and the 'sowing of seeds' through the faithful payments of tithes and offerings,"[39] created an awareness that everyone could escape poverty. The method and emphasis might have been abused by some church leaders. However, in congregations where it was balanced with teaching on work ethics, biblical business principles and workshops on building entrepreneurial and job seeking skills, the life of members who responded positively, were transformed from almost earning nothing to becoming business owners and hard workers who earned and maintained a living. This obviously fulfils Jesus' ministry of proclaiming good news to the poor.

J. Kwabena Asamoah-Gyadu, whom we celebrate in this collection of essays, has spent part of his academic career and ministerial vocation preaching, teaching and writing on issues that challenge materialism, ultimately calling for a balance in presenting the biblical message on wealth and prosperity.[40] In a presentation at the Lausanne Global Consultation on Prosperity Theology, Poverty, and the Gospel, Asamoah-Gyadu denounced "the theology of materialism." He called on Christians to condemn the gospel and the theology centered on living for "material things as if they were ends in themselves."[41] Asamoah-Gyadu acknowledges the contemporary churches who have designed social intervention programs for the poor. On the whole, however, he argues that "a proper theology that deals with poverty as a social and theological issue is missing."[42] He also warned against the behavior of some churches endorsing, uncritically, "the spirit of materialism," because it raises questions about "what the Bible says about the poor, poverty, and the marginalized in society." Asamoah-Gyadu concedes that "the Bible does not endorse poverty but enjoins those who have the power to do so, to pay attention to the needs of the poor."[43]

So, aside the above caveat, as Asamoah-Gyadu mentions, some Pentecostal and Charismatic Churches have programmes that aim at alleviating poverty. I focus here on the Church of Pentecost (CoP). For its many years of existence, the CoP has produced various forms of interventions to enhance the welfare of its members and also to affect the life of the communities they operate in. The flagship social justice scheme of the CoP is

39. Lausanne Theology Working Group, "Statement on the Prosperity Gospel," 99.
40. Asamoah-Gyadu, *Contemporary Pentecostal Christianity*; *African Charismatics*.
41. Asamoah-Gyadu, *Search for Balance*.
42. Asamoah-Gyadu, *Search for Balance*.
43. Asamoah-Gyadu, *Search for Balance*.

Pentecost Social Services (PENTSOS), which was established in 1980. This scheme is aimed at helping those in need within the church but broadly focuses on disaster prevention and relief services, economic empowerment, health services, and educational support schemes.[44] The church also raises funds throughout its congregations on "We Care Day," to help the poor.[45] Again, the CoP recently launched its five-year (2018–2023) vision, dubbed "Vision 2023." In this new document, there is the objective to revamp and empower PENTSOS to deal with issues of poverty reduction and social justice. One of the new ministries focusing on social issues is the "Ministry to Persons with Disabilities."[46] A documentary shown at the launch acknowledged that persons with disabilities are among the most marginalized in society and called on the Church to spearhead the inclusion of persons with disabilities for the world to follow. The programme as presented during the launch seems to focus on the spiritual needs of these persons with disabilities, without making references to how the church intends to help them to overcome their challenges and be self-sustaining. It was heartening, however, that the person with disability who spoke about how she had overcome her own disability through the grace of God and the help of the church and parents, called on the church to go beyond just presenting the gospel to persons with disabilities, to providing the environment to empower them to overcome their disability and be of a blessing to themselves, the church and the community.[47] If this call is positively heeded, the CoP will be seen to be adding social justice emphasis to the spiritual approach to "proclaiming good news to the poor."

Another major social justice issue that Pentecostals and Charismatics in Ghana need to address is the violence that women and girls suffer in contemporary Ghana. This will demonstrate that the church is concerned about physically liberating the captives as much as they care about their spiritual release. In spite of the many attempts at legal, social and religious remedies, women in Ghana suffer violence and discrimination through Widowhood Rites, Female Genital Mutilation and Shrine Slavery (Trokosi).[48] There are also reports of domestic and marital abuse in Ghana. One of the causes of such violence and discrimination is the perception of

44. Church of Pentecost, "PENTSOS."
45. Nyarko, *Poverty in Ghana*, 81.
46. Nyamekye, *Church of Pentecost*, 64.
47. Church of Pentecost, "Official Launch."
48. Amissah, "Reflection on the Prophetic Voice of Amos," 41–46.

society about women and the rhetoric that goes to promote the abuse.[49] Unfortunately, some Pentecostal and Charismatic Churches' attitude towards women and the utterance of their leaders about women, inadvertently festa these negative behaviors. For instance, Archbishop Duncan Williams, once told women that marriage is a privilege for which women must be thankful and stop misbehaving. He continued that no matter how pretty, beautiful and intelligent a woman is, she will rot in her beauty and intelligence unless a man proposes and marries her.[50] Around the same time, Bishop Dag Heward Mills, mocked Ghanaian girls, asserting that their inability to cook has devalued them to less than 10 percent of what Ghanaian men want.[51] Bishop Charles Agyinasare advised women abused in marriage: "You are not the first woman to be beaten by your husband, and you will not be the last. . . . Rise up with the Word of God and use your spiritual weapons."[52] Akosua Adomako Ampofo is thus right to interpret these statements to mean that these Charismatic church leaders put no value on women outside of marriage and that they present women as having no value within marriage "beyond providing domestic services." At the same time, these comments demand that women must "carry the responsibility for keeping the marriage intact, even at the cost of their personal well-being and safety."[53] This means that the church is endorsing the culturally constructed roles of men and women in marriage that work against the general wellbeing of women and which promotes injustice against women. Again, it is not a hidden fact that the major Pentecostal Churches in Ghana still do not ordain women and that means the leadership potential and influence of women are limited in those churches. All these utterances and attitudes towards women creates the environment within which abuse of women and violence against girls in all circumstances could be normalized. The practical and social justice effects of the good news of release from oppression and captivity seem thus to elude the approach of most Pentecostal and Charismatic churches.

49. Ghana Statistical Services, *Domestic Violence in Ghana*.
50. "Until a Man Proposes."
51. Haward-Mills, "Oh Ghana Girls."
52. Agyinasare, *Till Death Do Us Part*.
53. Ampofo, "Africa's Fast-Growing Pentecostal Mega Churches."

Conclusion

The chapter has established that the context within which the prophet spoke or wrote demands that Isaiah 61:1–2 be interpreted from both spiritual and social justice angles. Consequently, and given the context within which Jesus ministered, his use of part of this text to launch his ministry (Luke 4:18–19) calls for both spiritual and social justice application. In contemporary Ghana, poverty and oppression are some of the challenges to the church. The chapter has discussed the approach of Pentecostal and Charismatic Christianity in contemporary Ghana to poverty and oppression of women, calling for a balance in the interpretation of Isaiah 61:1–2 and Luke 4:18–19. Though there are evidence of a move towards this balance, more need to be done in the area of social justice to achieve that balance. The level of poverty and oppression of women in Ghana demands that Pentecostals and Charismatics proclaim the good news to the poor by going beyond presenting the gospel, seeking their salvation and praying for their spiritual liberation, to put in place more practical actions that will ameliorate poverty and liberate women physically from the oppression they suffer.

Section III

Media, Mediatization, and World Christianity

11

Second Generation Africans and the New Media as Agents of Demystification in the African Diaspora Church

Caleb Nyanni

Introduction

THE RELATIONSHIP BETWEEN RELIGION and media is not new either in the West or in the global south. As society in general changes with the influx of various forms of new media technologies, so has the church worldwide. The rapid growth of Pentecostal and Charismatic churches has been attributed to the power, presence and work of the Holy Spirit. The rise of these churches both in Africa and in the diaspora has been well documented in scholarly and lay circles.[1] Asamoah-Gyadu has argued that central to both Pentecostals and Charismatics is the emphasis they place on the Holy Spirit.[2] Hereafter, I use the word Pentecostals to refer to the various types of Pentecostal movements including their progenies, the neo-Pentecostals and Charismatic movements. Despite the recognition of the Holy Spirit as the main factor in propelling this growth, there is still another silent

---

1. Among the key works are Anderson, *Spreading Fires*; *To the Ends of the Earth*; Kalu, *African Pentecostalism*.

2. Asamoah-Gyadu, *African Charismatics*, 19.

yet potent factor that must be recognized as a coincidental factor in the dynamics of the growth of the Pentecostal movement especially in the last three decades. This is arguably the proliferation and use of various forms of media in the church. The past three decades have seen a rise in the use of media in Africa by many churches especially among the Pentecostals. Over the years, many African churches have adopted the use of one form of media or the other and sought to attract adherents through the media. This advancement and adaptation of the media by the churches is a consequence of the general trend of the use of technologies in Africa as a whole. From the old print media to the rise of the internet and modern forms of media technologies and social media platforms, there is an acceleration of a media revolution in Africa which cuts across the political, social and religious sectors. It is a misnomer to assume that Africa and especially African youth are still behind as far as media and social media is concerned. De Witte's observation captures this concisely: "Driven by technological developments, democratic and neo-liberal state policies, and new global infrastructures and interactions, the media landscape in Ghana, as in many African countries has been dramatically configured."[3]

In Ghana, like other African countries such as Nigeria, the Pentecostal churches were quick to embrace the media as an opportunity to propagate their message. This trend has continued among the African diaspora Pentecostal churches in Europe and the Americas. Recognizing the impact of media on these churches, Gifford asserts that "Christianity is a media phenomenon, to the extent that services are often built round the requirements of television."[4] Similarly, Hackett has demonstrated the dominance of Nigerian Pentecostals' use of the media and its implications with regards to other religions.[5] Meyer and Moors'[6] edited monograph looked at the cultural implications of media in African churches from the 1990s whilst Hackett and Soares subsequently examined how African religions have changed due to the rise of new media.[7] More recently Gabriel Faimau and William Lesitaokana's edited monograph looks at a

---

3. Witte, *Spirit Media*, 41.
4. Gifford, *Ghana's New Christianity*, 32.
5. Hackett, "Charismatic/Pentecostal Appropriation," 258–77.
6. Meyer and Moors, *Religion, Media, and the Public Sphere*.
7. Hackett and Soares, *New Media and Religious Transformations in Africa*.

wider perspective of how new media and mediatization of Africa is affecting religion across various African countries.[8]

All these works have rightly and carefully focused on the rise, use and impact of the various forms of media on the African church or churches. Arguably, Pentecostals lead the way in their use of media technologies in Africa.[9] Unlike the generation before, many African youth now have access to the internet with strong online presence on various social media apps. This has forced some of the historical churches to reluctantly but prudently embrace media technologies in their form of liturgy to some degree. African Pentecostals in the West continue to use the media to great effect in ways that connect them to Africa. Driven by the desire to connect Africans across the borders, the various forms of media are used to close spatial gaps that existed between Africans at home and abroad. Many of these African churches have now got branches in Europe and the Americas who are more connected to the world of media technology. These African-led churches whether established in the diaspora or transplanted from Africa are engaging with the media in ways that connect to their mother church or African culture. Amidst this rise in use of media is the next generation of African migrants in the West who appear to have a different emphasis on the use of the media. This paper focuses on the media as an agent of demystification of church culture among second generation African Pentecostals in the UK. The churches at the focus of this chapter are African Pentecostal and Charismatic churches in the UK.

The Mediatization of African Pentecostal Churches in the Diaspora

The mediatization of society generally refers to the rapid development of the various forms of media[10] and how media is transforming or interfering with societies and cultures.[11] Mediatization of the African diaspora church is target driven. From its adaptation into the African Pentecostal culture, media has been a positive, transformative and potent force in the praxis of the church. Seen as a weapon for the continual fight against evil spirits

---

8. Faimau and Lesitaokana, *New Media and the Mediatisation of Religion.*
9. Asamoah-Gyadu, "African Traditional Religion,"165.
10. Hjarvard, "Mediatization of Religion," 9–10.
11. Mazzoleni and Schulz, "'Mediatization' of Politics," 247–61.

and a tool to evangelize the world,[12] African Christians continue to use the media and the various social media network platforms for personal, global, social and economic gains. This has enabled first generation African diaspora churches to maintain an African identity, grow numerically and financially in the West. Thus, one can visit a church in London and yet feel as though they were in Ghana, Nigeria or Zimbabwe. The media has aided in continuity of practices and liturgy across borders. From doctrine, to fashion, many of these African diaspora churches are a replica of their counterpart church in Africa. Pentecostal media presence especially live streaming and social media is designed to meet the needs of Africans in the diaspora and those seeking a type of African Pentecostal Christianity. For African Pentecostal churches, the added value of having new digital media is the targeted diaspora audience. Asamoah-Gyadu's work on "Anointing through the Screen" highlights Ghanaian charismatic churches and their use of the media as a transnational tool.[13] For example, The Church of Pentecost in Ghana has its own TV and radio stations. Pastor Chris Oyakhilome of Nigeria has his renown Love World Incorporated media empire. Just like the churches in Africa, some of the diaspora charismatic churches in the West pay for TV and radio time on the airwaves in Europe and America. Kingsway International Christian Church (KICC) has its own TV network among the God channel TV stations in UK. Victory Bible Church, All Believers Church, International Central Gospel Church (ICGC), Redeemed Christian Church of God (RCCG), Faith TV among others, are all African based churches which either host their own platforms or buy airtime from major TV networks. More common however, among the diaspora churches is the streaming of live events on Facebook and YouTube channels which is relatively cheaper than buying airtime. These new and cheaper media platforms have drastically increased the African Pentecostal presence in the West. Some Charismatic churches in the diaspora organize special services and prayers online where they invite prophets and other anointed men and women of God to minister to them online. This practice increases the membership and attendances of these churches in the West and subsequently increases their finances.

---

12. Hackett, "Charismatic/Pentecostal Appropriation," 258.
13. Asamoah-Gyadu, "Anointing through the Screen," 21.

New Media and Continuity of African Praxis

The motives for the use of these online technologies by the African diaspora church are encoded in their theology. Mainly, healing, deliverance, wealth and prosperity. The theology of most of these African Pentecostal churches is fixated on deliverance and prosperity. Asamoah-Gyadu has distinguished the theology of the neo-Pentecostals and classical Pentecostals and argued that, whilst the neo-Pentecostals focus on prosperity, health and wealth, the classical Pentecostals have a strong emphasis on holiness and purity.[14] Nevertheless, for most African Christians, the belief in the spirit world and its effects on the material world means that whether classical or neo Pentecostal, Charismatic or neo-Charismatic, the underlying enemy to any form of progress or miracle is the devil and his evil emissaries, notable witches. Even among non-Pentecostal diaspora African Christians, their strong worldview on the influence of the demonic on their lives prompts them to seek help through the use of new media networks. Chigor showed in his research that regardless of their different denominations, Africans are generally inclined to a worldview of spiritual powers and spiritual warfare.[15] His research which included Africans from mainline churches such as Roman catholic, Church of England and Methodist churches showed that in spite of denominational differences, the emphasis on spirits and fear of evil spirits still drives many African diaspora communities to seek help.[16] What is interesting is that, in observing churches such as RCCG, Church of Pentecost, Light house and others, the first-generation members still hold on to their African worldview and beliefs which causes them to use various media networks as a means of getting their spiritual needs met.[17] Hence by connecting to new media technologies such as Facebook live, Africans in the diaspora can have access to their "super prophets" from Africa. Their purpose is to engage the power of God in healing, and the miraculous through the media technologies available to them. Some of the churches do not stream live services but rather focus on live web chats and video calls where they pray for people

---

14. Asamoah-Gyadu, "Anointing through the Screen," 13. See also Asamoah-Gyadu, *Sighs and Signs of the Spirit*, 12.

15. Chike, *Holy Spirit in African Christianity*. See also Anderson, *Spirit-Filled World*.

16. Chike, *Holy Spirit in African Christianity*, 224–25.

17. Hoover, *Religion in the Media Age*, 10.

with various issues. Just like the churches in Africa, the diaspora churches use their media presence to publicize their faith, promote their ministers and ministries and to generally demonstrate the power of God.

Through globalization processes and technological advancement, the African diaspora churches are able to disseminate information and practices, across borders without physically travelling. Whereas tracts, magazines and posters were used to exhibit the existential reality of the devil,[18] African Pentecostals use the new digital media in combat against witchcraft and satanic forces. For most of the first-generation African migrants, their struggles, whether physical, emotional or spiritual do not cease when they arrive in the West.[19] On the contrary, since witches do not need visas to travel abroad, they continue to wrestle with African migrants in the diaspora. In this context, the new media technologies have not necessarily changed the dominant socio-cultural epitomes of the African worldview. Rather the media technologies have become a vehicle which enables continuity of worldviews, appropriation of theology and significantly, a conduit through which African diaspora Pentecostals continue to engage the power of the Holy Spirit in the West. There is no doubt that the media in its various forms are both "shapers and products of culture" and society.[20] This dual perspective on the media means that it is difficult to completely ascertain the impact of media on religion. Indeed, for some of these African Pentecostal churches in Europe and the West, the media has not only changed their *modus operandi*, but it has significantly enhanced their experiential practice of their faith in the diaspora. In his work on *Anointing Through the Screens*, Asamoah-Gyadu describes how the television and radio sets is perceived as a talismanic object through which people receive their anointing and healing.[21] For the first-generation Pentecostals in the West, Facebook, WhatsApp, and YouTube are the primary media talisman. The theology of these churches notably; deliverance and prosperity are spectacular displayed using these forms of media and transmitted across the continents. They significantly highlight the pastors and bishops in their three-piece suits and flashy cars as examples of prosperous believers in the

---

18. Meyer, "Delivered from the Powers of Darkness," 65.

19. Asamoah-Gyadu, "On Mission Abroad," 95; Adogame, *African Christian Diaspora*, 87.

20. Hoover, *Religion in the Media Age*, 10.

21. Asamoah-Gyadu, "Anointing through the Screen," 23.

contemporary society.²² For some of these Pentecostals, the various media platforms have become the vehicle through which they continue to relate to practices of the church in Africa and receive their blessings.

The Second Generation and the Mediatization of the Diaspora Church

The emergence of the second-generation Pentecostals in the diaspora has contributed to the rise in African diaspora online presence and significantly, a shift in the content of some of the activities online. This increase in social activity by the African diaspora church is not only due to the accessibility of internet but significantly, the worldview of the next generation of African Pentecostals in the West. Indeed, the easily accessible internet and variety of media options available to the second generation has exposed the church to an unimaginable parade of online activities which some of the first-generation founders were oblivious to. The power of new media cannot be underestimated. With the rise of new digital media and social media apps such as Facebook, Twitter, WhatsApp, Snapchat, and Instagram, a generation of African diaspora media consumers are emerging who are changing the media scene and hence influencing the sociopolitical, cultural and religious landscape in Europe and the West. The new media technologies are not just merely used to receive information. They are sources of entertainment, a community hub, advisory center, image building tools and for some people, a source of boosting their self-image and creating new identities. These new media technologies such as Snapchat, and Instagram can make things and people appear more attractive and beautiful than they really are without going to beauty studios. Turkle describes this as life on a screen.²³ With life on a screen, people and organizations can develop an identity which they otherwise find difficult to project in real life. Through these media networks they create an image which is attractive and relevant to their consumers.²⁴

The adaptation of the various media networks and platforms has become part of the Pentecostal identity in the African diaspora church

---

22. Hackett, "Charismatic/Pentecostal Appropriation," 264.

23. Turkle, *Life on the Screen*, 5. On the impact of television, see Witte, "Television and the Gospel of Entertainment," 144–64.

24. For discussions on identity and media, see Kitchin, *Cyberspace*; Löveheim, "Identity," 41.

because it does not only advance their international status, but it also gives them an identity as a modern and relevant church. By using media in its various forms, these African diaspora churches remain present, visible and most importantly, relevant in the community.[25] African diaspora churches such as the church of Pentecost in UK, Jesus House-RCCG,[26] and Kingsway International Christian Center (KICC) have websites and social media feeds which highlight their involvement in community events. From Food banks to homeless initiatives and projects for children, young people and the elderly, African-Led Churches in the diaspora are demonstrating through the media their relevance in the society. Jubilee church in London have various community-oriented schemes on their website including support for school uniforms for poorer families in the community.[27] Light House International Church also advertise their community ministries including ministry to prisoners on their website.[28] Salem church in Wembley had this on their blog:

Salem PIWC Youth Ministry Participates in Red Nose Day, March 15, 2019.

> Salem PIWC Youth Ministry is proudly participating in this year's Red Nose Day, to raise funds to help the needy within the country and also across the world. We as a Church firmly believe in supporting our community in every way we can. With much Prayer and Giving, we can together help change the lives of the needy. You can support by donating as little as £1 towards Comic Relief. Deadline for giving is March 15, 2019.[29]

This post, along with the other websites, highlight the churches' intention in being part of national and social interventions. Most of these churches run these community projects which they proudly stream online, publish pictures on their social media feeds using vlogs, blogs, Instagram, Twitter and Snapchat to showcase their work in the community. At the heart of these initiatives and their daily actions are the second generation who do

---

25. Stolow, "Religion, Media, and Globalization," 544.
26. Jesus House is a branch of the Redeemed Christian Church of God (RCCG).
27. Jubilee Church London, "School Uniform Scheme."
28. Lighthouse Church, "Ministries."
29. Feltham PIWC Church, "Salem PIWC Youth Ministry." Salem is a parish of The Church of Pentecost in Wembley, UK.

not only ensure that they are running, but also ensure that they are published in the media. The second generation through new media technologies, are deconstructing an image of the African diaspora church which was primary based on spiritual warfare and aimed at first generation Africans. For some of these diaspora churches, the understanding is that unless they demonstrate their significance in the community through the media, they risk being irrelevant in the community and hence obsolete in the near future. Significantly, the use of these media platforms is purpose driven. With pictures showing multi-cultural congregations, youth on the streets in the communities and city centers, the youth are using various media to demonstrate and construct a new identity and brand of African Pentecostalism which is meeting both the spiritual and physical needs of the western community. The use of media in transmitting religious messages has been seen in various forms of radicalization in recent years.[30] The presence of this new media revolution has significantly changed the way some of these Pentecostal churches in the diaspora present their online materials.[31] Their aim is to present a different image of the African diaspora church in the western society. With the dual combination of new media and second generation diasporeans, the African diaspora church has shifted their attention from presence to relevance on a wider scale in the Western communities. Arguably, as young Pentecostals, the Holy Spirit is working through them via the various media networks.

The Media as a Weapon of Change for the Second-Generation African Pentecostals in the West

Discussions surrounding generational use of the media has been increasing since the incredible rise of the media in the last decade.[32] With easy access to the internet and competitive prices for internet access devices, more and more young people have unlimited access to the internet in the contemporary society. The younger generation are generally seen as consumers of the digital media whose focus has shifted from conventional television, film and radio to internet and social media. From a very young age, children today have online presence. There is no doubt that young people today are exposed to excessive use of digital media especially social media networks

---

30. Moberg, "Concept of the Post-Secular," 103–4.
31. Adogame, *African Christian Diaspora*, 153.
32. Hoover, *Media, Home, and Family*.

and platforms. This extravagant reliance and use of the internet by the second generation of Africans undoubtedly affects their view on religion especially their parents' practices and certain beliefs. Whilst first generation African Pentecostals and charismatics have mainly used the media to connect with various institutions in Africa and including receiving special prayers and ministries from home churches, the second generation to a large extent are using the new media technologies for different purposes. Hoover argues that whilst the consumption of old media such as television and home video was seen as undoing "childhood, family and importantly parental authority," the new media threatens to do more damage to these cultural traditions.[33] Again, whilst the new media is seen as an effective tool and game changer in transfer of information, there is also the underlining fears of those who see certain forms of media as detrimental to cultural and social values.[34] For some first generation parents these fears are genuine as they struggle to keep up with the various forms of media as well as the challenges in seeing their children burry their heads in their phones and gadgets constantly. However, the emerging generations have to some extent been able to espouse the use of new media such as online streaming, social media apps with their cultural and traditional expectations. The increase in the use of media and technology has aided the transfer of cultural practices to a new generation of Africans who were otherwise becoming increasingly detached from some of the traditions of their parents.

There is a sense whereby the second-generation Africans are not only using new media technologies to get cultural understanding from Africa but significantly, they are using it as a tool for exchanging of ideas transculturally. Wilson describes this transfer of ideas transculturally as a "new kind of relativism."[35] This has taken the participation and connection of intercultural ideas to a new level. The second generation connect with churches locally, nationally and internationally through the new forms of media. This participation of the second generation in globalization has enhanced their desire to see the migrant churches evolve and become more multi and intercultural. The new digital media has enhanced the second generation's cultural awareness and exposed them to church liturgy, practices and styles from other churches across the globe. Whilst first generation African migrants mainly use visual media to connect to events

33. Hoover, "Practice, Autonomy, and Authority," vii.
34. Faimau and Lesitaokana, "New Media and the Mediatization of Religion," 3.
35. Wilson, *Religion in Sociological Perspective*, 129.

back in Africa, most of the second-generation Pentecostals go beyond their immediate cultural background. For example, in January 2017 The Church of Pentecost in Ghana organized a global ministers conference for all its pastors worldwide in Accra, Ghana. This five-day conference was streamed online and was accessible to all its members worldwide. I have shown in a survey that most of the people in the UK who watched the live streaming were first generation members.[36] The small number of second-generation members who watched were impressed with the technology but not necessarily the ideas of how church should be conducted. This is because they saw some of the practices as irrelevant for the church in the West.[37] Young Africans in the RCCG, Light House and All Believers church frequently watch mega churches such as Ruach ministries, Hillsong church, Potters House and Lakewood church.[38]

The young and emerging generation log on to live streams from these mega churches in Europe and America to see how they do church services. In this case, the media is still used for both cultural and spiritual purposes but not in the context wished for by their first-generation parents. Through media and globalization processes, the young Africans are connecting with other forms of Pentecostal and Charismatic churches and seeking to create newer forms of liturgy. Elsewhere, I have demonstrated and argued that the influence of new media has fostered inquisitive minds and exposed second generation African migrants in the diaspora to ask questions of their parents' religious practices.[39] The motives behind these questions are often to help them resolve internal tensions of contemporary relevance of some of the practices of their parents in church. The caveat is that for the first-generation parents, the more they watch and connect to programs and services in Africa, the longer their religious and cosmological view remain African. These younger African progenies in the diaspora are however seeking for different ways to organize church that meets the society in which they live. They are using the media to enhance church liturgy such as preaching, singing and announcements or notices. Visits to African diaspora churches where there are significant numbers of second generation shows how they use various media in their church services. The youth use

---

36. I conducted a random survey of twenty first-generation and twenty second-generation members of the church in London. See Nyanni, "Spirits and Transition."
37. For more discussions, see Nyanni, "Spirits and Transition."
38. Nyanni, "Spirits and Transition."
39. Nyanni, "Spirits and Transition."

PowerPoint presentations in their sermons and project songs onto screens. Announcements which often take several minutes by one of the leaders are now condensed into two to three-minute video clips. Others condense them into an image and post them on Twitter, Instagram, and WhatsApp platforms. These are visible demonstrations of second-generation church communities where the youth are seeking to change the way church is conducted. Their ideas are undoubtedly borrowed from other churches through the various media networks.

The second generation's indulgence in new media technologies has also enhanced their evangelistic inventions. The rise of the various media technologies has made the world a competitive place. From the marketplaces to churches, people use the media as a tool to gain attraction and followers. The recourse to new alternatives to evangelism is therefore facilitated and necessitated by the emerging generations understanding of the power and influence of the media technologies. The second generation are using less of the conventional forms of evangelism such as door to door, open air evangelism and distribution of tracts for more sophisticated forms of evangelism. Significantly, they are using the perceived impersonal medium of communication to achieve personal and spiritual results. Second generation dominated churches such as Salem PIWC and Olympic City use their Twitter and Instagram pages effectively as an evangelism tool.[40] They promote their faith, advertise their events and market their churches through social media. For example, Olympic City church advertised their New Year's Eve event on Twitter with these words:

> Join us for our New Years' service tomorrow!! Don't miss out, it's going to be an AWESOME NIGHT!!! We will be entering a new decade, a new year full of Lord's blessings. #newyearseve#2020#NewDecade#OCP.[41]

With social media language and pictures to accompany them most of these second generation are attracting other people to their churches and their faith. Most African diaspora churches that are flourishing have second generation web designers and communicators who operate and manage their websites and social media feeds. The young people engage with their peers and the world through the church's websites, Instagram pages, Twitter feeds and often stream services on Facebook and you tube

---

40. Salem and Olympic City are parishes of The Church of Pentecost in UK.
41. Olympic City PIWC, "Join Us."

live. Through these sources, church programs and events have local and global reach.[42] Some of these churches have social media apps that can be downloaded on mobile phones and electronic gadgets and give real time information. Unlike the first generation whose modus operandi attract mainly Africans, the second generation are using the media to showcase the relevance of the African church in the diaspora. Some churches and faith groups are now beginning to recruit and encourage virtual members who follow them online and listen to podcasts and live stream services. Though this type of church has its challenges and critiques, there is a case for online church in the sense that it is a modern way of connecting people to faith.[43] For example, there is a group of young people in Birmingham who meet in online chatrooms during the weekdays to discuss scriptures then subsequently meet in person once a month for what they call "Link Up."[44] Online communities have led to Cyber churches and thus the potential of breeding more online believers. Whilst this is a challenge to the African culture, which is physical community oriented, the second generation use these forms of media to connect with other churches and Christians and not to necessarily create online churches. The desire for these second-generation Pentecostals to attend church and be present in the services has not diminished.

Arguably, the new forms of media are by nature consumeristic and has the propensity of keeping an individual glued to the screen and yet be part of an online community. The presence of new media enhances what Rosa calls "social acceleration."[45] Social acceleration enhances rapid transfer of information yet at the same time, has contributed to the surge in individualistic alienated consumerism society. Indeed, the new forms of media are challenging the very core of the physical and "presence" community as its known. Though this danger is real and seen among some of the western churches, there is currently no evidence or data to suggest that the African diaspora church is experiencing a decline in church attendance or membership yet. For now, there is very little evidence to suggest that the African second generation are running away from the physical church community or God due to the influence of social media. On the contrary, through these new media

---

42. Adogame, *African Christian Presence*, 156.
43. Murray, *Changing Mission*, 68.
44. Interview with a leader for Church Freaks Birmingham, October 18, 2019.
45. Rosa, *Social Acceleration*, 3–33.

technologies, the second generation are showing new inventive ways of connecting to God, their culture and their communities.

Conclusion

This chapter has shown that African migrants have not shied away from using technology in their praxis and practical experiences. Whilst the print media and television has remained the most used forms of media, new technological advancements in social media networks, such as Facebook live, and YouTube have been particularly used by first generation migrants in the diaspora to connect to Africa. The expectation is that through the various forms of media the people in the diaspora will continue to experience practices and faith similar to what they left back in Africa. For most of these first-generation migrants, the media and new technologies are a blessing if their spiritual needs are met through them. Though the fear of Satan and witchcraft is still prevalent, the use of social media and online streaming services ensures that if their spiritual needs are not met in the West, they can still be met online. The second generation, on the other hand, are using their extravagant access to some of these new social media, such as Instagram, Snapchat, and Twitter, to a more practical and relevant way in the western community. In other words, using various social/digital media technologies, the emerging generation of African Pentecostals express, transmit and project a new image of the church. Unlike their parents whose primary concern was to build a church which was home away from home, the second generation are redefining themselves as a church that belongs to the West. For many of these diaspora churches, the use of both digital and social media has become a permanent feature in their practice and self-identity. I have argued that without denigrating their cultural heritage, second generation African Pentecostals in the diaspora are using the media as a tool to redefine and reinvent the African diaspora church. By using new media technologies and social media apps, they are seeking new ways of doing church and establishing a connection with their communities that seeks to both stake their claim for relevance and attract new people to their churches.

12

Mass Media and the Dynamics between African Pentecostalism and African Neo-Traditionalism[1]

Marleen de Witte

Introduction

Scholars of Pentecostalism have usually studied people who embrace it and belong to it, but rarely those who do not subscribe to it or explicitly reject it. Taking inspiration from Kwabena Asamoah-Gyadu's work on the intimate relationship between African Pentecostalism and African traditional religiosity, in this chapter I present some material from my ethnographic study of a charismatic mega-church and a neo-traditional religious movement in Ghana and their media practices[2] to reflect on the possibilities and limits of "African Pentecostalism" as a distinct field of study. I argue that the increased mass mediation of religion complicates such a framing and compels us to widen our scope beyond Pentecostal churches, movements, and people.

My 2008 study concerns the public manifestation of religion in Ghana, where the synergy of mass media, commerce and democracy has

---

1. This chapter is an adapted version of my article, "Pentecostal Forms across Religious Divides: Media, Publicity, and the Limits of an Anthropology of Global Pentecostalism," published in *Religions* 9.7 (2018) 217.

2. Witte, "Spirit Media."

generated and enabled new religious forms. In Ghana, as in many other African countries, the liberalization of the media in the nineties has produced a new religious environment that is characterized by politics of representation and othering. In this environment I investigated the interrelationships between two mass-mediated forms of religion that are at first sight at opposed ends of Ghana's religious landscape, but on closer inspection show remarkable overlaps: the audio-visual culture of "charismatic Pentecostalism," with Mensa Otabil's International Central Gospel Church (ICGC) and its "media ministry" as a case study, and the public representation of "African Traditional Religion" (ATR) by the neo-traditional Afrikania Mission (Afrikania). Taking as a point of departure that one cannot sufficiently understand the rise of new religious movements without understanding how they influence each other, borrow from each other, and define themselves vis-à-vis each other, I examined the paradoxical dynamics between charismatic-Pentecostal revival and traditionalist revival in Ghana and the role of the mass mediation of religion in these dynamics. I discovered that due to its strong and mass-mediated public presence, neo-Pentecostalism has provided a powerful model for the public representation of religion in general and some of its forms are being appropriated by other religious groups seeking publicity and public recognition, including the decidedly anti-Pentecostal Afrikania Mission. The mass mediation of Pentecostalism, and of other religions, thus has consequences for how we conceive of the study of Pentecostalism in an African (or, in fact, any geographical) context and how we define its object.

In defining and delimiting our field of study, we should be wary not to uncritically reproduce religious self-categorizations and boundary setting. Both "African traditional religion" and "charismatic Pentecostalism" are academic constructs and must be problematized as such. Both designations are also used by leaders and adherents themselves. This does not mean, however, that we can take them for granted. The usage of such terminology for self-categorization and consolidation of religious identities forms part of religious groups' struggles for and over public presence and recognition and is thus inherently political. The definition of "Pentecostalism" is thus never only a theoretical problem, but is intimately bound up with the negotiations by religious people themselves over what/who is Pentecostal and what/who is not. By interrogating such self-definitions and asserted religious boundaries, instead of reproducing them in defining our research subject, we are better positioned to analyse these struggles and disagreements as part of a broader politics of self-representation and religious authentication.

"Charismatic Pentecostalism" and "African Traditional Religion": Beyond Compartmentalization

My choice for studying "Charismatic Pentecostalism" and "African Traditional Religion" together grew out of a certain discontent, although at the time not so consciously defined, with an anthropology of Pentecostalism/Christianity that remained too close to Christians' own emphasis on religious difference to account for the interreligious dynamics and relationships that interested me. I thus framed my project not as a study of "two religions" in Ghana, but as a study of religion as it manifests within and across the frameworks set up by two religious organizations in Ghana's religious field.

Official and popular representations of "religions in Ghana," including the population census, generally slice up Ghana's diverse and volatile religious field into the categories of "Christianity," "Islam," "African traditional religion," and "other." Sometimes the category of "Christian" is further subdivided into "Roman Catholic," "Anglican," "Presbyterian," "Methodist," "spiritualist," "Pentecostal/charismatic," and "other denominations."[3] Such neat categorization of people into religious tick-boxes forms part of the dominant discourse, which people of various religious affiliations also use to categorize themselves (in fact, the census is based on self-categorization). In practice, however, the boundaries between different religious categories are not all that rigid. People's religious itineraries involve moving back and forth and dual or multiple affiliations. Religious practice may vary according to context or specific needs. Religious identification or practice differs between the public and the private realm. Census taking or Sunday worship belong to the former, while visiting a shrine for spiritual consultation and healing is often kept strictly secret. It may not be understood as "religion" at all, and even less as "religious affiliation."

All this is common knowledge among scholars of religion in Africa (and elsewhere). And yet, even if they take the plurality of religious fields into account, they mostly take as their object of study one "religion," "religious group," or "religious movement." Like the people they study,

---

3. The Population and Housing Census of 2000 had a separate entry for "charismatic and Pentecostal," for the first time, indicating that charismatic and Pentecostal Christianity had by then become recognized as mainstream.

scholars of religion also group themselves into distinct academic communities—Islamic Studies, Pentecostal Studies—focusing on single religious traditions. Recent work from the anthropology of religion in Africa suggests new directions beyond such compartmentalization and offers productive frameworks for analyzing religious encounters, cohabitation, and entanglement in broader religious fields.[4] On the whole, however, a labor division structured by difference and distinction between "religions" still dominates scholarship on religion, including the burgeoning field of (global) Pentecostalism.

The spectacular rise of neo-Pentecostal or charismatic churches since the late seventies has been accompanied by an equally exponential growth of a body of scholarly work dedicated to understanding and explaining it. This scholarship, Matthew Engelke suggests, has tended to ascribe to Pentecostalism an exclusive urgency that echoes Pentecostalism's own "loud and domineering" self-presentations, (implicitly) claiming that if one seeks to understand Christianity (or even religion) in the world today one needs to study Pentecostal churches.[5] It may seem too obvious to state that Pentecostal Studies have focused on Pentecostals. It has examined the influence, effects, and significance of conversion to Pentecostalism, in converts' lives and in wider social and cultural realms. Those who study Pentecostalism have thus studied the people who embrace it and belong to it, but not those who do not belong, who do not subscribe to it.

I suggest that the study of global Pentecostalism should not remain limited to investigating Pentecostal churches and movements, and people who consider themselves Pentecostal. It should equally take into account the ways in which Pentecostal and charismatic ideas and forms have their repercussions outside Pentecostalism, on non-Pentecostal and non-Christian religions,[6] on broader popular cultural forms,[7] and on what counts as "religion" or "being religious." The entanglement of Pentecostalism and mass media plays a crucial role here. One of the most significant things about African charismatic-Pentecostal churches that Asamoah-Gyadu's work has called our attention to is their extensive media production and

---

4. Janson and Meyer, "Christian-Muslim Encounters"; Larkin, "Entangled Religions"; Larkin and Meyer, "Pentecostalism, Islam, and Culture"; Soares, *Muslim–Christian Encounters in Africa*; Peel, *Religious Encounter; Christianity, Islam, and Orişa Religion*.

5. Engelke, "Past Pentecostalism."

6. Witte, "Media Afrikania."

7. Meyer, "Praise the Lord."

powerful audiovisual presence in the public sphere.[8] Crucially, the new mass-mediated forms of Pentecostalism do not remain within the boundaries of the particular churches that produce it and their communities, but have produced and circulated paradigmatic formats for the public representation of religion that influence the styles of public performance and media representation adopted by other religious groups.[9] Some recent work on Islam in Africa has hinted at the impact of Pentecostal styles and televangelism on Islamic movements and their media use[10] and suggested new analytical frameworks for studying Christian-Muslim encounters and entanglements.[11] While this work resonates with my own work on Pentecostal-ATR encounters and offers fruitful connection points (to which I return below), African traditional religions have generally been placed outside the realms of public representation, media, and globalization, and hence, outside the influence of mass media Christianity.

In the field of African studies, interesting historical-anthropological work on Christianity has been done that generally has been more sensitive than the newer field of Pentecostal studies to the historical interaction between indigenous religious traditions and globalized forms of Christianity. Studies of older Pentecostal groups and African Independent Churches have thus paid much attention to traditional religiosity and the issue of "Africanization," both "from above" and "from below." Studies of the newer charismatic-Pentecostal churches have also noted continuities with traditional religiosity, and Asamoah-Gyadu's work has offered major contributions in this respect.[12] On the whole, however, studies of neo-Pentecostalism have tended to stress these churches' indebtedness to global Pentecostal networks more than to indigenous religious traditions. Conversely, in studies of traditional religions and neo-traditionalist movements in Africa, attention has been paid to the presence of Christianity, but most studies of traditional religion are ethnographies of relatively closed, rural communities. African charismatic Pentecostalism and African traditional religions are rarely studied together on an equal basis, without treating one

---

8. See, for instance, Asamoah-Gyadu, "Of Faith and Visual Alertness"; "Anointing through the Screen"; "Mediating Spiritual Power."

9. Witte, "Spectacular and the Spirits."

10. Larkin, "Ahmed Deedat"; Schulz, "Promises of (Im)mediate Salvation."

11. Janson and Meyer, "Christian–Muslim Encounters"; Larkin, "Entangled Religions"; Soares, *Muslim-Christian Encounters in Africa*.

12. See, for instance, Asamoah-Gyadu, *African Charismatics*; "Spirit and Spirits." See also Gifford, *Ghana's New Christianity*; Kalu, *African Pentecostalism*.

as the other's "context." The fact that charismatic churches and traditionalists groups appear so intrinsically different in terms of religious doctrines, practices, and outlook, and that they assertively position themselves as each other's opposites seems to have fuelled researchers' foci on single religious groups and their self-compartmentalization into sub-disciplines structured by religious boundaries and difference.

I suggest taking seriously, however, the inextricable intertwinement of charismatic Pentecostalism and (neo-)traditional African religion as part of one religious field with a shared history and partly overlapping audiences and examining the complex dynamics between them. My point is not only that African charismatic Pentecostalism, as part of a global religious movement, cannot be studied outside the local contexts in which it is lived and practiced and upon whose broader cultural dynamics it spreads and grows. It is also that African traditional religion, generally understood as "local," must equally be studied as part of the historical globalization of religion.[13] Just as Ghanaian charismatic Pentecostalism, despite the "complete break with the past" it requires[14] and the very real changes it produces,[15] shows remarkable continuities with traditional religion, neo-traditional reformulations of African traditional religion often show remarkable continuities with Christianity, despite their explicit rejection of Christianity.[16]

Charismatic Christian and traditionalist leaders operate and manifest themselves in a single religious arena, in which they seek to convince widely overlapping audiences of their claims to authority and authenticity. A dual focus on these two manifestations of religion in Ghana reveals the paradoxical dynamics at work in the relation between them: in opposing each other, the Afrikania Mission and charismatic Pentecostalism also become like each other. African charismatic-Pentecostal churches "fight" against traditional religion, yet implicitly incorporate the logic, spiritual forces, and ways of worship of local religious traditions as media through which Christian spirituality is communicated. The Afrikania Mission "fights" (charismatic) Christianity, yet adopts Christian formats in its reformulation of "African Traditional Religion." The entanglement of religion and mass media reinforces these dialectics. On the one hand, the growing public presence of

---

13. Chidester, *Savage Systems*; Witte, "Transnational Tradition"; Ranger, "African Traditional Religion"; Shaw, "Invention."
14. Meyer, "Complete Break."
15. Robbins, "Continuity Thinking."
16. Witte, "Neo-Traditional Religions."

religion extrapolates the antagonism. Religion increasingly becomes a site of public clash, especially between Pentecostals and traditionalists.[17] At the same time, religious mass media generate and disseminate similar religious formats that have a cross-religious impact on the public representation of religion. Charismatic Pentecostalism, being the dominant and most publicly present religion, has become the template for religion as such and, surprisingly, also for Afrikania's public representations.

While the importance of mass media is well recognized in the literature on African charismatic Pentecostalism, not in the least by Asamoah-Gyadu, media have often been treated as "a feature" of charismatic churches, as one of their distinctive "characteristics." In my work I have taken up the question of media, mediation, and publicity as its central problematic.[18] Exactly this problematic, I argue, complicates a demarcation of our field of study as restricted to Pentecostal movements alone. In the field of global Pentecostalism, quite some attention has been paid to how the mass mediatization of Pentecostal and charismatic churches and the circulation of their images across the globe drives the globalization of a particular "culture of Pentecostalism." Indeed, charismatic-Pentecostal performance in Ghana is strongly influenced, through mass media, by the styles of worship, preaching, prayer, dress, body movement, and facial expression exhibited by charismatics and Pentecostals across the world. What tends to be overlooked by this focus on "the global" is how in local religious and media landscapes, such styles move outside of Pentecostalism. Brian Larkin has called this process "the lability of religious form": "stylistic elements that emerge within a particular religious tradition but then are loosened from those origins and circulate into other domains."[19] Larkin's emphasis on religious *form*, my own attention to religious and media *formats*,[20] and Birgit Meyer's notion of a "Pentecostalite style"[21] are all part of a broader turn in the study of religion towards aesthetics[22] that in my view offers a more fruitful angle from which to analyse the dynamics of lived Pentecostalism in broader religious and non-religious contexts than a preoccupation with doctrines and beliefs does. Other religious groups' appropriations of Pentecostal formats and styles, cut loose from Pentecostal

17. Hackett, "Radical Christian Revivalism."
18. Witte, "Spirit Media"; "Religious Media, Mobile Spirits"; "Spectre of the Fake."
19. Larkin, "Entangled Religions," 635.
20. Witte, "Altar Media's *Living Word*"; "Spectacular and the Spirits."
21. Meyer, "Praise the Lord."
22. See Meyer, *Aesthetic Formations*.

teachings, are part and parcel of the culture of Pentecostalism and must be explored if we want to understand the full complexity of how Pentecostalism grows and operates in the world.

Two Movements in One Setting: The International Central Gospel Church and the Afrikania Mission

The two religious organizations that I studied appear diametrically opposed in many respects. With over ten thousand members, its four-thousand-seat Christ Temple in Accra and branches all over Ghana, in other parts of Africa as well as in Europe and the United States, a weekly prime time TV programme and daily radio broadcasts, the International Central Gospel Church is one of the largest and most influential charismatic churches in Ghana. Its leader Mensa Otabil is a public personality. His well-established media presence and flamboyant appearance have given him celebrity status. His "life-transforming teachings" strike chords with a broad audience across Ghana's religious field and he is widely perceived as "the teacher of the nation." The Afrikania Mission is dedicated to representing and reviving "African Traditional Religion" in Ghana's Christian-dominated public sphere and on the international stage of "world religions." In contrast to the ICGC's well-oiled and capital-driven media machine, the Afrikania Mission lacks resources and struggles to find alternative ways into the media. Intended as a counterweight to the Christian hegemony, it presents a strong voice for the defence of traditional cultural practices, but remains rather marginal. Although the movement seems to attract a growing number of followers in rural areas, the attendance of its worship services in Accra, where the movement originated and is still headquartered, is a far cry from the mass spectacles of charismatic worship. Lastly, the emphasis in traditional religion on secrecy and seclusion make Afrikania's relationship to the media and the public sphere a lot more problematic than the ICGC's with its explicit strategy of outreach and evangelization.

But there are also striking parallels between the two groups. Both celebrated their twentieth anniversary in the early 2000s in buildings that paled their humble beginnings in the early 1980s. In a period of political turbulence and renewed cultural awareness, the Afrikania Mission was founded in 1982. Two years later, amidst a new wave of Christian enthusiasm and spiritual awareness, the International Central Gospel Church was founded in 1984. Early meetings were held in a small classroom, but to accommodate the rapidly growing membership a garage, a cinema hall, and a scout hall were rented respectively. In 1996 the church completed its own, huge church hall, the Christ Temple, which it uses for regular services, conferences, concerts and a host of other activities. Meanwhile the Afrikania Mission moved from renting a drinking spot at the National Cultural Centre for its meetings and worship services to building its three-storey headquarters, used for services, celebrations, education, press conferences, and more.

There is also, surprisingly perhaps, a considerable overlap between the visions of the two movements' leaders. Behind the obvious antagonism of Pentecostal anti-traditionalism and traditionalist anti-Pentecostalism they express, both Mensa Otabil and the subsequent Afrikania leaders propagate an explicit message of Africanist emancipation. Both strive for values of African pride and self-confidence, seek to come to terms with the question of Africanness and modernity, and are well-versed in the Pan-Africanist discourse of "liberation from mental slavery." They differ fundamentally, however, in how they flesh out this emancipation. For Afrikania it implies a rejection of Christianity as "inherently foreign," the religion used to "dominate and exploit Africans," and a revitalization of "traditional religion and culture" as the only source of selfhood for Africans. For Otabil, it implies an Africanist re-reading of the Bible and a critical approach to "African culture."[23]

The ICGC and Afrikania also share a complex positioning in Ghana's broader religious field that in both cases produces a similar tension between intellectualism and spirit practice. In the ICGC Otabil's passion and plea for knowledge, education, and critical thinking stands in tension with the emotional expression and concern with spirits of charismatic-Pentecostal religiosity, also within his own church. He criticizes and sometimes even ridicules the spiritualist tendencies of many charismatics and his rationalist message of self-development sets him apart in the field of Ghanaian charismatic Pentecostalism today.[24] But at the same time he also depends (for his celebrity status, for his followers, and thus for his income) on the charismatic wave that sweeps the country. While his message sits uneasily with charismatic practices like exorcism, divine healing, and reliance on divine intervention, he has to tolerate them in his church.

---

23. Witte, "Buy the Future."
24. See also Gifford, *Ghana's New Christianity*; Larbi, *Pentecostalism*.

The Afrikania Mission aspires to be a "church" like all other churches, a "religion" like all other recognized "world religions." In this aspiration, as the next section will detail, it takes over many Christian forms. This "mimetic zeal,"[25] however, is paired with a "distinctive zeal," an explicit self-definition as non-Christian, as an authentically African alternative to Christianity. It fights for the revival of African Traditional Religion against Christian suppression and claims to represent all traditional religious practitioners and adherents. In practice, however, the specificities of particular cults are hard to fit into the "common religious form" Afrikania has created and undermine its "neutrality." Its concern with "cleanliness," "orderliness," and "beauty," moreover, is hard to match with practices like ecstatic spirit possession and blood sacrifice. For the people Afrikania seeks to attract and represent such practices are highly meaningful and powerful. Afrikania's intellectualist and modernizing approach to traditional religion, then, produces a tension not only with religious practitioners outside Afrikania, but occasionally also with those who have joined the movement.

Finally, the leaders of both the ICGC and Afrikania are media enthusiasts and their movements have drawn upon mass media from their beginnings. For both, however, it is complicated to mediate the spiritual power on which their authority and attraction ultimately thrive. It is only at first sight that Afrikania's hampered efforts at media representation stand in stark contrast to the explosion of seemingly unlimited publicity of charismatic-Pentecostal media activity. Both struggle with what I have elsewhere discussed as the problem of spirit presence and media representation.[26] For Otabil, his authority hinges on charisma, on his ability to set in motion what people experience as a flow of Holy Spirit power. This flow risks being broken by the fixity of Otabil's media format. The successful formula of his television broadcast threatens to overrun its own success and even established pastors like him constantly need to authenticate the implicit message that they are not "mere" media creations, but embody "real" and effective anointing from God, that is, divine, not human power. For Afrikania, the perpetual challenge is how to represent in public a religion in which authority is rooted in restricted access to spirit powers, mediated by practices of secrecy and seclusion, and threatened by openness. Its media representations are met with caution by shrine priests for whom images may not remain "mere" representations, but

25. Mary, "Pilgrimage to Imeko."
26. Witte, "Spectre of the Fake."

mediate spirit presence into unauthorized spaces. For both the ICGC and the Afrikania Mission, then, entering Ghana's new media sphere implies a constant negotiation of conflicting impulses.

Mass Media and the Dialectics of Religious Antagonism and Entanglement

How do charismatic Pentecostalism and African traditional religion relate to each other in Accra's religious landscape, and what does the mass mediation of both religions do to this relationship? By studying the International Central Gospel Church and the Afrikania Mission as part of a single religious field with a shared genealogy and a partly overlapping audience, I discovered that the relationship between charismatic Pentecostalism and African traditional religion in this field is characterized by a paradoxical dialectic of opposition and entanglement. In opposing each other and asserting difference, charismatic Pentecostalism and (neo-)traditional African religion not only influence each other, but are intimately bound up with each other. This dialectic is historically informed by the "long conversation" between Christianity and indigenous religions, but gets amplified in the present era, in which religious manifestation is increasingly mass mediated. The mass mediation of religion, which boomed with the liberalization of the Ghanaian media scene in the 1990s, both sharpens religious antagonism and generates religious forms that are shared across religious boundaries.

Both the charismatic and the traditionalist revival movement have been inherently mass mediated from their very beginnings in the early 1980s. In the 1990s, however, the synergy of democracy, media liberalization, and neo-liberalism brought about a revolution in the relationships between the Ghanaian state, mass media, religion, and commerce that fundamentally changed both movements' styles and strategies of public presence and representation. From 1992 onwards, Ghana's formerly state-controlled media scene gradually developed into a plural, liberalized, and commercialized field of interaction. Religious groups, and especially charismatic-Pentecostal churches, made use of the new opportunities for media access this offered. This has intensified religious competition for public presence, expressed in terms of public visibility and audibility, and tensions between born-again Christians and traditionalists in the public sphere. In this field charismatic

Pentecostalism and African traditional religion seem at first sight to be radically opposed in terms of media use and public presence.

The new commercialized media culture of personality creation, spectacle, and dramatization provides particular fertile ground for charismatic-Pentecostal media strategies. Charismatic Pentecostalism, with its emphasis on charismatic leaders, massive crowds, and embodiment and dramatic expression of spirit power, flourishes in Ghana's public sphere, where pastors become celebrities and mass mediated sounds and images facilitate the flow of the Holy Spirit. The success of the televisual culture of charismatic Pentecostalism in Ghana can be traced, I have argued elsewhere,[27] to the elective affinities between the formats, styles, and modes of address of commercial broadcast media and those of communicating spirit power in charismatic ritual. African "Men of God" such as Mensa Otabil tap into the globalized commercial formats of celebrity, spectacle, and branding as a source of power in a local religious context in which religious specialists are perceived to embody divine power. The convergence of these two kinds of power in the figure of the pastor-celebrity enhances his charismatic appeal.

The Afrikania Mission has more difficulty spectacularizing traditional religion and bridging the gap between the practices of shrines and the formats of the commercial public sphere. Having lost its earlier state sponsored radio broadcast to the liberalization of the broadcast media, Afrikania has adopted new strategies for the public representation of African Traditional Religion (ATR) that make it visually attractive for a broad media audience and seek to counter the demonizing representations of traditional religious practices that Pentecostals disseminate. Afrikania's efforts, however, are hampered by lack of resources and dependency on Christian-oriented media houses and professionals. On a deeper level, what complicates Afrikania's media activities is a clash between the requirements of the Christian dominated televisual public sphere, that presuppose certain formats for what "religion" is and should look like, and the dominant formats of spiritual mediation in shrines. The latter are not modes of visual attraction, spectacle, and mass address, but rather of seclusion, secrecy, and concealment. In representing ATR in the media, Afrikania thus has to negotiate with traditional priests and priestesses, who are often wary of audiovisual media.

This difference between charismatic Pentecostalism and African traditional religion is reinforced by their antagonistic position towards each other. In forming and authenticating religious identities, both strongly

27. Witte, "Spectacular and the Spirits."

affirm boundaries, and stress discontinuity and ultimate Otherness. Charismatic-Pentecostal framings of traditional religion as the evil Other find expression in sermons, healing and deliverance rituals, and media representations. Otabil's intellectualist stance towards African traditional religion takes some distance from the sensationalist demonization of it that inundates the popular media. Nevertheless, his message of radical cultural transformation equally identifies African traditional religion and culture as the root cause of Africa's problems. In a mirroring move, Afrikania holds Christianity, and charismatic Pentecostalism in particular, responsible for all evil in Ghanaian society. Only a return to traditional religious systems of morality, crime prevention, and social and spiritual control could save the country and the African continent.

Behind the plane of religious differentiation and antagonism, however, interesting continuities and mutual influences emerge. Particularly relevant here are four shared aspects of charismatic Pentecostalism and African traditional religions, all addressed by Asamoah-Gyadu in his various publications in much greater analytical depth than I am able to do here: first, a religious imaginary that recognizes the direct presence and influence of spirit beings in people's daily lifeworld; second, a practical, thisworldly (rather than otherworldly) focus that is directed at spiritual problem-solving and physical, material, and social wellbeing; third, an emphasis on the role and power of divinely elected religious specialists as intermediaries between human beings and spirit powers (despite the Pentecostal rejection of such mediation) and, by extension, a competition for clients between such religious specialists; and fourth, a bodily regime that values expressive, emotional modes of worship and constitutes the body as the prime medium of interaction with the spirit world. Despite its marked globalism and explicit distancing from African traditional religion, charismatic Pentecostalism thus resonates with much of indigenous religious traditions. This, as Asamoah-Gyadu has repeatedly argued, is crucial to understanding its tremendous appeal.

Conversely, the foundation of the Afrikania Mission and its neo-traditionalist revival can be understood only in direct connection with the historical and contemporary presence of Christianity in Ghana. The very notion of African Traditional Religion is a historical product of the close interaction with Christianity. Continuing this interaction, Afrikania has adopted a Christian derived form and concept of religion for its reformation of traditional religion, despite its fierce opposition to Christianity and its claim to provide an "authentically African" alternative. This "christianization" of ATR included the formulation of a systematic doctrine with religious creeds, holy scriptures, and authorized prophets; the possibility of "conversion" to ATR as a personal choice based on inner conviction; and the practice of Sunday worship service, clearly modelled after Catholic liturgy. Also, the terminology Afrikania uses indicates a borrowing from a Christian idea of what religion entails: church, bible, liturgy, preaching, communion. With the rapid rise and public appearance of charismatic-Pentecostal churches there has been a shift in what constitutes the format for religion. Whereas in the past Catholicism provided the format for Afrikania, more recent practices like public conventions, camp meetings, evangelization, all night prayers, and a general preoccupation with public audibility and visibility have been taken over from charismatic churches. The same type of Christianity that has pushed Afrikania into a more explicitly anti-Christian attitude, now also provides the dominant format for what religion looks like and drives Afrikania to borrow generously from its repertoire of practices and aesthetic forms through which public presence is established in Accra's urban landscape: a highly visible, huge and brightly colored building with a copious office for the leader; conspicuous signboards, banners and posters along road sides; the use of a loudspeaker van for public evangelization; passionate preaching styles broadcast into the neighborhood through a public address system at high volume.

Religious groups' increased use of mass media has strengthened both tendencies of mutual opposition and entanglement, thus amplifying the paradoxical dynamics between charismatic Pentecostalism and African traditional religion. On the one hand, with the adoption of mass media, religious groups establish an ever-stronger public presence. They become more assertive and self-assured while religious differences and antagonisms become ever more marked. Religion increasingly becomes a site of public clash and occasional violence, especially so between Pentecostals and traditionalists. At the same time, the global dissemination of religious messages through television, radio, audio and video tapes and CD's, print media, and Internet sites generates and reproduces similar religious formats not only across spatial boundaries, but also across religious boundaries. Clearly, mass media are more favorable to some religious formats than to others. Through their extensive media activity, charismatic churches have by now become mainstream and established a strong auditory and visual presence in the public arena, thus providing the format for "religion" in general and influencing not only other Christian denominations, but also non-Christian religions seeking publicity. The mass mediatization of charismatic Pentecostalism thus has a cross-religious impact on media representations and styles of performance, as other religions that do not accept or even radically reject its messages, do draw upon its formats of representing religion, albeit with varying success.

In the current religious and media climate, Afrikania employs the media mainly in response to charismatic Pentecostalism's repression of traditional religion and the encroaching "pentecostalization" of the nation. In attracting media coverage, however, it draws on dominant styles of representing religion that are heavily influenced by globally circulating images and sounds of charismatic-Pentecostal preaching and worship and emphasize visual attraction, sonic impression, spectacle, and crowd imagery. These formats of extraversion are at tension with the formats of religious practice found in traditional shrines. Paradoxically, however, the current Pentecostal hegemony in Ghana's public sphere at the same time pushes Afrikania closer to shrine practitioners. Pentecostal churches' emphasis on the reality of African spirits and the ways they offer to deal with them, widely publicized through their media ministries, drives Afrikania to also claim access to spiritual power and allow more room for spiritual practices than in its earlier years. This move also entails an economic aspect of competition in a spiritual marketplace. Operating in a single arena in which religious specialists of various traditions offer similar spiritual services for similar problems is another important dimension of the close and everyday entanglements of Pentecostalism, African traditional religion, and other religious movements.

Conclusion

In this chapter I have examined two religious organizations in Ghana, the charismatic-Pentecostal International Central Gospel Church (ICGC) and the neo-traditionalist Afrikania Mission, as they manifest themselves in the liberalized and commercialized media sphere. This dual focus on two religious groups that seemed at first sight so intrinsically different allowed me to lay bare their complex entanglement. I have argued that in the Ghanaian religious landscape charismatic Pentecostalism and African traditional religion are at once strongly opposed to each other and intimately bound up with each other. The ways in which religion gets mass mediated play an important role in reinforcing both the opposition and the intimacy between them.

On the basis of this conclusion I wish to suggest that, in studying Pentecostalism, in Africa as elsewhere, we must not limit ourselves to studying Pentecostalism per se. We also have to look at: (1) the history and politics of the very category of "Pentecostal" and its boundaries as it plays out *between* religions in broader religious fields, in local practices of religious identification and struggles for public representation and recognition; (2) relationships with other religions, not only from the perspective of Pentecostalism but also from that of those other religions, recognizing that explicit opposition is as much an engagement with Pentecostalism as is subscription; and (3) the spill-over of Pentecostalism into expressions of popular culture and political culture that may not be Pentecostal as such. Limiting our scope to Pentecostal churches may not be the most productive way to do so. By keeping the framework of Pentecostal Studies strong at the core and open at the edge we leave room for the contingencies and surprises that the religious field has to offer and may find significant traces of Pentecostalism in unexpected places.

13

Hallelujah Testimonies

Miracles, Memory, and Mediatization of Pentecostal Performances

OLUWASEUN ABIMBOLA

IN 2017, ONE OF Nigeria's foremost gospel artists, Nathaniel Bassey, kicked off an online worship experience called the #HallelujahChallenge, which has morphed into an annual ritual across social media platforms. Since inception, the viral #HallelujahChallenge provides a virtual empiricism to the emerging patterns of Nigerian Pentecostal mediatization and its reach beyond local space. The dynamics and digitization of the challenge's religious testimonies, archived on the Hallelujah Testimonies Blog and subsequently on hallelujahchallenge.ng, highlight the ways in which religious rituals are also shaping an online culture that gives agency to anonymity and performativity.

Retelling and archiving miracles in such foremost digitized manner also redefine how memory is mediated at both a personal and religious level. I examine how the appropriation of the new media platforms creates borderless, performative spaces for participants who shared testimonies of their miracles as though they were "gathered" in church. By doing a content analysis of the comments on the blog, this essay equally affirms how shared testimonies embrace the representational modes of "spectacularization and dramatization"[1] and the digital expressions of the Nigerian Pentecostal culture and language.

Ọlọ́wọ́gbọgbọrọ: The Symbol of Nigerian Pentecostal Reach and Mission

True to its implicative reference of God within Yoruba's linguistic and cultural interpretation, the #HallelujahChallenge's theme, Ọlọ́wọ́gbọgbọrọ, captures both the problematic definition and categorization of Nigerian Pentecostalism and the embracing, evangelical mission of Nigeria's Pentecostal influence and biblical ambition to reach the corners of the world. Ọlọ́wọ́gbọgbọrọ loosely translates as God whose hand is long enough to reach any length or space.

There are no clear, firm distinctives, structures and/or doctrinal espousers that broadly define what Nigerian Pentecostalism is or is not. I use the term here to demonstrate the peculiar practices of Pentecostalism in Nigeria, which in themselves are not absolute, and the cultural significations, temperaments and expressions it pursues in defining self and meaning. While considerable research on the external and internal shaping mechanisms for the historical growth and contemporary popularity of Nigerian Pentecostalism exists,[2] it has fallen shy of defining what should normatively qualify as Nigerian Pentecostalism. Instead, focus can be on the structural, historical, economic or political makeup depending on the critical basis the scholarly engagement is predicated upon.

In part, like the intended linguistic grasp of the term Ọlọ́wọ́gbọgbọrọ, Nigerian Pentecostalism also extends the contours of its flamboyant, audacious drive to gain international coverage and presence through the effective use of the media. As Pentecostalism became the dominant expression of Christianity across the continent, its explosion was supported by "policies instigated by the International Monetary Fund (IMF) to encourage the democratization, liberalization and commercialization of the media."[3] In the wake of technological advancement, part of the mission to reach any parts of the world has now equally been through the effective use of social media. The Nigerian Christian landscape in its almost six decades

---

1. Meyer, "Pentecostalism and Modern Audiovisual Media," 122.

2. Wariboko, *Nigerian Pentecostalism*; Adesoji, *New Pentecostal Movement in Nigeria*; Marshall-Fratani, "Mediating the Global and Local."

3. Meyer, *Pentecostalism*, 114.

of existence has been characterized by a lot of transformations and shifting internal dynamics. The shift to new media resources is a key component of changing dynamics within the Pentecostal movement in Nigeria.

Social media is conceived as a group of Internet based applications that build on the ideological and technological foundations of Web 2.0, and this allows the creation and exchange of User Generated Content.[4] According to Constantinides and Fountain:

> Web 2.0 is a collection of open-source, interactive and user-controlled online applications expanding the experiences, knowledge and market power of the users as participants in business and social processes. Web 2.0 applications support the creation of informal users' networks facilitating the flow of ideas and knowledge by allowing the efficient generation, dissemination, sharing and editing of informational content.[5]

This definition invariably covers social networking sites and online content communities like Facebook, Instagram, Twitter and Youtube, which became the dominant sites of community worship during the #HallelujahChallenge. The Instagram viewership of the online challenge grew from its opening day number of three thousand to one hundred sixty-two thousand at some point, ultimately averaging over fifty thousand throughout the initial twenty-one-day period. This number switched into millions in total viewership across other social media platforms in 2017 at the beginning of the worship campaign. On Twitter alone, users' shares and posts reached about two million viewers. The image below is Evolve Press' SWOT Analysis of the campaign and virtual numbers:

---

4. Kaplan and Haenlein, "Users of the World, Unite!," 61.
5. Constantinides and Stefan, "Web 2.0," 232–33.

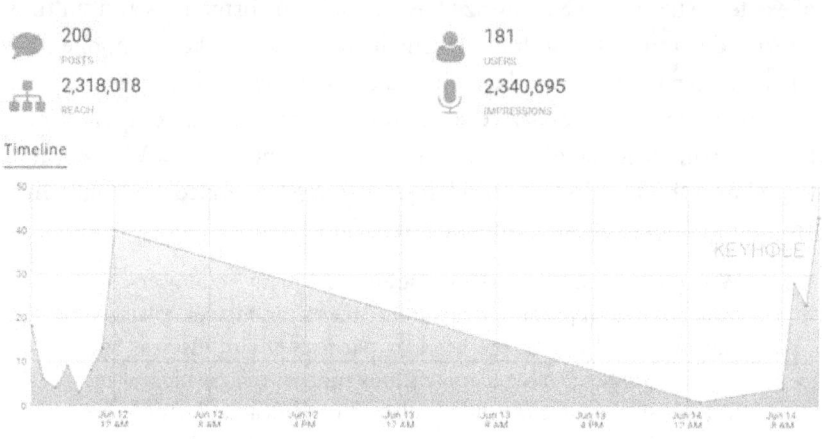

Figure 1. #HallelujahChallenge Twitter Viewers Statistics[6]

A little detour from the missional use of social media for Pentecostal churches, especially in Nigeria, to examining the peculiarities of the #HallelujahChallenge reveals that the new media became more than just an additional source of worship broadcast. It was not just an alternative location; it became the sole location. It was the site of worship. Down to its current congregation, it is still an online church. The #HallelujahChallenge continues to show an archetypal way in which online social networking sites can be mobilized as a worship space for digital church. As an important aside, this also has tremendous impact on the canonization of identity formation among religious adherents and their transnational networks. Nathaniel Bassey's deployment of the social media for the #HallelujahChallenge facilitated transnational connection within a borderless scope that also sought to unite participants across varied spatial, denominational, ethnic and religious ties.

The recent literatures on transnationalism, diaspora, migration and associated concepts reveal a significant and understandable shift in language, concepts, and praxis that reflect the growing influence of cultural significations and global capitalism on transnationalism. Transnational scholars have therefore interrogated theories that emphasize the importance of collective identities, cultural expressions, activities, and social spaces formed by groups with transnational extensions, by exploring their inherent functions. This shift has provoked a reflection and a critical extension of focus on the social, political and economic contexts that create flows. By its

6. "#HallelujahChallenge SWOT."

constitutive instigations, world religions are transnational.[7] If argued from the prism of what is transnational as "any relation which, deliberately or by its nature, constructs itself within a global space beyond the context of the nation-state, and which escapes, at least partially, the control or mediating action of State,"[8] transnationalism extends beyond the signifying context of nation-states which is constituted primarily within physical and ideological boundaries. Instead, the presence of multiple forms of transnational flux informs a reconsideration that convincingly accounts for the linked value and sophistication of "communications and media networks."[9]

While the thrust of this study does not concern itself with the transnational merit of the #HallelujahChallenge, it promotes a discussion on how designated virtual sites of worship become a performative space of multiple identities for users' responsive culture mirrored through the Nigerian Pentecostal languages of I-believe, I-receive and Amen. This reach extends to various nations of the world, affirming a transnational community connected in their religious interests and solidarity. In discussing the implications of social media for migration research, McGregor and Siegel[10] argue the usefulness of social media with regards to diaspora engagement. The #HallelujahChallenge is a critical plank in the (re)imagining of the digital church model, that is non-hierarchical, user-based, and interactive, with viewership and engagement that are not defined within a local, geographical setting. This rhetoric strengthens the conversation about the potential reach of the Nigerian Pentecostal churches ambition to be visible in every part of the globe. How important, therefore, is the mediatization of Nigerian Pentecostal activities in pursuit of that?

#HallelujahChallenge taps into an important Pentecostal culture of religious mediatization in Nigeria. Kuponu[11] believes Pentecostalism is synonymous with the religious media. A key significant factor in the missional culture of Pentecostal churches is the role of the media in their expansion theology. Part of the appeal of the Pentecostal churches to millennials, a term that equally captures most of the membership, is how the production and circulation of media items largely play into an avid media consumer culture that supports the reality of the postmodern age. This sentiment has

---

7. Marshall-Fratani, *Mediating the Global*, 278.
8. Badie and Smouts quoted in Marshall-Fratani, *Mediating the Global*, 81.
9. Marshall-Fratani, *Mediating the Global*, 278
10. McGregor and Siegel, "Social Media and Migration Research."
11. Kuponu, "Pentecostalism and Media."

been explored by several scholars who believe that the popularity of the Pentecostal mission is somewhat hinged on this fact.[12] Exploiting such savviness for religious motivations further undergirds why Pentecostalism is a little ahead of other Christian expressions.

Another dynamic in the expansionism of Pentecostalism is

> the place and role of money in the thinking and formation of founders/leaders as well as members. This new "Christian culture" is concerned with ideas and techniques of generating wealth, prosperity and health for Christians who are not unafraid to name and claim what is rightfully theirs as members of the body of Christ.[13]

Imperatively, it is important not to legitimize an assumption that Pentecostalism in Nigeria is the same as Prosperity Christianity. The attempt at such distinction is to dissociate from the gross attempt at animating all Pentecostal churches in Nigeria with the absolute brush of prosperity gospel. Prosperity Christianity, Yeku argues, "has as its chief aim a morbid desire for the accumulation of capital, which provides an ideological imaginary for the rituals of Christian behaviour that have come to be associated with a large section of Christianity in Nigeria in recent decades."[14]

Historically, Pentecostalism in Nigeria has been informed by a prosperity paradigm of religious worship. Buoyed by the failed economic experiments in the country, the rise, mutation and popularity of Pentecostalism in Nigeria have often been traced to specific moments of postcolonial deprivations in the nation's futile political history. However, emphasis on prosperity has different connotations to different Pentecostal expressions. I will be showing later how the prosperity gospel ties into the emphasis on testimonies around breakthrough, promotion, success and miracles. Here, what is evident within the online worship challenge is how the business strategies and practices that have become symptomatic of Nigerian Pentecostalism are equally mobilized.

---

12. Asamoah-Gyadu, "Pentecostal Media Images"; Ukah, "Roadside Pentecostalism."
13. Kuponu, *Pentecostalism and Media*.
14. Yeku, *Republic of Extraverted Pentecostals*.

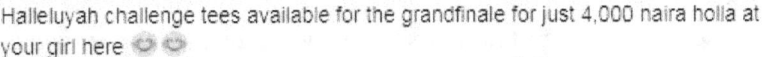

Nwanyi'Oma Retweeted

GbemieO @gbemie_O · 23h
Halleluyah challenge tees available for the grandfinale for just 4,000 naira holla at your girl here 🙌🙌

Figure 2. Branded Shirts Sold as a Result of the Online Challenge[15]

One consistent use of Pentecostal theatrics, events and displays as evident in the picture is how it provides the entrepreneurial acknowledgement and theorization of the profound impact of capital on Nigerian religious imagination. This is not an isolated content. It situates itself within the money bias that drives the Nigerian Pentecostal space. Branded wears, anointed scarfs and handkerchiefs, books authored by pastors, anointing oil, amongst others become transactional items in worship places. As with criticisms that trail such practices and money collections, notably the recurrent tithe debate in Nigeria, the #HallelujahChallenge has been criticized for reflecting the avarice and cosmetic showiness of the physical Nigerian Pentecostal churches. Daddy Freeze, a popular On-Air Personality in Nigeria, who also became notorious for criticizing tithe collection, the flamboyance and money culture in Nigerian Pentecostal churches, described the

15. https://twitter.com/gbemieO/status/874299374196719616?s=20.

challenge as a "celebrity screenshot challenge" and "an unverified testimony challenge."[16] He considered Nathaniel Bassey's appropriation of only good news at the time of the #HallelujahChallenge to the challenge as a reflection of selective truth and dishonesty. Daddy Freeze also represents the growing voices in Nigeria that have become loudly critical of the money culture of Nigerian Pentecostalism which shapes the psychology of disdain of an average Nigerian to matters of honesty and work ethic.

It is useful to interrogate here how criticisms have also been weaponized and given agency in the evangelical mission of the church. When Pentecostal leaders are often criticized or challenged about their doctrines and wealth, a biblical phrasal reference, "touch not my anointed," is used to absolve them from being held accountable. This lack of accountability is explored by Olson in what he calls the dark side of Pentecostalism.[17] Nigerian Pentecostal Christianity is oxygenated by revivalism and politics that insulate itself from accountability. In January 2017, for instance, the boss of the Financial Regulatory Council, the body vested with financial regulation of corporations in Nigeria, was fired for weighing heavily, albeit widely adjured contentious, on the need for tenure leadership and financial probity in corporate and religious institutions. The most popular and revered Pentecostal pastor in Nigeria, with 23,880 separate parishes in Nigeria and established congregations in 165 countries around the world,[18] had to reluctantly step aside and subsequently expressed his displeasure at this development amplifying his suspicion of political coloration. He thereafter asked his members to join political parties in order to influence the decision-making process. The next day, the FRC boss was sacked by the presidency, or perhaps "melted," for "moving too close to the sun." This signals the power wielded by Nigerian Pentecostal leadership vis-à-vis the political economy of their actions.

In highlighting the lack of accountability as a factor in his seven aspects of Pentecostalism dark side, Olson also bemoans the culture of uncritical loyalty and anti-intellectualism as dominant tropes in its governing philosophy. While Nathaniel Bassey did not play into the categorization of his challenge as an exclusive Pentecostal activity, the church he identifies with, the Redeemed Christian Church of God (RCCG), represents a core, prominent part of the Pentecostal voices and cultures in Nigeria. In his response to criticisms of the challenge, Bassey says:

16. "Daddy Freeze Hit at Nathaniel Bassey."
17. Olson, *Dark Side of Pentecostalism.*
18. Ukah, "Roots and Goals."

Jesus, our Lord and saviour, was criticized a lot and no one on earth has been criticized as much as Jesus Christ. What it does is that it puts us in good company. I am sure when Martin Luther King said he had a dream, people thought he was crazy. Criticisms come with our faith. I think with the way God works, all the criticisms only helped the project grow because it made people curious. What the devil meant for evil worked to our favor. The criticism has actually done a great awareness for what we are doing.[19]

Bassey had intelligently invoked a unique Pentecostal disposition to deflect having conversations about the validity of the criticisms against his worship movement. Pentecostal Christianity is often critiqued as emboldening emotionalism, escapism, and naivety amongst the followers. The conventional reactive culture is reflected in Bassey's choice of words and allusions to suggest that the ultimate triumphalism of Pentecostal Christianity's works trump the motivation behind the criticisms that attempt to define the strength of their reach and mission.

Mediatization of Hallelujah Testimonies

In Nigerian Pentecostal space, one of the most circulated texts for media visibility is the testimonies of the miraculous. It functions within the commercialized media culture of spectacle and the dramatic. In spreading the images of success for public visibility and audibility, it taps into a secularized, celebrity culture of branding and language of power for popular, charismatic appeal.[20] However, beyond the spectacle is the inherent purpose of a wider audience reach with what is normalized as the religious message of hope and faith. Moving from the dramatic to the specificity of community is how language is mobilized via the media to shape religious imagination as component features of popular culture. The relationship of the new media to religion is expanded in determining the intersectionality of Pentecostal practices with digital culture and new media technologies. This denarrativizes the independent roles of the new media in (re)producing socio-cultural and religious discourses. It speaks to the fact that cultural environments of the media, most specifically here, both digital and social media, "have taken over many of the

---

19. Olonilua, "Criticisms Made Hallelujah Challenge Bigger."
20. Meyer, *Pentecostalism*; Lynch and Lövheim, "Mediatization of Religion Debate."

social functions of the institutionalized religions, providing both moral and spiritual guidance and a sense of community."[21]

The long-term consequence is a mediatization process that legislates a novel approach to understanding and projecting cultural mnemonics. Hjarvard[22] argues that mediatization is the processes through which the various institutions of culture and society (family, politics, religion, etc.) become increasingly influenced by the media and their logics—a word he uses to represent the media's various technological, aesthetic, and social modus operandi.

This is peculiarly important because Nigeria is not immune from traditional media censorship that often changes with the disposition of every government to issues of news and information sharing. There was a high-profile case in 2004 brought against the Nigerian Broadcasting Commission (NBC) by a popular Pentecostal church, Christ Embassy, to oppose the NBC's attempt at that time to stop miracles broadcast. It is such restrictions and potential politically viewed censorship that is almost absent in respect to the new media. The #HallelujahChallenge does advance the democratization of the new media as people gleefully wrote about their miracles without restrictions or censorship. The critical assumption of this thesis is that the presence of new media has generally informed changes in the ways conventional Charismatic and traditional beliefs, norms and practices are expressed, with new forms of interpretation and understanding. Many popular Pentecostal churches in Nigeria broadcast programs on TV and radio stations to show the triumph of God's power and spiritual gift of healing over medical, physical, academic, social, marital or spiritual challenges. The language of supernatural encounters is couched in phrases like "Atmosphere of Miracles," "Healing Hour," "Night of Wonders," etc. This Pentecostal culture of sharing testimony premised on miracles experienced while in Christian worship is now extended to the new media as represented with the #HallelujahChallenge.

An important characteristic of the digitized testimonies from #HallelujahChallenge is anonymity of persons telling their testimonies. Unlike in physical churches where putting a face to a testimony is deliberately preferred to validate the authenticity of claims, not necessarily through critical channels of verification, the request for anonymity by participants reshape the attributes and character of testifiers on new media platforms.

21. Hjarvard, *Mediatization of Religion*.
22. Hjarvard, *Mediatization of Culture and Society*.

"Please, keep (me) anonymous" mostly precedes personalized narrations of testimonies sent to the convener of the challenge for public sharing on his personal social media accounts. On the question of anonymity, it is important to make a distinction between the shift from social media posts to the blogs under engagement here. No doubt, social media platforms have been dogged with criticisms of lack of privacy, but the conceptualization of anonymity precludes the extension of privacy as conceived in how user information is used and appropriated. Anonymity is not entirely an alien Christian culture despite the thriving Pentecostal culture of showmanship and visuality. Brachear quotes what St. John Cantius parish leaders once wrote in the church's bulletin saying, "[Facebook] is exactly the opposite of the Christian culture where people go into the secrecy and sacredness of the confessional to blot out their sins forever."[23] Such tradition could suggest that anonymous sharing is a preferred, popular choice among social media users.[24] Here are some of the randomly selected texts from the challenge's archived testimonies:

Anonymous said...

At exactly 7:12 a.m. of June 9, I received a disqualification mail from one of the applications I did, one of the highly competitive leadership fellowship in Africa—Young African Leaders Initiative by former president Barack Obama.

I knew quite well that I don't deserve the disqualification so I mailed them to request for the reasons and criteria used in selection but I got a mail that "they were sorry and all." I was pained and disturbed, then I spoke with one of my friends from South Africa about what I was going through, so she reminded me that Prayer and Fasting does a lot in successful applications, so I planned a prayer and fasting session for myself. After the first day of prayer, another friend of mine introduced me to the #halleluyahchallenge by Nathaniel Bassey and that she prayed for me already during her prayers, so I joined the following night June 13, I enjoyed it and I became optimistic about my testimonies, and the following night I did desame.

Today, June 15, after I had my regular one hour noon prayer too, I had a nudge to check my mail but I forgot, at past 3 p.m., I remembered and checked, and to my amazement, the foundation

---

23. Brachear, "Facebook and Christianity a Bad Mix."
24. Zhang and Kizilcec, "Anonymity in Social Media."

mailed me with a congratulatory message that I have been selected and I will be travelling by July 31.

This testimony is humbling because I have gotten a disqualification mail already. It's very unusual and I give God the glory that I have made me received my own share of the many miracles of #OneHourHalleluyahChallenge and I know this is just the beginning because Olowogbogboro has just started with me. Also I received another mail for the scholarship I applied for that I have been selected too for the first round and I know God will perfect it. This is Olowogbogboro ti'nyo omo're l'ofin aye!

I know you will read this when you are online, but if there's a mail for testimonies, I can as well forward all my testimonies there because I am going to have a landful of wonders and miracles!

Thank you pastor Nat!

Halleluyah!!!
#Olowogbogboro
#halleluyahchallenge
June 15, 2017, at 12:56 p.m.

Anonymous said . . .

Something was bothering me very much this week, especially yesterday, my brothers, both in their final year. The first one had issues with his exams and he's doing a re-sit that ends today and the other one that lives with me, because I travelled on work assignment, he was by himself at home and he slept off and missed his exam and even though his PMC (personal mitigating circumstances) was accepted, he was placed to write it in August, meaning his result won't be out until September which will affect his grad school offer so asides Nigeria and a few other things, they have been my prayer request. To cut the long story short, the one that lives with me called me that even with the exam he missed, the result came out today and somehow he still finished with a first class and is allowed to graduate.

So he can go and tell the school he doesn't need to write the exam again and no effect on grad school. Just waiting for the second one now

June 15, 2017, at 1:16 p.m.[25]

There is a constant thread in the shared testimonies, a religious imaginary that identifies an unseen hand (*Olowogbogboro ti'nyo omo're l'ofin aye*)

---

25. All testimonies are from Bassey, "#HalleluyahChallenge/Testimonies."

behind the miracles. The domain of the miraculous for these anonymous testifiers become an interrogative concern for the objective, amused observer. If indeed the testimonies are verifiable, what is miraculous about a reversal of fortune that is a disservice to the integrity of a process? Why should anyone pass an examination they never sat for? How about the triumph of basic civics and religious doctrines of honesty in exposing cheating? This plays into a nuanced symbolism of expression, the Pentecostal language of testimony, framed within that theatrics of the absurd that dispossesses active performers and audience of that community of a possible, alternative reality. The site of any different reality is non-existent aside the God who *did it just like that*. It is the intentionality of participants of the challenge to revisit and transfer words of such symbolic formulations of the practice of sharing these testimonies to new media that suggests how language of Nigerian Pentecostal Christianity simultaneously survives and collapses differing spaces.

> *Anonymous said...*
>
> *Praise God. I joined the hallelujah challenge on the 13th. Before that my nephew had been down for some days and I wrote down on a piece of paper for his healing, placed it on the floor and danced over it all through the one hour. And just like that, the Olowogbogboro restored his health by the time he woke up that morning. This God is too good ooo*
>
> *June 15, 2017, at 2:02 p.m.*
>
> *Anonymous said...*
>
> *This God is too good oooo. . . . I joined the halleluyah challenge on Friday and praised God with all my soul. At exactly 1 a.m. the live video ended but something in me just said I should check your profile and I saw it still continued. Immediately I clicked on it you faced the screen and said that person that is planning to squat that just like that God will provide accommodation immediately I keyed into that prophecy for my patner and told God that how it will happen I don't want to know, that by this week latest nextweek tuesday I want it to be settled. AND JUST LIKE THAT HE DID IT. this afternoon I got a call that a check has been issued to him an amount that will get a house and even furnish it. . . . This our God is true to his word. . . .*
>
> *June 15, 2017, at 3:23 p.m.*

SECTION III: MEDIA, MEDIATIZATION, AND WORLD CHRISTIANITY

> Anonymous said . . .
>
> *And just like that He did it! Thanks to God who has stretched out His mighty hands towards me. Olowgbogboro!*
>
> *Yesterday evening for the first time I took part in the Hallelujah challenge during which we were asked to make a request to God and ask Him to stretch out his hands into our situations. I asked a lot of things and in the morning eight hours at the end of the worship I received a job offer! But not a simple one. I am amazed at how the Lord aligned things for me. The salary was very good. It is the first permanent contract I have been offered so far and the office is like fifteen minutes away from my house. before getting the offer I was wondering "oh if they offer me the job, how do I take time off for my exams?" "Should I tell them now that I will not be available before August while I was told they absolutely need the applicant to start early July." I even started looking for another position somewhere. And this is where God does His magic: when I got the job offer, I was told that I needed to start asap but no later than August 1!!! Like really???? Only God!!!*
>
> *Now I pray God seems me through during my exams.*
>
> *No words to express how I feel now. But Glory Glory Glory to God alone!!!*
>
> *Hallelujah!!!!*
>
> *June 15, 2017, at 3:40 p.m.*

"Just like that" is a metaphor of the language of miracles in Nigerian Pentecostal churches. This metaphor manifests itself in shades of phrases and words that promote the understanding of God rooted in a cultural worldview in view of valorizing instantaneous miraculous. This language fits the postmodern economic culture of urgency; the fast-paced generation in search of meaning and answers. The vocabulary of Nigerian Pentecostalism imports, reformulates and transposes the phrasal indications of the psychology of the society to connect with the struggles and experiences of its members. These sentiments are expressed in the testimonies accompanied by animated emotions; often represented, in writing, with multiple exclamatory signs to show overt exhilaration and enthusiasm. The Hallelujah Testimonies split references of miracles as: Fruit of the Womb| Healing| Promotion| Protection| Provision| Turn Around| Other Testimonies| Screenshots|. The media is not just being used for communicative practices, a transplantation of a critical practice and culture of the Pentecostal church is rather being given virtual structure and agency.

Figure 3. Posts from the Hashtag Trend for #HallelujahChallenge over the Years on Twitter[26]

How is the archiving of these testimonies central to preserving the memories of both the experience and the shared community? I operationalize the use of memory here as I had argued elsewhere:

> A lay way to advance the argument of memory is to consider how we preserve information. This links with the role written texts facilitate in canonizing memory and cultural templates. This inevitably speaks to the preservation of a culture's ethos, values and

26. https://www.twitter.com/hashtag/hallelujahchallenge.

worldview through orality, whether it is primary or secondary. Memory, therefore, is conserved through the textual preservation it enjoys. Text, in this sense, goes beyond the traditional perception of it as every utterance or set of utterances fixed by writing; it represents also every resource that legitimizes memory conservation and a people's identity.[27]

My attempt was to show that canonical attempts of oral resources can inform how memory is mediated, especially through songs and folklores. I am equally arguing that beyond how media memory is conceptualized, in view of how media is deployed to narrate the collective pasts, in retelling testimonies of personal miracles during the #HallelujahChallenge, the challenge provides the virtual space for memorialization of religious rituals. Memory is incentivized through an archival attempt online to practice and preserve a major Pentecostal tradition. Pentecostalism thrives on the full gamut of "sharing testimonies." The Hallelujah Blog and website gave an extension to an erstwhile temporal and spatial practice, which grounds a sense of solidarity and understanding within the community of testifiers. This reflects the conceptual understanding of collective memory. The importance of the point being made here is that, unknown to the convener and participants of the challenge, they were sustaining and preserving a representational practice, of a community with shared beliefs and values, that has somewhat become institutionalized within Pentecostal rituals.

Conclusion

The impact of the #HallelujahChallenge echoes the tension of the Nigerian Pentecostal space in competing with pop culture. Pentecostal Christianity in Nigeria has been a major vehicle for, and at other times against, civic agency and socio-political consciousness. It carves a reputation for itself as a key aspect of Nigeria's popular culture, offering a scope for identification which extends far beyond local culture. This has major implications for many strictures in how development is conceived, and the language that shapes conversations in politics, social relations, inter-religious affairs, gender roles, work ethics and household economics.

The assumption that the Pentecostal republic represents an integral part of Nigeria's democratic process[28] is statistically backed by its growing

---

27. Abimbola, *Legend of Ajala's Travels*, 57.
28. Obadare, *Pentecostal Republic*, 5; Katenga-Kaunda, *Pentecostalism as a Political*

membership. Another pointer is to the enormous power of social engineering invested in Nigerian Pentecostal leaders which is premised on the popular respect they enjoy from their adherents. This positions the churches and various transnational expulsions as significant players in the construction of national narratives, regional alliances or global political economies. But much more, this tension is more of a testament to the Nigerian Pentecostal flexibility to evolve in realignment with the realities of a changing world. With every wave of its development, the constant shift continues to support a framework of transition in current negotiation of its religious place and practice in the context of a digital world. The #HallelujahChallenge provides the digital evidence of an online religion that can relive, and as well as reshape, the localized culture of Pentecostal Christianity with the spectacularization that defines it, without dwarfing its mission to win and cover the earth.

Movement.

Section IV

African Pentecostalism in Context

14

"Rise Up and Walk!" The Role of Pentecostals in Economic Development and Poverty Eradication

Philomena Njeri Mwaura

Introduction

SINCE THE MID-2000S, SOME African countries have experienced tremendous economic, social and political transformation. These include; widening of democratic space, infrastructural development and growth of their Gross Domestic Product (GDP). At independence, every country in Africa had visions of how they would rid their people of the three enemies of development namely; poverty, disease and ignorance. For most, this vision of the good life or development was to be achieved by the year 2000; when most households would have tap water, free education for their children and free health care. Close to sixty years later, for most countries, there are still glaring economic iniquities and inequalities among the populace.

According to a United Nations Report,[1] while global poverty rates have been cut by more than half since 2000, one in ten people in developing nations are still living with their families on less than two dollars a day. While significant progress has been made within eastern and south-eastern Asia, up to 42 percent of the population in sub-Saharan Africa continue to live below the poverty line. In Kenya, according to a World

---

1. United Nations, "Ending Poverty."

Bank Report,[2] poverty is still high at 29.9 percent. The same report observes that, at the rate of 1 percent reduction rate of poverty per year, Kenya cannot reduce poverty by 2030.[3]

Globally, there are 122 women aged 23–34 years living in extreme poverty for every 100 men. Many such poor people are found in fragile and conflict prone areas. Though the Sustainable Development Goals (SDGs) number eight talks of promoting sustained, inclusive and sustainable economic growth; full and productive employment and decent work for all; reports from the UN indicate that the situation is still dire. In Sub-Saharan-Africa, unemployment is still rife and women still get lower salaries than men for equal work. In Africa, over 60 percent of the workforce are engaged in the informal sector, including agriculture. According to the United Nations, this situation of poverty and unemployment continues to fuel crime, lack of food security and rural urban migration and out migration to countries of the Northern hemisphere in search of better livelihoods. The SDGs which articulate Agenda 2030, are an effort by member nations of the United Nations to transform the lives of their people socially, economically, politically and environmentally by 2030.

In view of the above, this chapter poses the following questions: What notions of development inform development initiatives at the global and national levels? What does development and sustainable development mean? How is religion related to development and what are Pentecostals in Africa doing to promote the well-being of their congregants in an integral way? What ideas or theologies inform their approaches to development? To respond to these questions, let us briefly examine some theories/notions of development since the twentieth century.

Some Notions of Development

Giovanni E. Reyes[4] postulates that development is a social condition within a nation, in which the needs of its population are satisfied by the rational and sustainable use of natural resources and systems. This utilization of natural resources is based on technology, which respects the cultural features of the population of a given country. He further says that, development in this sense includes the specification that; social groups have access to organizations,

2. World Bank, *Kenya Economic Update.*
3. World Bank, *Kenya Economic Update.*
4. Reyes, "Four Main Theories of Development," 2.

basic services such as education, health services, and nutrition and above all else, that their traditions are respected within the social framework of a particular country.[5] In an economic sense, development implies that, a given population of a country has access to employment opportunities, satisfaction of basic needs and fair distribution of resources. Development therefore is multifaceted and covers as well the political, cultural, environment, gender equity and equality and other aspects.

Sustainable development in a simple sense, is a way for people to use resources without the resources running out. It implies doing development without damaging the environment. Development with sustainability, meets the needs of the present without compromising the ability of future generations to meet their own needs.[6] This concept, has been in existence in the West for centuries. "Modernization, "westernization," and especially "industrialization" are other terms often used while discussing economic development. Economic development also has a direct relationship with the environment and environmental issues. Whereas economic development is a policy intervention that aims at improving the economic and social well-being of people, economic growth is a phenomenon of market productivity and rise in Gross Domestic Product (GDP). Consequently, as economist Amartya Sen points out, "economic growth is one aspect of the process of economic development."[7]

Some Theories of Development

There are several theories of development. I will however, only focus on modernization and globalization theories.

Modernization Theory

Modernization theory was used in the 1950s and 1960s to explain the process of modernization/progress within societies. It refers to a model of a progressive transition of societies from a "pre-modern" or "traditional" to a "modern" society. Modernization theory originated from the ideas of German sociologist Max Weber (1864–1920), which provided the basis for the modernization paradigm developed by Talcott Parsons

---

5. Reyes, "Four Main Theories of Development," 2.
6. Musoni, "African Pentecostalism and Sustainable Development," 76.
7. See Sen, *Development as Freedom*.

(1902–1979). The theory looks at the internal factors of a country while assuming that with assistance, "traditional" countries can be brought to development in the same manner more developed countries have been. Modernization theory disappeared and made a comeback after 1991, but remains a controversial model.

According to the Modernization theory therefore, modern societies are more productive, children are better educated, and the needy receive more welfare. According to Smelser's analysis,[8] modern societies have the particular feature of social structural differentiation, that is to say a clear definition of functions and political roles from national institutions. He further argues that, "although structural differentiation has increased the functional capacity of modern organizations, it has also created the problem of integration, and coordinating the activities of the various new institutions."[9] The major assumptions of the modernization theory of development basically are:

Firstly, modernization is a phased and homogenizing process. In this sense we can say that modernization produces tendencies towards convergence among societies. This means that as time goes on, societies will increasingly resemble one another because the patterns of modernization are such that; the more highly modernized societies become, the more they will resemble one another. Secondly, modernization is a westernization process. These nations are viewed as having unmatched economic prosperity and democratic stability. Thirdly, modernization is an irreversible process and once started, it cannot be stopped. Modernization is also perceived as a progressive process, which in the long run is not only inevitable but desirable. It is also a lengthy process that evolves, and not just a revolutionary process, but also transformative. This theory was based on Rostow's[10] model of five stages; traditional society, precolonial take off, the take-off process, the drive to maturity, and high mass consumption society.

Modernization was prescribed to the developing countries as a recipe for development. It was assumed that if their problem was productive investments, then they should be given aid in forms of capital, technology and expertise. This approach to development was faulted for being ethnocentric and aiming at eliminating traditional values. Nevertheless, on a positive note, it enhanced the importance of the individual and provided access to opportunities to marginalized groups. It is worth noting that many development

8. Smelser, *Towards a Theory of Modernization*, 268–74.
9. Smelser, *Towards a Theory of Modernization*, 26.
10. Reyes, "Four Main Theories of Development," 3.

approaches which have been prescribed to Africa and other developing countries have not worked as anticipated. A case in point are the Structural Adjustment Programmes, the Poverty Reduction Strategy Paper, rights approach, Gender and Development and many others since the 1980s.

Globalization Theory

This theory emerged from global mechanisms of greater integration with particular emphasis on the sphere of economic transactions. This theory also had focus on cultural elements and their communication worldwide. In this cultural communication, one of the most important factors is the increasing flexibility of technology to connect people around the world. According to Reyes,[11] the main elements of globalization theory are:

1. Recognition that global communications systems are gaining an increasing importance every day and through this process, nations are interacting every day and much more frequently at the government and citizenry level.

2. Communication systems are operating not only among the developed nations but among the poor ones as well.

3. That modern communication systems implies structural and important modifications in the social, economic, and cultural patterns of nations: "In terms of the economic activities, the new technological advances in communications are becoming accessible to small businesses as well. This situation is creating a completely new environment for carrying out economic transactions, utilizing productive resources, equipment, trading products, and taking advantage of the 'virtual monetary mechanisms.'"[12]

4. Globalization theories emphasize cultural factors as the main determinants which affect the economic, social and political conditions of nations. From this perspective, the systems of values, beliefs and the patterns of identity of dominant or hegemony and the alternative or subordinate groups within a society; are the most important elements to explain national characteristics in economic and social terms.

---

11. Reyes, "Four Main Theories of Development," 10.
12. Reyes, "Four Main Theories of Development," 10.

Globalization has been perceived as advantageous due to its widening of opportunities for business among nations, employment and education, flow of information, increase in trade, equal opportunities in relation to the global north. This theory has been faulted due to its ethnocentrism and attempts to homogenize the world and perpetuate domination of the poor by the rich; and eliminating identities and differences among people. It also has negative economic ramifications for the poor countries.

Some scholars like Paul Gifford attribute the rise of neo-Pentecostal churches in Africa to the effects of globalization, through the flows of information from the north to the south and as a response to the economic hardships of the 1990s. Gifford further argues that, African Neo-Pentecostalism is an import from global Pentecostalism. African scholars of Pentecostalism like Kwabena Asamoah-Gyadu,[13] Ogbu Kalu and Afe Adogame, have challenged this view. They argue that the message of global Pentecostalism especially on prosperity resonates well with traditional African notions of the good life and power.

Having explored the concept of development, let us examine what religion entails and how it relates to development.

Religion and Development

According to Gerrie ter Haar,[14] knowledge of religion and theologies of particular religions is crucial to understanding why religious believers act the way they do with positive and negative consequences for development. She further observes: "Many of the major flaws in the development process have arisen from failure to come to grips with the metaphysical questions concerning human life which provide the framework for any meaningful debate about the aims of development and how to understand and measure progress or the nature of the good life."[15] Religion has several important resources that can be harnessed for development purposes (i.e., social, moral and spiritual capital). Religion provides powerful emotional symbols of group identity which bring people together. Religion has the potential to liberate, empower and restore people's dignity. It supplies a special kind of moral anchorage which society yearns for. It provides meaning to life offering people hope, faith, and courage to overcome life's obstacles.

13. See Asamoah-Gyadu, *Pentecostal Christianity*.
14. Haar, *Religion and Development*, 4.
15. Haar, *Religion and Development*, 4.

Ellis and Haar argue that the most appropriate approach in relation to religion and development is to proceed from local epistemologies; exploring how people perceive themselves, view their world and explain their reality. They further note that, most Africans "understand and interpret the world through the prism of religion. Religion . . . is a mode of apprehending reality."[16] The linkage between culture and worldview and ecology has protected the centrality of religion in non-western contexts including Africa. Religion has always been influenced by these forces and in turn influenced them. As Ogbu Kalu again observes, the world view in African communities is charismatic as gods operate in the sky, land, sea and the ancestral world. They "destroy the boundaries between the sacred and the profane; sacralize reality and give religious value to everyday activities."[17]

African epistemologies have two basic concepts whose understanding is crucial to effective interventions in development and politics; this is the notion of the interconnectedness of reality material and non-material. Both are viewed as two sides of the same coin. Hence even to talk of religion/faith and development or politics would be absurd. Bujo aptly observes that the Africans still lives in a web of relationships that are in continual interaction. He continues to say, "according to African people's belief, not only human beings influence each other, but all forces possess a causal and ontological interdependence . . . all things can be traced to the highest being, who created everything."[18] The Cartesian worldview propounded by the modernization enterprise has therefore conflicted with the African worldview.

The other concept is what has been identified as the spirit idiom. This is the belief that the world is the arena where spirits operate influencing the life of communities and individuals. Promotion of well-being for individuals and communities is predicated upon maintaining an ontological balance between all the realms of being. These beliefs exist elsewhere but the crucial point is that the spirit language is used to image happenings in the secular world like economic decline and its attendant consequences like, poverty and poor governance or loss of legitimacy. This language persists in Pentecostal and Charismatic churches' rhetoric which displays a continuation rather than rapture with this world view. I argue that it is important to incorporate this epistemology in developing

---

16. Ellis and Haar, *Worlds of Power*, 13–14.
17. Kalu, *Power, Poverty, and Prayer*, 149.
18. Bujo, *Ethical Dimensions of Community*, 16.

any theory social or political of grappling with developmental issues; in the quest for explanatory or interventionist models.

Scholars of Pentecostalism have observed that, in Africa, the political realm is sacralized or enchanted and politics is a religious matter precisely because it is a moral performance. It is about the under girding values that determine how governance is executed or power is wielded in the task of governing.[19] Authority is legitimized or delegated power. Every ruler is situated in a subsidiary entity. So the questions of power are always: who wields power, for whom and to what end? Implicit in these views is the moral dimension of power which still asserts itself in diverse ways. There is however always the question of the source of authority and obligation.

Pentecostals and Economic Development

Pentecostal churches in Africa, whether classical, indigenous/independent or Neo-Pentecostal/Charismatic are providing safe spaces for their adherents and equipping them with spiritual, social and economic resources to enable them face life and transform their individual and communal circumstances. I argue that the Pentecostal ethos is such that it spurs economic growth of a country, individuals and communities because of its promotion of the values of thrift, hard work, mutual caring, strict moral codes (avoidance of alcohol, drugs, smoking, sexual immorality, etc.). These and other values are necessary for sustainable development and it is therefore important for those involved in development initiatives to understand a people's beliefs, values, fears and worldview in order to provide long lasting and sustainable processes. Some Pentecostal churches today run explicit development projects but others are very small congregations of the poor, and have a different approach to existential problems focusing more on spiritual resources.

Scholars like Ogbu Kalu and David Maxwel[20] claim that pauperization of African nations in the lost economic decade of the 1980s and 1990s fuelled the rise of these churches. The 1990s were characterized by economic crisis, poor governance, and narrowing of the democratic space. On the other hand, the quest for democracy led to the enlargement of political space for religious actors. Thus to Maxwell, Zimbabweans

---

19. See Gifford, *African Christianity*; *Christianity, Development, and Modernity in Africa*.

20. See Maxwell, *African Gifts of the Spirit*.

were drawn to the Zimbabwe Assemblies of God Africa (ZAOGA) by a process of rupture. He argues that Pentecostal discourse is replete with images of rupture and discontinuity.[21]

I argue in this chapter that, the greatest contribution to development by Pentecostals is not necessarily through consciously defined development activities, but rather, through the very nature of Pentecostal beliefs and practices. This is what scholars call social and spiritual capital.[22] Pentecostals maintain a holistic worldview that does not separate the secular from the sacred. The whole of life to them, is subject to God's judgement. I argue that, Pentecostalism does in deed shift peoples' belief's, values and morality in such a way that, when other factors are favorable, very often, these people make quite radical social and economic changes which then lead them in the direction of development.

Ogbu Kalu postulates that, one of the reasons for the appeal of Pentecostalism in Africa is the resonance of its world view with that of Africa.[23] Gifford has described this world view as an "enchanted worldview"; a perspective that sees the material world as an arena for the struggle between the forces of good and evil. Pentecostalism has held special appeal to young forward looking individuals seeking to leave behind the failures of their nations' past and embrace the possibilities of modernity, like material prosperity. In Neo-Pentecostalism, a discourse of demonology is also used to account for economic failure and dispossession. Hence, problems in the country, family, poverty, illness, and misfortune may be perceived to be the work of demonic forces which are ubiquitous. Their influence is hence at a personal, communal and national levels. To some extent, demonology and Pentecostal Prosperity theology are drawn on to explain generalized developing countries' failures, with sentiments like, "Economic collapse is a sign of national sin."[24]

Kalu further notes that, the rise of Pentecostalism is an aspect of African's attempt to link the resources of a new religiosity with an ongoing effort to solve problems in the ecosystem. It is a "continuation of Africa religiosity and emerges from the African worldview but critiquing the old solutions that lost efficacy as the old system fell apart."[25] Pentecostal churches today,

21. Maxwell, *African Gifts of the Spirit*, 185
22. Maselko et al., "Religious Social Capital."
23. Kalu, *Power, Poverty, and Prayer*, 149.
24. Maxwel, *African Gifts of the Spirit*, 185–86.
25. Kalu, *Power, Poverty, and Prayer*, 150.

especially the Neo-Pentecostals, openly attacks African Religion as an institution and draws its rhetoric from traditional notions of evil and Western based scholars of demonology like Derek Prince and others. While providing a means for understanding misfortune, the cognizant moral structure of the Pentecostal cosmology, also supplies hope, for this worldly, miraculous salvation through this break with spaces and narratives of failure. This promise is an active assertion of self-determination and rebirth into a larger world and the transcendence of former microcosms.

Robert Akoko, writing about Cameroon and the rise of Neo-Pentecostalism argues that, the movement has arisen in the context of economic decline, war and conflict, poor governance; and failure by the mainline churches to effect changes despite their utilization of several strategies to influence government.[26] He further observes that, the Pentecostal messages of individual prosperity and enrichment within a local-global context is appealing to people with little options in life.[27] The messages of hope drawn from the Bible and Prosperity Literature becomes a catalyst for individual and communal transformation. Dena Freeman in a seminal article on "Pentecostalism and Economic Development in Sub-Saharan Africa," identifies two types of transformation that occur or are promoted in Pentecostal Churches in Africa, namely, "transformation of subjectivity" and "transformation of values and relationships." This article agrees with Freeman's analysis on how the Pentecostal ethic/doctrines contributes to economic and social development in Africa. Transformation of subjectivity refers to change at the level of a person's being; at the level of feelings and agency.

Transformation of Subjectivity

Pentecostals and Charismatics are extremely effective in bringing about dramatic changes in subjectivity. This is a type of "remaking of the individual," or a "reorientation" of person's being. While "traditional economic system was an economy of affection, and the society was a tight knit web of relationships with mutual help especially for the needy in society; the ideal Pentecostal African is an individual with no economic demands beyond his/her immediate household."[28] Freeman further observes—and I agree with her:

26. Akoko, "New Pentecostalism."
27. Aoko, "New Pentecostalism," 359–76.
28. Freeman, "Pentecostalism and Economic Development," 5.

While the traditional African is reticent to become wealthier than his/her peers, lest he/she be accused of witchcraft, the African Pentecostal, strives to become rich because he/she believes that this is what God wants for him. While the traditional African is generally rather fatalist and accepts his/her lot; the African Pentecostal has a strong sense of agency and thinks that he/she can improve the situation with hard work and fervent prayer. While the traditional African favors stability and is slow to take risks, the African Pentecostal strives for improvement and is more likely to try something new.[29]

This transformation in the individual and the social networks may have an impact on economic and social behavior. Victor Shumba, in an article on "The Role of Christian Churches in Entrepreneurial Stimulation," observes that sermons by Neo-Pentecostal preachers on spiritual and financial breakthroughs, wealth creation, and general prosperity have a positive influence in encouraging people to venture in business and to believe in themselves.[30]

Pentecostal churches are therefore effective at bringing about the type of change that is often called development at the subjective and overt levels. This happens as we have earlier mentioned due to personal transformation, empowerment and shift in values; behavior change and reconstruction of personality.[31] Most members of Neo-Pentecostal churches in Africa come from either among the rural and urban poor or the new middle class. Each group have particular needs that are met within the congregations. Maxwell has observed that most poor people first come to a Pentecostal church when they are feeling wretched, desperate, hopeless and despised. Their self-esteem is low and feel unable to change their situations. People in these situations in South Africa, Kenya, and Tanzania complain of being turned into "zombies." Joining a Pentecostal church and their ensuing conversion, can radically change the people's sense of themselves and their place in the world. Participating in prayer, healing, anointing services enables these people to begin to see themselves as valued individuals, a part of God's people, somebody, rather than a nobody. They move beyond fatalism and come to realize that they have agency.[32] This is healing in an integral way.

This transformation is often brought about by deliverance and spiritual healing. May Pentecostal churches carry out deliverance and healing

29. Freeman, "Pentecostalism and Economic Development," 5.
30. Shumba, "Role of Christian Churches," 154.
31. Freeman, "Pentecostals and Economic Development," 6.
32. Maxwell, *African Gifts of the Spirit*, 198.

rituals like exorcism, Jericho walks, healing the family tree all perceived as engaging in a spiritual warfare where God and Satan are engaged in a cosmic struggle and in which God always wins. Christians are encouraged to be patient, persistent, and warriors in prayer and to know that "He who is in us, is greater than him who is in the world," and "in Christ, they are new creations." These subjective transformations can radically change a person's life and enable him/her to find purpose and meaning in life. Most importantly, "they develop a sense of agency and personal power. People experience a sense of newness. Such charismatic experiences make possible a fundamental rapture in the social order and then lead to the possibility of the establishment of a new order."[33] Many people from being dependents to depending on themselves. They also become productive members of the society. It is important to note that these transformations do not change the life threatening circumstances in which people live. They do not deal with structural sin and macro issues. Nevertheless, Pentecostals are able to transcend their circumstances and do their part as they wait for God. The state and non-state actors should therefore continue providing opportunities for economic empowerment to the citizens and if possible harness the enthusiasm and transformed subjectivities in their membership.[34]

Pentecostals today have become mega churches with investments in schools, universities, hospitals, transport industry, real estate business, ICT and others. For example the Christ Is the Answer Ministries, formally Nairobi Pentecostal Church is said to be one of the wealthiest churches in the Kenya with huge Sunday collections mounting to hundreds of millions of shillings a year. Some own banks, media houses and all the equipment associated with them. So too the independent/Independent African Pentecostal churches like Redeemed Christian Church of God and Winner's Chapel from Nigeria. These churches encourage people to do business and they play a major role in stimulating and shaping behavior. They empower people to be courageous, and to aim higher, take risks, and follow their dreams. Many of these churches train their members in project planning, starting a business, monitoring and evaluation. Pentecostal churches in Ghana[35] and Botswana, also invest extensive time and energy to the particular matter of how a modern believer is to be transformed and developed into a proactive and goal oriented agent.

33. Freeman, "Pentecostals and Economic Developemnt," 7.
34. Freeman, "Pentecostals and Economic Development," 7.
35. See Asamoah-Gyadu, "Prosperity and Poverty in the Bible."

Transformation of Values and Social Relationships

Pentecostal teachings encourage their followers to withdraw from social obligations which would block them from achieving their financial goals. The social bonds of African extended family are seen as demanding and destructive to a person's wellbeing. Pentecostal theology also views African culture as demonic from which it is their mission to deliver people. In this new movement, kinship patterns are based on a shared faith and not blood. This lack of involvement in social occasions and the financial costs associated with them, is linked to accumulation of savings in terms of money and time. This thus looks like the Weberian Protestant ethic and the spirit of capitalism. Though Pentecostals do not lead a puritanical lifestyle like the puritans of Calvin's time, they nevertheless accumulate savings due to avoidance of wanton behavior. They become more responsible parents and raise "God fearing" children.

Pentecostals call upon their followers to abstain from alcohol, tobacco, gambling and extra-marital affairs, embezzlement of public funds and drug use. As believers make strong efforts to change their behavior, in the name of Jesus, they bring about a highly significant change in their spending patterns. Money that is earned is no longer given out to destitute and demanding kin among relatives, but may be used in investment and accumulation of wealth.

Conclusion

Pentecostalism is a Christian movement that contributes to the economy by creating communities of affection, love and concern where each member puts their talents to the service of the church community and where in turn they experience affirmation. Modern day Pentecostalism in Africa stimulates transformation of behavior that can lead to success and upward mobility in the contemporary neo-liberal economy. It motivates new behaviors and renders them moral. It promotes hard work, saving and a limitation on certain types of unproductive consumption. As such it leads people to participate, and succeed in uplifting their lives and those of their families. This way, Pentecostals contribute to individual and community development.

15

The Need for Theologizing from the Experience of the "Other"[1] in Contemporary Christianity in Africa

Faith K. Lugazia

Introduction

CHRISTIANITY IN AFRICA HAS been gaining freedom in transforming her church after the independence of African countries from colonial and missionary powers since the early 1960s. Such transformation made the African Church become self-indigenizing, self-innovating, and self-criticizing of her theology and practices. In this twenty-first century, there are some traces of transformation in its theology and practices. For example, African Christian theology has been taught as a module and not part of Western Systematic theology in many African Theological Universities. The contents of such a module are not confirmed by Western philosophers and theologians like Dietrich Bonheoffer, Claus Westermann, or Elizabeth Fioeranza but scholars like Mercy Oduyoye, Kwame Bediako, John Mbiti, Musimbi Kanyoro, Kwabena Asamoah-Gyadu, Allan Anderson, and Charles Nyamiti—to mention but a few. Of course, western scholar's wisdom is cited in the above mentioned work to inform readers that any

---

1. In this article, the word "other" will always refer to women in the Church in Africa.

theology constructed is borne from the experiences of different and diverse communities. Also, developments of different kinds within the African Church are taking place in the continent. For example, many churches in Africa are ordaining women to pastoral ministry. In some denominations in Africa we have female bishops, deans, and chaplains, and in some others, women and youths are holding position in decision-making bodies. However, it is still equally important to mention that African theology modules do not still include the experiences of the "other" since women in African Churches are still experiencing unequal sharing of power in the whole process of witnessing Christ.

This chapter deploys the critical feminist and feminist hermeneutical methods to argue that contemporary theology in Africa should include the "other's" experiences and perspectives. The facts of African, Biblical, and Western cultures of the past should not forestall the initiatives of inclusion of the experiences and perspectives of the other. African theologies should instead use opportunities given to reconstruct an inclusive theology which respect others in their otherness. Christian theologies, which for a long time have exalted men, should be critiqued in order to allow transformation and change. My argument is validated by the reality that, constructed theologies in Africa so far, still exclude women in the life and mission of the Church. And the feminist critical approach is an ongoing project which involves, "criticizing, analyzing in order to eradicate the misinterpretation, distortion and oppression resulting from historically male perspectives," in the use, understanding and practices of religious scripts.[2] With this approach, we will be able to ask some questions with regard to why the "other" is discriminated against, and how the Bible can provide liberating tools despite the misinterpretation and distortion of the Bible in African Christianity? Feminist hermeneutical method then will give directions on how African theology can include women as the "other" in the life of the Church.

Need for Theologizing from the Experiences and Perspectives of the "Other"

Why do we argue that there is a need to theologize from the experiences of the "other"? Is this simply adding new "frills" and supplement to the solid core of theology that has been established by many generations of

---

2. Scatlas, *Do Feminist Ethics Encounter Feminist Aims?*, 18.

accumulated theological traditions? In this chapter, I argue that theologizing from the perspective of the other is a fundamental shift of perspectives that throws the traditional systems of Christian theology in Africa into question, and at the same time gives directives on how to include the others in the mission of God. One of the reasons why African Christian theology fails to deal with the experiences and perspectives of women derives from the negative picture of the women yielded by the society. For example, African communities still believe women to be witches. This representation is so much like that of the medieval women characterized by William Perkins. In his *A Discourse on the Damned Art of Witchcraft*, Perkins asserted:

> Women are more prone to demons and hence to witchcraft than men. A woman's proneness to witchcraft is due not only to her weak intellect and less firm control on her emotions, but also because she is prone to rebelliousness against her state of subjugation.... [For Puritans] the woman who departs from her divinely appointed place by rejecting male authority is not only a moral subversive but a heretic and witch. She is heretic because she is denying her divinely intended subjugation as clearly revealed in the Bible and taught by the Church. She is an incipient witch because she incorporates thereby with the devil in subverting the moral order of the society.[3]

Even though Perkins' characterization of the woman represents a Western medieval narrative, such a narrative unfortunately is the reality for most women in African societies. Rather than been seen and even venerated as mothers as well as human co-creators with God, women are looked upon as the destroyers of human creation. For example, in Tanzania, women whose eyes had turned red due to constant contact with firewood smoke in their daily struggles for survival are branded as witches, and sometimes even killed.[4] Such African belief, when combined with Christian mythology about women, not only justifies their social oppression, their reduction to servile labor in the home, but also denies them education, civic rights, and participation in public leadership. Though the status of women in the African churches has gradually started to change, their presence is still insignificant.

Theologizing from the side of the "other" then is an imperative for African Christian communities to include the experiences and perspectives

---

3. Ruether, "Theologizing from the Side of the 'Other,'" 69.
4. Edgar, "Success Stories."

of women in their theologies. Somewhere else, I narrated how Neo-Pentecostal and Charismatic churches in Africa includes the experiences and perspectives of women in their theologies. In these churches, women are given the opportunity to give testimonies about their life experiences, their encounter with Jesus Christ and their perspectives on Christian faith. These churches also have healing and deliverance ministries; ministries mostly needed by women because of the heavy emotional burden they carry as mothers and wives.[5]

Women in Africa have been defined by their experience of oppression. This include oppression in such mystical forms like been bewitched, being possessed by demons or ancestral spirits whose consequence is to hinder the life progress of the women. In Tanzania, there is a belief that the ancestral spirit that possesses a women becomes a spirit husband that prevents any physical marriage. Testimonies especially from men who married such women are challenging. In short, what is experienced by African women as mystical and mysterious oppression by principalities and powers are part of the experiences they wish to include in the contextual theologies born and grown on the African continent. Also, women have been and are still experiencing injustices on ethical issues related to sexuality in their churches. For example, where both a boy and a girl are caught in adultery, and the girl becomes pregnant, she is punished by the church by being put under church discipline as if committing adultery is only a woman's misconduct. The argument of considering these experiences of the other is that giving attention to their positive achievement and their significance will serve as encouragement that will limit the need for church discipline.

Theologizing from the other will help the church to first bring into question negative experiences which women encounter, by naming and owning these stories and experiences, and looking for ways to challenge and get rid of them. In terms of social, economic and political injustices, the African woman bears the brunt more than the men, since both religion and culture subordinate her. When we talk about poverty be it of mind or of economy,[6] a woman is much more affected due to lack of formal and informal education that gives her skills and enables her to cope with challenging

---

5. Lugazia, "Theology of Presence," 316.

6. I am aware that economy in Africa is described not from a material point of view but a communal one. I agree, then, with Mercy Oduyoye when she said that her mother is rich not because she has a lot of money and other properties but a community of people whose joys and sorrows are hers. See Oduyoye, *Beads and Strands*, 61

situation and emerge positively. In some parts of African there are still some cultural beliefs that insist women should not be educated since they will get married and only be of benefit to the husband and his family.[7] The few who are highly educated have many responsibilities which still keep them fighting for competence with their male counterparts to the extent that they do not have time to empower uneducated women on the continent. And a few others have been lost to western societies because their governments could not accommodate their competence, or do not just care to. The essence of theologizing from the experience of these women "other" is not to narrate how their experience orbit those of the men; rather, it is to highlight their predicament in ways that will facilitate the emergence of a theology of empowerment for the women.

Cultural Mythologies and Biblical Mythology of Creation Confirms the Need of Theologizing from the Side of the Other

The stories/myths of creation from many African cultures confirm that God created men and women at the same time and for the same purpose. Some of the stories are similar to the Biblical story which puts the creation of humans at the very end. Man and woman are created either simultaneously or a man first, and shortly after, a woman, created to be his wife.[8]

African creation myths also speak about different methods by which human were created. Many African cultures "speak of God using clay in creating human beings."[9] Others, though accept that it is God who created, however express the methods of creation in different ways. Among the Bahaya of North-Western Tanzania, for example, the story of creation goes thus: there were primordial giants, with their specific boundaries—the male giants live on land, while the female live in the water. One day, a female giant saw flowers on land, moved out of the water to pick them, met a male giant, and got pregnant. The offspring, which was cuter than both giants, resembled humans. This was the beginning of the knowledge that if two different giants go beyond their boundaries and commingle, they will produce humans.[10] The Akamba of Kenya, for example, believe that God created humans in a marsh or a hole. They have a rock at a place called

---

7. Lugazia and Rwamunyana, "Effect of Culture on Gender Roles," 76.
8. Buberwa, "Spirits and Ancestors," 19.
9. Mbiti, *African Religions and Philosophy*, 91
10. Theophilos Balige Ihangiro, interview with the author, November 2, 2019.

Nzaui in the West-central part of Akambaland, which has a hole believed to be the origin of the first man and his wife. Myths from the people living on the coastal areas of Angola down to the Zambezi River and some communities in Zaire and Sudan speak of humans originating from trees.[11] Among the Maasai of Kenya and Tanzania, there is a belief in another world which is older than this one and is invisible. In this older world, God created the first man and his wife, then at an opportune time, this first couple came out and entered our world.[12]

The essence of the creation stories is to demonstrate that there was no discrimination in the creation of humans. These stories also revealed the significant role of the woman in procreation. Even though these stories tell us that one was created before the other, there is nothing to show that one was created to wield authority over the other. On the contrary, both were created to live in harmony, and with complementary and shared responsibilities.

Where then did the difference, discrimination and oppression of the woman as the other come from? Further elements of some of these creation stories reveal that after humans were created, they made some guidelines which will make them live and work in the world they find themselves in. These guidelines are embedded in what we today call culture. Culture is the "artificial, secondary environment which man superimpose on the natural. It comprises language, habits, ideas, beliefs, customs, social organization, inherited artifacts, technical process and values."[13] It is with the emergence of culture that a division of labor was established that separated between men and women, placed men in the place of authority over women, and women as mere observers. By being observers, it followed that women were removed from being subject and placed as objects in the life and work of the community.

The culture created distance between men and women. Men claimed the role of leadership while women continued to be receivers of whatever is imposed on them. Culture denied women's voices in decision making from the family by claiming that it is a man, the head, who is the leader in the family. When Christianity was introduced in Africa by missionaries, and though it transformed many cultural practices, the question of the rights and responsibilities of women in the *Mission Dei* was left untouched

---

11. Mbiti, *African Religions and Philosophy*, 91–92.
12. Mbiti, *Introduction to African Religion*, 78–79.
13. Niebuhr, *Christ and Culture*, 32.

because the missionaries also participates in the androcentric, patriarchal and kyriarchal systems that dominate the woman as the other. Patriarchy is defined as "power of the fathers, which defines women as the other of men, as subordinate to men in power. A structure which is not sorely based on gender differentiation; it governs the relationship between the rests of the family members as well."[14] Being androcentric is about "'male centeredness.' It considers the male are normative human beings while their counterpart women are derivative and subordinate and are deficient type of beings."[15] Fiorenza goes on to assert that "Kyriarchy" (derived from the Greek *Kyrios*) is a "social-political system of domination in which elite educated propertied men hold power over women and other men."[16]

Misinterpretation of the Bible due to Literal Reading and Its Effects on Women

The interpretation of Genesis 2–3 began in rabbinic thought during the inter-Testament period and was incorporated into the Pauline concept of the fallen Adam by the post-Pauline Church which wishes to suppress the earlier participation of women in the ministry that has been current in some of the early churches.[17] The creation story has been understood wrongly because of the literal reading of the Bible. Christians have understood words Adam to mean a man and Eve to mean a woman and that creation produced only these two people. I argue that, the creation story is a myth since nobody was there to see the procedures and process of creation of him/herself. But the feminist hermeneutic informs that:

> Adam, in the Hebrew language, has no masculine connotation. It comes from the word "adamah" (earth) to mean that a human was made of earth. The masculine pronoun comes from the fact that Hebrew has no neuter gender, so all words are either masculine or feminine.[18]

The differentiation of man (*Adam*) from human person into man (*ish*) and woman (*Ishah*) gives rise to difference between the male and female

---

14. Fiorenza, *Bread Not Stone*, 103.
15. Rakoczy, *In Her Name*, 11.
16. Fiorenza, *Wisdom Ways*, 20.
17. Fiorenza, *In Memory of Her*.
18. Barton, "Woman and Man in Creation," 37.

gender identity. This then implies that both were created at the same time. The mutuality of men and women carries no suggestion of male headship or female submission.

When we come to the second story of creation which explains the process of creation, we see that God was completing the mutuality of equal partners since all other created beings were not qualifying. This equality is expressed in the "one flesh" language (Gen 2:24). Hence, the meaning of "helper" to characterize the woman cannot be taken in the sense of "a helpful assistant to a man." In the Old Testament, helper (*Ezer*) is used sixteen times to refer to God coming alongside humans to help them. So woman is said to be the helper in the sense that she serves God with the man and not helping man to serve God. The naming of the women (*Isha*) as "bone from my bones and flesh from my flesh" mean neither Eve nor headship or authority; but confirms the mutuality of both coming from the same substance. It is also important to know that the name Eve was not given during creation but it appeared immediately after the fall (Gen 3:20).

When discussing the fall, feminist scholars insist on two interpretations. The first contends that "when man was receiving the instructions, the woman was not with him (Gen 2:17) since she was not created yet. The second added that in the discussion with the serpent, the woman used the plural form of "you" (Gen 3:1b) which indicated the man and the woman were together. Therefore, both fell together into disobedience. This further means that both are thereby accountable. Jesus had several women as devoted disciples like Mary his mother, Mary Magdalene, the "other" Mary. Mary of Bethany, Johanna, Susan and Salome.[19] Mary, mother of John, provided the room where the disciples took shelter after the death of Jesus Christ.

The argument of this section is that the biblical God, Father, Son and the Holy Spirit looked at women differently from how the societies looked at them. While most cultures and societies saw women as weaker and inferior sex, the God of the Bible intentionally portrayed the woman as a powerful human creation who, like man, has been called to care for creation and subdue it (Gen 1:28). Christ, who liberates human creation from all cultural constraints which hinders women from not seeing freedom brought out by him, not only spoke against these cultural constraints, but equally acted publicly against them by including women in his mission.

---

19. Scholler, *Biblical Basis for Equal Partnership*, 3

SECTION IV: AFRICAN PENTECOSTALISM IN CONTEXT

Critical Feminism as a Tool in Theologizing from the Experiences and Perspectives of the Other

McKinnon asserts that "critical feminism is based on the assumptions that gender oppression is endemic in our society; traditional claims of gender neutrality and objectivity must be contested; social justice platforms and practices are the only way to eliminate gender discrimination."[20]

Critical feminism criticizes the cultural ideology which claims that women are weak creatures, and their thinking capacity is lower compared to that of men. Critical feminists rejects the biblical ideas that women are the glory of the men (1 Cor 11:7), and they cannot have inheritance (Num 27:4). Rather, the objective of critical feminism is to de-objectify women, and make them subjects who can participate fully in God's *oikos*.

The liberating experiences which African women have had, especially in their fight against principalities and powers, the burden they carry as mothers, and the suffering of childbirth and child rearing, ought to be part of what African theologies should consider in becoming more inclusive of these experiences of the other. In other words, African women need social platforms where such experiences and perspectives could facilitate their participation in communal and social endeavors as partners. Social platforms will also give chances to challenge the history and historical contexts and their policies and practices, especially those affecting women negatively. The challenge for critical feminist theory is that it must also be interdisciplinary since oppressive culture is found in all disciplines in theology.[21] This, among other things, demands the emergence of a gender curriculum across all disciplines.

Feminist Biblical Hermeneutic as a Tool in Theologizing from the Side of the Other

> Feminist biblical hermeneutic seeks to look at the scriptures but instead of focusing on arguments that support the submission or objectivation of women, it seeks to discuss scripture in a light of a number of feminist concerns, including whether women are equal to men.[22]

20. MacKinnon, "Feminism, Marxism, Method, and State." See MacKinnon, "Reflections on Sex Equality."

21. Geisinger, "Critical Feminist Theory, Rape, and Hooking Up," 13.

22. Wood, "Dialogue on Feminist Biblical Hermeneutics."

Feminist biblical hermeneutic also looks at the Bible from a feminist hermeneutical standpoint which discusses texts not only to fit them into women experiences, but also to open up the realities and validity of such texts. For example, in 1 Corinthians, feminist hermeneutic would be worried as to why Paul refused to record the vital fact of Jesus appearing to women (given the scriptural witness that the women were the first to see Jesus)? Feminist hermeneutic also queries why Paul, in 1 Tim 2:12, forbids a woman to teach when there are women teachers today? And lastly, why women who worked day and night to make sure that Christ is proclaimed by giving their belongings like houses for prayers, time and even income for the sake of the Gospel are not uplifted in the lectionaries and sermons of the Church? For example, the conversation of Nicodemus (John 3) and that of the Samaritan woman (John 4) both have the same intention of revealing who Jesus is.[23] But African Christianity insists on second birth of Nicodemus than that of the "come and See the Messiah," a call which brought Samarians to Christ. Looking at the Bible with women eyes reveals all these facts and directs the theologians to construct a theology which counts "others" in the mission of God.

Testimonies from Women in Churches and From the Bible

Concrete experiences of women which are spelled out through testimonies have become the balm of Gilead that soothes their wounds. For them, testimonies actualize the presence of God in their misery. Some women ministers, for example, have been raped and impregnated at a young age.[24] Some of them are also divorcees because in their marriages, these women experienced oppression, their powers to act were restricted, and their voices were silenced.[25] Some were abused by their families as witches, kept at home unmarried against their wish as wives of the clan spirits, and jailed because of the mistakes or moral sin committed willingly or unwillingly. They in turn, after being delivered, "have started deliverance and healing ministries as part of divine plan for them and legitimized by an encounter with God

---

23. Between 2015 and 2019, I did research on different sermons/Bible studies about Samaritan woman, aiming at listening to the educative content of the text. 82 percent of what taught was about the behavior of the Samaritan woman, while only 12 percent was talking about Missiological and ecumenical character of the text.

24. Margret Wanjiru, a leader of the "Jesus Alive Ministry" (JIAM) in Kenya, was impregnated at the age of sixteen.

25. Dr. Gertrude Rwakatare of "Mount of Fire" Assemblies of God Church, Tanzania, Dar es Salaam.

either through a conversion experience or through a subsequent endowment with divine power that manifests itself in the ability to heal and deliver from demonic powers."[26] Their testimonies, when heard by other women with similar situations and challenges, move such women to surrender their lives to Christ. Biblical women testimonies also support the importance of theologizing from the side of women. Hagar testified that indeed, it is God who not only saw her desperate situation, but also sees the affliction and oppression of His people (Gen 16:13 NRSV). There are also women, like Mary, who testified about their readiness to obey God's call and do His will in circumscribed environment (Luke 1:34, 38 NRSV).

Conclusion

Some women in African Churches confess to finding God who is present in their faith, the "faith which seeks understanding," in their joy and above all in their struggle with life's questions. As Bridges would say, when talking about women in church generally that, "Jesus Christ who reconciled them to himself, and in order to do this marvelous action he dared to enter their world of alienation and pain and critiqued the numbness of his society.[27] Reading of the Bible from a feminist perspective will also build a hermeneutic theology and support the significance of theologizing from the side of the other. Women will participate in the mission of God not as objects but subjects of the mission. And not as observes but as active participants in God's oikos.

---

26. Kalu, *African Pentecostalism*, 152.
27. Johns, "Pentecostal Spirituality and Conscietization of Women," 153–55.

16

Religion and Development in European-African Dialogue

Exploring Learning Processes with Independent and Charismatic Churches in Africa on Sustainability and Integral Social Development

Dietrich Werner

THERE IS NO DOUBT that religion plays an important role as a factor both to stimulate and to hinder social and political development on the African continent. Religion (the interpretation of the whole of life within a spiritual worldview) is part of the very African social fabric and the mental settings, which influence the majority of African societies, particularly in sub-Saharan Africa. Any proper understanding of sustainability and integral social development on the African continent has to be informed by a specific perception of the role of religious dimensions within the political and social process, particularly in faith-based organizations. As even secular discourses in governments and ministries for development cooperation have become explicitly interested in and open for understanding the religious dimension of development, it is an important task of ecumenical learning and the role of Faith Based Organizations (FBOs) to build bridges between different world views and to highlight the role of those new actors on the ground which for cultural, colonial or political reasons have been marginalized in current discourses on sustainability and integral development.

Western scholars of intercultural theology and western development agencies have started to realize how deeply the changing landscapes of World Christianity are affecting their conceptual understandings, their work and their ways of collaboration. Kwabena Asamoah-Gyadu is one of the most distinct African scholars who has developed much of his research and reflections on understanding the scope, root causes and consequences of these changes with regard to African Christianity not only on the African continent but also in the African Diaspora abroad.[1] Some scholars have described this as the Charismatization of World Christianity which on the African continent takes on the form of the "Pentecostalization of the public sphere in African Christianity."[2] It is known that Pentecostal, Charismatic and Independent churches have grown disproportionately from representing 1.5 percent of World Christianity in the year 1910 to 16.2 percent in 2010 on global scale. Annual growth rates of Pentecostal and Charismatic churches in many parts of Africa are often almost twice as high as those from historical mainline or mission churches. Pentecostals ("Renewalists") are currently represent 25.8 percent of World Christianity (2010), i.e., around six hundred million Christians, and are therefore as significant numerically as the historical mainline ecumenical churches which are represented in the WCC and in most of the member organizations of Action of *Churches* Together (ACT)Alliance.

The picture has become more complicated as there are several types and different forms of Charismatic Churches, which sometimes are also grouped differently. Classical Pentecostal churches, rooted in the Pentecostal awakening of the early twentieth century due to the combination of African spiritual traditions and leadership, the liberative experience of Christian worship and charismatic gifts in a situation of racial discrimination and suppression, are something different than charismatic renewal experiences within some of the historical mainline denominational traditions which presented a genuine form of spiritual renewal in worship and prayer across the whole range of Christian denominational traditions in the Sixties of the twentieth century. The emergence of Neo-Pentecostal churches in the last decades of the twentieth century which was influenced by new concepts of individualized power-evangelism, the aggressive use of new media and

---

1. See Asamoah-Gyadu, "God is Big in Africa"; "To the Ends of the Earth."
2. Meyer, "Going and Making Public," 53.

the emergence of highly commercialized spiritual power leadership figures within predominantly White American middle class cultural frameworks is something completely different than African Initiated Churches (AICs) which are rooted in an anti-colonial re-appropriation process of African initiatives and African indigenization efforts of Christian faith and its reconciliation with forms of traditional African wisdom and leadership traditions. Thus, great care has to be applied in order to refrain from generalized and sweeping statements concerning the understanding of different forms of new churches and players around in African Christianity.

There are some pioneers of research and intercultural dialogue between academic intercultural theology, research in religious studies and in developmental discourses, which have contributed to an emerging body of research papers and publications concerning the understanding of the changing landscape of World Christianity for common concepts of development cooperation and issues of sustainability.[3] However, dialogue between Pentecostal and Independent churches and development organizations is still less advanced than with historical mainline and mission instituted churches. Earlier attempts of dialogue, like the international consultation "Encounter beyond the routine" in Missionsacademy in the year 2010 between Protestant Development Service (EED), Protestant Association of Churches and Mission (EMW) and selected African scholars as well as with a network of key players, including Historic, Independent and Charismatic Churches in Ghana on the campus of Church of Pentecost in 2018, in which Kwabena Asamoah-Gyadu participated, need intentional continuation.[4] As it has been estimated that each day around twenty-two thousand Africans find their spiritual and social anchor in one of the new churches of Independent, Charismatic and Pentecostal Orientation in Africa, these types of churches and social organizations cannot be bypassed in the future in any meaningful dialogue concerning models of integral development for African societies, as development approaches should be intentional to be inclusive and not to leave anybody behind.

There are growing concerns of World Christianity scholars that the future might see a widening gulf between one quarter of World Christianity, representing the ecumenical or historical churches, focusing on

---

3. See Freeman, "Pentecostalism and Economic Development"; *Pentecostalism and Development*. See also Öhlmann et al., *African Initiated Christianity*, the work of a research team at Humboldt University, Berlin.

4. See Boersma and Neusel, *Encounter Beyond Routine*.

solid self-understandings in terms of apostolic tradition, catholicity and the achievements of social Protestantism and ethics (including development programs), and the other major part of World Christianity, representing churches of the new type, focusing on the understanding of the church as a vibrant charismatic fellowship of spiritual empowerment, experiences with the Holy Spirit and healing or deliverance prayers and rooted in different social, generational and cultural realities. An emerging global apartheid and non-communication between these two types of churches could happen if the efforts to build bridges and to identify learning areas where mutual interests are involved will be neglected. Wesley Grandberg-Michaelson has identified the communication gap and intercultural challenges between the different families of Christian churches as one major challenge for the future of ecumenical unity and inner cohesion of World Christianity.[5] What historically has been a major challenge in the period of the Ancient Church with the tension and communication problems between the Jerusalem types of Christianity, remaining strict to the standards of purity and doctrinal identity of Jewish Christianity and the Antiochia type of Christianity which took seriously the missionary dynamic of early Christianity to transcend its early Jewish cultural boundaries and to reach out to Hellenistic and non-circumcised parts of the population in Asia Minor and much beyond in the Mediterranean region, repeats itself in the twentieth/twenty-first century as a cultural tension and/or partly clash between north-Atlantic born historical mainline churches as well as indigenous and independent and charismatic types of churches from below.

A deepened dialogue between church development organizations, rooted in the tradition of the ecumenical movement and social Protestantism, and the new type of Independent and charismatic churches on the African continent—this paper argues—is needed for at least four strategic reasons:

1. Christian development organizations, which are part of ACT Alliance, which stands for Action of *Churches* Together, should make any effort to observe and analyze carefully ongoing changes within World Christianity. Successful development cooperation certainly includes careful attention to certain standards and standards of professionalization, which belong to any given framework of accountability and transparency—this all should not be loosened. At the

---

5. Granberg-Michaelson, *From Times Square to Timbuktu*.

same time ACT member organizations should be open to consider whether their own efforts in development cooperation can become more successful and more broad based in case they recognize the potential for broader working alliances on issues like agro-ecological transformation, food security and land rights with some of those churches or Christian organizations which for historical and cultural and theological reasons have remained outside the established circles of communication and existing ecumenical partnership. Western development agencies need to be aware of certain dangers of cultural captivity by being related mainly to those partners, which are more easily to be related to for them. Going beyond established comfort zones in listening, learning and relating also with more difficult partners might involve risks which have to be carefully monitored and reflected, but it can—if practiced carefully—also involve potentials for new learning processes which are of benefit for the inclusivity and broader working coalitions in the regions which can be beneficial for integral social development and ecological sustainability within a broader sector of African Christianity;

2. Independent and Charismatic churches in the African continent, like Church of Pentecost in Ghana, Church of the Lord Aladura in Nigeria, the Redeemed Christian Church of God in Nigeria,[6] Efata Ministries Tanzania or Soweto Pentecostal Church are not any more just small congregations only, but huge social organizations with followings of millions of faithful and often organized even as multi-national church networks with global impact. Some of them play an increasingly public role also in their own national or regional political arena and particularly with their media networks—thus they have to be taken seriously as new players in the area of social and political development. The Church of Pentecost in Ghana for instance has played a pioneering role in issues of environmental stewardship, climate change and waste issues, reaching out in national campaigns and even promoting lobbying work and critical engagement with the Ghanaian government;

3. A challenge, however, is the very diverse and heterogeneous landscape of African churches at present. Just in Kenya there are said to exist some four thousand Christian denominations. How to develop an appropriate understanding of the diverse characters and profiles

---

6. Akhazemea and Adedibu, "Redeemed Christian Church of God," 53.

of African churches involved? Even if Church-based development organizations rooted in western contexts try to develop a more accurate and detailed understanding on how "Renewalist churches" on the African continent are presenting and shaping their own specific concept for integrating African spirituality, Christian tradition, social development and modernization, this will never be sufficient to have a complete and sufficiently deep insight in the realities and complexities of African Independent and Charismatic churches. One key argument and prudent solution therefore has been that new churches who belong to the category of Charismatic and Independent Churches should turn to their respective neighbor churches within the regions and try to develop cooperative approaches on the local and regional level rather than avoiding the test of more regional ecumenical collaboration in their own contexts and turning directly to external and international western partners. There seem to be much wisdom in this approach to strengthen inner-African ecumenical collaboration and not trying to put external Christian development actors in a position of discerning which church or Christian organization might become a potential partner for international development cooperation on a global scale. With the Organization of African Instituted Churches (OAIC) which cooperates with Christian development organization from western background there have been successful projects for instances in the area of training local farmers for issues of food security and agriculture which then involve also people from other Christian churches as beneficiaries and cooperation partners. Thus regional collaboration in African contexts is strengthened instead of enhancing denominational competition and interference from outside.

4. A final reason for exploring learning processes and dialogues between AICs and Charismatic Churches and Christian development actors from external partners is that we face some hopeful signs for a growing learning movement for social competency, Christian ethics and explorations around integral development concepts within at least some of the AICs and Charismatic Churches.[7] Some of the new churches in Africa express an increasing interest to be more open to dialogue with partners from western churches, as the younger generation of church leaders becomes more educated and academically trained and

---

7. Öhlmann et al., *African Initiated Christianity*.

also wants to benefit from the historical achievements of western social Protestant thinking and critical concepts of development in facing some of the shortcomings and distortions within African spiritualities and church concepts. Thus there emerges a situation where there is a learning potential for both sides: Concepts for development which are more shaped and supported in a milieu marked by secularization and modernization can to be enriched and challenged by concepts and practice models of development which are rooted in African spiritual worldviews allowing them to become more integrated not only with issues related to social and political transformation, but also spiritual, ethical and value transformation in African societies.[8] African Christian views and mindsets are equally enriched and challenged to learn from the long history of Social Protestantism and professional diaconal and development related work and collaboration with state actors in western churches.

The more interaction and mutual learning processes there are between historical mainline churches within the African context and Independent and Charismatic churches of FBOs from this background, the more easy it will become also for western Christian development actors to engage in dialogue and collaboration with some of the new churches. This is not an easy process at all as prejudices and stereotypes, which hinder proper communication, are involved on both sides. For some people in western church development agencies the churches of the new type in Africa (like in some of established western traditional academic theology) are viewed still with suspicion. They are stereotyped as religious movements relapsing into pre-enlightenment positions such as the belief in spirits, demons, exorcism and to propagate and produce patriarchal and oppressive structures, thus leading more to further dependence, lack of autonomy and freedom and questionable social values. These churches sometimes are also reproached as being apolitical, socially disinterested and not a progressive factor in African societies, ergo not to be considered in any way as partners either for project support or for mutual learning

---

8. The majority of Evangelical and Pentecostal churches on the African continent are uneasy for some of the western partners as they "don't consent necessarily with that distinction between mission and development (which has been formative for the identity of some western development agencies). They would rather say that that sound development is only possible on the basis of an intimate relation between Christ the Redeemer, respectively the Holy Spirit, and the believer" (Boersma and Neusel, *Encounter Beyond Routine*, 10).

on development.⁹ Unfortunately there are also in reality many cases in the realm of Charismatic, Pentecostal and Independent churches which present real instances of a distorted identity and perception of the liberative Christian Gospel and of an ideological instrumentalization of Christian faith or political misuse of Christian leaders. On the other hand there is an increasing body of recent research which supports the other perception, arguing that many Pentecostal churches in Africa have developed an amazing variety and intensity of social networking, charity project building, health care for HIV/AIDS, training of skills, development of entrepreneurial mentalities and a positive value change that poverty can be changed with both spiritual and social power which have led some scholars even to believe, that Pentecostal churches are apparently "more successful in bringing about change that is effective, deep-rooted, and long-lasting" than mainline Christianity and even most of the NGOs. Research done for instance on Grace Bible Church, a Pentecostal mega-church in South Africa, has shown, that members of this church are more compassionate towards poor and needy, have better awareness of social problems and have a common understanding that education, skills training programs and hard work are important factors to alleviate poverty.

It belongs to the honesty of an ecumenical approach, however, to admit that the picture is far from being unified and remains contradictory. In deed one cannot deny that there have been cases and examples of churches, leading apostles and senior pastors which certainly might be perceived more as obstacles to integral development then as facilitator and driving force due to blunt violation of standards of human dignity in some charismatic or healing worship events, due to financial mismanagement, corruption or appropriation of huge amounts of funds from the faithful by few leading figures. Some prejudices are involved also on the side of AICs or Charismatic churches: Mission instituted or mainline churches and their agencies are often viewed with stereotypes, conveniently labeled as "dry bones" or "churches of the law" and not spiritually engaged churches.¹⁰ It is interesting in this regard that the All African Conference of Churches in 2019 started a continent-wide process (in which Kwabena Asamoah-Gyadu was heavily involved) to explore core criteria for dealing with "misleading theologies" around in several churches in African. It is the first time that an ecumenical umbrella organization on the continental level dares to address such

---

9. See Biehl, "Religion, Development, Mission," 105.
10. Boersma and Neusel, *Encounter Beyond Routine*, 11.

sensitive issues. It has been agreed to deepen and continue this process towards discerning proper and sound biblical teachings and to distinguish them from misleading theologies in at least three major thematic areas, namely health and healing, power and authority and prosperity and development. It has been stated clearly during the conference that misleading theologies can be found everywhere and not just in one denominational camp, so the process of purification and correction becomes an issue of one type of denomination accusing the other. The very fact that churches are taking up issues of mutual self-correction, brotherly critique and apologetics against distortions of the liberating Gospel of Jesus Christ is encouraging also for ecumenical partners as this—if followed up strategically and systematically both on continental, regional and national levels—can restore and strengthen the reputation and reliability of churches in Africa which has been damaged by a number of scandals and ill-practices which partly were inspired and influenced also by misleading theologies. We are reminded once again that the renewal of Christian faith and ecclesial life always involves aspects of an *ecclesia semper reformanda*. Thus the process started has the potential to lead to both a genuine reformation of African Christianity (commercialization and ideological misuse of the Gospel and central Christian symbols was the topic already in sixteenth-century Reformation in Europe) as well as to strengthen the authentic social witness of the church and its relevance for social and ecological transformation.

It remains a crucial task on all sides to develop more research and more direct dialogue with Independent and Pentecostal churches within regional settings and to some extent in international encounter in terms of their actual understanding, impact and their models to contribute to social and sustainable development, social uplift and human rights. Neither blunt and generalized statements praising Pentecostals as the only attractive and solid new social agent of development nor a blatant rejection of Independent or charismatic churches as opponents to any social development will help and be appropriate. Accompanying, identifying, analyzing, supporting and nurturing the slowly emerging *new types of an African Independent or Charismatic Churches Social Ethics and related Independent and Charismatic Christian Leadership Training Programs*, including Business and Management Values Training systems, might become *one of the most important conceptual and strategic tasks of furthering capacity building and competence training* in a broader sector of African Christianity in the decades to come if western Christian *development actors* want to make an impact for broadening the alliances for a future generation of leaders in African Christianity and for common work on eco-social transformation in African societies.

A diverse range of concepts and issues certainly will play a major role in deepening honest dialogue. This is the whole area of what traditionally is called "Prosperity Gospel," as it is alive in many different facets and shapes in African Christianity. A stream involved with this terminology has become an overarching feature for the majority of Pentecostal churches, also for quite a significant number of many mainline churches on the African continent. While a theological critique at some aspects of certain types and distortions within of Prosperity Gospel rhetoric remains necessary and legitimate, nowadays increasingly also happening within some of the Pentecostal African circles themselves (like a critique of the equation or causal relationship between material growth and spiritual blessings), it should first be understood that some of the language of Prosperity Gospel in the context of African cultures, which always and for centuries have associated deities with abundant life and the presence of God with the visibility of earthly blessings,[11] is an expression of the indigenization and adaptation of Christian faith to African worldviews. The language of prosperity teaching often answers needs of a situation often marked by abject poverty, precarious living conditions and hopelessness. Some variations of Prosperity Gospel in this perspective can be also seen as a vigorous refutation of the spiritualization of poverty in which lack of livelihood is seen as a fate, which cannot be changed. Encountering and dialoguing with different streams of Prosperity Gospel therefore should be guided by the overarching question where and how spiritual assets in fighting poverty can be identified, which religious energies and concepts to rise out of apathy and passivity can be promoted and sustained in theologically responsible ways. Spiritual resources and *spiritual sustainable development goals (SSDGs)* (which go beyond just secularist and reductionist concepts of development) are to be taken seriously and identified without which no lasting way out of dependency, social misery and decay but also out of materialist consumerism can be identified and sustained in African contexts.

There is another aspect for development cooperation, which relates to the ongoing critical discourse in western development cooperation to what extend it is wise, prudent and responsible to involve private actors and economic corporations into development cooperation. In many

---

11. Heuser, "Concepts of 'Development,'" 55.

Pentecostal African churches (as well as in other parts of World Christianity, like China) we have a growing number of entrepreneurial Christians or Christian entrepreneurs, which have considerable economic power and impact, even beyond their own churches in national or global economy and want to do good with their financial means (particularly in Nigeria, Ghana, Kenya, South Africa). Partnering with networks of associations of entrepreneurial Christians and Christian businessmen (often coinciding with church leadership positions) in the global South is a field which is less developed—might be also due to the fact that it contradicts the western typologies of partners in the global South being always poor and disadvantaged. Western development agencies can mainly deal with partners which need money and send applications to get funds or with those who need personnel and experts. But what if there are partners in Africa (or Asia) who need neither money nor staffing, because they have both in abundance, but would be interested in conceptual learning, in consultancies and dialogue on the spiritual side of development? If western church development agencies fail to realize the importance of these new players and trends they will be marginalized in processes both on the African continent as well as globally relating to new trendsetters in terms of development, poverty eradication, church growth and social modernization. Publications like from the former chair of the Church of Pentecost in Ghana, Apostle Michael Kwabena Ntumi, on good financial practice and stewardship (Financial Breakthrough: Discovering God's Secrets to Prosperity, 2004),[12] indicate a new approach to financial planning, to charity projects and early forms of social diakonia within the African Pentecostal milieu. These initial signs of some embryonic concepts of financial stewardship and social responsibility of wealth which can be compared to the early first beginnings of organized social work and diakonia in the history of European social Protestantism should not be rejected lightly, but critically evaluated, accompanied and qualified in international ecumenical dialogue with new partners on international development cooperation.

A key issue which will come up earlier or later in discourses like this is the question which type of relations in development partnership and ecumenical cooperation might be promoted and most suitable for unequal partners and for new partners in this context. Classically Western Christian development agencies have been involved in project partnership where according to agreed goals and measurable outcomes projects funds

---

12. Heuser, "Concepts of 'Development,'" 56.

are channeled to partner NGOs, churches or civil society organizations to achieve their objectives. Certainly there is a mature critical awareness that project partnership cannot work with solid dimensions of ongoing ecumenical partners dialogue, which is less centered around project agreements and achievement reports. But people are also aware of the fact that each partner relationship which involves sharing or sending of funds has a critical dimension of potential inequality and the unequal power-relationships involved can affect also the relationships in the region between the partner (organization) involved and benefitting and those actors on the local and regional ground which are not involved. Each partnership has implicit implications for the power-relationships on the ground. With the special case of new types of churches in the changing landscapes of African Christianity the question emerges whether the dominant model of project related fund sharing partnerships are the most appropriate to offer. It might well be that particularly for churches who have created their own mechanisms of self-funding and financial self-reliance the paradigm and *model of project funding* is not the most promising and helpful, but could be even harmful as this could lead to entering into forms of relationship which run the risk of undermining the essential self-understanding of African churches as being African Initiated and African Independent. The question therefore has emerged whether the most appropriate form of partnership could be involved with a *strategic learning partnership* where emphasize is put more on capacity-building for public theology, conceptual work on sustainability issues and integral concepts of social development rather than on direct financial project support.

This brings us back to a major topic which has to be mentioned here and which has been an issue of frequent conversations with Kwabena Asamoah-Gyadu: Where and how is the future generation of African Christian leaders and pastors being trained and equipped to develop their own sound and Biblically-based concept of socio-ecological transformation and model of development which affirms the dignity of all African people? The component of theology of development and public theology is strong only in a limited number of institutes and curriculum outlines within African theological education. There is a grave lack of resources in many churches, including Independent and Charismatic churches concerning insights of eco-theology and ethics of sustainability as has been found out in a major research and inquiry project carried out recently by the ETE program of WCC in Geneva.[13]

13. Jeglitzka and Werner, *Eco-Theology*.

A remedy must be found to invest and increase joint theological training and capacity building for sound and proper theologies of development with Independent and Charismatic and Mainline Churches in the African continent. Without investment into the quality, depth and accessibility of theological education, also the envisaged process of clarifications concerning misleading theologies in African Christianities will be futile, because it is the matter of education which counts in the area of integrity, quality and critical awareness in theological concepts in Africa.

It has become clear in recent dialogues both on regional as well as continental levels that there are several hopeful processes at work which can enhance mutual learning between the different types of churches within the changing landscapes of African Christianity. A lot of cross-fertilization between AICs, APCs and mainline churches takes already place. In several NCCs African Pentecostal Churches are members already—but certainly the enormous fragmentation of African Christianity still continues, as until now there always will remain churches which prefer to stay apart and view those who collaborate on a broader ecumenical platform with suspicion. Many younger Pentecostal or Independent church leaders have also studied in mainline churches seminaries or faculties and many people know each other across the complete wide range of denominational identities. There are four areas in which a continuation of dialogue and research seems advisable and of interest for all sides for the future:

1. One field of intense interest and huge contemporary relevance is the range of topics under the umbrella theme *church, society, and corruption*. Many church leaders have an interest to protect their churches from charlatans and grave distortions in Christian faith and practices. One step towards better standards is a deliberate training in areas of corruption and also in certain basic criteria for a sound Christian ministry and pastoral counselling (where forms of misuses can be observed);

2. Another area is the huge interest to learn from each other in *biblically founded and integral concepts of development and sustainability*: It will be crucial to revive and remind church leaders about their assets and potentials to contribute to environmental awareness building and ethics of sustainability. AICs can contribute a lot from their traditional African wisdom traditions as the symbols of water, trees, hills and sacred places in nature play an important role in their self-understanding;

3. A third area might be the sensitive area of *gender relations, human rights and violence within families.* Knowing that education for women and affirming the rights fo women is a vital key for social development in African societies there are many positive signs of interest that this can become a joint field of interest between churches involved from all denominational traditions;

4. A last area relates to the ongoing *international dialogue on the core concepts of biblical Diaconia* as expressed in the new WCC study document on Ecumenical Diaconia—Called to Transformative Action." This study document which will be released during Central Committee meeting in June 2021 gives recognition to different regional contextual expressions of Diaconia (even the different languages and key sematic fields in referring to this in different churches) while maintaining some root principles all churches need to reflect in order to remain rooted within the biblical tradition of diaconal witness of Christianity as expressed in Biblical Tradition. Studying aspects of this document[14] together with mixed groups of theologians, pastors and social action practitioners and development agencies could become a major push for a broad based learning movement on the potentially huge African Christian contribution to integrqal and sustainable development which is so much needed as part of the ongoing genuine Reformation of African Christianity.

---

14. See WCC, "Ecumenical Diakonia"; "WCC Explores Ecumenical Diakonia"; LWF, "New Ecumenical Study."

17

African Pentecostalism and Prosperity
Continuity and Discontinuity

Allan H. Anderson

Introduction

I HAVE KNOWN KWABENA Asamoah-Gyadu since he was a PhD researcher at the University of Birmingham, where I first met him on taking up my post in 1995. I was also internal examiner of his thesis. We have kept in regular contact since, and have met on several occasions. I want to begin by paying tribute to Asamoah-Gyadu's informative and copious research on African Pentecostalism—especially in Ghana—over more than two decades. His penetrating insights based on participant observation and fieldwork, and his practical experience as a Charismatic Methodist minister himself are notable. Perhaps above all, his evangelical spirituality and dedication to his calling as both a scholar and minister of the gospel have been exemplary. This spirituality and dedication exudes from his academic writings and are not "secularized" or separated from his faith, as so often happens with us academics, especially when we sit in the ivory towers of a university.

This paper concentrates on one aspect of African Pentecostalism that Asamoah-Gyadu often alludes to in his many writings, the prevalent so-called "prosperity gospel," also known as "health and wealth" by its detractors, and the "Faith Message" or "Word of Faith" by its promoters. This was the subject of my first published academic paper over thirty years ago, amid rising concerns in South Africa about the growth of this movement.[1] There I gave a summary of the "prosperity message" coming from the USA, which was the main influence on the white Charismatic churches in South Africa in the 1980s, especially the most influential Rhema Bible Church led by Ray McCauley in the affluent Johannesburg suburb of Randburg. My article was somewhat apologetic, as it sought to balance the negative press in church and academic circles, but was a little over-reliant on the teachings given by "Word of Faith" preachers themselves (especially American ones) without thoroughly interrogating them. However, I did treat some of the critiques seriously, such as the role of faith used in some cases as a magic lever to move God into action, and placing human faith in the center, where people can measure faith by results. I pointed out the danger of the idea that attaining prosperity and health becomes evidence of spirituality. Faith does please God, even when there are no results whatever, as the "heroes of faith" in Hebrews 11 testify by their sufferings. The emphasis on prosperity also neglects the New Testament warnings of the dangers of riches, and the rewards for suffering and persecution. Perhaps the most penetrating and thorough study of the American version of the prosperity gospel is the ethnographical history by Kate Bowler,[2] but that excellent study is a world apart from that of Africa—which is not to say that American prosperity preachers did not have influence there.

When I completed this article back in 1987, black-led churches in South Africa had been relatively untouched by the prosperity gospel. This is no longer the case. The sub-Sahara as a whole is a region where this message is prominent in the preaching and teaching of Pentecostalism. Asamoah-Gyadu defines "prosperity gospel" as "the popular teaching that material things and wellbeing constitute the only sure indicators of God's favor."[3] An academic compendium on the subject defined "prosperity theologies" (because there are several versions) as teaching "more than material well-being; prosperity includes emotional, physical, and spiritual health, although the material aspects are often disproportionately emphasized."[4] One of the most critical voices in the collection, Daniela Augustine remarks that "the prosperity gospel offers a spiritualization and moral justification for the capitalist

1. Anderson, "Prosperity Message," 72–83.
2. Bowler, *Blessed*.
3. Asamoah-Gyadu, *Contemporary Pentecostal Christianity*, 107.
4. Attenasi, "Introduction," 4.

primacy of greed and self-indulgence" and consequently "blinds its subscribers to the value and dignity of human life" experienced in suffering and marginalization.[5] Some scholars have equated the African version of this message with some of the extreme teachings coming out of the USA.[6] However, we should not apply this indiscriminately to African preachers lest we misunderstand the African context, even in the case of megachurches who sell American televangelists' books in their bookstores. As Amos Yong points out, because the prosperity teaching is so pervasive across many different kinds of Pentecostalism, "it is very difficult to make reliable generalizations about it."[7] Interacting with the work of Asamoah-Gyadu, in this chapter I examine this teaching from the perspective of ancient African beliefs on prosperity and success, and discuss whether it represents continuity with African religious beliefs or a transformative discontinuity with past beliefs. I argue that it is in both continuity and discontinuity that we can best understand the popularity of this teaching.

Continuity and Discontinuity

Scholarly studies about the rapid expansion of Pentecostalism in different regions worldwide have not explored thoroughly what I argue is a principal reason for its popularity—the extent to which Pentecostalism, through its experience of the Spirit, often unconsciously taps into deep-seated religious and cultural beliefs.[8] It is its flexibility, not to be bound by European or North American forms of Christian faith and practice, but to be free to engage with different cultural and religious contexts, that makes it attractive all over the world. Pentecostalism draws from these ancient sources in continuity with them, while also simultaneously confronting some of their practices in discontinuity. It is therefore able to maintain tension between the past and the present, between the old and the new, between continuity and discontinuity. Whether in continuity or discontinuity, it uses a biblical rationale for its beliefs and practices. Pentecostalism makes a "radical break with the past," but this is not an either/or situation. What often appears as continuity is often at the same

---

5. Augustine, "Pentecost and Prosperity," 207.

6. In particular, Gifford, *African Christianity*; *Ghana's New Christianity*; *Christianity, Politics*.

7. Yong, "Typology," 15.

8. Part of what follows is adapted from my *Spirit-Filled World*, 3–9.

time discontinuity, because of the interpretation and meaning given to the phenomenon. The reverse is also the case, where practices found throughout global Pentecostalism are invested with new meanings through the encounter with a local religious and cultural context.

Difficulties arise when one side of this tension is emphasized to the detriment of the other. Until relatively recently, social scientists have considered Pentecostalism to be continuous with African and other "traditional" religions, and have not considered the discontinuity that pervades the global movement.[9] Although the theme of continuity has dominated the social sciences, it also appears in theological and religious studies. Walter J. Hollenweger wrote that Pentecostalism is based on its "black roots," mediated through its African American founders at Azusa Street, Los Angeles. These aspects of African religion cause it to flourish in similar cultures where "orality" is the dominant feature.[10]

Harvey Cox takes this a step further in his book *Fire from Heaven*, where he states that the rapid spread of Pentecostalism is because of its "heady and spontaneous spirituality," which he calls "primal spirituality." Pentecostalism's emphasis on experience is spread through testimony and personal contact.[11] In one of his most telling paragraphs, Cox suggests that for any religion to grow it must include two underlying factors: "be able to include and transform at least certain elements of pre-existing religions which still retain a strong grip on the cultural subconscious," and "also equip people to live in rapidly changing societies." He sees these two "key ingredients" in Pentecostalism, which helps "people recover vital elements in their culture that are threatened by modernization." Many of the beliefs and practices found in, say, Korean Pentecostalism, Cox traces back to Korean ancient shamanistic religion. He describes Korean Pentecostalism as "a massive importation of shamanic practice into a Christian ritual."[12] However, Cox gleaned this idea from Hollenweger, whose only Korean PhD student's thesis on "Korean Pentecostalism" was aimed at charismatic practices in the Presbyterian Church, which he considered to be a resurgence of shamanism. He did not study Korean Pentecostalism itself. What Cox hinted at when referring to "preexisting religions" with "a strong grip on the cultural subconscious" is the equivalent of an overemphasis on continuity.

9. Anderson, *Spirit-Filled World*, 4–5.
10. Hollenweger, *Pentecostalism*, 269–71.
11. Cox, *Fire from Heaven*, 71.
12. Cox, *Fire from Heaven*, 219–28, 240.

Similarly, many who have written on African Pentecostalism and independent churches have attributed their success to their continuation of an "enchanted worldview" that retains ideas from pre-Christian African religion—as Swedish missionary bishop Bengt Sundkler famously put it, creating a "bridge back to the past"—in other words, continuity. Sundkler later retracted this view, and insiders to Pentecostalism are quick to point out that Pentecostals *confront*, rather than accommodate the spirit world, so they would almost invariably point to a radical *discontinuity*. The result is two contrasting views of insiders and outsiders, and fierce battles between them. Nigerian Pentecostal scholar Nimi Wariboko describes the ability of Nigerian Pentecostals to be simultaneously "inside and outside African traditional religions," representing "both continuity and rupture in the same Nigerian religious landscape."[13] This inside/outside tension, though not developed in an explicit way, remains an underlying theme of his significant research.

The Holy Spirit occupies an important place in charismatic Christianity in Africa, whether it be the beliefs of Pentecostal or new charismatic churches, Charismatics in older churches, or older African independent "Spirit churches." At the same time, this becomes more meaningful when placed in the context of the spirit world that permeates most aspects of African life. This is the subject of my most recent book, *Spirit-Filled World*. While recognizing that the ideas concerning the spirit world are by no means homogeneous throughout sub-Saharan Africa, certain foundational similarities exist. In Africa, Pentecostalism permeates every historic denomination and independent church. It has not only contributed to the reshaping of the nature of Christianity but has also left an indelible mark on popular religion and culture. The ordinary adherents of Pentecostalism and related independent churches are usually on the cutting edge of encounters with the dynamic, popular religion that has existed for generations and still permeates African societies, albeit in interaction with a constantly changing context with globalizing tendencies.

Witchcraft and Power in Africa

In order to understand the prosperity message in Africa it is first necessary to consider the African spirit world. This is a ubiquitous realm of

---

13. Wariboko, *Nigerian Pentecostalism*, 5, 26.

witchcraft and misfortune or "bad luck."[14] Full of curses, evil spirits, nature spirits, and witch familiars, this is a dreadful and powerful world from which people need constant protection. In this world of pervasive spirits, there are disembodied spirits (both good and evil ones), which have mysterious and unknown forms, in contrast to the "embodied" ancestors, who are always recognizable. Through the influence of Christianity, the biblical words "demon" and "devil" are often applied to these spirits. How people address questions of evil and suffering, including "bad luck" (misfortune) in this spirit-filled world, and what the causes of this might be, are important considerations. Many Africans want to know *who* is responsible for affliction and trouble, rather than *what* the cause might be medically or psychologically—the focus of inquiry in western societies. "African" afflictions—distinguished from other illnesses—are caused by curses and witchcraft for which there is no medical solution. This belief in the fearful spirit world can have devastating consequences for human social relations. Beliefs about these spirits still continue, and the tension between continuity and discontinuity is maintained in contemporary African societies. For people all over the world, spirits are everywhere. One study among Protestant churches in Africa and Asia found

> most members . . . believe in spirits both good and evil, in witchcraft and sorcery. These beliefs are held by city dwellers, even highly educated ones, and by villagers in "backward" rural areas. Many church members are afraid that evil spirits may harm them, and look for ways to be protected from them or freed from their influence.[15]

Social scientist Adam Ashforth spent several years in Soweto, near Johannesburg, in the 1990s. His disturbing book *Madumo: A Man Bewitched* is set in the years following the end of apartheid. It tells the factual story of his pseudonymous friend Madumo, raised in the Zion Christian Church, who spent years struggling to free himself from the power of witchcraft and family curses. His story is tragic, though not unusual. His family rejected him after his mother died, accusing him of using witchcraft to kill her. He resorted to a diviner to free him from the curses he believed he had received, and he followed the diviner's harrowing prescriptions for ritual strengthening against them. He also consulted a prophet in his church who blamed his siblings for his troubles, and then through a feast at the ancestral home he

14. Adapted from Anderson, *Spirit-Filled World*, 113–16.
15. Währisch-Oblau, "Towards," 189.

tried to appease the ancestors whose protection he was deprived of—all to no avail. The book concludes with Madumo remaining with an overwhelming sense of powerlessness to change his dire circumstances. In his analysis, Ashforth points out that the "primary motivation" of witchcraft is jealousy. He defines witchcraft as "loosely understood as the capacity to cause harm or accumulate wealth by illegitimate occult means," and he adds that witchcraft "permeates every aspect of everyday life."[16] Ashforth depicts witchcraft as a complex system both reflecting and providing an explanation for the spiritual insecurity and misfortune felt by many people in African townships, especially those who are unemployed and desperately poor. His book, which offers no explanations or solutions, reveals the claim made often by social scientists that even when more "secular" reasons can be given for misfortune, in Africa it is almost always given a spiritual reason—witchcraft being the overwhelming one.

Throughout Africa, missionaries often contributed towards a rejection of the ambiguous and holistic nature of the spirit world and promoted a dualistic understanding of religion in which the Christian God was set over against the "pagan," "heathen" world of African religions, which they usually assigned to the realm of Satan. This had consequences. Birgit Meyer's ethnographic study on Charismatic Presbyterian churches in eastern Ghana, *Translating the Devil* is an important text and refers to how Pentecostals "translate" the spirit world. Meyer examines whether African Charismatics have simply transferred biblical concepts into already existing beliefs, without change. In particular, beliefs about spirits and evil are translated into the biblical idea of Satan and demons. This argument is not unusual in anthropological writing. Behrend and Luig, for example, write that "the conversion of African spirits into Christian ones is often accompanied by their devaluation, turning, for instance in Zambia, former respectable *Basangu* spirits symbolizing fertility, health, and wealth into malevolent spirits or the devil himself."[17]

Meyer takes this "conversion" a step further. In her case study, the missionaries of the Evangelical Presbyterian Church in Ghana believed in the realm of Satan but did not allow any ritualized practices of exorcism, or any emotional outbursts, during church activities. This eventually resulted in Pentecostal secessions. What they did in effect was to render "the Devil" as "a sort of sponge absorbing the old spiritual beings . . . a process

---

16. Ashforth, *Madumo*, 9.
17. Behrend and Luig, *Spirit Possession*, xv.

of diabolization."[18] Because there were no solutions offered by missionary Christianity to the "African" problems that people continued to experience, Africans turned to traditional remedies. As Meyer shows, the lack of a solution for their "difficult life conditions" created a situation for African Christians that had "split them away from the possibility of undertaking ritual action against evil powers."[19] The new churches created as a result, however, emphasized the ministry of deliverance from Satan and demons, an emphasis of most forms of African Pentecostalism. Through this emphasis, people transferred these new Christian ideas into the concepts that they were already familiar with. They were now able to bring their age-old fears and insecurities into the church and receive "deliverance" from them through the exorcism of demons.[20] In effect "the Devil" now defined almost all African traditional religious concepts and drove a wedge between those ideas and those who had been "born again." This will be no surprise to all who are familiar with the "born again" movement in Africa. To participate in the traditional rituals was tantamount to inviting the devil back into one's life. Meyer also examines the process that occurs when Africans encounter modernity. Modernity creates ambivalence for people who believe in a spirit-filled world. Pentecostalism (with its focus on message) is thoroughly "modern," and we might add, "discontinuous." Yet because it has no fixed form ("the Spirit moves where she wills"), it takes on local cultural forms effortlessly, and in this way provides a forum and ritual place for the spirit world to be dealt with. In this way the "old" becomes part of the "new," so this is the "continuous" aspect. Again, we must be careful to distinguish between *form* and *content* in this discussion. As Meyer argues, "Rather than offering new *content*, Pentecostalism offers converts above all a new, more adequate *form* through which to express their ideas."[21]

Ogbu Kalu takes a similar view when he notes that African Pentecostals have directly addressed the problem of evil forces "by turning the Bible into a canon of tribal history and weaving it into the indigenous worldviews."[22] Asamoah-Gyadu has made a valuable contribution to this discussion. He points to the "supreme power of the Holy Spirit who is considered to be able to overcome the demons of the traditional spiritual world, which is

18. Meyer, *Translating the Devil*, 103.
19. Meyer, *Translating the Devil*, 138–39.
20. Meyer, *Translating the Devil*, 211–12.
21. Meyer, *Translating the Devil*, 215.
22. Kalu, "Sankofa," 148.

a world of power."²³ In my own study, the conversations and testimonies recounted make it clear that both Pentecostals and other Christians continue to believe strongly in a spirit world hindering their every attempt at spiritual and economic progress. They see their faith in contradiction to and a means of escape from that world, and so they confront this world of evil spirits and demons. In doing so, their faith allows them to deal with fears and insecurities as they solve their ambivalence by keeping the old spirits and the new faith in creative tension. What has happened is that Pentecostal forms of Christianity, in advocating a complete break with the past—discontinuity—also and at the same time deal with the African spirit world ("the Devil") as the cause of every form of affliction and spiritual insecurity, and so in continuity with the past. Although there is a fervent belief that the past has gone and the new has come, this is tempered by the possibility that the past spirit world may still threaten and pursue the new Christian, who must remain vigilant and delivered.²⁴

The African Prosperity Gospel

Understanding this tension between continuity and discontinuity in African Pentecostalism, and the issues of witchcraft, spirits and misfortune are vitally important in a discussion about the prosperity gospel in Africa.²⁵ As Asamoah-Gyadu points out, witchcraft "remains the single most important explanation for the lack of material prosperity, progress and promotion in life."²⁶ Poverty and hardship in African popular religious thought is the result of a diminishing of power, and cannot easily be separated from the concept of omnipresent witchcraft, the work of evil spirits. As Ogbu Kalu puts it, "religious ardour may appear very materialistic as people strive to preserve their material sustenance in the midst of the machinations of pervasive evil forces."²⁷ If people believe that bad luck is evidence of the working of witchcraft and malice, and is the diminishing of power in an all-encompassing spirit world, then the opposite is also true: good luck, success, progress and relative prosperity is the blessing of God, the increasing of power and influence. Asamoah-Gyadu again writes of "African beliefs in the reality of

23. Asamoah-Gyadu, "Spirit and Spirits," 42.
24. Anderson, *Spirit-Filled World*, 179–82.
25. Anderson, *Spirit-Filled World*, 137–40.
26. Asamoah-Gyadu, "African Pentecostalism," 20.
27. Kalu, "Sankofa," 143.

the spirit world and the ardent desire to engage with it for the purposes of human survival, health, fruitfulness, and longevity."[28] So there is a direct connection between the spirit world and human flourishing.

The Pentecostal message of the power of the Holy Spirit, and especially its focus on healing, deliverance, and abundant living, resonates well with people who live in constant fear of a threatening invisible world of spirits and evil forces. In Africa, misfortune, illness, barrenness, and all forms of trouble are attributed to a loss of power and are brought about through witchcraft and curses. People feel trapped in a world from which there is no obvious escape. It is evidence of the widespread spiritual insecurity and fear that permeates African communities, especially experienced by people who are poor and unemployed. It follows that the opposite of this, success, prosperity and health, are evidence of the blessing of God, of an increase of abundant life-force, and of being a person with more power to live life in enjoyment and security. No human being can be blamed for wanting that, especially in those parts of Africa so ravished by poverty. Yong asks a very pertinent question about how the Christian message can be contextualized "in contexts marked by poverty, disease, and underdevelopment?"[29]

In recent years and for all the above reasons, it is little wonder that the "prosperity gospel" has become widespread in African Pentecostalism. Charismatic preachers throughout the continent proclaim a God who not only heals and delivers from demons, but promises success and prosperity to those who have faith. Christians are urged to "sow seeds" of their tithes and offerings to bring about the abundant blessing of financial and physical prosperity that is assured to every person who believes. Preachers invoke biblical promises, especially the prophet Malachi's command to bring in a tenth so that God would pour out abundant blessing, to encourage the faithful to give generously. This is not without its downside and its critics, even those sympathetic to African Pentecostalism, show how dangerous it can be.

Asamoah-Gyadu writes of how many contemporary African Pentecostals "have developed a certain penchant and proclivity for things that reflect glory and power, which includes seeing material acquisitions as reflective of God's favor almost to the total exclusion of any discussion of why people suffer." This, he points out, "is partly informed by the instrumental purposes that religions serve in African traditions."[30] Not only is suffering ignored,

---

28. Asamoah-Gyadu, "Spirit and Spirits," 41.
29. Yong, "Typology," 24.
30. Asamoah-Gyadu, *Contemporary Pentecostal Christianity*, 113–14.

but if the prosperity does not happen or suffering takes place, it is because of witchcraft: "witchcraft is easily invoked to explain the shortfalls of the prosperity gospel."[31] In another place he links the prosperity gospel with the fear of evil: "any form of misfortune is an indication of the supernatural evil in one form or another."[32] This can "deliberately create the impression that the Spirit-filled Christian becomes almost completely insulated from certain misfortunes that afflict other people."[33] These are serious shortcomings, and even worse, some of these preachers include a crass emphasis on financial giving and increase their own personal wealth at the expense of their followers. Asamoah-Gyadu describes "the main indicators of God's approval" as "luxurious cars, frequent trips abroad on first-class tickets, palatial homes and . . . testimonies of good health without any hint of illness."[34] These preachers have usually received their wealth through what are often the sacrificial gifts of their many followers. Some of these preachers can only be described as exploiting the aspirations of those who seek a life that is better than the dire circumstances they find themselves in.

It should be clear by now that the prosperity gospel is often in direct continuity with traditional African ideas, even in those places where ministries of "deliverance" constantly confront the "demons" of the old religion. However, some preachers sincerely believe that the prosperity message is a contextual message in a continent filled with misfortune and poverty. They also promote self-help schemes for better living, and business initiatives providing employment. Wariboko has shown how African prosperity preachers have different "paradigms," some of which promote economic development through hard work and professional excellence.[35] In South Africa, the "distinguishing feature" of the new Pentecostal churches is that they "encourage a sense of agency in its participants" with a positive message to people living on the margins of society: "you are a worthy person, and you can change and improve your life."[36] Chesnut points out that studies throughout the world "reveal a theology that encourages adherents to realize their potential through hard work, entrepreneurship, sobriety, and

---

31. Asamoah-Gyadu, "African Pentecostalism," 31.
32. Asamoah-Gyadu, *Contemporary Pentecostal Christianity*, 107.
33. Asamoah-Gyadu, *Contemporary Pentecostal Christianity*, 109–10.
34. Asamoah-Gyadu, *Contemporary Pentecostal Christianity*, 116.
35. Wariboko, "Pentecostal Paradigms," 35–59.
36. CDESA, "Under the Radar," 80.

wise investments."[37] We sorely need these efforts and should applaud them. African Pentecostal preachers everywhere proclaim a positive message of God's material provision. The reasons for this and the context in which this is found are very different from those of the notorious preachers of health and wealth in the American Bible Belt.

Prosperity is defined in a different way in African religions and has always been an important sign of the blessing of the Creator God. God is the ultimate source of power, the sustainer of life-force, success and prosperity. To have power is to be prosperous, successful, and healthy; to have less power is to be poor and to fail and suffer. There is no dichotomy in African religious thought between physical and spiritual poverty, or between physical blessings and spiritual ones. Salvation is holistic and covers the whole of life. When Africans say "God is good," "God is love," etcetera, they do not separate God's moral attributes from God's provision. As Kenyan theologian John Mbiti put it, traditional beliefs about God are inextricably linked to God's physical provision for creation:

> This is one of the most fundamental beliefs about God, and examples of it come from all over Africa. In various ways God provides for the things He has made, so that their existence can be maintained and continued. He provides life, fertility, rain, health and other necessities needed for sustaining creation. . . . It is also widely believed that God shows His providence through fertility and health of humans, cattle and fields, as well as through the plentifulness of children, cattle, food and other goods.[38]

So the question is not whether the "prosperity gospel" is compatible with African religions, because the answer should be obvious from this discussion. A question which might not yet have been answered sufficiently is how the prosperity gospel relates to the continuity/discontinuity tension and has been appropriated and transformed in Pentecostalism. We cannot simply regard the popularity of the teaching in Africa as a repetition of the American version. Rather, we need to see it in its context, in which we put the discontinuity of the global trend within Pentecostalism to confront the old religions together with the continuity of the African world. There, the only way to live above a hostile spirit world is to have more power, life-force, and material possessions—all of which only God can supply. When Pentecostal preachers back this up with biblical verses to show that the

---

37. Chesnut, "Prosperous Prosperity," 215.
38. Mbiti, *African Religions*, 41.

power of God's Spirit can enable people to live above their dire circumstances, this message is welcomed. However, when the message is linked to exploitation, where the only person really benefitting is the preacher, we should recoil in horror.

Pentecostalism worldwide reflects both the dynamic nature of Christianity and the religious background of its participants. Pentecostalism is popular in Africa precisely because, as Asamoah-Gyadu puts it, "it affirms traditional worldviews of mystical causality and provides the appropriate Christian ritual contexts within which the fears and insecurities of ordinary people may be dealt with."[39] In a book based on some of his sermons treating the Holy Spirit, he shows how central the Spirit is to Pentecostalism, and the "most critical" reason for its growth.[40] The Holy Spirit directs the life and worship of believers, enabling them to succeed in business, in politics, and to prosper in every area of life, including physical health and deliverance from evil forces. Sometimes there may be play-acting, manipulation, and even deception—but Africa does not have a monopoly on religious charlatans, and neither does Pentecostal Christianity.

The popular fringes of Pentecostalism promise unconditional health and wealth through faith in God. Asamoah-Gyadu warns of the dangers of accumulating wealth through dishonest means, evoking the story of Ananias and Sapphira, and he calls out some of the abuses found in churches in Africa.[41] In one of his most revealing passages he makes the direct connection between the prosperity gospel and African tradition. After writing of the one-sided emphasis that overlooks the "painful cost of discipleship," he writes:

> As a result, success and promotion, wellbeing and empowerment, fruitfulness and breakthrough theologies have become the dominant themes of neo-Pentecostalism. Such an emphasis finds fertile soil in Africa because traditional religions themselves constitute survival strategies that attempt, by whatever means possible . . . to exterminate obstacles to power and prosperity in order to achieve wellbeing in this life."[42]

---

39. Asamoah-Gyadu, "Spirit and Spirits," 50.
40. Asamoah-Gyadu, *Holy Spirit*, 228–30.
41. Asamoah-Gyadu, *Holy Spirit*, 173–74.
42. Asamoah-Gyadu, *Contemporary Pentecostal Christianity*, 114.

He goes on to state that the overemphasis "has the potential to undermine the central message of the cross in demonstrating God's power or glory through weakness."[43]

Conclusion

The new forms of African Pentecostalism that emerged towards the end of the twentieth century show that there are still unresolved questions to be answered. Pentecostalism, in keeping with traditional questions relating to the role of "success" and "prosperity" in God's economy, shows that God's gifts of healing and material provision and the holistic dimension of "salvation" are particularly meaningful in an African context of widespread poverty and inadequate health provision. The "here-and-now" challenges these churches address still challenge the church as a whole. But there are seldom instant solutions to life's challenges and certainly not on a "name it and claim it" basis. We should not measure Christian faith in terms of success. People are not only convinced by the successes in living out Christian faith, but also by perseverance under its trials, as Asamoah-Gyadu has pointed out. A one-sided triumphalist, power theology is dangerous and must be balanced. Pentecostalism is claimed to be a movement of the Holy Spirit. The Spirit is not only a Spirit of power, but also a "holy" Spirit, a gentle dove, a Spirit of humility, patience and meekness, of love, joy and peace. The Spirit is the tender Comforter, the one who comes alongside to help and strengthen people through life's trials and challenges. This ministry of the Spirit needs to be emphasized in an Africa plagued with spiritual insecurity, famine, poverty, economic and political oppression, and disease. Overemphasizing outward success often leads to bitter disappointment and disillusionment when that success does not evidently and immediately happen. Our theology must not only focus on power when there is a lack of it—it must also be able to sustain people through life's tragedies and failures, especially when there is no visible or instant success. My first academic article agonized over the "prosperity message" and warned that although its preachers are sometimes guilty of always seeing the "not yet" as "already," there was also the danger of always seeing the "not yet" as "not yet." I concluded with the rhetorical question:

---

43. Asamoah-Gyadu, *Contemporary Pentecostal Christianity*, 115.

"Would not our message be more relevant . . . if it provided for the *whole* of human needs and not only 'spiritual' needs?"[44]

Christianity is affected by and affects religious beliefs in many fundamental ways. Both in its similarities and in its differences with African beliefs and rituals, Pentecostalism has succeeded in remarkable ways to integrate these throughout the sub-Sahara. The world of ancestors, witchcraft, evil spirits, witch familiars, and demonic forces is believed to be responsible for all kinds of events—including misfortune, illness, poverty, and a host of other social, economic, and political problems bringing spiritual insecurity. These beliefs are in continuity with the past. In its encounter with this spirit world, Pentecostalism offers radical, discontinuous solutions to all these problems through its emphasis on the power of the Spirit and the exercise of "spiritual gifts." In confronting this pervasive spirit world, however, Pentecostalism also helps preserve it. This may be a compelling explanation for the popularity of Pentecostalism outside what has become a rational, largely secularized, western world.

---

44. Anderson, "Prosperity Message," 81.

Bibliography

Abbott, Lyman. *The Acts of the Apostles*. New York: A. S. Barnes, 1876.
Abimbola, Oluwaseun. "The Legend of Ajala's Travels and Transnational Backpacking in Africa." MA thesis, University of Ibadan, Nigeria, 2015.
Achebe, Chinua. *Things Fall Apart*. London: Heinemann, 1958.
Adam, S., and J. Vercoutter. "The Importance of Nubia: A Link between Central Africa and the Mediterranean." In *Ancient Civilizations of Africa*, edited by G. Mokhtar, 298–321. Berkeley: University of California Press, 1981.
Adams, William Y. *Nubia: Corridor to Africa*. Princeton: Princeton University Press, 1977.
Ade Ajayi, J. F. *Christian Missions in Nigeria 1841–1891: The Making of a New Elite*. Evanston, IL: Northwestern University Press, 1969.
Adeleye, Femi B., et al. "A Call for Biblical Faithfulness amid the New Fascism." *INFEMIT* (blog), January 20, 2017. Online. https://infemit.org/call-biblical-faithfulness.
Adeoti, Ezekiel Oladele. "African History and the Tradition of Historical Writing." *Journal of Social Sciences* 3.2 (2014) 317–22.
Adesoji, Abimbola O. "The New Pentecostal Movement in Nigeria and the Politics of Belonging." *Journal of Asian and African Studies* 52.8 (2017) 1159–73.
Adogame, Afe. *The African Christian Diaspora: New Currents and Emerging Trends in World Christianity*. London: Bloomsbury, 2013.
Afulike, C. C. "Luke's Portrayal of the Social Dimension in the Ministry of Jesus and the Apostles (Luke-Acts) according to Isaiah's Message of Social Justice in Chapters 61:1–2 and 58:6." *Journal of Religious & Theological Information* 17.2 (2018) 41–54.
Agbeti, J. Kofi. *West Africa Church History: Christian Missions and Church Foundations 1482–1919*. Leiden: Brill, 1986.
Agyarko, Robert Owusu. "Libation in African Christian Theology: A Critical Comparison of the Views of Kwasi Sarpong, Kwesi Dickson, John Pobee, and Kwame Bediako." MA thesis, University of the Western Cape, South Africa, 2005.
Agyinasare, C. *Till Death Do Us Part: Building a Fire Proof Marriage*. Second ed. Accra: Breakthrough, 2018.

BIBLIOGRAPHY

Akhazemea, Daniel, and Babatunde Adedibu. "The Redeemed Christian Church of God, A Missionary Global Player: What Is Her Message Regarding Human Development?" In *Encounter Beyond Routine: International Consultation, Academy of Mission, Hamburg, January 17–23, 2011*, edited by Owe Boersma and Wilfried Neusel, 53–64. Hamburg: Evangelisches Missionswerk in Deutschland eV, 2011.

Akoko, Matthew A. *The Ngwo Blue Print*. Bamenda: Ngwo Cultural and Development Association, 2014.

Akoko, Robert. *"Ask and You Shall Be Given": Pentecostalism and the Economic Crisis in Cameroon*. Leiden: African Studies Centre, 2007.

———. "New Pentecostalism in the Wake of the Economic Crisis in Cameroon." *Nordic Journal of African Studies* 11.3 (2002) 359–76.

Allman, Jean. "Fashioning Africa: Power and the Politics of Dress." In *Fashioning Africa Power and the Politics of Dress*, edited by Jean Marie Allman, 1–12. Indianapolis: Indiana University Press, 2004.

———. "'Let Your Fashion Be in Line with Our Ghanaian Costume': Nation, Gender, and the Politics of Clothing in Nkrumah's Ghana." In *Fashioning Africa Power and the Politics of Dress*, edited by Jean Marie Allman, 144–65. Indianapolis: Indiana University Press, 2004.

Amissah, Patrick K. "Justice and Righteousness in the Prophecy of Amos and Their Relevance to Issues of Contemporary Social Justice in the Church in Ghana." PhD diss., King's College London, 2016. Online. https://kclpure.kcl.ac.uk/portal/files/51215526/2016_Amissah_Patrick_Kofi_0848210_ethesis.pdf.

———. "A Reflection on the Prophetic Voice of Amos on Social Injustice in Ghana." *Trinity Journal of Church and Theology* 20.1 (2019) 31–57.

Ampofo, A. A. "Africa's Fast-Growing Pentecostal Mega Churches Are Entrenching Old Injustices Against Women." *Quartz Africa*, June 16, 2017. Online. https://qz.com/africa/1007819/pentecostal-churches-in-ghana-and-nigeria-are-entrenching-sexist-gender-roles-for-women.

Anderson, Allan H. *African Reformation: African Initiated Christianity in the Twentieth Century*. New Jersey: Africa World, 2001.

———. *Bazalwane: African Pentecostals in South Africa*. Pretoria: University of South Africa, 1992.

———. *An Introduction to Pentecostalism*. Cambridge: Cambridge University Press, 2004.

———. "The Prosperity Message in the Eschatology of Some New Charismatic Churches in South Africa." *Missionalia* 15.2 (1987) 72–83.

———. *Spirit-Filled World: Religious Dis/Continuity in African Pentecostalism*. Cham, Switzerland: Palgrave Macmillan, 2018.

———. *Spreading Fires: The Missionary Nature of Early Pentecostalism*. London: SCM, 2007.

Andrews, Edward E. "Christian Missions and Colonial Empires Reconsidered: A Black Evangelist in West Africa, 1766–1816." *Journal of Church and State* 51.4 (2009) 663–91.

Anim, Emmanuel Kwesi. "The Prosperity Gospel and the Primal Imagination." *Trinity Journal of Church and Society* 17.2 (2009) 32–53.

———. "Who Wants to Be a Millionaire? An Analysis of Prosperity Teaching in the Charismatic Ministry (Churches) in Ghana and Its Wider Impact." PhD diss., All Nations Christian College, Hertfordshire, UK, 2003.

Annor-Antwi, Gibson. *Myth or Mystery: The "Bio-Autobiography" of Professor Opoku Onyinah*. London: Ived, 2016.
Ansah, N. Gladys. "Harnessing our Multilingual Heritage for National Development." Lecture delivered at the Inter-College Lecture Series, ISSER Conference Facility, University of Ghana, May 2, 2019.
Anti, K. K. Amos. "Libation in the Old Testament and Akan Life and Thought: A Critique." PhD diss., Selly Oak College, Birmingham, UK, 1987.
Armah, Ayi Kwei. *Fragments*. London: Heinemann, 1974.
Asamoah-Gyadu, J. Kwabena. *African Charismatics: Current Developments within Independent Indigenous Pentecostalism in Ghana*. Leiden: Brill, 2005.
———. "African Pentecostalism, Deliverance, and Healing: Recent Developments and New Challenges." In *Witchcraft, Demons, and Deliverance: A Global Conversation on an Intercultural Challenge*, edited by Claudia Währisch-Oblau and Henning Wrogemann, 17–40. Zürich: LIT, 2015.
———. "African Traditional Religion, Pentecostalism, and the Clash of Spiritualities in Ghana." In *Fundamentalisms and the Media*, editors Stewart M. Hoover and Nadia Kaneva, 161–78. London: Continuum, 2009.
———. "Anointing through the Screen: Neo-Pentecostalism and Televised Christianity in Ghana." *Studies in World Christianity* 11 (2005) 1–28.
———. "'Broken Calabashes and Covenants of Fruitfulness': Cursing Barrenness in Contemporary African Christianity." *Journal of Religion in Africa* 37.4 (2007) 437–60.
———. "'Christ Is the Answer': What is the Question? A Ghana Airways Prayer Vigil and its Implications for Religion, Evil, and Public Space." *Journal of Religion in Africa* 35 (2005) 93–117.
———. "Christianity and Sports: Religious Functionaries and Charismatic Prophets in Ghana Soccer." *Studies in World Christianity* 21.3 (2015) 239–59.
———. *Contemporary Pentecostal Christianity*. Oxford: Regnum, 2013.
———. *Contemporary Pentecostal Christianity: Interpretations from an African Context*. Eugene, OR: Wipf & Stock, 2013.
———. "From Every Nation Under Heaven." In *Global Renewal Christianity: Spirit-Empowered Movements Past, Present, and Future*, edited by Vinson Synan et al., xxvii–liv. Florida: Charisma, 2016.
———. "'Get Up . . . Take the Child . . . and Escape to Egypt': Transforming Christianity into a Non-Western Religion in Africa." *International Review of Mission* 100.2 (2011) 337–54.
———. "'Go Near and Join Thyself to This Chariot . . .': African Pneumatic Movements and Transformational Discipleship." *International Review of Mission* 106.2 (2017) 336–55.
———. "God Bless Our Homeland Ghana: Religion and Politics in a Post-Colonial African State." *Studies in World Christianity & Interreligious Relations* 48.1 (2014) 165–83.
———. "God Is Big in Africa: Pentecostal Mega Churches and a Changing Religious Landscape." *Material Religion: The Journal of Objects Art and Belief* 15.3 (2019) 1–4.
———. "Growth and Trends in African Christianity in the Twenty-First Century." In *Anthology of African Christianity*, edited by Isabel Apawo Phili and Dietrich Werner, 65–75. Oxford: Regnum, 2016.

———. *The Holy Spirit Our Comforter: An Exercise in Homiletic Pneumatology*. Accra: Step, 2017.

———. "An Introduction into the Typology of African Christianity." In *Anthology of African Christianity*, edited by Isabel Apawo Phili and Dietrich Werner, 65–75. Oxford: Regnum, 2016.

———. "Kwame Bediako and the Eternal Christological Question." In *Seeing New Facets of the Diamond: Christianity as a Universal Faith—Essays in Honor of Kwame Bediako*, edited by Kwame Bediako et al., 38–55. Akropong-Akuapem, Ghana: Regnum Africa, 2014.

———. "Learning to Prosper by Wrestling and by Negotiation: Jacob and Esau in Contemporary African Pentecostal Hermeneutics." *Journal of Pentecostal Theology* 21.1 (2012) 64–86.

———. "Mediating Spiritual Power: African Christianity, Transnationalism, and the Media." In *Religion Crossing Boundaries: Transnational Religious and Social Dynamics in Africa and the New African Diaspora*, edited by Afe Adogame and James V. Spickard, 87–105. Leiden: Brill, 2010.

———. "Of Faith and Visual Alertness: The Message of 'Mediatized' Religion in an African Pentecostal Context." *Material Religion* 1.3 (2005) 336–56.

———. "On the 'Mountain of the Lord': Healing Pilgrimages in Ghanaian Christianity." *Exchange* 36.1 (2007) 65–86.

———. "Pentecostal Media Images and Religious Globalization in Sub-Saharan Africa." In *Belief in Media: Cultural Perspectives on Media Christianity*, edited by Peter Horsfield et al., 65–79. Aldershot: Ashgate, 2004.

———. "Pentecostalism and the Influence of Primal Realities in Africa." In *The Many Faces of Global Pentecostalism*, edited by Harold D. Hunter and Neil Ormerod, 139–61. Cleveland, TN: CPT, 2013.

———. "Prosperity and Poverty in the Bible: Ghana's Experience." In *Prosperity Theology and the Gospel: Good News for the Poor?*, edited by J. Daniel Salinas, 99–114. Peabody: Lausanne Movement, 2017.

———. "Pulling Down Strongholds: Evangelism, Principalities, and Powers and the African Pentecostal Imagination." *International Review of Mission* 96 (2007) 306–17.

———. "Renewal within African Christianity: A Study of Some Current Historical and Theological Developments within Independent Indigenous Pentecostalism in Ghana." PhD diss., University of Birmingham, 2000.

———. "The Search for Balance: Prosperity and Poverty in the Bible." Lecture delivered at the Lausanne Global Consultation on Prosperity Theology, Poverty, and the Gospel, São Paulo, Brazil, March 30–April 2, 2014. *YouTube* video, 33:38. May 28, 2014. https://youtu.be/Gk7slNftZuc.

———. *Sighs and Signs of the Spirit: Ghanaian Perspectives on Pentecostalism and Renewal in Africa*. Eugene, OR: Wipf & Stock, 2015.

———. "Sighs and Signs of the Spirit: Ghanaian Perspectives on Pentecostalism and Renewal in Africa." *PentecoStudies: An Interdisciplinary Journal for Research on the Pentecostal and Charismatic Movements* 17.2 (2018) 230–32.

———. "Spirit and Spirits in African Religious Traditions." In *Interdisciplinary and Religio-Cultural Discourses on a Spirit-filled World: Loosing the Spirits*, edited by Veli-Matti Kärkkäinen et al., 41–53. Cham, Switzerland: Palgrave Macmillan, 2013.

———. *Taking Territories and Raising Champions: Contemporary Pentecostalism and the Changing Face of Christianity in Africa 1980-2010.* Legon: Trinity Theological Seminary, 2010.

———. "Theological Education." In *West Africa in Handbook of Theological Education in Africa*, edited by Isabel Apawo Phili and Dietrich, 146–53. Oxford: Regnum, 2013.

———. "Therapeutic Strategies in African Religions: Health, Herbal Medicines and Indigenous Christian Spirituality." *Studies in World Christianity* 20.1 (2014) 70–90.

———. "'To the Ends of the Earth': Mission, Migration, and the Impact of African-Led Pentecostal Churches in the European Diaspora." *Mission Studies* 29.1 (2012) 23–44.

———. "You Shall Receive Power: Empowered in Pentecostalism/Charismatic Christianity." In *Pentecostal Mission and Global Christianity*, edited by Wonsuk Ma et al., 45–66. Oxford: Regnum, 2014.

———. "'Your Miracle Is on the Way': Oral Roberts and Mediated Pentecostalism in Africa." *Spiritus: ORU Journal of Theology* 3.1 (2018). Online. https://digitalshowcase.oru.edu/spiritus/vol3/iss1/4.

Ashforth, Adam. *Madumo: A Man Bewitched.* Chicago: University of Chicago Press, 2000.

Attenasi, Katherine. "Introduction: The Plurality of Prosperity Theologies and Pentecostalisms." In *Pentecostalism and Prosperity: The Socio-Economics of the Global Charismatic Movement*, edited by Katherine Attenasi and Amos Yong, 1–12. Cham, Switzerland: Palgrave Macmillan, 2012.

Augustine, Daniela C. "Pentecost and Prosperity in Eastern Europe: Between Sharing of Possessions and Accumulating Personal Wealth." In *Pentecostalism and Prosperity: The Socio-Economics of the Global Charismatic Movement*, edited by Katherine Attenasi and Amos Yong, 189–212. Cham, Switzerland: Palgrave Macmillan, 2012.

Aune, David E. *The Westminster Dictionary of New Testament and Early Christian Literature and Rhetoric.* Louisville: Westminster John Knox, 2003.

Awolalu, Joseph Omosade. *Yoruba Beliefs and Sacrificial Rites.* London: Longman, 1979.

Ayandele, Emmanuel A. *African Historical Studies.* London: Frank Class, 1979.

———. *Holy Johnson: Pioneer of African Nationalism 1836-1917.* London: Longmans, Green & Co., 1970

———. *The Missionary Impact on Modern Nigeria, 1842-1914.* London: Longmans, Green & Co. 1966.

Babalola, E. O. *Christianity in West Africa.* Ibadan: Bamboye, 1988.

Badie, Bertrand, and Mane-Claude Smouts. *Le retoumement du monde: Sociologie de la scine internationale* Paris: Presses de la Foundation Nationale des Sciences Politiques & Dalloz, 1992.

Baeta, Christian G., ed. *Christianity in Tropical Africa.* London: Oxford University Press, 1968.

———. *Prophetism in Ghana: A Study of Some "Spiritual" Churches.* London: SCM, 1962.

Balz, Heinrich. *Where the Faith Has to Live: Studies in the Bakossi Society and Religion.* Berlin: Dietrich Reimer Verlag, 1984.

Bame, Michael. *The Supernatural Powers of Evil.* Yaounde: Agwecam, 1985.

Barber, Lionel, et al. "Vladimir Putin Says Liberalism Has 'Become Obsolete.'" *Financial Times*, June 28, 2019. Online. https://www.ft.com/content/670039ec-98f3-11e9-9573-ee5cbb98ed36.

Barnes, Andrew E. *Global Christianity and the Black Atlantic.* Waco, TX: Baylor University Press, 2017.

BIBLIOGRAPHY

Barrett, C. K. *A Critical and Exegetical Commentary on the Acts of the Apostles*. 2 vols. Edinburgh: T & T Clark, 1994, 1998.

Barrow, Christine, and Peter Aggleton. "'Good Face, Bad Mind?' HIV Stigma and Tolerance Rhetoric in Barbados." *Social and Economic Studies* 62.1/2 (2013) 29–52.

Barton, Mukta. "Woman and Man in Creation." In *Women of Courage: Asian Women Reading the Bible*, edited by Lee Oo Chung, 39–51. Seoul: Asian Women Resource Center, 1992.

Basham, Don. *Can a Christian Have a Demon?* Monroeville, PA: Whitaker, 1971.

Bassey, Nathaniel. "#HalleluyahChallenge/Testimonies." *Hallelujah Testimonies* (blog), June 14, 2017. Online. https://hallelujahchallenge.blogspot.com/2017/06/halleluyahchallenge-testimonies.html.

Baur, John. *Two Thousand Years of Christianity in Africa: An African Church History*. Nairobi: Pauline Africa, 1994.

Bediako, Kwame. *Christianity in Africa: The Renewal of a Non-Western Religion*. Edinburgh: Edinburgh University Press, 1995

———. *Theology and Identity*. Oxford: Regnum, 1992.

Behrend, Heike, and Ute Luig, eds. *Spirit Possession: Modernity and Power in Africa*. Oxford: James Currey, 1999.

Beti, Mongo. *The Poor Christ of Bomba*. Long Grove, IL: Waveland, 1971.

Bevans, Stephen B. "Plenary Address." Delivered at World Council Churches Assembly, Busan, South Korea, November 4, 2013.

Biehl, Michael. "Religion, Development, Mission." In *Religion: Help or Hindrance to Development?*, edited by Kenneth Mtata, 97–120. Geneva: Lutheran World Federation, 2013.

Bitrus, D. "Biblical Perspectives on Wealth Creation, Poverty Reduction, and Social Peace and Justice." *Transformation* 20.3 (2003) 139–43.

Bock, D. L. *Luke*. 2 vols BECNT. Grand Rapids: Baker Academic, 1994, 1996.

Boersma, Owe, and Wilfried Neusel, eds. *Encounter Beyond Routine: International Consultation, Academy of Mission, Hamburg, January 17–23, 2011*. Hamburg: Evangelisches Missionswerk in Deutschland eV, 2011.

Bongmba, Elias, ed. *Routledge Companion to Christianity in Africa*. New York: Routledge, 2016

Boni, Stefano. *Clearing the Ghanaian Forest: Theories and Practices of Acquisition, Transfer, and Utilization of Farming Cities in Sefwi-Akan Area*. Legon/Accra: Institute of African Studies, 2005.

Bosch, David J. "The Structure of Mission: An Exposition of Matthew 28:16–20." In *Exploring Church Growth*, edited by Wilbert R. Shenk, 218–48. Grand Rapids, MI: Eerdmans, 1983.

———. *Transforming Mission: Paradigm Shifts in Theology of Mission*. Maryknoll, NY: Orbis, 1991.

Bowcott, Owen, et al. "Johnson's Suspension of Parliament Unlawful, Supreme Court Rules." *Guardian*, September 24, 2019. Online. https://www.theguardian.com/law/2019/sep/24/boris-johnsons-suspension-of-parliament-unlawful-supreme-court-rules-prorogue.

Bowler, Kate. *Blessed: A History of the American Prosperity Gospel*. New York: Oxford University Press, 2013.

BIBLIOGRAPHY

Brachear, Manya. "Facebook and Christianity a Bad Mix, Chicago Parish Warns." *Chicago Tribune*, April 6, 2011. Online. https://www.chicagotribune.com/news/ct-xpm-2011-04-06-ct-talk-catholics-facebook-0407-20110406-story.html.

Bradshaw, Paul F. *The Search for the Origins of Christian Worship*. London: SPCK, 2002.

Bridges, Johns Cheryl. "Pentecostal Spirituality and Conscientization of Women." In *All Together in One Place*, edited by H. D. Hunter and P. D. Hoocker, 155–67. Sheffield: Sheffield Academic, 1993.

Brown, Rebecca. *He Came to Set the Captive Free*. Springdale, PA: Whitaker, 1992.

———. *Prepare for War*. Springdale, PA: Whitaker, 1987.

Bruce, F. F. *The Acts of the Apostles: The Greek Text with Introduction and Commentary*. Grand Rapids: Eerdmans, 1951.

———. *Commentary on the Book of the Acts: The English Text with Introduction, Exposition, and Notes*. NICNT. Grand Rapids: Eerdmans, 1977.

Buberwa, Elisa. "Spirits and Ancestors in African Traditional Religion (in the Context of Eastern Africa) and the Christian Teaching about the Holy Spirit: Convergences and Divergences." MA thesis, Wartburg Seminary, Dubuque, IA, 1996.

Bujo, Benezet. "Distinctives of African Ethics." In *African Theology on the Way: Current Conversations*, edited by Diane B. Stinton, 79–89. London: SPCK, 2010.

———. *Ethical Dimensions of Community: The Africa Model and the Dialogue between North and South*. Nairobi: Pauline's Publications, 1998.

Bultmann, Rudolf Karl. *Jesus Christ and Mythology*. New York: Scribner, 1958.

Burridge, Richard A. *What Are the Gospels? A Comparison with Graeco-Roman Biography*. SNTSMS 70. Cambridge: Cambridge University Press, 1992.

Burrus, Virginia. "The Gospel of Luke and the Acts of the Apostles." In *A Postcolonial Commentary on the New Testament Writings*, edited by F. F. Segovia and R. S. Sugirtharajah, 133–55. London: Continuum, 2007.

Burstein, Stanley. *Ancient African Civilizations: Kush and Axum*. Princeton: Marcus Wiener, 1998.

Byfield, Judith. "Dress and Politics in Post-World War II Abeokuta (Western Nigeria)." In *Fashioning Africa: Power and the Politics of Dress*, edited by Jean Marie Allman, 31–49. Indianapolis: Indiana University Press, 2004.

Byrskog, Samuel. *Story as History—History as Story: The Gospel Tradition in the Context of Ancient Oral History*. Boston: Brill, 2002.

Cabrita, Joel, et al., eds., *Relocating World Christianity: Interdisciplinary Studies in Universal and Local Expressions of the Christian Faith*. Leiden: Brill, 2017.

Carey, Hilary M. *God's Empire: Religion and Colonialism in the British World, 1801–1908*. New York: Cambridge University Press, 2011.

Casson, Lionel. *The Ancient Mariners: Seafarers and Sea Fighters of the Mediterranean in Ancient Times*. 2nd ed. Princeton, NJ: Princeton University Press, 1991.

Center for Development and Enterprise, South Africa (CDESA). "Under the Radar: Pentecostalism in South Africa and its Potential Social and Economic Role." In *Pentecostalism and Prosperity: The Socio-Economics of the Global Charismatic Movement*, edited by Katherine Attenasi and Amos Yong, 63–85. Cham, Switzerland: Palgrave Macmillan, 2012.

Central Intelligence Agency (CIA). "Africa: Egypt." *The World Factbook*. Online. https://www.cia.gov/library/publications/the-world-factbook/geos/eg.html.

Che, Beicho Vivian. "The Origin and Evolution of Obang Village from Pre-Colonial Period." Unpublished Paper, University of Buea, 1996.

Chesnut, R. Andrew. "Prosperous Prosperity: Why the Health and Wealth Gospel is Booming across the Globe." In *Pentecostalism and Prosperity: The Socio-Economics of the Global Charismatic Movement*, edited by Katherine Attenasi and Amos Yong, 215–23. Cham, Switzerland: Palgrave Macmillan, 2012.

Chidester, David. *Savage Systems: Colonialism and Comparative Religion in Southern Africa*. Cape Town: University of Cape Town Press, 1996.

Chike, Chigor. *The Holy Spirit in African Christianity*. Milton Keynes: Paternoster, 2016.

The Church of Pentecost. "Annual Statistics Report." Accra: Pentecost, 2019.

———. *The Church of Pentecost Ministerial Handbook*. Accra: Pentecost, 2018.

———. "Official Launch of MPWD, HUM, Counselling Ministry & Chaplaincy." Facebook video, 2:31:44. December 15, 2019. https://www.facebook.com/thecophq/videos/489915214963372.

———. "PENTSOS: Pentecost Social Services." Online. http://pentsos.org/our-history.

Clines, D. J. A. *The Dictionary of Classical Hebrew*. Sheffield: Sheffield Phoenix, 2011.

Cobba-Biney, Augustine. "Do Our Churches Need Dress Codes?" *Spectator*, February 20, 2010.

Collins, J. C. *Introduction to the Hebrew Bible*. Third ed. Minneapolis: Fortress, 2018.

Commission on World Mission and Evangelism (CWME). "Together Towards Life: Mission and Evangelism in Changing Landscapes." *World Council of Churches*, September 5, 2012. Online. http://www.oikoumene.org/en/resources/documents/commissions/mission-and-evangelism/together-towards-life-mission-and-evangelism-in-changing-landscapes.

Constantinides, E., and Stefan, J. Fountain. "Web 2.0: Conceptual Foundations and Marketing Issues." *Journal of Direct, Data, and Digital Marketing Practice* 9.3 (2007) 232–33.

Conzelmann, Hans. *A Commentary on the Acts of the Apostles*. Edited by Eldon Jay Epp and Christopher R. Matthews. Translated by James Limburg et al. Philadelphia: Fortress, 1987.

Cook, Arthur B. *Zeus: A Study in Ancient Religion*. Vol. 1. Cambridge: Cambridge University Press, 1940.

Cox, Harvey. *Fire from Heaven: The Rise of Pentecostal Spirituality and the Reshaping of Religion in the Twenty-First Century*. London: Cassell, 1996

Creswell, John W. *Research Design: Qualitative, Quantitative, and Mixed Methods Approaches*. London: Sage, 2009.

Crocker, P. T. "The City of Meroe and the Ethiopian Eunuch." *BurH* 22.3 (1986) 53–72.

Crosby, R. C. "A New Kind of Pentecostal." *Christianity Today*, August 3, 2011. Online. https://www.christianitytoday.com/ct/2011/august/newkindpentecostal.html.

"Daddy Freeze Hit at Nathaniel Bassey's 'Hallelujah Challenge.'" *Information Nigeria*, June 26, 2017. Online. https://www.informationnigeria.com/2017/06/daddy-freeze-hit-nathaniel-basseys-hallelujah-challenge-see-photos.html.

Dah, Jonas N. *The Angry Gods and the Eruption of the Cameroon Mountain 1999: A Report*. Kumba: Presprint, 1999.

———. *The Challenges of Spiritual Healing*. Bamenda: PCC DLTE, 2011.

———. *Christian Chiefs: Fallen Between Stools*. Bamenda: Peaceberg, 2014.

———. *Missionary Motivations and Methods: A Critical Examination of the Basel Mission in Cameroon 1886–1914*. Basel: University of Basel, 1983

———. "The Vision and Challenges of an Autonomous Church." In *Presbyterian Church in Cameroon: Fifty Years of Selfhood*, edited by Jonas N. Dah, 15–55. Limbe: Presprint, 2007.

Daughrity, Dyron B. *Rising: The Amazing Story of Christianity's Resurrection in the Global South*. Minneapolis: Augsburg Fortress, 2018.

Deissmann, Adolf. *Light from the Ancient East*. Grand Rapids: Baker, 1978.

DeLancey, Mark Dike, et al. *Historical Dictionary of the Republic of Cameroon*. Historical Dictionaries of Africa 113. Lanham: Scarecrow, 2010.

Denis, Philippe. "Christianity in Southern Africa." In *Anthology of African Christianity*, edited by Isabel Apawo Phili and Dietrich Werner, 248–58. Oxford: Regnum, 2016.

Denzin, Norman K., and Yvonne S. Lincoln, eds. *Handbook of Qualitative Research*. Third ed. Thousand Oaks, CA: Sage, 2005.

Dibelius, Martin. *Studies in the Acts of the Apostles*. Edited by H. Greeven. Translated by M. Ling. New York: Scribner's Sons, 1956.

Dickson, Kwesi A., and Paul Ellingworth. *Biblical Revelation and African Beliefs*. London: Lutterworth, 1969.

Dickson, Kwesi W. *Theology in Africa*. Maryknoll, NY: Darton, Longman & Todd, 1984.

Dijk, Rijk van. "Pentecostalism, Cultural Memory, and the State: Contested Representations of Time in Postcolonial Malawi." In *Memory and the Postcolony: African Anthropology and the Critique of Power*, edited by Richard Werbner, 155–81. London: Zed, 1998.

Domeris, W. R. "אביון." In *New International Dictionary of Old Testament Theology and Exegesis*, edited by W. A. Vangemeren, 228–32. Grand Rapids: Zondervan, 1997.

———. *Touching the Heart of God: The Social Construction of Poverty among Biblical Peasants*. London: T & T Clark, 2007.

Douglas, Mary. *Purity and Danger: An Analysis of Concept of Pollution and Taboo*. London: Routledge, 1966.

Downe-Wamboldt, Barbara. "Content Analysis: Method, Applications, and Issues." *Health Care for Women International* 13 (1992) 313–21.

Du Bois, W. E. B. *The World and Africa*. New York: International, 1965.

Duchrow, U., and G. Liedke. *Shalom: Biblical Perspectives on Creation, Justice, and Peace*. Geneva: WCC, 1989.

Dutton, Edward. "Fashion." In *The Routledge Companion to Religion and Popular Culture*, edited by John C. Leyden and Eric Michael Mazur, 246–60. London: Routledge, 2015.

Dyer, B. R. "Good News to the Poor: Social Upheaval, Strong Warnings, and Sincere Giving in Luke-Acts." In *The Bible and Social Justice: Old Testament and New Testament Foundations for the Church's Urgent Call*, edited by C. L. Westfall and B. R. Dyer, 102–24. Eugene, OR: Pickwick, 2016.

Dzokoto, Vivian. "Adwenhoasem: An Akan Theory of Mind." *Journal of the Royal Anthropological Institute* 26.s1 (2020) 77–94.

Ecke, Jonas Paul. "Continuity and Discontinuity: Pentecostalism and Cultural Change in a Liberian Refugee Camp in Ghana." *PentecoStudies* 14.1 (2014) 42–71.

Eckey, Wilfried. *Die Apostelgeschichte: Der Weg des Evangeliums von Jerusalem nach Rom*. 2 vols. Neukirchen-Vluyn: Neukirchener Verlag, 2000.

"An Economy for the 99 Percent." *Oxfam*, January 15, 2017. Online. https://www.oxfamamerica.org/explore/research-publications/an-economy-for-the-99-percent.

Edgar, Sarah. "Success Stories." *SaveeldersTanzania* (blog), May 1, 2018. Online. https://saveelders2016.wordpress.com/2018/05/01/success-stories-save-elders-tz.

Ela, Jean Marc. *My Faith as an African*. Eugene, OR: Wipe & Stock, 1988.
Elizabeth, Fiorenza S. *Bread Not Stone: The Challenge of Feminist Biblical Interpretation*. Boston: Beacon, 1984.
———. *In Memory of Her: A Feminist Reconstruction of Christian Origins*. York: Crossroads, 1983
———. *Wisdom Ways: Introducing Feminist Biblical Interpretation*. Maryknoll, NY: Orbis, 2001.
Ellis, Stephen, and Gerrie ter Haar. "Religion and Politics in Sub-Saharan Africa." *Journal of Modern African Studies* 36.2 (1998) 175–201.
Engelke, Matthew. "Discontinuity and the Discourse of Conversion." *Journal of Religion in Africa* 34.1 (2004) 82–109.
———. "Past Pentecostalism: Notes on Rupture, Realignment, and Everyday Life in Pentecostal and African Independent Churches." *Africa* 80 (2010) 177–99.
Esoh, Felix Kang. "Christianity and Sar'h/Ezul (Libation) in Obang, Cameroon: A Cultural Historical Reconstruction." PhD diss., Yonsei University, Seoul, 2019.
Essel, Osuanyi Quaicoo. "Libation Art in Art of Ghana: Linking the Unlinked." *International Journal of African Society, Culture, and Traditions* 1.1 (2014) 39–49.
Evangelischen Missionswerks in Deutschland (EMW). *Von allen Enden der Erde: Die neuen Landschaften der Weltchristenheit*. Hamburg: EMW, 2014.
Faimau, Gabriel, and William O. Lesitaokana. *New Media and the Mediatization of Religion: An African Perspective*. Cambridge: Cambridge Scholars, 2018.
Falk, Peter. *The Growth of the Church in Africa*. Grand Rapids: Zondervan, 1979.
Farhadian, Charles E. *Introducing World Christianity*. Malden, MA: Blackwell, 2012.
Feltham PIWC Church. "Salem PIWC Youth Ministry." Facebook Post. March 10, 2019. Online. https://web.facebook.com/felthampiwc/photos/a.1960058924278037 /2302294483387811/?type=3&eid=ARAp2_5_ZBpNPqoB2oauNd2roT3UR KcgrwqaiJNloSkJlAYL8o_lVzkk5LHNekyG7fyLggPkQDwftJoG&_rdc=1&_rdr.
Fiedler, Klaus. *The Story of Faith Mission: From Hudson Taylor to Present Day Africa*. Oxford: Regnum, 1994.
Fitzmyer, Joseph A. *The Acts of the Apostles: A New Translation with Introduction and Commentary*. AB31. New York: Doubleday, 1998.
———. *The Gospel According to Luke: Introduction, Translation, and Notes*. Garden City, NY: Doubleday, 1981.
Flichy, Odile. *L'oeuvre de Luc: L'Évangile et les Actes des Apôtres*. CaÉ 114. Paris: Cerf, 2000.
Fomum, Zacharias Tanee. *The Way of Spiritual Warfare*. Yaounde: Christian, 1985.
Fossouo, Pascal. *Croyance Africaine aux Ancestres et Foi Christian: Debat pour une Reconciliation Spirituelle*. Ndoungue: Doudou, 2014.
Foucault, Michel. *The History of Sexuality*. Vol. 1. Translated by R. Hursley. London: Penguin, 1977.
Freeman, Dena. *Pentecostalism and Development: Churches, NGOs, and Social Change in Africa*. Basingstoke: Palgrave Macmillan, 2012.
———. "Pentecostalism and Economic Development in Sub-Sahara Africa." In *The Routledge Handbook of Religions and Global Development*, edited by Emma Tomalin, 114–26. Abingdon: Routledge, 2015.
Gabbatt, Adam. "Donald Trump's Tirade on Mexico's 'Drugs and Rapists' Outrages US Latinos." *Guardian*, June 15, 2015. https://www.theguardian.com/us-news/2015/ jun/16/donald-trump-mexico-presidential-speech-latino-hispanic.
Gaventa, Beverly Roberts. *Acts*. Nashville, TN: Abingdon, 2003.

BIBLIOGRAPHY

Geisinger, N. B. "Critical Feminist Theory, Rape, and Hooking Up." PhD diss., Iowa State University, 2011.

Gerloff, Roswith I. H. "The Holy Spirit and the African Diaspora: Spiritual, Cultural, and Social Roots of Black Pentecostal Churches." *EPTA Bulletin: Journal of the European Pentecostal Theological Association* 14 (1995) 85–103.

Gerrish, B. A. *A Prince of the Church: Schleiermacher and the Beginnings of Modern Theology.* London: SCM, 1984.

Gerson, Michael. "Trump Isn't Just Telling Lies, He's Inviting Loyalists to Live in His Own Political Reality." *Washington Post*, June 24, 2019. Online. https://www.washingtonpost.com/opinions/trump-isnt-just-speaking-lies-hes-inviting-loyalists-to-live-in-his-own-political-reality/2019/06/24/2be2bcc0-96c0-11e9-8d0a-5edd7e2025b1_story.html.

Ghana Statistical Services. *Domestic Violence in Ghana: Incidence, Attitudes, Determinants, and Consequences.* Brighton: Institute of Development Studies, 2016.

———. *Population and Housing Census 2000.* Accra: Ghana Statistical Service, 2002.

Gifford, Paul. *African Christianity: Its Public Role.* London: Hurst & Co., 1998.

———. *Christianity and Development and Modernity in Africa.* London: Hurst & Co., 2015.

———. *Christianity, Politics, and Public Life in Kenya.* London: Hurst, 2009.

———. *Ghana's New Christianity: Pentecostalism in a Globalizing African Economy.* Bloomington: Indiana University Press, 2004.

Gitau, Wanjiru M. *Megachurch Christianity Reconsidered: Millennials and Social Change in African Perspective.* Downers Grove, IL: InterVarsity, 2018.

Gonzales, Justo L. *Acts: The Gospel of the Spirit.* Maryknoll, NY: Orbis, 2001.

Gooder, Paula. "The Gospel of Luke: An Introduction." *YouTube* video, 24:59. January 4, 2013. https://youtu.be/X098Bs8u3lU.

Goodwin, J. M. "Social Justice: A Manifesto to the Missio Dei." *Didache: Faithful Teaching* 12.1 (2012) 1–10.

Goulder, M. D. *Type and History in Acts.* London: SPCK, 1964.

Granberg-Michaelson, Wesley. *From Times Square to Timbuktu: The Post-Christian West Meets the Non-Western Church.* Grand Rapids: Eerdmans, 2013.

———. *Future Faith: Ten Challenges Re-Shaping Christianity in the Twenty-First Century.* Philadelphia: Fortress, 2018.

Green, J. B. "Good News to Whom? Jesus and the 'Poor' in the Gospel of Luke." In *Jesus of Nazareth: Lord and Christ: Essays on the Historical Jesus and New Testament Christology*, edited by J. B. Green and M. Tuner, 59–74. Grand Rapids: Eerdmans, 1994.

Gyekye, Kwame. *An Essay on African Philosophical Thought: The Akan Conceptual Scheme.* Pennsylvania: Temple University Press, 1995.

Haar, Gerrie ter. *Religion and Development: Ways of Transforming the World.* London: Hurst & Co., 2011.

Hackett, Rosalind I. J. "Charismatic/Pentecostal Appropriation of Media Technologies in Nigeria and Ghana." *Journal of Religion in Africa* 27.3 (1998) 259–77.

———. "Radical Christian Revivalism in Nigeria and Ghana: Recent Patterns of Conflict and Intolerance." In *Proselytization and Communal Self-Determination in Africa*, edited by Abdullahi An-Na'im, 246–67. Maryknoll, NY: Orbis, 1999.

———. "Revitalization in African Tradition Religion." In *African Traditional Religions in Contemporary Society*, edited by Jacob K. Olupona, 135–48. St. Paul: Paragon, 1991.

BIBLIOGRAPHY

Hackett, Rosalind I. J., and B. F. Soares, eds. *New Media and Religious Transformations in Africa*. Bloomington: Indiana University Press, 2015.

Haenchen, Ernst. *The Acts of the Apostles: A Commentary*. Philadelphia: Westminster, 1971

Haers, J., and P. de Mey. *Theology and Conversation: Towards a Relational Theology*. Leuven: Leuven University Press, 2003.

Hakem A. A., et al. "The Civilization of Napata and Meroe." In *Ancient Civilizations of Africa*, edited by G. Mokhtar, 298–321. Berkeley: University of California Press, 1981.

"#HallelujahChallenge SWOT/Digital Audit—Day 14." *Evolve Press*, June 14, 2017. Online. https://www.facebook.com/notes/evolve-press/hallelujahchallenge-swot-digital-audit-day-14/1414145608678180.

Hamilton, V. P. "פקח." In *Dictionary of Old Testament Theology and Exegesis*, edited by W. A. Van Gemeren, 665–66. Grand Rapids: Zondervan, 1997.

Hanciles, Jehu H. *Beyond Christendom: Globalization, African Migration, and the Transformation of the West*. Maryknoll, NY: Orbis, 2008.

Hansberry, William Leo. *Africa and Africans as Seen by Classical Writers*. Edited by Joseph E. Harris. Washington, DC: Howard University Press, 1981.

Hanson, P. D. *The People Called: The Growth of Community in the Bible*. Louisville: Westminster John Knox, 2002.

Harris, R. Geoffrey. *Mission in the Gospels*. Peterborough: Epworth, 2004.

Hartmut, Rosa. *Social Acceleration: A New Theory of Modernity*. New York: Columbia University Press, 2015.

Harvey, Fiona, and Jillian Ambrose. "Pope Francis Declares 'Climate Emergency' and Urges Action." *Guardian*, June 14, 2019. Online. https://www.theguardian.com/environment/2019/jun/14/pope-francis-declares-climate-emergency-and-urges-action.

Hassan, Rumy. *Religion and Development in the Global South*. Cham, Switzerland: Palgrave Macmillan, 2017

Hasting, Adrian. *The Church in Africa 1450–1950*. Oxford: Clarendon, 1994.

Hauser-Renner, Heinz. "'Obstinate' Pastor and Pioneer Historian: The Impact of Basel Mission Ideology on the Thought of Carl Christian Reindorf." *International Bulletin of Missionary Research* 33.2 (2009) 68–69.

Haward-Mills, Daag. "Oh Ghana Girls." *YouTube* video, 3:19. November 12, 2014. https://youtu.be/XPudqyDeYoA.

Hays, R. B. *The Moral Vision of the New Testament: A Contemporary Introduction to New Testament Ethics*. San Francisco: HarperSanFrancisco, 1996.

Hayward, Victor E. W., ed. *African Independent Church Movements*. London: Edinburgh House, 1963.

Hegel, George Wilhelm Friedrich. *The Philosophy of History*. Kitchener: Batoche, 2001.

Hemer, Colin J. *The Book of Acts in the Setting of Hellenistic History*. Edited by Conrad H. Gempf. WUNT 49. Tübingen: Mohr, 1989.

Heuser, Andreas. "Concepts of 'Development' in Contemporary African Pentecostal Christianity." In *Religion: Help or Hindrance to Development?*, edited by Kenneth Mtata, 51–68. Minneapolis: Lutheran University Press, 2013.

Hickling, Frederick W., and Caryl James. "Traditional Mental Health Practices in Jamaica: On the Phenomenology of Red Eye, Bad-mind, and Obeah." In *Perspectives in*

Caribbean Psychology, edited by Frederick W. Hickling et al., 465–86. Kingston: Caribbean Institute of Mental Health and Substance Abuse, 2008.
Hjarvard, Stig. *The Mediatization of Culture and Society*. London: Routledge, 2013.
———. "Mediatization of Religion: A Theory of the Media as Agents of Religious Change." *Northern Lights: Film & Media Studies Yearbook* 6.1 (2008) 9–26.
———. "The Mediatization of Religion: Theorizing Religion, Media, and Social Change." *Culture and Religion* 12.2 (2011) 119–35.
Hjarvard, Stig, and Lövheim Mia, eds. *Mediatization and Religion: Nordic Perspectives*. Gothenburg: Nordicom, 2012.
Hodari, Askhari Johnson, et al. *Lifelines: The Black Book of Proverbs*. New York: Broadway, 2013.
Hollenweger, Walter J. *Pentecostalism: Origins and Developments Worldwide*. Peabody: Hendrickson, 1997.
Hoover, Stewart M. *Media, Home, and Family*. New York: Routledge, 2004.
———. "Practice, Autonomy, and Authority in the Digitally Religious and Digitally Spiritual." In *Digital Religion, Social Media, and Culture: Perspectives, Practices, and Futures*, edited by Pauline Hope Cheong, vii–xi. New York: Peter Lang, 2012.
Houston, W. J. *Contending for Justice: Ideologies and Theologies of Social Justice in the Old Testament*. London: T & T Clark, 2008.
Idowu, E. Bolaji. *Olodumare: God in Yoruba Belief*. London: Longman, 1962.
Irvin, Dale T., and Scott W. Sunquist. *History of the World Christian Movement*. Vol. 1. Maryknoll, NY: Orbis, 2001.
Irvine, Doreen. *From Witchcraft to Christ: My True Life Story*. London: Concordia, 1973.
"Isaiah 61: Cambridge Bible for Schools and Colleges." *Bible Hub*, 2019. Online. https://biblehub.com/commentaries/cambridge/isaiah/61.htm.
Isichei, Elizabeth. "A Soul of Fire." *Christian History* 22.3 (2003) 22.
Janson, Marloes, and Birgit Meyer. "Introduction: Towards a Framework for the Study of Christian–Muslim Encounters in Africa." *Africa* 86 (2016) 615–19.
Jeglitzka, Elisabeth, and Dietrich Werner. *Eco-Theology, Climate Justice, and Food Security*. Geneva: Theological Education and Christian Leadership Development, 2016.
Johnson, Luke Timothy. *The Acts of the Apostles*. SP 5. Collegeville, MN: Liturgical, 1992.
Johnson, Todd M., and Kenneth R. Ross, eds. *Atlas of Global Christianity*. Edinburgh: Edinburgh University Press, 2009.
Johnstone, Patrick, et al. *Operation World: Twenty-First Century Edition*. 6th ed. Carlisle: Paternoster Lifestyle, 2001.
Jørgensen, Knud. *Equipping for Service: Christian Leadership in Church and Society*. Oxford: Regnum, 2012.
Jubilee Church London, "School Uniform Scheme." *SENT*. Online. https://www.communityspiritlondon.org/enfield-school-uniform-scheme.
Jukko, Risto, and Jooseop Keum, eds. *Moving in the Spirit: Report of the World Council of Churches Conference on World Mission and Evangelism, March 8–13, 2018, Arusha, Tanzania*. Geneva: WCC, 2019.
Jumbam, Kenjo. *The White Man of God*. Oxford: Heinemann, 1980.
Kalu, Ogbu U., ed. *African Christianity: An African Story*. Pretoria: Department of Church History, University of Pretoria, 2005.
———. *African Pentecostalism: An Introduction*. Oxford: Oxford University Press, 2008.
———. *Power, Poverty, and Prayer: The Challenges of Poverty and Pluralism in African Christianity, 1960–1996*. Trenton, NJ: Africa World, 2006

———. "Sankofa: Pentecostalism and African Cultural Heritage." In *The Spirit in the World: Emerging Pentecostal Theologies in Global Contexts*, edited by Veli-Matti Kärkkäinen, 135–52. Grand Rapids: Eerdmans, 2009.

———. "The Shape and Flow of African Historiography." In *African Christianity: An African Story*, edited by Ogbu U. Kalu, 1–23. Pretoria: University of Pretoria, 2005.

———. "The Third Response: Pentecostalism and the Reconstruction of Christian Experience in Africa, 1970-1995." *Journal of African Christian Thought* 1.2 (1998) 3–16.

Kaplan, Andreas M., and Haenlein Micahel. "Users of the World, Unite! The Challenges and Opportunities of Social Media." *Business Horizons* 53 (2010) 59–68.

Karecki, Madge. "A Missiological Reflection on 'Together Towards Life: Mission and Evangelism in Changing Landscapes.'" *International Bulletin of Missionary Research* 38.4 (2014) 191–92.

Katenga-Kaunda, Mkotama. "Pentecostalism as a Political Movement in Africa." *International Association for Political Science Students (IAPSS)*, June 27, 2015. Online. https://www.iapss.org/2015/06/27/pentecostalism-as-a-political-movement-in-africa.

Kato, Byang H. *African Cultural Revolution and the Christian Faith*. Jos: Challenge, 1975

———. *Biblical Christianity in Arica*. Achimota: African Christian, 1985

———. *Theological Pitfalls in Africa*. Kisumu: Evangelical, 1975.

Kaunda, Chammah J. *The Nation That Fears God Prospers: A Critique of Zambian Pentecostal Theopolitical Imaginations*. Minneapolis, MN: Fortress, 2018.

Keener, Craig S. *Acts*. Cambridge: Cambridge University Press, 2020.

———. *Acts: An Exegetical Commentary*. 4 vols. Grand Rapids: Baker Academic, 2012–2015.

———. "The Aftermath of the Ethiopian Eunuch." *The AME Church Review* 118.385 (2002) 112–24.

———. "Novels' 'Exotic' Places and Luke's African Official (Acts 8:27)." *Andrews University Seminary Studies* 46.1 (2008) 5–20.

Keum, Jooseop, ed. *Together Towards Life: Mission and Evangelism in Changing Landscapes*. Geneva: WCC, 2013.

———. "Transforming Discipleship: Faith, Love, and Hope after Empire." Lecture delivered at 15th Joe A. and Nancy Vaughn Stalcup Lecture, Dallas, TX, 2019.

Kim, Elijah F. *The Rise of the Global South: The Decline of Western Christendom and the Rise of Majority World Christianity*. Eugene, OR: Wipf & Stock, 2012.

Kim, Kirsteen. "Christians without Borders and Churches on the Move." In *Catholicity Under Pressure: The Ambiguous Relationship between Diversity and Unity*, edited by Dagmar Heller and Peter Szentpétery, 93–116. Leipzig: Evangelische Verlagsanstalt, 2016.

———. *The Holy Spirit in the World: A Global Conversation*. Maryknoll, NY: Orbis, 2007.

———. *Joining in with the Spirit: Connecting World Church and Local Mission*. London: SCM, 2012.

———. *Mission in the Spirit: The Holy Spirit in Indian Christian Theologies*. Delhi: ISPCK, 2003.

Kim, Kirsteen, and Andrew Anderson, eds. *Edinburgh 2010: Mission Today and Tomorrow*. Oxford: Regnum, 2011.

Kim, Sebastian C. H., and Kirsteen Kim. *Christianity as a World Religion*. Second ed. London: Bloomsbury, 2016.

BIBLIOGRAPHY

———. *A History of Korean Christianity*. Cambridge: Cambridge University Press, 2015.
Kincaid, Jamaica. *A Small Place*. London: Daunt, 2018.
Kitchin, R. *Cyberspace: The World in Wires*. Chichester: Wiley, 1998.
Klauck, Hans-Josef. *Magic and Paganism in Early Christianity: The World of the Acts of the Apostles*. Translated by Brian McNeil. Minneapolis: Fortress, 2003.
Klein, Naomi. "Let Them Drown: The Violence of Othering in a Warming World." *London Review of Books* 38.11 (2016). Online. https://www.lrb.co.uk/the-paper/v38/n11/naomi-klein/let-them-drown.
Koduah, Alfred. *The Woman's Head-Covering in Church: Controversies Surrounding the Issue*. Accra: Excellent Printing, 2010.
Koehler, L., and W. Baumgartner. *Hebrew and Aramaic Lexicon of the Bible*. Leiden: Brill, 2001.
Kollmann, Bernd, "Philippus der Evangelist und die Anfänge der Heidenmission." *Bib* 81.4 (2000) 551–65.
Kraft, Charles H. *Christianity with Power*. Ann Arbor: Servant, 1989.
———. *Defeating the Dark Angels*. Kent: Sovereign World, 1993.
Kraybill, J. Nelson. *Imperial Cult and Commerce in John's Apocalypse*. JSNTSup 132. Sheffield: Sheffield Academic, 1996.
Kreamer, M. Christine. "Practical Beauty: Headgear for Daily Wear." In *Crowning Achievements: African Arts of Dressing the Head*, edited by Mary Jo Arnoldi et al., 83–98. Los Angeles: Folwer Museum of Cultural History, University of California, 1995.
Kuponu, Selome I. "Pentecostalism and Media: A Reflection on Space Contestation on the Internet." *International Journal of Social Sciences and Humanities Reviews* 5.1 (2015) 74–78.
Kwiyani, Harvey C. *Sent Forth: African Missionary Work in the West*. Maryknoll, NY: Orbis, 2014.
Lake, Kirsopp, and Henry J. Cadbury. *English Translation and Commentary*. Vol. 4 of *The Beginnings of Christianity*. Edited by F. J. Foakes Jackson and Kirsopp Lake. Grand Rapids: Baker, 1979.
Lanchester, John. "Brexit Blues." *London Review of Books* 38.15 (2016). Online. https://www.lrb.co.uk/the-paper/v38/n15/john-lanchester/brexit-blues.
Larbi, Emmanuel K. "The Nature of Continuity and Discontinuity of Ghanaian Pentecostal Concept of Salvation in African Cosmology." *Asian Journal of Pentecostal Studies* 5.1 (2002) 87–106.
———. *Pentecostalism: The Eddies of Ghanaian Christianity*. Accra: Centre for Pentecostal and Charismatic Studies, 2001.
Larkin, Brian. "Ahmed Deedat and the Form of Islamic Evangelism." *Social Text* 26 (2008) 101–21.
———. "Entangled Religions: Response to J. D. Y. Peel." *Africa* 86 (2016) 633–39.
Larkin, Brian, and Birgit Meyer. "Pentecostalism, Islam, and Culture: New Religious Movements in West Africa." In *Themes in West Africa's History*, edited by Emmanuel Akyeampong, 286–312. Oxford: James Currey, 2006.
Latourette, Kenneth Scott. *A History of the Expansion of Christianity*. 7 vols. New York: Harper Brothers, 1937–1945.
Lausanne Movement. *The Cape Town Commitment: A Confession of Faith and a Call to Action*. October 2010. Online. https://www.lausanne.org/content/ctcommitment#capetown.

Lausanne Theology Working Group. "Statement on the Prosperity Gospel." *Evangelical Review of Theology* 34.3 (2010) 99–102.
Leclant, J. "The Empire of Kush: Napata and Meroe." In *Ancient Civilizations of Africa*, edited by G. Mokhtar, 278–95. Vol. 2 of *General History of Africa*. Berkeley: University of California Press, 1981.
Leclerc, T. L. *Introduction to the Prophets: Their Stories, Sayings, and Scrolls*. New York: Paulist, 2007.
Lee, S. *A New Kind of Pentecostalism*. Amsterdam: Foundation, 2011.
Lefkowitz, Mary R. *Women in Greek Myth*. Baltimore: Johns Hopkins University Press, 1986.
Leonard, Christine. *A Giant in Ghana: The Story of James McKeown and the Church of Pentecost*. West Sussex: New Wine, 1985.
Levisen, Carsten, and Melissa Reshma Jogie. "The Trinidadian 'Theory of Mind': Personhood and Postcolonial Semantics." *International Journal of Language and Culture* 2.2 (2015) 169–93.
Lewis, Alan E. *Between Cross and Resurrection: A Theology of Holy Saturday*. Grand Rapids: Eerdmans, 2001.
Lewis, Jovan Scott. "A So Black People Stay: Bad-mind, Sufferation, and Discourses of Race and Unity in a Jamaican Craft Market." *The Journal of Latin American and Caribbean Anthropology* 20.2 (2015) 327–42.
The Lighthouse Church. "Ministries." *TLHC* (blog). Online. http://tlhc.church/ministries.
Littlewood, Margaret. "Bamum and Bamileke." In *Peoples of the Central Cameroons*, edited by Daryll Forde, 53–129. Ethnographic Survey of Africa 9. London: International African Institute, 1954.
Losch, Stephan. "Der Kämmerer der Königen Kandake (Apg. 8,27)." *ThQ* 111 (1930) 477–519
Löveheim, Mia. "Identity." *Digital Religion: Understanding Religious Practice in New Media Worlds*, edited by Heidi A. Campbell, 41–56. London: Routledge, 2013.
Lüdemann, Gerd. *Early Christianity according to the Traditions in Acts: A Commentary*. Minneapolis: Fortress, 1989.
Lugazia, Faith K. "'Theology of Presence' in African Christianity: A Transforming Missiological Factor for Women in Contemporary Pentecostal Churches in Africa." *International Review of Mission* 106.2 (2017) 307–21.
Lugazia, Faith K., and J. Rwamunyana. "The Effect of Culture on Gender Roles in the Protestant Church: A Case Study of the Protestant Churches in Huye District of Southern Province of Rwanda." *Family, Gender, and Community Development* 5 (2014) 53–82.
Luhrmann, Tanya M. "Thinking about Thinking: The Mind's Porosity and the Presence of the Gods." *Journal of the Royal Anthropological Institute* 26.s1 (2020) 148–62.
———. *When God Talks Back: Understanding the American Evangelical Relationship with God*. New York: Knopf, 2012.
Lutheran World Federation (LWF). "New Ecumenical Study Aims to Strengthen Diakonia." *Lutheran World Federation*, May 24, 2018. Online. https://www.lutheranworld.org/news/new-ecumenical-study-aims-strengthen-diakonia.
Lynch, Gordon, and Löveheim Mia. "The Mediatization of Religion Debate: An Introduction. Culture and Religion," *Culture and Religion: An Interdisciplinary Journal* 12.2 (2011) 111–17.

BIBLIOGRAPHY

MacKinnon, C. "Feminism, Marxism, Method, and State: Towards Feminist Jurisprudence." *Signs* 8.4 (1983) 635–58.

———. "Reflections on Sex Equality under the Law." *Yale Law Journal* 100.5 (1991) 1281–1328.

Magesa, Laurenti. *What Is Not Sacred?: African Spirituality*. Maryknoll, NY: Orbis, 2013.

Malina, B. J. "Wealth and Poverty in the New Testament and Its World." *Interpretation: A Journal of Bible and Theology* 41.4 (1987) 35–67.

Mangena, F. "Natural Law Ethics, Humanism, and the Concept of Retributive Justice among the Korekore-Nyombwe People of Northern Zimbabwe: An Ethical Investigation." PhD diss., University of Zimbabwe, 2008.

Marguerat, Daniel. *The First Christian Historian: Writing the "Acts of the Apostles."* Translated by Ken McKinney et al. SNTSMS 121. Cambridge: Cambridge University Press, 2002.

Markwei, Lawrence. "Church of Pentecost Relaxes 'Morality' Rules." *Ghanaian Times*, February 17, 2010.

Marshall, I. H. *The Gospel of Luke: A Commentary on the Greek Text*. New International Greek Testament Commentary (NIGTC). Grand Rapids: Eerdmans, 1978.

Marshall-Fratani, Ruth. "Mediating the Global and Local in Nigerian Pentecostalism." *Journal of Religion in Africa* 28.3 (1998) 278–315.

Mary, André. "Pilgrimage to Imeko (Nigeria): An African Church in the Time of the 'Global Village.'" *International Journal of Urban and Regional Research* 26 (2002) 106–20.

Maselko, Joanna, et al. "Religious Social Capital: Its Measurement and Utility in the Study of the Social Determinants of Health." *Soc Sci Med* 73.5 (2011) 759–67.

Masok, Emmanuel Basam. "How Should the Presbyterian Church in Cameroon Respond to Global Pentecostalism?" MA thesis, Presbyterian Theological Seminary, Kumba, 2010.

Maxwell, David. *African Gifts of the Spirit: Pentecostalism and the Rise of a Zimbabwean Transformational Religious Movement*. Oxford: James Curry, 2006.

———. "'Delivered from the Spirit of Poverty?' Pentecostalism, Prosperity, and Modernity in Zimbabwe." *Journal of Religion in Africa* 28.3 (1998) 350–73.

Maxwell, David, and Ingrid Lawrie, eds. *Christianity and the African Imagination*. Leiden: Brill, 2013

Mays, J. L. "Justice Perspectives from the Prophetic Tradition." In *Prophecy in Israel: Search for an Identity*, edited by D. L. Petersen, 144–58. London: SPCK, 1987.

Mazzoleni, Gianpietro, and Winfried Schulz. ""Mediatization" of Politics: A Challenge for Democracy?" *Political Communication* 16.3 (1999) 247–61.

Mbembe, Achille. "The Age of Humanism Is Ending." *Mail & Guardian*, December 22, 2016. Online. https://mg.co.za/article/2016-12-22-00-the-age-of-humanism-is-ending.

Mbiti, John S. *African Religions and Philosophy*. Garden City, NY: Anchor, 1970.

———. *Introduction to African Religion*. London: Heinemann, 1975.

———. "Theological Impotence and the Universality of the Church." *Lutheran World* 21.3 (1974) 251–60.

McCoskey, Denise Eileen. *Race: Antiquity and Its Legacy*. New York: Oxford University Press, 2012.

BIBLIOGRAPHY

McCulloch, Merran. "Tikar." In *Peoples of the Central Cameroons*, edited by Daryll Forde, 11–49. Ethnographic Survey of Africa 9. London: International African Institute, 1954.

McGregor, Elaine, and Siegel Melissa. "Social Media and Migration Research." United Nations University (UNU) and Maastricht Economic and Social Research Institute on Innovation and Technology (MERIT) Working Paper 68. 2013. Online. https://www.merit.unu.edu/publications/working-papers/abstract/?id=5334.

McLoughlin, William G. *Revivals, Awakenings, and Reform: An Essay on Religion and Social Change in America, 1607–1977*. Chicago: University of Chicago Press, 1978.

Medica, Hazra C. "The Influence of Anxiety: Re-Presentations of Identity in Antiguan Literature from 1890 to the Present." PhD diss., St. Anne's College, University of Oxford, 2014.

Mesthrie, Rajend, et al., eds. *Introducing Sociolinguistics*. Second ed. Edinburgh: Edinburgh University Press, 1949.

Meyer, Birgit, ed. *Aesthetic Formations: Media, Religion, and the Senses*. New York: Palgrave, 2013.

———. "Christianity in Africa: From African Independent to Pentecostal-Charismatic Churches." *Annual Review of Anthropology* 33 (2004) 447–50.

———. "Going and Making Public: Pentecostalism as Public Religion in Ghana." In *Christianity and Public Culture in Africa*, edited by H. Englund, 149–66. Athens: Ohio University Press, 2011.

———. "'Make a Complete Break with the Past': Memory and Postcolonial Modernity in Ghanaian Pentecostal Discourse." *Journal of Religion in Africa* 28.3 (1998) 316–49.

———. "Pentecostalism and Modern Audiovisual Media." In *Media and Identity in Africa*, edited by Kimani Njogu and John Middleton, 114–23. Bloomington: Indiana University Press, 2009.

———. "'Praise the Lord': Popular Cinema and Pentecostalite Style in Ghana's New Public Sphere." *American Ethnologist* 31 (2004) 92–110.

———. *Translating the Devil: Religion and Modernity among the Ewe in Ghana*. Edinburgh: Edinburgh University Press, 1999.

Meyer, Birgit, and Moors, A., eds. *Religion, Media, and the Public Sphere*. Bloomington: Indiana University Press, 2006.

Minns, Ellis H. *Scythians and Greeks: A Survey of Ancient History and Archaeology on the North Coast of the Euxine from the Danube to the Caucasus*. Cambridge: Cambridge University Press, 1913.

Mishra, Pankaj. *Age of Anger: A History of the Present*. London: Allen Lane, 2017.

Moberg, Marcus, and Kennet Granholm. "The Concept of the Post-Secular and the Contemporary Nexus of Religion, Media, Popular Culture, and Consumer Culture." In *Post-Secular Society*, edited by Peter Nynäs et al., 103–4. New York: Routledge, 2012.

Mokoko Gampiot, Aurélien, and Cécile Coquet-Mokoko. *Kimbanguism: An African Understanding of the Bible*. University Park, PA: Pennsylvania State University Press, 2017.

Motyer, J. A. *The Prophecy of Isaiah: An Introduction Commentary*. Downers Grove, IL: IVP Academic, 1993.

Müller, Jan-Werner. *What Is Populism?* Philadelphia: University of Pennsylvania Press, 2016.

Munck, Johannes. *The Acts of the Apostles*. AB 31. Garden City, NY: Doubleday, 1967.

Murray, Stuart. *Changing Mission: Learning from the New Churches*. London: Churches Together in Britain and Ireland, 2006.
Musoni, Philip. "African Pentecostalism and Sustainable Development: A Study on the Zimbabwe Assemblies of God Africa, Forward in Faith Church." *International Journal of Humanities and Social Science Invention* 2.10 (2013) 75–82.
Ncozana, Silas S. *The Spirit Dimension in African Christianity: A Pastoral Study Among the Tumbuka People of Northern Malawi*. Blantyre: Christian Literature Association, 2002.
Ndip, Philip Nkongho. *Prayer Blast: Seven Steps Journey of the Soul: Deliverance and Healing Handbook*. Yaounde: Book House, 2008.
Neba, Gala Otto. *Healing Services and Anointing: A Divine Sanction*. Yaounde: Messie, 2009.
Nehusi, Kimani S. K. *Libation: An Afrikan Ritual in the Circle of Life*. Lanham, MD: University Press of America, 2016.
Neville, R. "The Relevance of Creation and Righteousness to Intervention for the Poor and Needy in the Old Testament." *Tyndale Bulletin* 52.2 (2001) 307–10.
Niebuhr, Richard. *Christ and Culture*. New York: Harper Torch, 1956.
Nyamekye, E. *The Church of Pentecost—Vision 2023*. Accra: Church of Pentecost, 2019.
Nyanni, Caleb. "The Spirits and Transition: The Second Generation and The Church of Pentecost-UK." PhD diss., University of Birmingham, 2018.
Nyarko, G. A. *Poverty in Ghana: Theological Reflection on the Response of Some Churches in Kumasi Metropolitan Area*. Kumasi: KNUST, 2012.
Obadare, Ebenezer. *Pentecostal Republic: Religion and the Struggle for State Power in Nigeria*. London: Zed, 2018.
Oduyoye, Mercy Amba. *Beads and Strands: Reflections of an African Woman on Christianity in Africa*. Maryknoll, NY: Orbis, 2004.
Ofoe, Stephen Ofotsu. *The "Newness" Theology of Opoku Onyinah: For Christian Spirituality, Mission, and Thinking*. London: MSI, 2018.
Öhlmann, Philipp, et al. *African Initiated Christianity and the Decolonization of Development: Sustainable Development in Pentecostal and Independent Churches*. New York: Routledge, 2020.
Ojo, Matthew A. "The Church in the African State: The Charismatic/Pentecostal Experience in Nigeria." *Journal of African Christian Thought* 1.2 (1998) 25–32.
Oldham, J. H. *A Devotional Diary*. London: SCM, 1925.
Oliver, Roland, and J. D. Fage. *A Short History of Africa*. New York: Facts on File, 1989.
Olonilua, Ademola. "'Criticisms Made Hallelujah Challenge Bigger'—Nathaniel Bassey." *Punch*, June 24, 2017. Online. https://punchng.com/criticisms-made-hallelujah-challenge-bigger-nathaniel-bassey.
Olson, Roger E. "The Dark Side of Pentecostalism." *Roger E. Olson* (blog), October 31, 2016. Online. https://www.patheos.com/blogs/rogereolson/2016/10/the-dark-side-of-pentecostalism.
Olwa, Alfred. "Christianity in Eastern Africa." In *Anthology of African Christianity*, edited by Isabel Apawo Phili and Dietrich Werner, 222–36. Oxford: Regnum, 2016.
Olympic City PIWC (@OlympicCityPIWC). 2019. "Join Us for Our New Years' Service Tomorrow." Twitter, December 30, 2019, 6:56 a.m. https://twitter.com/OlympicCityPIWC/status/1211662455367196672.
Onyinah, Opoku. "African Christianity in the Twenty-First Century." *Word and World: Theology for Christian Ministry* 27.3 (2007) 305–14.

BIBLIOGRAPHY

———. "Akan Witchcraft and the Concept of Exorcism in the Church of Pentecost." PhD diss., University of Birmingham, 2002.

———. "Contemporary 'Witch-Demonology' in Africa." *International Review of Mission* 93.3 (2004) 330–45.

———. *Pentecostal Exorcism: Witchcraft and Demonology in Ghana*. Blandford: Deo, 2012.

Oosterwal, Gottfried. *Modern Messianic Movements as a Theological and Missionary Challenge*. Elkhart, IN: Institute of Mennonite Studies, 1973.

Orr, James Edwin. *The Second Great Awakening in Great Britain*. London: Marshall, Morgan & Scott, 1949.

Pachuau, Lalsangkima. *World Christianity: A Historical and Theological Introduction*. Nashville: Abingdon, 2018.

Pao, David W. "Waiters or Preachers: Acts 6:1–7 and the Lukan Table Fellowship Motif." *Journal of Biblical Literature* 130.1 (2001) 127–44.

Parrinder, George. *Religion in an African City*. London: Oxford University Press, 1953.

Peel, John. *Christianity, Islam, and Orişa Religion: Three Traditions in Comparison and Interaction*. Oakland: University of California Press, 2016.

———. *Religious Encounter and the Making of the Yoruba*. Bloomington: Indiana University Press, 2000.

Pervo, Richard I. *Dating Acts: Between the Evangelists and the Apologists*. Santa Rosa, CA: Polebridge, 2006.

Pilkington, Ed. "Donald Trump: Ban All Muslims Entering US." *Guardian*, December 8, 2015. Online. https://www.theguardian.com/us-news/2015/dec/07/donald-trump-ban-all-muslims-entering-us-san-bernardino-shooting.

Pleins, J. D. "Poor, Poverty." In *The Anchor Bible Dictionary*, edited by D. N. Freedman, 402–14. New York: Doubleday, 1992.

Plümacher, Eckhard. *Geschichte und Geschichten: Aufsätze zur Apostelgeschichte und zu den Johannesakten*, edited by Jens Schröter and Ralph Brucker, 1–32. Tübingen: Mohr Siebeck, 2004.

———. *Lukas als hellenistischer Schriftsteller: Studien zur Apostelgeschichte*, SUNT 9. Göttingen: Vandenhoeck & Ruprecht, 1972.

Porterfield, Amanda. *The Power of Religion: A Comparative Introduction*. Oxford: Oxford University Press, 1998.

Presbyterian Church in Cameroon (PCC). "The Administration of the Sacrament of Holy Baptism to Infants." In vol. 2 of *Book of Divine Services*, 37–47. Hamburg: Tron KG, 1984.

———. "The Blessing of a Private or Pastor's House." In *Special Services, Special Blessings and Special Thanksgiving*, 428–32. Vol. 6 of *Book of Divine Services*. Hamburg: Tron KG, 1984.

Price, T. "The Missionary Struggle with Complexity." In *Christianity in Tropical Africa: Studies Presented and Discussed at the Seventh International African Seminar, University of Ghana, April 1965*, edited by C. G. Baeta, 101–46. Oxford: Oxford University Press, 1968.

Prince, Derek. *Blessings or Cursing*. Milton Keynes: Word Publishing, 1990.

———. *From Cursing to Blessing*. Lauderdale, UK: Derek Prince Ministries, 1986.

———. *They Shall Expel Demons: What You Need to Know about Demons: Your Invisible Enemies*. Harpenden, UK: Derek Prince Ministries, 1998.

BIBLIOGRAPHY

Quayesi-Amakye, Joseph. "Prophetism in Ghana's New Prophetic Movement." *Journal of European Pentecostal Theological Association* 35.2 (2015) 163–73.

Rakoczy, Suzan. *In Her Name: Women Doing Theology.* Pietermaritzburg: Cluster, 2004.

Ramsay, William M. *Pictures of the Apostolic Church: Studies in the Book of Acts.* London: Hodder & Stoughton, 1910.

Ranger, Terence. "African Traditional Religion." In *The World's Religions: The Study of Religion, Traditional, and New Religion,* edited by Stewart Sutherland and Peter Clarke, 106–14. London: Routledge, 1988.

Ray, Benjamin C. *African Religions: Symbol, Ritual, and Community.* Eaglewood Cliffs, NJ: Prentice-Hall, 1976.

Rayan, Samuel. *The Holy Spirit: Heart of the Gospel and Christian Hope.* Maryknoll, NY: Orbis, 1978.

Redditt, P. L. *Introduction to the Prophets.* Grand Rapids: Eerdmans, 2008.

Reese, Robert. "John Gatu and the Moratorium on Missionaries." *Missiology* 42.3 (2014) 245–56.

Reindorf, Christian. *History of the Gold Coast and Asante: Based on Traditions and Historical Facts, Comprising a Period of More Than Three Centuries from about 1500 to 1860.* Second ed. Basel: Basel Mission, 1889.

Reyes, Giovani, E. "Four Main Theories of Development: Modernization, Dependency, Word-System, and Globalization." *Nomadas: Revista Critica de Ciencias Sociales y Juridicas* 4 (2001) 1–18.

Rios, Elizabeth D. "Pentecostals, the Church, and Justice." *Pentecostals & Charismatics for Peace & Justice* (blog), January 27, 2019. Online. https://pcpj.org/2019/01/27/pentecostals-the-church-and-justice.

Robbins, Joel. "Continuity Thinking and the Problem of Christian Culture: Belief, Time, and the Anthropology of Christianity." *Current Anthropology* 48 (2007) 5–38.

Robert, Dana Lee. *Converting Colonialism: Visions and Realities in Mission History, 1706–1914.* Studies in the History of Christian Missions. Grand Rapids: Eerdmans, 2008.

———. "Naming 'World Christianity': Historical and Personal Perspectives on the Yale-Edinburgh Conferencein World Christianity and Mission History." *International Bulletin of Mission Research* 44.2 (2019) 111–28.

Rodriguez, D. L. "The God of Life and the Spirit of Life: The Social and Political Dimension of Life in the Spirit." *Studies in World Christianity* 17.1 (2011) 1–11.

Roeder, Günther. "Die Geschichte Nubiens und des Sudans." *Klio* 12 (1912) 51–82.

Rothschild, Clare K. *Luke-Acts and the Rhetoric of History: An Investigation of Early Christian Historiography.* WUNT 2. Tübingen: Mohr Siebeck, 2004.

Ruether, Rosemary. "Theologizing from the Side of the 'Other': Women, Blacks, Indians, and Jews." In *Faith that Transforms: Essays in Honor of Gregory Baum,* edited by Robert McAfee Brown and Douglas J. Hall, 62–81. New York: Paulist, 1987.

Rushe, Dominic, et al. "What You Need to Know about Trump's First Speech as President." *Guardian,* January 20, 2017. https://www.theguardian.com/world/2017/jan/20/donald-trump-inauguration-speech-analysis.

Sanneh, Lamin, and Joel A. Carpenter, eds. *The Changing Face of Christianity: Africa, the West, and the World.* Oxford: Oxford University Press, 2005.

Sanneh, Lamin, and Michael McClymond, eds. *The Wiley Blackwell Companion to World Christianity.* Malden, MA: Blackwell, 2016.

Sapir, Edward. *Culture, Language, and Personality: Selected Essays.* Los Angeles: University of California Press, 1949.

Sarpong, Peter Kwesi. *Libation*. Accra: Anansesem, 1996.
Satyavrata, Ivan. "Pentecostals and Charismatics." In *Christianity in South and Central Asia*, edited by Kenneth R. Ross et al., 287–300. Edinburgh: Edinburgh University Press, 2019.
Scatlas, P. W. *Do Feminist Ethics Encounter Feminist Aims?* Bloomington: Indiana University Press, 1992.
Schliesser, C. *On a Long Neglected Player: The Religious Dimension in Poverty Alleviation: The Example of the So-Called "Prosperity Gospel" in Africa*. Zurich: Open Repository and Archive, 2014.
Schnelle, Udo. *Apostle Paul: His Life and His Theology*. Translated by M. E. Boring. Grand Rapids: Baker Academic, 2005.
Scholler, M. David. *A Biblical Basis for Equal Partnership: Women and Men in the Ministry of the Church*. Covenant Companion. Valley Forge, PA: American Baptist Women in Ministry, 1997.
Schulz, Dorothea. "Promises of (Im)mediate Salvation: Islam, Broadcast Media, and the Remaking of Religious Experience in Mali." *American Ethnologist* 33 (2006) 210–29.
Sen, Amartya. *Development as Freedom*. New York: Anchor, 1999.
Shabangu, Andries. "The Gospel Embodied in African Traditional Religion and Culture with Specific Reference to the Cult of Ancestor Veneration and the Concept of Salvation: An Inculturation Hermeneutic." PhD diss., University of Pretoria, 2004.
Shaw, Rosalind. "The Invention of 'African Traditional Religion.'" *Religion* 20 (1990) 339–53.
Shepperson, George, and Thomas Price. *Independent African: John Chilembwe and the Origins, Setting, and Significance of the Nyasaland Native Rising of 1915*. Edinburgh: Edinburgh University Press, 1958.
Shillington, V. George. *An Introduction to the Study of Luke-Acts*. London: T & T Clark, 2007.
Shumba, Victor. "The Role of Christian Churches in Entrepreneurial Stimulation." *The International Journal of Business & Management* 3.7 (2015) 152–57.
Silverman, David. "Indians, Missionaries, and Religious Translation: Creating Wampanoag Christianity in Seventeenth-Century Martha's Vineyard." *William and Mary Quarterly, Third Series* 62.2 (2005) 141–74.
Simpson, St. John. "Bone, Ivory, and Shell: Artifacts of the Persian through Roman Periods." In vol. 1 of *The Oxford Encyclopedia of Archaeology in the Near East*, edited by Eric M. Meyers, 343–48. 5 vols. New York: Oxford University Press, 1997.
Smelser N. *Towards a Theory of Modernization*. New York: Basic, 1964.
Smith, Abraham. "'Do You Understand What You Are Reading?': A Literary Critical Reading of the Ethiopian (Kushite) Episode (Acts 8:26–40)." *JITC* 22.1 (1994) 48–70.
Snowden, Frank M., Jr. *Blacks in Antiquity: Ethiopians in the Greco-Roman Experience*. Cambridge, MA: Harvard University Press, 1970.
Soards, Marion L. "Review of *Profit with Delight: The Literary Genre of the Acts of the Apostles* by Richard I. Pervo." *JAAR* 58.2 (1990) 307–10.
Soares, Benjamin F., ed. *Muslim-Christian Encounters in Africa*. Leiden: Brill, 2006.
Sobol, Donald J. *The Amazons of Greek Mythology*. South Brunswick: A. S. Barnes, 1972.
Spencer, F. Scott. "A Waiter, a Magician, a Fisherman, and a Eunuch: The Pieces and Puzzles of Acts 8." *Forum* 3.1 (2000) 155–78.
Spencer, Herbert. *The Principles of Sociology*. Vol. 1. New York: D. Appleton, 1898.

Stolow, Jeremy. "Religion, Media, and Globalization." In *The New Blackwell Companion to the Sociology of Religion*, edited by Bryan S. Turner, 544–62. Chichester: Blackwell, 2010.

Strohbehn, Ulf. *Pentecostalism in Malawi: A History of the Apostolic Faith Mission in Malawi, 1931–1994*. Zomba: Kachere Series, 2005.

Stulman, Louis, and Hyun Chul Paul Kim. *You are My People: An Introduction to Prophetic Literature*. Nashville: Abingdon, 2010.

Sundkler, Bengt. *Bantu Prophets in South Africa*. Second ed. Oxford: Oxford University Press, 1961.

Sundkler, Bengt, and Christopher Steed. *A History of the Church in Africa*. Cambridge: Cambridge University Press, 2000.

Sutherland, Marcia E. "The Need for an African-Centered Jamaican Psychology." *Journal of Black Psychology* 39.3 (2013) 330–32.

Tamale, Sylvia. "Nudity, Protest, and the Law in Uganda." Inaugural Lecture delivered at Makerere University, Kampala, Uganda, October 28, 2016.

Tasie, G. O. M. *Christian Missionary Enterprise in the Niger Delta 1864–1918*. Leiden: Brill, 1978.

Taylor, Charles. *A Secular Age*. Cambridge, MA: Harvard University Press, 2007.

Taylor, John. *The Primal Vision: Christian Presence amid African Religion*. London: SCM, 1963.

Taylor, John H. *Egypt and Nubia*. Cambridge, MA: Harvard University Press; Trustees of the British Museum, 1991.

Taylor, John V. *The Go-Between God*. London: SCM, 1972.

Taylor, William Ernest, and William Salter Price. *African Aphorisms; or, Saws from Swahili-land*. London: Christian Knowledge Society, 1891.

Thomas, Keith. *Religion and the Decline of Magic: Studies in the Popular Beliefs in Sixteenth and Seventeenth-Century England*. London: Weidenfeld and Nicolson, 1971.

Todd, N. R., and Rufa A. K. "Social Justice and Religious Participation: A Qualitative Investigation of Christian Perspectives." *American Journal of Community Psychology*, 51.3/4 (2013) 315–31.

Trump, Donald. "Inauguration Speech." *Guardian*, January 20, 2017. Online. https://www.theguardian.com/world/2017/jan/20/donald-trump-inauguration-speech-full-text.

Turkle, S. *Life on the Screen: Identity in the Age of the Internet*. New York: Touchstone, 1995.

Turner, Harold W. *The Church of the Lord (Aladura)*. Vol. 1 of *History of an African Independent Church*. Oxford: Clarendon, 1967.

Ukah, Asonzeh F. "The Redeemed Christian Church of God (RCCG) Nigeria: Local Identities and Global Processes in African Pentecostalism." PhD diss., Universität Byareuth, 2003.

———. "Roadside Pentecostalism." *Critical Interventions* 2.1–2 (2008) 125–41.

———. "Roots and Goals: Nigeria's Redeemed Christian Church of God." *Pulitzer Center*, January 13, 2014. Online. https://pulitzercenter.org/reporting/roots-and-goals-nigerias-redeemed-christian-church-god.

United Nations. "Ending Poverty." Online. https://www.un.org/en/sections/issues-depth/poverty.

United Nations Human Rights Council (UNHRC). "Climate Change and Poverty: Report of the Special Rapporteur on Extreme Poverty and Human Rights." A/HRC/41/39. Online. https://www.ohchr.org/EN/Issues/Poverty/Pages/SRExtremePovertyIndex.aspx.

BIBLIOGRAPHY

"'Until a Man Proposes, You'll Rot in Your Beauty, Intelligence'—Duncan-Williams Tells Women." *Modern Ghana*, October 27, 2014. Online. https://www.modernghana.com/news/577248/until-a-man-proposes-youll-rot-in-your-beauty-intelligen.html.

VanGemeren, W. A. *Interpreting the Prophetic Word: An Introduction to the Prophetic Literature of the Old Testament*. Grand Rapids: Zondervan, 1990.

Vries, Jacqueline de. *Catholic Mission, Colonial Government, and Indigenous Response in Kom, Cameroon*. Leiden: African Studies Centre, 1998.

Wagner, C. Peter. *Confronting the Powers: How the New Testament Church Experienced the Power of Strategic Level Spiritual Warfare*. Ventura: Regal, 1996.

———, ed. *Engaging the Enemy: How to Fight and Defeat Territorial Spirits*. Ventura: Regal, 1993.

———. *Warfare Prayer*. Ventura: Regal, 1991.

———. *Warfare Prayer: How to Seek God's Power and Protection in the Battle to Build His Kingdom*. Ventura: Regal, 1992.

Währisch-Oblau, Claudia. "Towards a Protestant Ministry of Deliverance—Experiences, Insights, and Reflections from a Process of the UEM Community." In *Witchcraft, Demons, and Deliverance: A Global Conversation on an Intercultural Challenge*, edited by Claudia Währisch-Oblau and Henning Wrogemann, 187–207. Zürich: LIT, 2015.

———. "We Shall be Fruitful in the Land: Pentecostal and Charismatic New Mission Churches in Europe." In *Fruitful in this Land: Pluralism, Dialogue, and Healing in Migrant Pentecostalism*, edited by Andre Droogers et al., 32–46. Zoetermeer: Uitgeverij Boekencentrum, 2006.

Wara, Solomon Che. *Seven Great Prayer Weapons, "Seven Keys to Help Yourself": An Amazing Discovery in the Ministry of Healing and Deliverance*. Bamenda: Agwecam, 2009.

———. *The Student Prayer Passport*. Bamenda: Agwecam, 2009.

Wardle, Huon. "On 'Bad Mind': Orienting Sentiments in Jamaican Street Life." In *An Anthropology of the Enlightenment: Moral Social Relations Then and Today*, edited by Nigel Rapport and Huon Wardle, 51–68. London: Bloomsbury, 2020.

Wariboko, Nimi. *Nigerian Pentecostalism*. Rochester: University of Rochester Press, 2014.

———. "Pentecostal Paradigms of National Economic Prosperity in Africa." In *Pentecostalism and Prosperity: The Socio-Economics of the Global Charismatic Movement*, edited by Katherine Attenasi and Amos Yong, 35–59. Cham, Switzerland: Palgrave Macmillan, 2012.

Weaver, Matthew. "Hate Crimes Soared After EU Referendum, Home Office Figures Confirm." *Guardian*, October 13, 2016. Online. https://www.theguardian.com/politics/2016/oct/13/hate-crimes-eu-referendum-home-office-figures-confirm.

Wedderburn, Alexander J. M. *A History of the First Christians*. London: T & T Clark, 2004.

Weever, Jacqueline de. "Candace in the Alexander Romances: Variations on the Portrait Theme." *RomPhil* 43 (1990) 529–46.

Weinfeld, M. "Ancient Near Eastern Patterns in Prophetic Literature." In *The Place is Too Small for Us: The Israelite Prophets in Recent Scholarship*, edited by R. P. Gordon, 32–49. Winona Lake: Eisenbrauns, 1995.

———. *Social Justice in Ancient Israel and in the Ancient Near East*. Jerusalem: Magnes, 1995.

Welbourn, F. B., and Ogot, B. A. *A Place to Feel at Home: A Study of Two Independent Churches in Western Kenya*. London: Oxford University Press, 1966.

BIBLIOGRAPHY

Welsby, Derek A. *The Kingdom of Kush: The Napatan and Meroitic Empires.* Princeton: Markus Wiener, 1998.

West, Martin L. *Greek Epic Fragments: From the Seventh to the Fifth Centuries BC.* Cambridge, MA: Harvard University Press, 2003.

White, Peter, and Niemandt, Cornelius J. P. "Ghanaian Pentecostal Churches." *Mission: Journal of Pentecostal Theology* 24 (2015) 241–69.

Williams, Rowan. *Being Disciples: Essentials of the Christian Life.* London: SPCK, 2016.

Wilson, Bryan. *Religion in Sociological Perspective.* Oxford: Oxford University Press, 1982.

Wiredu, Kwasi. "The Concept of Mind with Particular Reference to the Language and Thought of the Akans." In *African Philosophy*, edited by Guttorm Fløistad, 153–79. Vol. 5 of *Contemporary Philosophy: A New Survey.* Dordrecht: Martinus Nijhoff, 1987.

Wireko, Vicky. "Invitation to Worship: Dress Codes and Other Matters." *Daily Graphic*, March 3, 2010.

Witherington, Ben, III. *The Acts of the Apostles: A Socio-Rhetorical Commentary.* Grand Rapids: Eerdmans, 1998.

Witte, Marleen de. "Altar Media's *Living Word*: Televised Charismatic Christianity in Ghana." *Journal of Religion in Africa* 33 (2003) 172–202.

———. "Business of the Spirit: Ghanaian Broadcast Media and the Commercial Exploitation of Pentecostalism." *Journal of African Media Studies* 3.2 (2011) 189–204.

———. "Buy the Future: Charismatic Pentecostalism and African Liberation in a Neoliberal World." In *Pentecostalism and Politics in Africa*, edited by Adeshina Afolayan et al., 65–85. Cham, Switzerland: Palgrave Macmillan, 2018.

———. "Media Afrikania: Styles and Strategies of Representing African Traditional Religion in Ghana's Public Sphere." In *New Media and Religious Transformation in Africa*, edited by Rosalind Hackett and Ben Soares, 207–26. Bloomington: Indiana University Press, 2015.

———. "Neo-Traditional Religions." In *The Wiley Blackwell Companion to African Religions*, edited by Elias Bongmba, 173–83. Oxford: Blackwell, 2012.

———. "Religious Media, Mobile Spirits: Publicity and Secrecy in African Pentecostalism and Traditional Religion." In *Travelling Spirits: Migrants, Markets, and Mobilities*, edited by Gertrud Hüwelmeier and Kristine Krause, 83–100. New York: Routledge, 2010.

———. "The Spectacular and the Spirits: Charismatics and Neo-Traditionalists on Ghanaian Television." *Material Religion* 1 (2005) 314–34.

———. "Spirit Media: Charismatics, Traditionalists, and Mediation Practices in Ghana." PhD diss., University of Amsterdam, 2008.

———. "Spirit Media and the Spectre of the Fake." In *Christianity and the Limits of Materiality*, edited by Minna Oppas and Anna Haapalainen, 37–55. Bloomsbury, 2017.

———. "Television and the Gospel of Entertainment in Ghana." *Exchange* 41 (2012) 144–64.

———. "Transnational Tradition: The Global Dynamics of 'African Traditional Religion.'" In *Religion Crossing Boundaries: Transnational Religious and Social Dynamics in Africa and the New African Diaspora*, edited by Afe Adogame and Jim Spickard, 253–85. Leiden: Brill, 2010.

Wood, David. *Poet, Priest, and Prophet: Bishop John V. Taylor.* London: CTBI, 2002.

Wood, Maureen Maeve. "A Dialogue on Feminist Biblical Hermeneutics: Elisabeth Schüssler Fiorenza, Musa Dube, and John Paul II on Mark 5 and John 4." MA thesis, University of Dayton, 2013.

Wood, R. L. "Pentecostal Christianity: Retrogressive Force or Dynamic Ally?" *OpenDemocracy*, September 9, 2014. Online. https://www.opendemocracy.net/en/openglobalrights-openpage/pentecostal-christianity-retrogressive-force-or-dynamic-ally-0.

World Bank. *Kenya Economic Update: Policy Options to Advance the Big 4—Unleashing Kenya's Private Sector to Drive Inclusive Growth and Accelerate Poverty Reduction*. Nairobi: World Bank, 2018.

World Council of Churches (WCC). "Ecumenical Diakonia." June 7–12, 2017. Online. https://kirken.no/globalassets/kirken.no/smm/dokumenter/2019/wcc-ecumenical-diakonia-study-document.pdf.

———. "WCC Explores Ecumenical Diakonia as Way Towards Renewed Unity." *World Council of Churches*, June 16, 2018. Online. https://www.oikoumene.org/en/press-centre/news/wcc-explores-ecumenical-diakonia-as-way-towards-renewed-unity.

Wright, N. T. *The New Testament and the People of God*. London: SPCK, 1992.

Yamauchi, Edwin M. *Africa and the Bible*. Grand Rapids: Baker, 2004.

Yeku, James. "A Republic of Extraverted Pentecostals: A Response to Ebenezer Obadare." *Medium*, June 25, 2019. Online. https://medium.com/@yeku.james/a-republic-of-extraverted-pentecostals-a-response-to-ebenezer-obadare-64632fdd1ba6.

Yong, Amos. *The Spirit Poured Out on All Flesh: Pentecostalism and the Possibility of Global Theology*. Grand Rapids: Baker Academic, 2005.

———. "A Typology of Prosperity Theology: A Religious Economy of Global Renewal or a Renewal Economics?" In *Pentecostalism and Prosperity: The Socio-Economics of the Global Charismatic Movement*, edited by Katherine Attenasi and Amos Yong, 15–33. Cham, Switzerland: Palgrave Macmillan, 2012.

Zhang, Kaiping, and Kizilcec, Rene F. "Anonymity in Social Media: Effects of Content Controversiality and Social Endorsement on Sharing Behavior." Paper Presented at the Eight International AAAI Conference on Weblogs and Social Media, ICWSM, University of Michigan, June 1–4, 2014. Online. https://www.aaai.org/Library/ICWSM/icwsm14contents.php

Zurlo, Gina, and Todd Johnson. "Religious Demographies of Africa, 1970–2025." In *Anthology of African Christianity*, edited by Isabel Apawo Phiri et al., 155–69. Oxford: Regnum, 2016.

Name Index

Adelaja, Sunday, 43
Anderson, Allan, 6, 12, 15, 20, 31, 38, 150, 234
Anim, Emmanuel, 26, 27
Asamoah-Gyadu, Johnson Kwabena, xi, xii, 5, 6, 8, 9, 10, 11, 12, 15, 16, 20, 24, 30, 31, 32, 34, 44, 45, 107, 108, 110, 111–19, 120, 121, 122, 124, 126, 127, 128, 129, 130, 131, 132, 134, 135, 136, 137, 165, 171, 174, 175, 176, 185, 188, 189, 191, 197, 226, 234, 246, 247, 252, 256, 259, 260, 261, 266, 267, 268, 269, 271, 272
Athanasius, 17
Augustine of Hippo, 17

Babalola, Joseph, 19
Baeta, C. G., 20, 113
Bassey, Nathaniel, 201, 204, 208–9, 211
Bediako, Kwame, 31, 33, 109, 112, 114, 121, 234
Bonnke, Reinhard, 24
Bolsonaro, Jair, 88
Braide, Garrick Sokari, 19, 36
Bultmann, Rudolf, 34, 35n7, 114, 116

Cerullo, Morris, 24

Chilembwe, John, 39
Clement of Alexandria, 17
Considine, John Joseph, 3
Cox, Harvey, 18, 262

Duterte, Rodrigo, 88

Erdogan, Recip, 88

Harris, Willam Wade, 19, 36, 38, 39, 111
Heidegger, Martin, 1n1
Herodotus, 66–67

Idahosa, Benson Andrew, 25
Isaiah, 72–73, 154–55, 156, 158, 159, 160–61, 164

Jesus Christ, 35, 36, 51, 84, 98, 99, 135, 153, 164, 209, 237, 241, 244, 253
Jinping, Xi, 88
Johnson, Boris, 88
Joshua, T. B., 144

Kalu, Ogbu, 24, 121, 137, 226, 227, 228, 229, 266–67
Kimbangu, Simeon, 20, 36, 39, 40–41
Koschorke, Klaus, 53
Kraft, Charles, 25

NAME INDEX

Kumi-Larbi, Alexander Nana Yaw, 77–78

Livingstone, David, 19
Lindsay, Gordon, 25
Luke, 10, 46, 47, 48, 49, 51, 53, 57, 58, 59, 60, 61, 64, 67, 69, 70, 71–73, 74, 98, 159, 160, 161, 162, 164

Macchia, Frank, 6
Magesa, Laurenti, 34
Marshall, Ruth, 6
Mbiti, John, 31, 33, 35n7, 109, 116, 141, 234, 270
McKeown, James, 78, 80
Mills, Dag Heward, 163, 167
Modi, Narendra, 88

Ojo, Matthew, 6
Orban, Viktor, 88
Origen of Alexandria, 17
Osborn, T. L. 24
Otabil, Mensah, 132–33, 163, 186, 192–93, 194, 196–97

Paul, 46–49, 51, 56, 80, 98, 101, 115, 240, 243

Philip, 16, 47, 51, 58, 67, 70, 72–73
Putin, Vladimir, 88–89

Reindorf, Carl Christian, 109n2
Robert, Dana, 2, 53

Sanneh, Lamin, 4, 31, 52, 53
Salvini, Matteo, 88
Shembe, Isaiah, 19, 39

Tetteh, Lawrence, 119–20
Trump, Donald, 88–92, 94–95, 101

Queen Candace (Kandake), 58n8, 59, 64, 69–70, 71–72

Van Dusen, Henry P., 3

Wagner, Peter, 25
Walls, Andrew, 31, 52, 53, 55
Wariboko, Nimi, 6, 263, 269
Williams, Duncan, 167

Xenophon, 66

Yong, Amos, 6, 42, 261, 268

Subject Index

Action of *Churches* Together (ACT), 246, 248
Africa/Africanness, xi, 2, 4, 5–6, 8–9, 10, 16, 17, 20, 22, 27–29, 30–31, 32, 33–35, 36, 38–42, 44, 59, 61n24, 62, 66n71, 74, 109, 114, 121, 140, 144, 172, 174–75, 180–81, 193, 227–29, 245, 247, 251, 264–65, 268
Africanization, 21, 31–32 189
African Christians, ii, 16, 27, 28, 38, 41, 42, 43, 108, 114, 116, 138, 174–75, 236, 251, 256, 258, 266
African Christianity, 9, 26, 27, 29, 30–31, 32, 38n18, 40, 41, 42, 43–44, 45, 111, 138, 141, 235, 243, 246, 247, 249, 253–54, 256, 257, 258, 276, 277, 278, 282, 283, 287, 290, 293
African churches, 19, 28, 40, 108, 111, 115, 116, 128, 172–73, 183, 234–35, 236, 244, 249–50, 255, 256, 291
African culture/s, 31, 36, 40, 41, 44, 86, 173, 183, 193, 233, 238
African diaspora, 11, 31, 41, 125, 171, 172–74, 175–79, 183, 246, 275, 278, 285

African Initiated/Independent Christianity/Churches (AIC), 5, 19–20, 23, 28, 29, 31, 32, 36–37, 38, 39–41, 127, 189, 247, 250, 256, 284, 293, 297
African ontology, 108–9, 111, 114, 116, 121
African Pentecostalism, xi, xii, 5–8, 9, 10, 11, 12, 43, 45, 117, 137–38, 179, 185, 259, 263, 266, 267–68, 272, 276, 277, 287, 288, 293
African Pentecostals, 6–7, 30, 41, 44, 127, 137, 173–75, 176, 177, 180, 184, 231, 255, 266
Africa's religio-culture, 110, 111, 112, 115, 138, 142
African spirituality, 35, 45, 113, 246, 250, 251, 291
African theology, 121, 142, 234–36, 242, 275
African traditional religion, 7, 8, 9, 10, 19, 27, 30, 32, 33, 34, 35, 36, 38, 39, 45, 110, 112, 130, 138, 172, 185–87, 189, 190, 192, 194–98, 199, 262–63, 265, 266, 270, 277, 281, 285, 295, 296
African worldview, 21, 27, 119, 124, 134, 141, 175, 176, 227, 229, 254

303

SUBJECT INDEX

Afrikania Mission, 186, 190, 192, 193–95, 196, 197, 199
Akan, 10, 77, 80, 84, 85, 86, 87, 115, 120, 123, 124–25, 130–32, 133, 136, 277, 280, 283, 285, 294, 299
Akwankyere, 130, 133
Aladura, 39, 41, 249, 297
Amazons, 64, 66–67, 72n110, 124, 296
anawim, 154, 155, 156, 157
ancestor, 34–35, 109n2, 112, 135, 140, 149–50, 264–65, 273, 281, 296
Anointed One, 155–59, 164
anonymity, 11, 201, 210–11, 300
Apostolic Church, 21, 41, 85, 295
Apostolic Faith Mission, 21, 297
apostolicity, 9, 45–46, 50–51, 56
Apostolisation, 78
Arusha Call to Discipleship, 97
Arusha Conference, 97, 100
Asia, 2, 4, 48, 52, 55, 66, 101, 221, 248, 255, 264, 280, 296
Assemblies of God, 21, 41, 43, 229, 293
Atheist Club, 18n9
Azusa Street, 42, 262

baptism, 22, 49, 50, 148, 294
Berlin Conference, 1884, 32
Bible, 20, 21, 24, 28, 33, 34, 36, 84, 93, 100, 114, 116, 125, 146, 151, 157–58, 165, 193, 198, 230, 235, 236, 240, 243, 244, 266, 270, 282, 283, 286, 292, 300
born again, 21, 144, 195, 266

Cape Town Commitment, 96, 99, 100, 289
Catholic Mission, 17, 142, 298
catholicity, 2, 9, 46, 52, 55, 56, 248, 268
cause/causality, 7, 10, 107–8, 109, 110, 111, 114, 115, 116, 119, 120, 121, 132, 134–35, 267, 271
charismatic triad, 126, 128
Charismatics, 24, 25, 42, 112, 127, 144, 163, 164, 166, 168, 171, 180, 191, 193, 230, 263, 265, 277, 295, 296, 299

Christian development actors, 250, 251, 253
"Christians without borders", 56, 288
Christendom, 3, 46, 286, 288
Christianity, African. See African Christianity
Christianity, Africanization. See Africanization
Christianity, American Evangelical Pentecostal, 9
Christianity, charismatization, 9, 30, 32, 246
Christianity, enthusiastic, 9, 30, 32, 41, 44
Christianity, missionary, 19, 29, 112, 142, 143, 149, 266
Christianity, Pentecostalization, 9, 16, 21, 22, 23, 28, 199, 246
Christianity, Western/European, 2, 16, 34, 55, 56
Christianity, World, ii, xi, xii, 1–7, 10, 11, 12, 20, 30, 31, 32, 45–46, 52, 53–56, 96, 98, 102, 103, 246, 247–48, 255, 275, 281, 284, 288, 294, 295
Church Missionary Society (CMS), 17
Church of God Mission International, 25
Church of Pentecost (CoP), 10, 21, 43, 75–76, 82, 86, 165, 174, 175, 178, 181, 247, 249, 255, 290, 291, 293, 294
climate change, 94–96, 101, 249
Cold War, 4
colonialism/colonization, 3, 4, 33n2, 37, 39, 40, 41, 52, 282, 295
Communism, 3, 4, 56
continuity/discontinuity, 10–11, 12, 137–38, 139, 142, 143, 145, 152, 174, 176, 197, 229, 261–64, 267, 269, 270, 273, 276, 283, 284, 289
Coptic Orthodox Church, 17
creation myth, 238
culture, 11, 19, 34, 39, 40, 44, 47, 55, 67, 74, 75, 76, 79, 80, 86, 87, 97, 108, 151, 163, 176, 184, 193, 201, 205, 209, 210, 211, 214, 227, 235, 237, 239, 241, 242, 262, 263, 290
culture, media, 196, 209, 287

SUBJECT INDEX

culture, Pentecostal, 173, 186, 191–92, 196, 202, 205, 206, 207–9, 210, 211, 215, 217
culture, political, 91, 94, 200
culture, popular, 200, 209, 216, 283, 292

deliverance, 25, 26, 115, 117, 119, 128, 133, 134, 135–36, 138, 143, 144, 146, 148n58, 151, 156, 175, 176, 197, 231, 237, 243, 248, 266, 268, 269, 271, 277, 293, 298
demon/demonization/demonology, 18, 19, 21, 25, 26, 35n7, 47, 115, 119, 120, 121, 130, 134, 135, 141, 146, 175, 196, 197, 229–30, 233, 236, 237, 244, 251, 264, 265, 266–69, 273, 277, 280, 294
deror, 154, 158
development, ii, 7, 11, 19, 30, 31, 38, 53, 74, 77, 95, 119, 132, 172, 173, 193, 216, 221, 222–27, 229, 231, 233, 235, 245–54, 255, 258
   development, economic, 5, 11, 134, 223, 269
   development, integral, 246, 247, 250, 252
   development, sustainable, 11, 222, 223, 228, 253, 258
devil, 18, 19, 21, 120, 175, 176, 209, 236, 264, 265, 266, 267
discipleship, 92, 97–98, 99, 100, 271, 277, 288

East African Revival, 38, 103
ecclesiology, ii, 10, 39, 40, 41, 108, 117, 118
ecumenism, ii, 3, 4, 55
Egypt/Egyptian, 17, 48, 59, 60, 62–63, 64n47, 65, 68, 70, 73
Elim Pentecostal Church, 21, 43
English assemblies, 75–81
Enlightenment, 18, 19, 34, 44, 92, 112n11, 251
ethics, 79, 85, 87, 110, 165, 216, 248, 250, 256, 257

Ethiopia/Ethiopian, 17, 19, 48, 59–65, 67, 68, 72, 73
Ethiopian eunuch/official, 10, 16, 57, 58, 59, 60, 64, 67, 69, 70, 72, 73n115, 74, 288
Europe/European, 2, 3, 4, 10, 21, 32, 33, 34, 37–40, 43, 44, 46, 48, 50, 52, 53, 55, 66, 72, 83, 85, 89, 91, 98, 111, 112n11, 121, 122, 141, 142, 143, 172, 174, 176, 177, 181, 192, 253, 255, 261
evangelism, 22, 33, 36, 52, 79, 117, 127, 163, 182, 189, 246, 278, 282, 288
evil, 25, 26–27, 37, 89, 101, 115, 118, 120, 128, 129, 132, 134, 136, 139, 146, 147, 148, 150, 152, 156, 173, 175, 197, 209, 229, 230, 264, 265–69, 271, 277, 279
exorcism, 22, 25, 26, 115, 118, 128, 136, 151, 193, 232, 251, 265, 266, 294
exotic, 10, 44, 58, 59, 60, 61, 64, 66, 74

faith, 16, 17, 21, 23, 25, 28, 36, 47, 52, 55, 56, 69, 92, 96, 98, 108, 129, 130, 142, 145, 165, 176, 182, 183, 184, 209, 226, 227, 233, 237, 244, 247, 252, 253, 257, 259, 260, 261, 267, 268, 271, 272, 278, 279
Faith-Based Organization (FBO), 11, 245
fascism, 90, 101, 275
Fellowship of Christian Union (FOCUS), 22
feminist/feminism, 12, 235, 240, 241, 242, 243, 244, 284, 285, 291, 296, 300
folk theory of mind, 10, 123, 124
Foursquare Gospel Church, 21, 41
Full Gospel Business Men's Fellowship (FGBMF), 22

gender, 77, 81, 87, 216, 223, 225, 240, 241, 242, 258, 290
Gentiles, 47, 48, 49, 50, 98
Global Christian Forum, 55
globalization, 1n1, 2, 52, 119, 134, 139, 176, 180, 181, 189, 190, 191, 223, 225–26, 278, 286, 297

SUBJECT INDEX

God, 1n1, 7, 8–11, 16, 18, 21–23, 24, 35, 40, 41, 43, 50, 51, 52, 54, 73, 81, 84, 86, 90, 93, 96, 101, 102, 103, 108, 110, 112, 113, 114, 115, 116, 117, 118, 120, 122, 127, 129, 131, 133, 134, 135, 140, 148, 150–55, 156, 159, 160, 176, 183–85, 202, 212–14, 231, 232, 236, 238–43, 244, 254, 260, 265, 268–72
God, kingdom of, 3, 24, 43, 48, 161, 162–64
God, Spirit of, 7, 8, 50, 51, 100, 157, 158
god/goddess, 18, 19, 26, 27, 34, 42, 63, 70, 107, 125–26, 147, 227
good luck/bad luck, 264, 267
good news, 36, 47, 48, 153, 154, 155, 156, 159, 160, 161, 162, 164, 165, 166, 167, 168, 208, 278
Gospel Faith Mission, 21
gospel/Gospel, xi, xii, 7, 10, 17, 20, 25, 47, 48, 60, 82–83, 96, 98, 100, 111, 126, 138, 141, 142, 150, 160, 161, 165, 166, 168, 243, 252, 253, 259
Gross Domestic Product (GDP), 221, 223

#HallelujahChallenge, 201–5, 207–8, 210, 213, 214, 216, 217
Hallelujah Testimonies, 201, 209, 214
Harvard Divinity School, 18
healing, 19, 22, 25, 26, 36, 39, 40, 79, 113, 115, 116, 117, 118, 119, 120, 126, 127, 128, 135, 138, 139, 141, 142, 143, 144, 148n58, 149, 151, 175, 176, 187, 193, 197, 210, 213, 214, 231–32, 243, 248, 252, 268, 272, 277, 278, 282, 293
heaven/hell, 18, 40, 48, 49, 79, 127, 128, 132
hermeneutics, 23, 132, 278, 300
"Holiness unto the Lord", 85
Holy Spirit, xii, 8–9, 22, 23, 36, 42, 46, 49, 50, 52, 56, 87, 99, 102, 107, 108, 113, 115, 117, 118, 121, 125, 127–28, 129, 130, 135, 136, 153, 155, 163, 171, 176, 179, 194, 196, 241, 248, 251n8, 263, 266, 268, 271, 272
holy water, 144, 145, 146, 148, 149, 150, 151

idol/idolatry/idol worship, 18, 49n10, 147n57
imperialism, 2, 4, 48
Industrial Revolution, 2
injustice, 95, 99, 156, 157, 159, 160, 161, 167, 237
International Central Gospel Church, 132, 174, 186, 192, 195, 199
International Fellowship of Mission as Transformation, 90, 101
International Monetary Fund (IMF), 202
Israel/Israelite, 135, 145, 151, 155, 156, 158, 161

Jerusalem Council, 49

Kingdom of God. See God, Kingdom of
Kingsway International Christian Church (KICC), 174, 178
knowledge, 5, 26, 60, 61, 62, 65, 73, 82, 100, 130, 139, 187, 193, 203, 226, 238

Latin America, 2, 4
Lausanne Movement, 96, 99
leadership, 16, 24, 40, 75, 76, 80, 81, 83, 87, 88, 90, 93, 94, 95–103, 147, 155, 167, 208, 211, 236, 239, 246–47, 253, 255
Legon discourse, 6
libation, 10, 137–42, 143, 146, 147–49, 150, 151, 152
liberalism, 18, 36, 89, 90, 195

mainline churches, 16, 17, 20, 22, 23, 24, 149, 175, 230, 248, 251, 252, 254, 257
media technologies, xi, 5, 11, 171, 172, 173, 175, 176, 177, 179, 180, 182, 184, 209
media/mediation//mediatization, xii, 5, 11, 12, 24, 26, 111, 171, 172, 173,

SUBJECT INDEX

174, 175–78, 179, 180–84, 185, 186, 188–91, 192, 194–98, 199, 201, 205, 209, 210, 213, 214, 232, 246, 249
megachurches, 56, 261
memory, 201, 215, 216
Meroe, 59–62, 67, 68, 69, 70, 71, 72, 73
mind, 10, 113, 123, 124–26, 130, 131, 133, 136, 237
Mind and Spirit Project, 124n5, 130–31, 133
miracle, 35, 42, 138, 175, 201, 206, 210, 212–14, 216
mission/missionaries, 1, 2, 3, 4, 7, 8, 9, 16, 17, 18–21, 22, 28, 30, 32–33, 34–35, 36–38, 40–44, 46–49, 50, 51–52, 54, 55, 56, 80, 83, 85, 96, 99, 102, 103, 111, 112, 116, 119, 127, 128, 139, 141, 142, 144, 201, 205, 239–40, 247, 251n8, 265
modernist, 10, 82
modernization, 119, 223, 224, 227, 250, 251, 255, 262
money, 97, 100, 145, 206, 207, 208, 233, 237n6, 255

neo-Pentecostal/ism, 9, 10, 38, 41, 42, 43, 115, 116, 138, 139, 144, 145–48, 151, 152, 171, 175, 186, 188, 189, 226, 228, 229–30, 231, 237, 246, 271
neo-traditionalist, 11, 189, 199
New Testament, 16, 35, 46, 56, 116, 117, 260
nnoboa, 78
Nubia, 58, 59, 62, 64, 67, 68, 70, 71, 72n114, 73, 74
nudity, 83, 84

okra, 123
Old Testament, 27, 93, 153, 241
Ọlọwọgbọgbọrọ, 202, 212, 213
ontology, 109, 110, 112, 113, 119, 146
  ontology, African. See African ontology

oppression, 11, 135, 154, 157, 159, 160, 161, 164, 167, 168, 235, 236, 237, 239, 242, 243, 244, 272
orality, 23, 216, 262
Other/Otherness, 197, 234n1, 235, 236, 237, 238, 240

pagan, 83, 265
Pentecost International Worship Centers (PIWCs), 75
Pentecostalism, xi, 5, 6, 7, 8, 10, 21, 22, 23, 31, 42, 44, 45, 77, 85, 126, 128, 150, 163, 185, 186, 188, 189, 191, 192, 196, 200, 202, 206, 208, 216, 229, 233, 261, 262, 266, 271, 272
  Pentecostalism, African. See African Pentecostalism
  Pentecostalism, American, 43, 49
Pentecostal performance, 11, 136, 148, 189, 191, 199
pietist/pietism, 18, 49, 112n11, 128
pneumatic/pneumatology, 5, 10, 108, 112, 124, 127, 128, 131, 137, 153
Poor Christ of Bomba, 37n12
popular culture. See Culture, popular
porosity, 125, 134, 135
poverty, 11, 25, 27–28, 95, 135, 154, 156, 157, 159, 160, 164–66, 168, 221, 222, 225, 227, 229, 237, 252, 254, 255, 267, 268, 269, 270, 272, 273
power, 7, 17, 19, 21, 22, 24, 25, 35, 36, 42, 44, 45, 46, 47, 49, 51, 53, 70, 71, 91, 92, 96, 97, 98, 100, 102, 108, 112, 113, 115, 116, 117–21, 127, 128, 130, 132, 134, 135, 139, 144, 145, 146, 155, 163–65, 171–75, 176, 177, 194, 196, 199, 208, 210, 226, 237, 240, 243–44, 247, 253, 263–68, 270, 272
prayer, 23, 24, 26, 27, 40, 51, 78n9, 100, 116, 118–20, 126, 127, 128, 129, 131, 133, 142, 143, 145, 147n57, 148, 149, 174, 178, 180, 191, 198, 211, 212, 231–32, 243, 246, 248
priest/priestess/priesthood, 17, 23, 72, 111n7, 116, 118, 155, 194, 196
primitive solidarity, 10, 77, 78

307

SUBJECT INDEX

prophets/prophetism, 19, 20, 26, 27, 40, 51, 87, 97, 100, 101, 118, 119, 120, 130, 143, 144, 150, 155, 156, 157–58, 159, 160, 168, 174, 175, 198, 264
prosperity, 12, 25, 26, 27, 28, 45, 69, 90, 119, 120, 127, 157, 164, 165, 175, 176, 206, 224, 226, 229, 230, 231, 253, 260, 261, 263, 267, 268–70, 272
prosperity gospel, 7, 12, 25, 27, 28, 132, 164, 206, 254, 259, 260, 267–71
publicity, 186, 191, 194, 199

racism, 4, 93
reality, 10, 18, 34, 35, 91, 92, 108–112, 114, 116, 144, 146, 161, 199, 213, 227
Redeemed Christian Church of God (RCCG), 41, 43, 174, 208, 232, 249
religion, 2, 5, 9, 11, 16, 17, 18, 28, 34, 35, 36, 38, 42, 52, 53, 54, 81, 112n10, 115, 119, 120, 126, 127, 138, 146, 150, 171, 172, 176, 180, 185, 186, 187, 188–90, 191, 193–95, 198, 199, 200, 205, 209, 210, 217, 222, 226, 227, 230, 237, 245, 262, 263, 268
    religion, traditional African. See African traditional religion
religious imaginary, 197, 212
revivalism, 208
Rome, 48, 62n34, 71

salvation, 26, 49, 80, 127, 128, 134, 161, 163, 168, 230, 270, 272
Satan, 115, 117, 120, 130, 133, 144, 176, 184, 232, 265, 266
Scripture Union (SU), 22
Second generation African Pentecostals, 11, 173, 177, 178–84
self-advancement, 124, 131, 132, 133, 135, 136
servant leader, 97, 98, 99–103
sex/sexuality/sexualization, 83–85, 101, 228, 237, 241

social justice, 11, 153–56, 158, 159, 160–68, 242
social media, 27n36, 76, 94, 172, 173, 174, 177, 178, 182–84, 202–4, 205, 211
sorcery, 21, 140, 264
speaking in tongues, 22, 42, 79, 129
spirit, 9, 19, 25–26, 30, 33, 34, 35, 110, 116, 124, 135, 141, 146, 147, 151, 237, 243, 251, 264
    spirit, evil. See evil.
    spirit, Holy. See Holy Spirit
spirit-oriented Christianity, 32, 40, 41, 42
spirit-world, 9, 30, 33–34, 42, 120, 146, 175, 197, 263–68, 270
spiritual gift, 27, 79, 117, 118, 210, 273
spirituality, 16, 23, 27–28, 29, 35, 45, 51, 79, 100, 102, 112, 113, 138, 148n58, 159, 190, 250, 251, 259, 260, 262
    spirituality, African. See African spirituality
spiritual sustainable development goals (SSDGs), 254
strongman, 10, 88, 89, 90, 92, 93, 94, 96
subjectivity, 84, 230
Sumsum Sore, 111, 117, 118
sunsum, 115, 123
sustainable development. See Development, sustainable
Sustainable Development Goals (SDG), 222
syncretism, 16, 39, 151

the poor, 48, 78, 79, 90, 101, 153, 156, 157, 160, 161, 162, 164–66, 168, 225, 226, 228
theology, 4, 6, 15, 19, 23, 34, 35, 39, 40, 41, 48, 53, 54, 55, 56, 108, 118, 135, 145, 165, 175, 176, 205, 229, 234–35, 236, 238, 242, 243, 244, 246, 247, 251, 256, 269, 272
    theology, African. See African theology.
    theology, liberal, 18
    theology, liberation, 48, 132

SUBJECT INDEX

theology, Pentecostal, 31, 108, 128–29, 136, 152, 233
"To the ends of the earth", 9, 45, 46, 60, 127
traditions of response, 112n10
Translating the Message, 4
transnational/transnationalism, 174, 204, 205, 207
trinitarian, 107, 118
truth/post-truth, 9, 23, 65, 88, 90, 91, 92, 116, 208

values, 79, 96, 180, 193, 197, 215, 216, 224, 225, 228–30, 231, 239, 251

warfare, spiritual, 25–26, 129, 175, 179, 232
well-being, 27, 97, 128, 167, 222, 223, 227, 260
Wesleyan Methodist Society, 17
wisdom, 64, 101, 132, 133, 157, 234, 247, 250, 257
witch/witchcraft, 5, 7, 18, 19, 21, 26, 119, 136, 175, 176, 184, 231, 236, 243, 263–65, 267, 268–69, 273
witchdemonology, 26
woman
World Christianity, 3
World Christianity: Yesterday, Today, Tomorrow, 3
World Council of Churches, 3, 52, 55, 97, 99
World Missionary Conference, 2, 37
worldview, 3, 7, 11, 27, 41, 42, 44, 119, 120, 134, 136, 137, 142, 150, 175, 176, 177, 214, 216, 227, 228, 229, 245, 263, 266, 271
worldview, African. See African worldview
worship, 16, 18, 20, 23, 24, 27, 39, 76, 80, 82, 85, 86, 113, 117, 125, 129, 140, 141, 144, 146–47, 150, 187, 190–92, 193, 197, 198, 199, 201, 203, 204, 205, 206, 207, 209, 210, 214, 246, 252, 271

xenophobia, 92, 93

Zimbabwe Assemblies of God Africa, 229